Tokens of Power

War presents a curious paradox. Interstate war is arguably the most carefully planned endeavor by states, yet military history is filled with disasters and blunders of monumental proportions. These anomalies happen because most military history presumes that states are pursuing optimal strategies in a competitive environment. This book offers an alternative narrative in which the pillars of military planning – evaluations of power, strategy, and interests – are theorized as social constructions rather than simple material realities. States may be fighting wars primarily to gain or maintain power, yet in any given historical era such pursuits serve only to propel competition; they do not ensure military success in subsequent generations. Allowing states to embark on hapless military ventures is fraught with risks, while the rewards are few.

ANN HIRONAKA is Professor of Sociology at the University of California, Irvine. She studies war, politics, and the environment from a global perspective. Her book, *Neverending Wars* (2005), examined the intractable civil wars of the contemporary era and the role of the international community in perpetuating these conflicts. Her recent book, *Greening the Globe* (Cambridge University Press, 2014), examined the historical emergence of the global environmental regime and its impact on national policy and environmental practices around the world.

Tokens of Power

Rethinking War

ANN HIRONAKA

University of California, Irvine

CAMBRIDGE
UNIVERSITY PRESS

CAMBRIDGE
UNIVERSITY PRESS

One Liberty Plaza, 20th Floor, New York, NY 10006, USA

Cambridge University Press is part of the University of Cambridge.

It furthers the University's mission by disseminating knowledge in the pursuit of
education, learning, and research at the highest international levels of excellence.

www.cambridge.org
Information on this title: www.cambridge.org/9781316662682 5
10.1017/9781316796290

© Ann Hironaka 2017

First published 2017

Printed in the United States of America by Sheridan Books, Inc.

A catalogue record for this publication is available from the British Library.

Library of Congress Cataloging-in-Publication Data
NAMES: Hironaka, Ann, author.
TITLE: Tokens of power : rethinking war / Ann Hironaka.
OTHER TITLES: Rethinking war
DESCRIPTION: New York, NY : Cambridge University Press, [2016] |
Includes bibliographical references and index.
IDENTIFIERS: LCCN 2016040381 | ISBN 9781107175112 (hardback : alk. paper)
SUBJECTS: LCSH: War. | Balance of power. | Power (Social sciences) | Strategy.
CLASSIFICATION: LCC U21.2 .H548 2016 | DDC 355.02–dc23
LC record available at https://lccn.loc.gov/2016040381

ISBN 978-1-107-17511-2 Hardback
ISBN 978-1-316-62682-5 Paperback

For my father, Minoru Hironaka

Contents

Preface and Acknowledgments

On the first day of my freshman political science course, the professor announced three assumptions that would undergird our study of international relations for the quarter. The first assumption was that states were rational actors. At the time I thought it odd to assume the rationality of states a priori, and the dubiousness of that proposition has only grown in my mind over the years. This book represents my attempt to look at the planning of interstate warfare without the assumption that states are acting rationally. This does not necessarily mean that states are acting irrationally – it simply does not insist on forcing historical events into a rational framework. I focus instead on the origin of broad assumptions about the nature of warfare and the international system that provide the taken-for-granted parameters within which decision-making takes place. This book seeks to develop an explanation for the basis for military planning, evaluation of state power, and the identification of national interests that underlies calculations for war.

The writing of this book was funded in part by fellowships at the University of Minnesota Institute for Advanced Study and the Stanford Center for International Security and Cooperation. I thank participants at the Stanford CISAC seminars, the political science department at Columbia University, the Comparative Social Analysis Seminar at UCLA, and the sociology departments at the University of Arizona, Stanford University, Emory University, the University of Minnesota, the University of North Carolina-Chapel Hill, and the University of California-Irvine for the many thoughtful comments that have enriched this work.

I have also benefited greatly from stimulating discussions with my friends and colleagues in political science, who helped me cross the

disciplinary divide between sociology and political science. I would par-
ticularly like to thank Fiona Adamson, Deborah Avant, Michael Barnett,
Aaron Belkin, Raymond Duvall, Theo Farrell, Tanisha Fazal, Jim Fearon,
Martha Finnemore, Ron Hassner, David Holloway, Stephen Krasner,
Barry O'Neill, Richard Price, Scott Sagan, Jack Snyder, and Sidney
Tarrow. I also thank an anonymous reviewer for Cambridge University
Press for extremely helpful comments.

   I also owe significant intellectual debts to conversations over the years
with Edwin Amenta, Andy Andrews, Colin Beck, Al Bergesen, Patricia
Bromley, Bruce Carruthers, Wade Cole, Frank Dobbin, Gili Drori, Lynn
Eden, Dana Eyre, Marion Fourcade, Joe Galaskiewicz, Selina Gallo-Cruz,
Heather Haveman, Ralph Hosoki, Ron Jepperson, Georg Krücken,
Charles Kurzman, Frank Lechner, Wes Longhofer, Jim Mahoney, Doug
McAdam, Peter Meyer, Susan Olzak, Pam Paxton, Francesca Polletta,
Woody Powell, Joachim Savelsberg, Marc Schneiberg, Kristen Shorette,
Dave Snow, Sarah Soule, Yasmin Soysal, Mitchell Stevens, David Strang,
David Suarez, Mark Suchman, Ann Swidler, George Thomas, Marc
Ventresca, and Christine Min Wotipka.

   Many individuals have also generously given their time and intellectual
energy to review parts of the book. I would particularly like to thank
Pertti Alasuutari, John Boli, Elizabeth Boyle, Patricia Chang, Susan
Cherco, Dan Chirot, Thad Domina, David Frank, Roger Haydon, Kieran
Healy, David Holloway, Jacques Hymans, Jim March, David Meyer,
Andrew Penner, Charles Ragin, Francisco Ramirez, Wayne Sandholtz,
Kiyo Tsutsui, and Andreas Wimmer. And I especially would like to
extends my thanks to John Meyer for his always-insightful comments,
and to Evan Schofer for his unstinting encouragement and relentless
editing.

The Ambiguity of Military Planning

War presents a curious paradox. Interstate war is arguably the most carefully planned endeavor pursued by states, yet the pages of military history are filled with military blunders of monumental proportions. For centuries, the Great Powers states devoted substantial resources to the planning and preparation of war. Militaries employed cadres of bright analysts to refine strategy and tactics and to analyze every facet of warfare in minute detail. Despite this painstaking preparation, the history of warfare is littered with failures on an almost inconceivable scale.

It is difficult to find a major war in which things did not go massively awry. The Franco-Prussian War proved a humiliating miscalculation for France and led to embarrassing defeat and loss of territory.[1] The First World War was a huge debacle, fought for reasons that remain opaque to this day and employing strategies that served principally to wipe out a generation of young European men.[2] The Second World War was another disaster for the aggressor as well as for millions more worldwide. In Vietnam, America's brilliant "whiz kids" led the world's most powerful military into a dismal muddle that has come to epitomize the term "quagmire."

This book, which examines military planning and war, offers a simple resolution to this puzzle. Militaries make egregious errors because

---

[1] Michael Howard, *The Franco-Prussian War: The German Invasion of France, 1870–1871*. New York: Macmillan, 1962; Geoffrey Wawro, *The Franco-Prussian War: The German Conquest of France in 1870–1871*. Cambridge: Cambridge University Press, 2003.

[2] Michael Howard, *The First World War*. Oxford: Oxford University Press, 2002.

warfare is exceedingly complex, while information about war is ambiguous and usually outdated. As any social scientist knows, it is difficult or even impossible to understand complex systems with limited data.[3] The number of potential military threats is vast, and upgrades in military strategy and technology occur with sufficient speed that lessons from the past provide poor guides for the future. Perhaps most importantly, the unpredictability of battle events – the fog of war – ensures that the course of campaigns never follows the plans drawn up in the war room. The sheer complexity of military affairs overwhelms the efforts of even the most skilled military planners.

In particular, this ambiguity undercuts conventional understandings of power. States cannot easily evaluate the power of enemy forces, or even reliably evaluate their own relative power.[4] It seems inconceivable that the American military could struggle against a militarily feeble insurgency in Vietnam only two decades after the impressive Allied victories in the Second World War. Yet such reversals are not uncommon throughout history, as the resources, strategies, and weapons that appeared decisive in one geographic, historical, and political situation prove less effective in a different situation. Military power is much less transferable across context than is often imagined.

Nevertheless, this answer simply begs further questions. Why do states march to war so confidently if war is complex and fraught with risk? Why don't states see the fragility of their plans? Why do states fight wars at all? Historically, the stakes of war have often been puzzlingly small in comparison to the enormous outlay of life and treasure. As James D. Fearon puts it, "the central puzzle" is that "war is costly and risky, so rational states should have incentives to locate negotiated settlements that all would prefer to the gamble of war."[5] One solution to this puzzle put forth by scholars is to argue that wars represent an error made by one or more participants. Stephen Van Evera notes, "Many modern wars have been wars of illusions, waged by states drawn to war by misperceptions of international power realities."[6] Scholars are increasingly recognizing the

---

[3] Gary King, Robert O. Keohane, and Sidney Verba, *Designing Social Inquiry: Scientific Inference in Qualitative Research*. Princeton: Princeton University Press, 1994.

[4] William C. Wohlforth, "Unipolarity, Status Competition, and Great Power War." *World Politics* 61 (2009): 28–57.

[5] James D. Fearon, "Rationalist Explanations for War." *International Organization* 49 (1995): 380.

[6] Stephen Van Evera, *Causes of War: Power and the Roots of Conflict*. Ithaca: Cornell University Press, 1999, 255.

prevalence of misperception and error in military and political decision-making.[7] Yet if every war must be explained as a mistake by one or both sides, the puzzle remains: Why don't states learn that military calculations are highly prone to error?[8]

This book develops a different explanation for this puzzle and other perplexing features of military competition by exploring the social dimensions of the international system. Over the course of centuries, the European state system developed a set of rule-like expectations that defined the hierarchy of Great Powers and channeled competition among states. Amid ambiguity, military planners turned to these widely accepted social facts of the international system; in particular, they focused on the recognized hierarchy of the Great Power states. However, these foundational aspects of military planning and competition – ideas about power, interests, and strategy, as well as the identity of Great Powers themselves – can ultimately be seen as socially constructions. The social agreement regarding power, interests, and strategy reduced perceived ambiguity and focused military competition, paving the way for war. However, social agreement does not erase the underlying empirical complexity and ambiguity. As a result, the Great Powers became embroiled in a hubris-filled quest to be masters of a hopelessly complex universe.

In this account, the Great Power hierarchy stands as the preeminent social fact of the state system, serving as a beacon in an ocean of

---

[7] Fearon, "Rationalist Explanations for War"; Darren Filson and Suzanne Werner, "A Bargaining Model of War and Peace." *American Journal of Political Science* 46 (2002): 819–838; Andrew Kydd, "Which Side Are You On? Bias, Credibility and Mediation." *American Journal of Political Science* 47 (2003): 597–611; Robert Powell, "Uncertainty, Shifting Power, and Appeasement." *The American Political Science Review* 90 (1996): 749–764; Robert Powell, "War as a Commitment Problem." *International Organization* 60 (2006): 169–203; Robert Powell, "The Inefficient Use of Power: Costly Conflict with Complete Information." *American Political Science Review* 98 (2004): 231–241; Robert Powell, *In the Shadow of Power: States and Strategies in International Politics.* Princeton: Princeton University Press, 1999; Alastair Smith and Allan C. Stam, "Bargaining and the Nature of War." *The Journal of Conflict Resolution* 48 (2004): 783–813; R. Harrison Wagner, "Bargaining and War." *American Journal of Political Science* 44 (2000): 469–484; Alex Weisiger, *Logics of War: Explanations for Limited and Unlimited Conflicts.* Ithaca: Cornell University Press, 2013; Suzanne Werner, "Deterring Intervention: The Stakes of War and Third Party Involvement." *American Journal of Political Science* 44 (2000): 720–732; Scott Wolford, Dan Reiter, and Clifford J. Carrubba, "Information, Commitment, and War." *The Journal of Conflict Resolution* 55 (2011): 556–579.

[8] Robert Jervis, *Perception and Misperception in International Politics.* Princeton: Princeton University Press, 1976; Jack S. Levy "Misperception and the Causes of War: Theoretical Linkages and Analytical Problems." *World Politics* 36 (1983): 76–99; Barbara W. Tuchman, *The March of Folly: From Troy to Vietnam.* London: Abacus, 1984.

ambiguity. The route to objective power and security may be elusive, but the pecking order of states in the Great Power hierarchy is well defined. One consequence is that efforts to pursue security frequently devolve into one-upmanship among the Great Powers. The hierarchy of the Great Power system also serves to define "best practices" in military planning, which subsequently diffuse across the state system. Just as ambitious university presidents look to Harvard as an exemplar, military analysts look to the preeminent Great Powers to inform their strategies and theories of war. This social consensus disguises the overwhelming ambiguity of warfare, allowing states to confidently embark on hapless military ventures.

The empirical chapters of this book examine the way states prepare for war and engage in military competition. How do states evaluate the power of their competitors or determine the most valuable resources? How do states identify the best strategies? How do they decide which technologies hold promise for the future? How do they identify their enemies? The chapters uncover greater complexity and ambiguity than is commonly acknowledged. Each one of these calculations proves devilishly challenging. Under pressure to plan, states resolve ambiguity by turning to others. States seek to emulate their peers and copy the popular military doctrines of the era in hopes of replicating the successes of the major Great Powers. Ultimately, preparation for war is a transnational process that is both social and collective in nature rather than the result of military planners operating in isolation from each other in the bowels of top-secret military facilities.

The threads of this book, intertwined over many chapters, weave a tapestry that suggests a new understanding of war. The pillars of military planning – power, strategy, and interests – can be seen as evanescent social constructions rather than hard material realities. States may be fighting wars to obtain power, but understandings of power and the means to achieve it are mirages that do little to ensure military success in subsequent generations. Later chapters explain how socially constructed beliefs about power, strategy, and interests – and thus patterns of military competition – change over time. The patterns of war shift when the social hierarchy of the Great Powers is disrupted, prompting states to construct new lessons and reorient around a different set of supposed best practices. One might say that the Great Powers are embarking on a string of fools' errands, chasing after new strategies and competing over new resources that will prove fruitless in subsequent wars. Yet the potent expectations of the Great Power system encourage states to press on to folly. States that compete and win wars may gain prestige and deference in the short term, but power and security prove elusive in the long run.

The perspective developed over the course of this book helps explain a number of puzzling features of interstate war, such as the tendency for states to engage in war despite the huge uncertainty and costs, the frequency of blunder, the rapid European-wide gyrations in accepted military strategy following Great Power wars, and the tendency for nations to "fight the last war" over again. These represent anomalies or puzzles precisely because much of the literature – especially classical military history – presumes that states are pursuing relatively optimal strategies in a competitive environment. That assumption must be articulated and reconsidered.

THE EFFICIENT WAR PERSPECTIVE

War is commonly viewed as the inevitable consequence of strategic actors pursuing their self-interest in a competitive system. We imagine that states are simply doing what they need to do to survive. This image of a struggle for survival in a dog-eat-dog world slants military thought in a materialist and evolutionary direction. States must generally be doing things right – namely, pursuing strategies and goals that enhance their power – because foolish and weak states would not survive. According to this logic, the winners of major wars must be the best of all.

Traditional military scholarship has been anchored by an implicit assumption: the latent military power of states is revealed through the mechanism of military competition.[9] Warfare is seen as a crucible, a test that identifies powerful militaries and reveals the weak and the foolish. Power is both the means by which states achieve victory in war and the

[9] Bernard Brodie and Fawn M. Brodie, *From Crossbow to H-Bomb*. Bloomington: Indiana University Press, 1973; J. F. C. Fuller, *The Conduct of War, 1789–1961*. New Brunswick: Rutgers University Press, 1961; Colin S. Gray, *Modern Strategy*. Oxford: Oxford University Press, 1999; Basil H. Liddell Hart, *Strategy, the Indirect Approach*. New York: Praeger, 1954; William McElwee, *The Art of War: Waterloo to Mons*. Bloomington: Indiana University Press, 1974; William H. McNeill, *The Pursuit of Power: Technology, Armed Force, and Society since A.D. 1000*. Chicago: University of Chicago Press, 1982; Barry R. Posen, *The Sources of Military Doctrine: France, Britain, and Germany between the World Wars*. Ithaca: Cornell University Press, 1984; Theodore Ropp, *War in the Modern World*. Durham: Duke University Press, 1959. Robert L. O'Connell, *Of Arms and Men: A History of War, Weapons, and Aggression*. Oxford: Oxford University Press, 1989.

stakes over which wars are fought. States may initiate a war to prevent a rival from acquiring more power, or wars may occur when there is uncertainty over the distribution of power. In either case, those states that are victorious acquire more power by gaining resources and humbling their enemies in battle. Interstate military competition thus becomes the ultimate measure of state power.

In other words, traditional military scholars have implicitly tended toward an *efficient war hypothesis*, analogous to the efficient market hypothesis in economics that posits that market prices accurately reflect value.[10] The efficient war hypothesis presumes that past wars reveal the most powerful militaries, the best strategies, and the most effective technologies.[11]

The efficient war hypothesis is simplistic, to the point that it seems like a straw man. Few would admit to following such a crude rule. Military theorists and planners routinely acknowledge (or at least pay lip service to) complexity and contingency. Nevertheless, the efficient war hypothesis is a potent undercurrent that pulls on military theorists and planners and even scholarly traditions such as realism. In a complex world with limited data, the notion that certain militaries (or strategies or technologies) were "proven" in battle is compelling. Time and again, major debates about strategy or technology are settled by reference to the outcomes of recent wars (as will be argued in Chapter 3).

This idea that winners embody "best practices" is seductive precisely because it opens the pages of history to contemporary military planners and scholars. Without the efficient war assumption, military debates become a morass of unresolvable complexity. However, if victorious states are militarily superior to the losers, history becomes a dataset from which military planners can discern the underlying rules of war. Unfortunately, the allure of the efficient war hypothesis pulls in the direction of materialist and teleological accounts of the past, causing scholars to

---

[10] I draw heavily on March's observation that conventional scholarship frequently assumes that history is efficient. See James G. March and Johan P. Olsen, "The Institutional Dynamics of International Political Orders." *International Organization* 52 (1998): 943–969.

[11] Many scholars have criticized this view: for instance, see Jason Sharman, "War, Selection, and Micro-States: Economic and Sociological Perspectives on the International System." *European Journal of International Relations* 21 (2015): 194–214 and Tanisha Fazal, *State Death: The Politics and Geography of Conquest, Annexation and Occupation.* Princeton: Princeton University Press, 2007.

systematically underappreciate the extent of ambiguity, contingency, and sheer luck involved in war.

As scholars such as James G. March and William C. Wohlforth have recognized, the efficient war hypothesis leads inevitably to teleology: the argument claims by definition that the most powerful state must have been the one that won the war; the strategies victorious nations utilized must generally have been good ones; and the objects of interstate competition must have advanced the interests and military power of the victor.[12] Military errors and blunders are easily dismissed as exceptions if one believes that a competitive environment reliably separates the powerful states from the weak ones.

Economists continue to debate whether markets, with billions of transactions a day, are truly efficient. But the rarity and complexity of military conflict raises far more serious questions about the efficiency of military competition. Drawing lessons from the winners of war is reasonable only if victory accurately reflects objective superiority rather than historical circumstance or chance. Any number of contingent events – weather, disease, terrain, or technology, not to mention the foibles of leaders – can drastically affect the outcome of war. Were a given war to be replayed a hundred times with the same outcome, we might have greater confidence that the victorious military was indeed superior. The results of any single war can be very misleading. The emulation of victors only makes sense if historical wars are representative of those conflicts fought in the future. To the extent that the next war will be substantially different – which later chapters will argue is almost inevitable – emulation of victors may lead to disaster.

Generations of military scholars have made their careers analyzing the last major war, offering sophisticated accounts of the necessary material resources and savvy strategies that contributed to the military power of the victorious state. Yet these strategies usually fall apart in subsequent wars and are quickly dismissed. In turn, subsequent victories become grist for future generations of teleological analyses. The only thing that remains constant, ironically, is the confidence that military planners have finally gotten things right this time around.

---

[12] March and Olsen, "The New Institutionalism," and William Curti Wohlforth, *The Elusive Balance: Power and Perceptions during the Cold War*. Ithaca: Cornell University Press, 1993. This criticism is developed in greater detail in Chapter 2.

AMBIGUITY AND THE INEFFICIENCY OF HISTORY

Military theorists often speak as though history holds lessons for all to see. The twentieth-century Italian visionary Douhet, for instance, provides the following formula:

> To prepare for war demands then, exercise of the imagination. We shall glance at the war of the past long enough to retrace its essential features; we shall ask of the present what it is preparing for the future; and, finally, we shall try to decide what modifications will be made in the character of war by the causes at work today in order to point out their inevitable consequences.[13]

Unfortunately, Douhet inconveniently omits guidelines for deciding which "war of the past" to study, how to identify that which is "essential," and which "modifications" will be needed for the wars of the future. Historically, military planners have made catastrophic errors on these points. Indeed, Douhet's own prediction – that the invention of the airplane would decide the Second World War "in a matter of days, by terrible lightning strikes ... from the air" – was not borne out.[14] Warfare is simply too complex to provide an empirical basis for efficient learning. The material attributes and strategies that are pivotal under one set of circumstances often prove irrelevant in another.

The challenge of devising optimal strategies from past experience lies with the cognitive dimensions of the problem.[15] Theorists of organizational learning have argued that even rational actors are unable to make optimal decisions under conditions of extreme ambiguity. According to Karl Weick, ambiguity occurs when the quantity of explanations for a particular phenomenon overwhelms the set of empirical facts available to distinguish among the explanations.[16] Rathbun similarly distinguishes between the "*ignorance* (in a nonpejorative sense) endemic to bargaining

---

[13] Ropp, *War in the Modern World*, 371.

[14] John Lukacs, *The Last European War*. Garden City: Anchor Press, 1976, 255.

[15] Richard M. Cyert and James G. March, *A Behavioral Theory of the Firm*. Cambridge: Blackwell Publishers, 1963; Barbara Levitt and James G. March, "Organizational Learning." *Annual Review of Sociology* 14 (1988): 319–338; Daniel A. Levinthal and James G. March, "The Myopia of Learning." *Strategic Management Journal* 14 (Winter 1993): 95–112; James G. March, "Bounded Rationality, Ambiguity, and the Engineering of Choice." *The Bell Journal of Economics* 9.2 (1978): 587–608.

[16] Karl E. Weick, "Educational Organizations as Loosely Coupled Systems." *Administrative Science Quarterly* 21 (1976): 1–19; Karl E. Weick, *Sensemaking in Organizations*. Thousand Oaks: Sage, 1995, pp. 91–92; J. Douglas Orton and Karl E. Weick, "Loosely Coupled Systems: A Reconceptualization." *The Academy of Management Review* 15 (1990): 203–223.

games of incomplete information and enforcement" and ambiguity, which Rathbun refers to as the "indeterminacy of . . . [the] socially constructed world that lacks meaning without norms and identities."[17] As Weick explains, "The problem in ambiguity is not that the real world is imperfectly understood and that more information will remedy that. The problem is that information may not resolve misunderstandings." Ambiguity exists when factual knowledge cannot provide the answer because the key social processes are fundamentally based on contingencies and complex causal loops.[18]

The flaws in military planning cannot be chalked up to lack of wit among military planners. In fact, militaries are masterful at improving the detailed aspects of their operations. Unfortunately, the challenges of ambiguity are exponentially greater when it comes to the big questions about future wars. In the case of military planning, decision-makers face profound ambiguity regarding the most fundamental issues, including: (1) the evaluation of the military power of states, (2) the determination of optimal military strategies, and (3) the identification of national interests. These complexities and ambiguities of military planning are discussed briefly here and unpacked in greater detail in subsequent chapters.

The Ambiguity of Power

The measurement of military power is fundamental to planning and the decision to go to war. States must be able to assess their own military capabilities relative to potential enemies and develop strategies that highlight strengths and minimize weaknesses. Yet scholars have found that devising a reliable measure of power is a surprisingly difficult task.[19] "No concept is more central to international relations theory than power; and none is more elusive," declares Wohlforth.[20]

---

[17] Brian C. Rathbun, "Uncertainty about Uncertainty: Understanding the Multiple Meanings of a Crucial Concept in International Relations Theory." *International Studies Quarterly* 51 (2007): 533–534.

[18] Recent scholars have tended to use the term "uncertainty" rather than "ambiguity." In many cases, the meanings of the two terms overlap.

[19] Risa A. Brooks, *Shaping Strategy: The Civil-Military Politics of Strategic Assessment.* Princeton: Princeton University Press, 2008; James G. March, "The Power of Power." In David Easton (ed.) *Varieties of Political Theory*, pp. 39–70. Englewood Cliffs: Prentice Hall, 1966.

[20] Wohlforth, *The Elusive Balance*, 2.

This bleak assessment is borne out in the frequent and often egregious errors that statesman and scholars have made in assessing state power throughout European history. As Sullivan notes, "[W]e know from observing the outcomes of wars that the political leaders who opt for war are frequently wrong about their ability to attain their war aims at an acceptable cost."[21] Austria, for instance, was widely considered a Great Power throughout the nineteenth century until its dismal performance in the First World War – at which point scholars vigorously pointed out "obvious" weaknesses with perfect hindsight. France was also considered a leading Great Power until its defeat in the Franco-Prussian War and was still viewed favorably until its even more disastrous accounting in the Second World War.[22] The United States was vastly more powerful than Vietnam based on every military metric of the day, yet the United States still suffered an embarrassing defeat. And, as Stephen Biddle points out, "As recently as 1991, a massive effort using state-of-the-art methods and the nation's best analysts radically overestimated U.S. losses in the upcoming Gulf War . . .. The majority were off by more than an order of magnitude."[23]

Scholars have developed elaborate theories of misinformation and bias that befoul rational decision-making. Even those academics that remain hopeful about the possibility of measuring power suggest the need for reams of historical data and a great deal of computing power. This book suggests another theoretical option: ambiguity is fundamental, and we must let go of the belief that military power can reliably be evaluated. Amid the messiness of empirical reality, it may not be possible to identify which aspects of military effort will have the greatest utility for future wars. The basis of military calculations must be rethought.

The Ambiguity of Military Strategy

A second dimension of ambiguity lies in the determination of optimal military strategies and technologies.[24] In many ways, militaries are able to

---

[21] Patricia L. Sullivan, *Who Wins: Predicting Strategic Success and Failure in Armed Conflict*. Oxford: Oxford University Press, 2012, p. 6.

[22] Derek McKay and H. M. Scott, *The Rise of the Great Powers, 1648–1815*. New York: Longman, 1983; J. A. S. Grenville, *Europe Reshaped, 1848–1878*. Hassocks: Harvester Press, 1976.

[23] Stephen Biddle, *Military Power: Explaining Victory and Defeat in Modern Battle*. Princeton: Princeton University Press, 2006; Risa A. Brooks and Elizabeth A. Stanley (eds.) *Creating Military Power: The Sources of Military Effectiveness*. Stanford: Stanford University Press, 2007, 1.

[24] Biddle, *Military Power*; Brooks and Stanley, *Creating Military Power*.

plan on a phenomenal scale, utilizing their massive resources, manpower, and organizational capacities. The Manhattan Project turned a farfetched academic theory into the destructive reality of the atomic bomb. Armies are able to train, equip, transport, and marshal huge numbers of personnel to distant fronts. Militaries excel at optimizing specific tasks when conditions can be held constant and ample data is available to refine their methods.

However, the broader task of planning a war is vastly more complex, and ultimately incomparable to optimizing a particular piece of technology or refining tactics toward a specific objective. Militaries face the essentially impossible task of planning for a war several decades in the future, on unknown terrain, against an enemy that has not yet been determined. As military planners are painfully aware, even basic variables such as weather and terrain have tremendous implications for the waging of war. The plans, strategies, technologies, and military training needed for a land war in the Russian winter are quite different from the requirements for a guerrilla war in the tropics or a fight against non-state terrorist networks.

Despite the lack of knowledge on key variables, militaries must train men and acquire resources using their best guesses. Plans must be laid for an unknown enemy, whose capabilities – and even the capability of one's own future military – cannot adequately be predicted since new technologies will have developed in the interim that may necessitate radically different military strategies. Under these circumstances, even the most prescient of military planners will be overwhelmed by the uncertainties.[25]

As a result, the development of military strategy is typically muddled and punctuated by failure.[26] The First World War exemplifies the

---

[25] Daniel Kahneman, Paul Slovic, and Amos Tversky, *Judgment under Uncertainty: Heuristics and Biases*. Cambridge: Cambridge University Press, 1982; Charles Perrow, *Complex Organizations: A Critical Essay*, third edition. New York: Random House, 1986; Scott D. Sagan, *The Limits of Safety: Organizations, Accidents, and Nuclear Weapons*. Princeton: Princeton University Press, 1993; Herbert Simon, *Models of Bounded Rationality*, vol. 3. Cambridge, MA: The MIT Press, 1997; Diane Vaughan, *The Challenger Launch Decision: Risky Technology, Culture, and Deviance at War*. Chicago: University of Chicago Press, 1996.

[26] For insight into the conditions under which change may be beneficial to an organization, see Heather A. Haveman, "Between a Rock and a Hard Place: Organizational Change and Performance under Conditions of Fundamental Environmental Transformation." *Administrative Science Quarterly* 37.1 (1992): 48–75 and Georg Krücken, "Learning the 'New, New Thing': On the Role of Path Dependency in University Structures." *Higher Education* 46 (2003): 315–339.

difficulties of recognizing the impact of new technology. Planners failed to anticipate the effect that the machine gun would have on the battlefield. Expecting a brief conflict, militaries were unprepared for a relentless war of attrition that called for completely different strategies. This type of error is the rule rather than the exception. In the Second World War, militaries likewise failed to foresee the effects of technologies such as the airplane, the submarine, and the tank. In the Cold War, the United States prepared for a nuclear showdown in Europe that never happened, leaving it unprepared for the Korean War that did. While each generation of military planners is determined not to repeat the errors of its predecessors, this determination is based on the belief that the outlines of war can be foreseen and planned. This presumption must be reconsidered.

The Ambiguity of Interests

A third dimension of ambiguity involves the national interests that impel states to initiate war.[27] All states have an interest in increasing their security, but the route to security is by no means obvious. Which resources and strategic territories are worth the cost of war? Is it more essential to control the territorial heartland of Europe or peripheral nations that may be targets of superpower expansion? The answers depend on fragile predictions about the military value that resources will have decades in the future. Here, again, the literature is plagued by teleological accounts. The assumption is often made that the inciting issue of a war *must* have been critical to the national interest. The fact that leaders were willing to fight a costly war is taken as evidence that the objects of contention were valuable. Yet even the most cursory analysis of major wars in history will raise obvious questions on this point. Many conflicts center on unclear or baffling objectives.

War is the most costly tool in the political repertoire. Not only do wars consume human lives and economic resources, but the fate of states hangs in the balance as well, since states may be destroyed or ripped apart through warfare. One would expect the astronomical costs of war to be motivated by even more compelling gains. States should go to war only

---

[27] Robert Axelrod, *Conflict of Interest: A Theory of Divergent Goals with Applications to Politics*. Chicago: Markham Publishing Company, 1970; Robert Gilpin, *War and Change in World Politics*. Cambridge: Cambridge University Press, 1981; James N. Rosenau, *The Scientific Study of Foreign Policy*. New York: Free Press, 1971; Van Evera, *Causes of War*.

over the most essential and indispensable of interests. Yet one of the enduring puzzles of military history, addressed in Chapter 4, is that major wars are often fought over minor issues or uncertain objectives. In many cases, it is unclear why a war is being fought even while it is under way. For instance, the national interests that impelled the First World War were puzzling to both scholars and statesmen at the time.[28] The interests underlying the Vietnam War and the Boer War were even more enigmatic. Indeed, the absence of any obvious national interest encouraged both laypeople and academics to theorize that these wars were driven by domestic conspiracies.

The fundamental ambiguities in the assessment of power, military strategy, and national interest fatally undermine efforts at learning and planning. As Van Evera has argued, "[A] root cause of war lies in the opacity of the future and in the optimistic illusions that this opacity allows. These illusions lead states to fight in false hope of victory, or for Pyrrhic victories."[29] These ambiguities are concealed by the advantages of hindsight, which allows military historians to gloss over the errors and omissions – and sheer luck – of the victorious army while highlighting the deficiencies of the defeated.

THE CONSTRUCTION OF MILITARY REALITY

If key concepts such as power, strategy, and interests are fundamentally ambiguous, where do states find a starting point for their military plans? It is conventional to assume that states generally know what they want and that military competition is the means to obtain it. By contrast, this book argues that the foundations of war can be traced to features of the international system. In particular, the pecking order of the international system becomes the primary social fact that allows military planning to move forward.

This book draws on world society theory,[30] a sociological perspective that shares intellectual roots with constructivism in political

---

[28] Basil H. Liddell Hart, Basil H. *The Real War, 1914–1918.* Boston: Little, Brown and Company, 1930.

[29] Van Evera, *Causes of War*, 14.

[30] John Boli and George M. Thomas, (eds.) *Constructing World Culture: International Nongovernmental Organizations since 1875.* Stanford: Stanford University Press, 1999; Elizabeth Heger Boyle, *Female Genital Cutting: Cultural Conflict in the Global Community.* Baltimore: Johns Hopkins University Press, 2002; Paul J. DiMaggio and Walter W. Powell, "The Iron Cage Revisited: Institutional Isomorphism and Collective

science.[31] World society theory posits that the international community is bound by a set of shared understandings. These common understandings, or shared "social facts," within the international community guide political and military calculations and fundamentally shape military dynamics among states in the international system. The primary "social fact" in this case is the composition and dynamics of the Great Power hierarchy, which provides *terra firma* for military plans and calculations.

Great Power Hierarchy

First and foremost, there is widespread consensus throughout the international community regarding the hierarchy of the Great Powers. Despite

Rationality in Organizational Fields." *American Sociological Review* 48 (1983): 147–160; Frank Dobbin, *Forging Industrial Policy: The United States, Britain, and France in the Railway Age.* Cambridge: Cambridge University Press, 1994; Martha Finnemore, *National Interests in International Society.* Ithaca: Cornell University Press, 1996; Martha Finnemore, "Norms, Culture, and World Politics: Insights from Sociology's Institutionalism." *International Organization* 50.2 (1996): 325–347; Ronald L. Jepperson, Alexander Wendt, and Peter J. Katzenstein. "Norms, Identity, and Culture in National Security." In *The Culture of National Security: Norms and Identity in World Politics*, edited by Peter J. Katzenstein, 33–75. New York: Columbia University Press, 1996; John W. Meyer, John Boli, and George M. Thomas, "Ontology and Rationalization in the Western Cultural Account." In *Institutional Structure: Constituting State, Society, and the Individual*, edited by George M. Thomas, John W. Meyer, Francisco O. Ramirez, and John Boli, 12–37. Newbury Park, CA: Sage, 1987; Francisco O. Ramirez and John W. Meyer, "Comparative Education: The Social Construction of the Modern World System." *Annual Review of Sociology* 6 (1980): 369–399; Francisco O. Ramirez and John Boli, "The Political Construction of Mass Schooling: European Origins and Worldwide Institutionalization." *Sociology of Education* 60 (1987): 2-17; Yasemin Nuhoğlu Soysal, *Limits of Citizenship: Migrants and Postnational Membership in Europe.* Chicago: University of Chicago, 1994; Mark C. Suchman and Dana P. Eyre, "Military Procurement as Rational Myth: Notes on the Social Construction of Weapons Proliferation." *Sociological Forum* 7 (1992): 137–161.

[31] James Der Derian, *On Diplomacy: A Genealogy of Western Estrangement.* New York: Basil Blackwell, 1987; Ronald L. Jepperson, Alexander Wendt, and Peter J. Katzenstein, "Norms, Identity, and Culture in National Security." In *The Culture of National Security: Norms and Identity in World Politics*, edited by Peter J. Katzenstein, 33–75. New York: Columbia University Press, 1996; Peter J. Katzenstein (ed.), *The Culture of National Security: Norms and Identity in World Politics.* New York: Columbia University Press, 1996; Richard M. Price, *The Chemical Weapons Taboo.* Ithaca: Cornell University Press, 1997; Jutta Weldes, Mark Lafffey, Hugh Gusterson, and Raymond Duvall (eds.), *Cultures of Insecurity: States, Communities and the Production of Danger.* Minneapolis: University of Minnesota Press, 1999; Alexander Wendt, *Social Theory of International Politics.* Cambridge: Cambridge University Press, 1999; Alexander Wendt, "Anarchy Is What States Make of It: The Social Construction of Power Politics." *International Organization* 46 (1992): 391–425.

ambiguity in the concrete assessment of military power, there is near-unanimity on which states are the Great Powers and their relative ranking in each historical era.[32] The mechanisms for promotion and demotion to Great Power status are widely agreed on. At first glance, Great Power status appears to be reliably founded on objective measures of military power. The recognized Great Powers have typically been the winners of recent major Great Power wars. These Great Powers continue to be victorious – right up until they suffer a disastrous defeat. A major defeat by another Great Power is universally acknowledged as prompting demotion in the Great Power hierarchy. Through the lens of the efficient war hypothesis, the Great Powers appear to have proven their mettle on the battlefield.

Chapter 2 argues that the status of being a Great Power is not simply a reflection of military prowess, but is an identity that is actively pursued by some states and eschewed by others. The expectations of the international community place strong pressure on the Great Power states to compete. This urgency, compounded by the knowledge that other Great Powers in the community are also preparing for war, propels the Great Powers into competitions with rival Great Powers. States that do not aspire to Great Power status opt out of these competitions, implicitly accepting a more peripheral status in the international system. Military competition principally occurs among those battling for Great Power status (or regional status, which involves analogous dynamics as discussed in Chapter 9).

As Chapter 2 argues, it is by no means simple to generalize from an observed Great Power victory to the more abstract qualities of military power that yielded victory. The indices that military pundits develop to measure military power are essentially teleological – mere summaries of the attributes of the recognized Great Powers of the era. Consequently, the empirical basis for Great Power rankings is largely fictional. Nevertheless, the Great Power hierarchy has very real consequences. Those at the top of the hierarchy gain substantial prestige and deference from all members of the state system. Moreover, the hierarchy guides competition, as those among the top jostle for dominance. And the hierarchy becomes a reference point that shapes other facets of military reality, including the dominant military theories of a given era. Unfortunately, the one thing

[32] Derek McKay and H. M. Scott. *The Rise of the Great Powers, 1648–1815.* New York: Longman, 1983; John J. Mearsheimer, *The Tragedy of Great Power Politics.* New York: W. W. Norton and Company, 2001; Kenneth N. Waltz, *Theory of International Politics.* Reading, MA: Addison-Wesley, 1979; Wohlforth, *The Elusive Balance,* 1993.

that the hierarchy does not provide is assurance of future military victory for the Great Powers.

Planning for War

Military planners navigate the ocean of ambiguity by drawing on the example of the leading Great Power states. On the assumption that the battles of the Great Powers demonstrate state-of-the-art military practices, military theorists comb the pages of history to distill the enduring rules of warfare. The efficient war hypothesis discourages recognition of the endemic errors, chance, and contingency that occur in military competition. Since the system is assumed to select against foolishness, observed conflicts tend to be interpreted as reasonable. Error is attributed mainly to the defeated military, and it is usually presumed that savvier planners could have sidestepped errors by correctly apprehending the military facts of the day. Victors are lauded for their foresight and planning, so the prolixity of error on the part of the victors has been given only marginal attention in the traditional military literature. This stance might seem more reasonable if the victors of the last war were not so often the losers of the next. By contrast, if one recognizes that ambiguity is the norm, the frequent and egregious errors and blunders that are observable throughout the history of warfare make more sense.

How do militaries plan in an ambiguous world? As Chapter 3 discusses, the dominant military paradigm of a given era is distilled from the practices of the Great Powers.[33] European military experts settle on key theories or paradigms that come to represent conventional wisdom. For instance, military thinkers such as Clausewitz and Jomini drew on the exemplary battles of Napoleon to develop the military paradigm that dominated nineteenth-century European military thought. Their military theories were widely accepted, driving military and political calculations

---

[33] See also: David Strang, *Learning by Example: Imitation and Innovation at a Global Bank.* Princeton: Princeton University Press, 2010; David Strang and Michael W. Macy, "In Search of Excellence: Fads, Success Stories, and Adaptive Emulation." *The American Journal of Sociology* 107 (2001): 147–182; David Strang and John W. Meyer, "Institutional Conditions for Diffusion." *Theory and Society* 22 (1993): 487–511; David Strang and Sarah A. Soule, "Diffusion in Organizations and Social Movements: From Hybrid Corn to Poison Pills." *Annual Review of Sociology* 24 (1998): 265–290; Chang Kil Lee and David Strang, "The International Diffusion of Public-Sector Downsizing: Network Emulation and Theory-Driven Learning." *International Organization* 60 (2006): 883–909.

across the Great Power system. Unfortunately, the next set of Great Power wars showed that many of the lessons drawn from Napoleonic battles were idiosyncratic. This led to the development of a new military paradigm, touted as embodying a new set of supposedly universal military principles. Alas, these were again overturned in the next round of wars. Despite their dubious empirical foundation, widely accepted theories or paradigms in the European military community provide an answer to the overwhelming ambiguity of warfare, allowing states to confidently pursue military ventures.

Motivation for War

The Great Powers of each historical era tend to be the states most frequently engaged in interstate wars.[34] Conventional scholarship assumes that the Great Powers wage war because they can – the Great Powers have the military capability to enforce their national interests at the point of the sword. I suggest an alternative explanation: the Great Powers wage war to maintain their identity and status as Great Powers. A Great Power that refrains from fighting will decline in status over time, replaced by another Power with a continual string of victories. Consequently, Great Powers enact their Great Power status by vying with other states in competitions large and small.

While the route to objective national security is ambiguous, the mechanism for enhancing Great Power status is straightforward. Defeating a Great Power rival leads to an increase in status and prestige in the eyes of the international community. Victory in war brings the greatest increase in status, but minor competitions also affect Great Power prestige and reputation. Consequently, the Great Powers engage in competitions of many sorts: scrambles for territory, arms races, and ancillary competitions such as the "space race." Conflicts shift from being merely a disagreement over a particular piece of land or strategic fortification to being a determinant of social standing in the Great Power hierarchy. The victorious state ascends higher in the Great Power hierarchy, while the defeated Great Power falls down a notch.

---

[34] A. F. K. Organski, *World Politics*. New York: Alfred A. Knopf, 1958; A. F. K. Organski and Jacek Kugler, *The War Ledger*. Chicago: University of Chicago Press, 1980; Meredith Reid Sarkees and Frank Wayman, *Resort to War: 1816–2007*. Washington, DC: CQ Press, 2010.

Given this system, the Great Powers feel urgency over the need to identify potential rival Great Powers.[35] The original motivation for the rivalry may be ambiguous or sometimes erroneous. Once a Great Powers identifies another as a rival, however, hostility and conflict become part of a self-fulfilling prophecy (see Chapter 8).[36] When one of the Great Powers seeks to acquire a territory or strategic resources, the rival quickly jumps into the competition, regardless of its prior assessment of strategic interests. The reputational value of victory quickly overshadows the ambiguous value of the initial stakes. Pyrrhic victories – in which the costs of victory outweigh the tangible gains – are common in Great Power competitions.

This system creates an environment in which Great Powers are more prone to engage in interstate wars than non–Great Power states. The onset of any particular war, of course, is not inevitable. Any state can choose to pull back from the brink of war. Indeed as I argue in Chapter 3, military events might usefully be viewed as probabilistic, including the initial decision to engage in war. Nevertheless, the implicit rule that Great Power status is maintained by engagement in international affairs encourages frequent Great Power military involvements.

The efficient war hypothesis presents a view of military competition as a sensible endeavor that is necessary to ensure power and security. This book reframes the issue entirely. States are embedded in a social system that encourages hubris. Efforts to obtain security become a continual

[35] William R. Thompson, ed., *Great Power Rivalries*. Columbia: University of South Carolina Press, 1999; Paul F. Diehl and Gary Goertz, *War and Peace in International Rivalry*. Ann Arbor: University of Michigan Press, 2000; Colaresi 2005; Rasler and Thompson 1994; Michael P. Colaresi, Karen Rasler, and William R. Thompson, *Strategic Rivalries in World Politics: Position, Space and Conflict Escalation*. Cambridge: Cambridge University Press, 2007; Karen Rasler and William R. Thompson, "Explaining Rivalry Escalation to War: Space, Position, and Contiguity in the Major Power Subsystem." *International Studies Quarterly* 44 (2000): 503–530; Paul Poast, "Can Issue Linkage Improve Treaty Credibility?" *Journal of Conflict Resolution* 57 (2013): 739–764.
[36] Deborah Welch Larson, *Anatomy of Mistrust: U.S.-Soviet Relations during the Cold War*. Ithaca: Cornell University Press, 1997; Robert Jervis, "Cooperation under the Security Dilemma." *World Politics* 30 (1978): 167–214; Jonathan Mercer, *Reputation and International Politics*. Ithaca: Cornell University Press, 1996: 19; Barry O'Neill, *Honor, Symbols, and War*. Ann Arbor: University of Michigan Press, 1999; Richard Ned Lebow, *A Cultural Theory of International Relations*. Cambridge: Cambridge University Press, 2008; T. V. Paul, Deborah Welch Larson, and William C. Wohlforth (eds.), *Status in World Politics*. New York: Cambridge University Press, 2014; William C. Wohlforth, "Unipolarity, Status Competition, and Great Power War." *World Politics* 61 (2009): 28–57.

march up the Great Power hierarchy that often ends with catastrophic defeat. In such a system, military competition may be quite disconnected from "true" security – if such a thing could be objectively measured. Since security means climbing the social hierarchy, competition never ends. Success brings prestige, but also creates a target for other Great Powers seeking to climb the hierarchy. Indeed, Great Powers frequently end up defeated and dismembered as a result of unending competition and over-extension.[37] In the end, "security" is a mirage that leads Great Powers to embark on an unending series of conflicts.

THEORETICAL CONTEXT AND CONTRIBUTIONS

The following chapters draw on a range of recent and classical scholar-ship to develop an alternative framework for understanding war. In this section I briefly review some points of commonalities and divergence with prior work.

Realism

Classic realist scholarship by Hans J. Morgenthau, Kenneth N. Waltz, and others focused on power, military strategy, and national interests as key determinants of war.[38] The unfolding of Great Power competition and war was explained as the natural result of strategic actors pursuing their interests in an anarchic environment.[39] While the realist tradition acknowledges that interests and power are complex, the notion that they are fundamentally ambiguous is anathema to the enterprise. Realists

---

[37] Paul Kennedy, *The Rise and Fall of the Great Powers: Economic Change and Military Conflict from 1500 to 2000*. New York: Random House, 1986.

[38] Edward Hallett Carr, *The Twenty Years' Crisis, 1919–1939: An Introduction to the Study of International Relations*. New York: Palgrave, 2001 [1939]; Inis L. Claude, Jr., *Power and International Relations*. New York: Random House, 1962; Robert Gilpin, "The Theory of Hegemonic War." *The Journal of Interdisciplinary History* 18 (1988): 591–613; Gilpin, *War and Change in World Politics*; Organski, *World Politics*; Organski and Kugler, *The War Ledger*; Hans J. Morgenthau, *Politics among Nations*. New York: Alfred A. Knopf, 1973 [1948]; Posen, *The Sources of Military Doctrine*; Mearsheimer, *The Tragedy of Great Power Politics*; Waltz, *Theory of International Politics*; Arnold Wolfers, *Discord and Collaboration: Essays on International Politics*. Baltimore: Johns Hopkins Press, 1962.

[39] Stephen D. Krasner (ed.), *Problematic Sovereignty*. New York: Columbia University Press, 2009; Stephen D. Krasner, "Logics of Consequences and Appropriateness in the International System." In *Organizing Political Institutions*, edited by Morten Egeberg and Per Laegrid. Oslo: Scandinavian University Press, 1999.

recognize that errors occur, but generally explain them as the result of exogenous factors such as technological change or the foibles of particular leaders. As a result, realist scholars never developed a general line of empirical research that examines how decision-makers identify military strategies and interests in practice. My arguments seek to fill this gap – and thus in some ways could be seen as complementary to realism. However, my conclusion – that military competition is a never-ending game of one-upmanship that may undermine "real" security – is very much at odds with the main thrust of realist scholarship.

Recent Responses to Realism

The theoretical dominance of realism has fragmented into a multiplicity of amendments and alternatives, several of which provide foundational steppingstones for the arguments in this book.

Bargaining Theory and the Causes of War. James Fearon and subsequent scholars offer an important starting point by questioning why rational states would go to war. Their answer emphasizes complexity and an endemic tendency toward misperception in military calculations. Much of the ensuing literature elaborates this key insight by unpacking the kinds of uncertainties that might lead rational states to enter into war. The bargaining theory perspective, in particular, emphasizes uncertainty and misperception, which parallels the concept of ambiguity emphasized in this book.[40]

This book offers a different answer to the puzzle raised by Fearon at the beginning of this chapter. Rather than starting with the assumption that states are generally rational, this book began with a more inductive and historical approach: Empirically, what did states compete over? Why did they start wars? Although the argument begins with ambiguity, as an empirical matter one finds substantial consensus in each historical era. The social realities of the system – the social fact of the Great Power hierarchy and episodes of consensus among military theorists – generate widespread agreement regarding power, strategy, and interests, which reduces perceived ambiguity and greases the wheels of competition and war. This perceived reduction in ambiguity is illusory, however, as later events typically demonstrate.

---

[40] Fearon, "Rationalist Explanations for War"; Powell, "War as a Commitment Problem." *International Organization* 60 (2006): 169–203; Powell, *In the Shadow of Power*; Smith and Stam, "Bargaining and the Nature of War"; Wagner, "Bargaining and War"; Weisiger, *Logics of War*.

Domestic Politics and Culture. Scholars have long recognized that international and domestic factors combine to influence military planning.[41] A substantial literature has arisen to unpack the domestic factors that affect military planning and the decision to go to war.[42] Military organizations develop their own internal cultures, which independently encourage changes in particular directions.[43] Political structures may allow some military strategies and prevent others.[44] Interaction between political decision-making and perceived international threats also affect states' military planning.[45] Global cultural models influence domestic adoption of military practices.[46]

---

[41] Deborah D. Avant, *Political Institutions and Military Change: Lessons from Peripheral Wars*. Ithaca: Cornell University Press, 1994; Deborah Avant, "Political Institutions and Military Effectiveness: Contemporary United States and United Kingdom. In *Creating Military Power: The Sources of Military Effectiveness*, edited by Risa A. Brooks and Elizabeth A. Stanley, 80–105. Stanford: Stanford University Press, 2007; Lynn Eden. *Whole World on Fire: Organizations, Knowledge, and Nuclear Weapons Devastation.* Ithaca: Cornell University Press, 2004; Matthew Evangelista, *Innovation and the Arms Race: How the United States and the Soviet Union Develop New Military Technologies.* Ithaca: Cornell University Press, 1988; Kimberly Marten Zisk, *Engaging the Enemy: Organization Theory and Soviet Military Innovation, 1955–1991.* Princeton: Princeton University Press, 1993.

[42] Risa A. Brooks, "Introduction: The Impact of Culture, Society, Institutions, and International Forces on Military Effectiveness." In *Creating Military Power: The Sources of Military Effectiveness*, edited by Risa A. Brooks and Elizabeth A. Stanley, 1–26. Stanford: Stanford University Press, 2007; Theo Farrell, "Culture and Military Power," *Review of International Studies* 24 (1998): 407–416.

[43] Avant, *Political Institutions and Military Change*; Evangelista, *Innovation and the Arms Race*; Elizabeth Kier, *Imagining War: French and British Military Doctrine between the Wars.* Princeton: Princeton University Press, 1997; Stephen Peter Rosen, *Winning the Next War: Innovation and the Modern Military.* Ithaca: Cornell University Press, 1991; Zisk, *Engaging the Enemy*.

[44] Risa A. Brooks, "Civil-Military Relations and Military Effectiveness: Egypt in the 1967 and 1973 Wars." In *Creating Military Power: The Sources of Military Effectiveness*, edited by Risa A. Brooks and Elizabeth A. Stanley, 106–135. Stanford: Stanford University Press, 2007; Avant, "Political Institutions and Military Effectiveness; Dan Reiter and Curtis Meek, "Determinants of Military Strategy 1903-1994: A Quantitative Empirical Test." *International Studies Quarterly* 43 (1999): 363–387; Michael C. Horowitz, *The Diffusion of Military Power: Causes and Consequences for International Relations.* Princeton: Princeton University Press, 2010.

[45] Emily O. Goldman, "International Competition and Military Effectiveness: Naval Air Power, 1919–1945." In *Creating Military Power: The Sources of Military Effectiveness*, edited by Risa A. Brooks and Elizabeth A. Stanley, 158–185. Stanford: Stanford University Press, 2007; Risa A. Brooks, *Shaping Strategy: The Civil-Military Politics of Strategic Assessment.* Princeton: Princeton University Press, 2008.

[46] Theo Farrell and Terry Terriff (eds.), *The Sources of Military Change: Culture, Politics, Technology.* Boulder: Lynne Rienner, 2002; Emily O. Goldman, "The Spread of Western Military Models to Ottoman Turkey and Meiji Japan." In *The Sources of Military*

Most importantly, scholars have argued that domestic constituencies may provide an audience akin to the international audience watching the outcome of Great Power wars.[47] As Fearon writes, decision-makers face a domestic audience that metes out rewards and punishments for "loss of credibility, face, or honor" in international engagements, similar to the allocation of status awarded by the international audience.[48] Depending on the country, these domestic audiences may prove influential for the decisions of elites.

The arguments in this book complement these diverse studies by exploring how the international system provides the grist that domestic actors utilize to promote their interests or interpretations. Political leaders may wish to enhance the status of the country, but as I argue, the rules of Great Power promotion and demotion are beyond the influence of any single country.[49] Military planners may leverage the dominant military paradigm to gain advantages for their domestic coalition, but that leverage depends on the strength of the international consensus for those military theories.[50] Wars may be promoted with domestic goals in mind, but warmongering will be more successful if based on appeals to increased status and prestige of the state in the Great Power hierarchy. This book lays out these components of the international system that provide important context for domestic actors.

The arguments of this book echo some themes of domestic politics arguments, but focus principally on a different level of analysis. My theory attends to the macro level of the international system and seeks to explain how the rules of the international system lead to Great Power competition. However, domestic factors in each state must also align to bring about the decision to go to war, and these domestic factors lie

Change: Culture, Politics, Technology, edited by Theo Farrell and Terry Terriff, 41–68. Boulder: Lynne Rienner, 2002.

[47] Bruce Bueno de Mesquita, Alastair Smith, Randolph M. Siverson, and James D. Morrow. *The Logic of Political Survival.* Cambridge, MA: MIT Press, 2003; James D. Fearon, "Domestic Political Audiences and the Escalation of International Disputes." *American Political Science Review* 88 (1994): 577–592.

[48] Fearon, "Domestic Political Audiences and the Escalation of International Disputes," 581.

[49] Jacques Hymans, *The Psychology of Nuclear Proliferation: Identity, Emotions, and Foreign Policy.* Cambridge: Cambridge University Press, 2006; Bueno de Mesquita, Smith, Siverson, and Morrow, *The Logic of Political Survival.*

[50] Scott D. Sagan, "Why Do States Build Nuclear Weapons? Three Models in Search of a Bomb." *International Security* 21 (1996–1997): 54–86; Scott D. Sagan, "1914 Revisited: Allies, Offense, and Instability." *International Security* 11 (1986): 151–175; Jack Snyder, *The Ideology of the Offensive: Military Decision Making and the Disasters of 1914.* Ithaca: Cornell University Press, 1984.

outside the scope of the theory of this book. In short, the arguments outlined in this book are potentially complementary for much of the scholarship focused on domestic politics.

Constructivism

Constructivist theory is central to the arguments developed in this book. The tradition, which shares intellectual roots with world society theory in sociology, argues that key realist concepts such as power and interests as well as the identities of states themselves, are socially constructed.[51] Following constructivist theory, the book resists the notion that strategy, interests, or power are the simple product of material circumstances, or that war evolves merely due to exogenous factors such as technological determinism. Ideas matter, and they shape international military competition in ways that cannot be predicted a priori.[52]

Alexander Wendt's classic declaration that "the identities and interests of purposive actors are constructed by these shared ideas rather than given by nature" is a rallying cry for the perspective.[53] One of the primary assumptions of the constructivist perspective is that power is socially constructed rather than inherent in material properties. As Wendt puts it, "[I]deas constitute those ostensibly 'material' causes in the first place."[54] This book develops a constructivist view of power by showing that the indicators used to measure military power in any given historical era are developed from lessons "learned" from history within the

---

[51] Wendt, *Social Theory of International Politics*; Wendt, "Anarchy Is What States Make of It"; Finnemore, *National Interests in International Society*; Katzenstein, *The Culture of National Security*; Finnemore, "Norms, Culture, and World Politics." For excellent reviews, see: Theo Farrell, "Constructivist Security Studies: Portrait of a Research Program." *International Studies Review* 4 (2002): 49–72; John Gerard Ruggie, "What Makes the World Hang Together? Neo-Utilitarianism and the Social Constructivist Challenge." *International Organization* 52 (1998): 855–885; Martha Finnemore and Kathryn Sikkink, "Taking Stock: The Constructivist Research Program in International Relations and Comparative Politics." *Annual Review of Political Science* 4 (2001): 391–416.

[52] Michael Barnett and Martha Finnemore, *Rules for the World: International Organizations in Global Politics*. Ithaca: Cornell University Press, 2004; Farrell, "Constructivist Security Studies"; Theo Farrell, *The Norms of War: Cultural Beliefs and Modern Conflict*. Boulder: Lynne Rienner, 2005; Theo Farrell, "World Culture and Military Power." *Security Studies* 14 (3): 448–488, 2005; John S. Duffield, Theo Farrell, Richard Price, and Michael C. Desch. "Isms and Schisms: Culturalism versus Realism in Security Studies." *International Security* 24.1 (1999): 156–180.

[53] Wendt, *Social Theory of International Politics*, 1.

[54] Wendt, *Social Theory of International Politics*, 94.

international community. These understandings then become reified as the basis of the Great Power hierarchy. In other words, Great Powers are seen as powerful in part because the accepted indicators of power are reflexive descriptions of the Great Powers.

Similarly, constructivist scholars have argued that national interests are constituted by the social system rather than by exogenous forces. Martha Finnemore argues that "[i]nterests are not just 'out there' waiting to be discovered; they are constructed through social interaction."[55] As she points out, states may want security, but figuring out what that entails is highly ambiguous. Emanuel Adler and Michael Barnett and their coauthors also show that understandings of security are constructed within "security communities."[56] I argue similarly that national security interests are constructed in part through Great Power efforts to outdo their rivals.

Some have misinterpreted constructivism as claiming that the entire world exists "in our heads," or that battle outcomes and weapon effects are mere figments of the imagination. This book makes no such ridiculous claims. However, subsequent chapters highlight the complexities and ambiguities of material reality, which allow for a multiplicity of plausible interpretations and for ample room for social construction processes to influence the course of military competition and warfare.

While the book primarily uses the sociological language of world society theory, described later here, the core ideas map directly onto constructivist scholarship in international relations. Thus, the book can be seen as an effort to contribute to constructivist scholarship by tracing the evolving constructions of power, interests, and strategy in the Great Power system, and their implications for the course of Great Power competition and conflict.

World Society Theory

World society theory is best known for predicting the global diffusion of ideas and policies in areas such as education, human rights, the environment, and law.[57] World society theory argues that a common global

[55] Finnemore, *National Interests in International Society*, 2.
[56] Emanuel Adler and Michael Barnett, eds. *Security Communities*. Cambridge: Cambridge University Press, 1998.
[57] John W. Meyer, John Boli, George M. Thomas, and Francisco O. Ramirez, "World Society and the Nation-State." *American Journal of Sociology* 103 (1997): 144–181; John W. Meyer, "World Society, Institutional Theories, and the Actor." *Annual Review*

culture has created a global society.[58] For instance, ideas and norms regarding environmental protection, espoused by the United Nations and other international groups influence policy and activity on a global scale.[59] Along these lines, Eyre and Suchman show that military procurement follows global norms and fads rather than just serving local military needs.[60] This book contains many examples of conventional world society diffusion. For instance, following the Franco-Prussian War, militaries around the globe sought to emulate nearly every facet of the Prussian military, from the Prussian General Staff to Prussian strategy. Many even adopted Prussian-style military gear and its educational system.

However, the book largely employs world society theory in novel ways to address new questions and key shortcomings in the theory. Drawing on the broader literature of cultural sociology in a search to understand the emergence of new institutional forms and the dynamics of institutional change, the book focuses on the center of world society rather than diffusion to the periphery.[61] Why did the Great Powers start pursuing

of Sociology 36 (2010): 1–20; Evan Schofer, Ann Hironaka, David John Frank, and Wesley Longhofer, "Sociological Institutionalism and World Society." In *The Wiley-Blackwell Companion to Political Sociology*, edited by Edwin Amenta, Kate Nash, and Alan Scott, 57–68. New York: Wiley-Blackwell, 2012; John Boli and George M. Thomas, "World Culture in the World Polity: A Century of International Non-Governmental Organization." *American Sociological Review* 62.2 (1997): 171–190; Georg Krücken and Gili S. Drori (eds.), *World Society: The Writings of John Meyer*. New York: Oxford University Press, 2010; Michael Lounsbury and Marc Ventresca, "The New Structuralism in Organizational Theory." *Organization* 10 (2003): 457–480; Walter W. Powell and Paul J. DiMaggio, *The New Institutionalism in Organizational Analysis*. Chicago: University of Chicago Press, 2012; Gili S. Drori, John W. Meyer, and Hokyu Hwang, *Globalization and Organization: World Society and Organizational Change*. New York: Oxford University Press, 2006; Gili S. Drori, John W. Meyer, Francisco Ramirez, and Evan Schofer, *Science in the Modern World Polity: Institutionalization and Globalization*. Stanford: Stanford University Press, 2003.

[58] Pertti Alasuutari, *The Synchronization of National Policies: Ethnography of the Global Tribe of Moderns*. New York: Routledge, 2016; Elizabeth Boyle, Minzee Kim, and Wesley Longhofer, "Abortion Liberalization in World Society." *American Journal of Sociology*, Forthcoming; Selina Gallo-Cruz, "Organizing Global Nonviolence: The Growth and Spread of Nonviolent INGOs, 1948–2003." *Research in Social Movements, Conflict, and Change* 34 (2012): 213–256.

[59] Ann Hironaka, *Greening the Globe: World Society and Environmental Change*. Cambridge: Cambridge University Press, 2014.

[60] Mark C. Suchman and Dana P. Eyre, "Military Procurement as Rational Myth: Notes on the Social Construction of Weapons Proliferation." *Sociological Forum* 7 (1992): 137–161.

[61] Bruce G. Carruthers and Wendy Nelson Espeland, "Accounting for Rationality: Double-Entry Bookkeeping and the Rhetoric of Economic Rationality." *American Journal of Sociology* 97 (1991): 31–69; Marion Fourcade, *Economists and Societies: Discipline and*

certain resources or strategies in one era, and why did they change in the next? The emergence of new military paradigms or rubrics in world society resembles a process of organizational learning. However, the book sticks to world society theory's roots in social constructivism, arguing that the process of organizational learning involves highly arbitrary lessons in an ambiguous world, rather than functional adaptation.[62] The process could be likened to March's idea of "superstitious learning," operating at a collective level in world society.[63]

It is generally presumed that new military strategies or technologies are adopted and diffuse because of their instrumental utility. By contrast, this book argues that military plans are anchored in quite arbitrary ideas and interpretations of the Great Power hierarchy that are widely accepted in world society. Those ideas are legitimated by reference to the existing hierarchy. Consequently, disruptions to the Great Power hierarchy provoke episodes of rethinking and institutional change, as the community of European military scholars seeks to make sense of the emergence of a new Great Power. Newly constructed narratives propel the military plans and competitions of the next generation. Arguments build on the work of David Strang, who has highlighted how organizations draw on exemplary firms in industry to inform their plans.[64] Drawing on Strang's insights, in the case of European military affairs the process is very much a collective one, whereby a transnational group of military theorists generate new narratives in world society.

Profession in the United States, Britain, and France, 1890s to 1990s. Princeton: Princeton University Press, 2010; Heather A. Haveman, "Follow the Leader: Mimetic Isomorphism and Entry into New Markets." *Administrative Science Quarterly* 38 (1993): 593–627; Kieran Healy, *Last Best Gifts: Altruism and the Market for Human Blood and Organs.* Chicago: University of Chicago Press. 2006; Alexander Hicks, *Social Democracy and Welfare Capitalism: A Century of Income Security Politics.* Ithaca: Cornell University Press, 1999; Mitchell L. Stevens, *Creating a Class: College Admissions and the Education of Elites.* Cambridge, MA: Harvard University Press, 2009; Ann Swidler, "What Anchors Cultural Practices." In *The Practice Turn in Contemporary Theory,* edited by Theodore R. Schatzki, Karin Knorr Cetina, and Eike von Savigny, 74–92. London: Routledge, 2001; Ann Swidler, "Culture in Action: Symbols and Strategies." *American Sociological Review* (1986): 273–286.

[62] Frank Dobbin, *Inventing Equal Opportunity.* Princeton: Princeton University Press, 2011.

[63] James G. March, *The Ambiguities of Experience.* Ithaca: Cornell University Press, 2010.

[64] David Strang, *Learning by Example: Imitation and Innovation at a Global Bank.* Princeton: Princeton University Press, 2010; David Strang and Michael W. Macy, "In Search of Excellence: Fads, Success Stories, and Adaptive Emulation." *The American Journal of Sociology* 107 (2001): 147–182.

The book also draws on the world society insight that the modern nation-state is fundamentally constructed and sustained by the international system.[65] The identity of being a Great Power – and the expanded sense of actorhood and agency that goes with it – is not a natural result of military prowess, but rather a historically emergent feature of the European system. The hubris associated with the Great Power identity can be understood in terms of the broader expansions of actorhood observed in the Western system.[66]

Finally, this book addresses an issue that world society scholars frequently ignore: war and conflict.[67] World society scholars have mainly focused on the diffusion of progressive global norms related to education, environment, and human rights.[68] However, world society constructs and empowers states to address a range of goals, including improvements in their security. The Great Power identity and narratives about the strategies and resources that lead to power are institutionalized in world

---

[65] John W. Meyer and Ronald L. Jepperson, "The 'Actors' of Modern Society: The Cultural Construction of Social Agency." *Sociological Theory* 18 (2000): 100–120.

[66] Meyer and Jepperson, "The 'Actors' of Modern Society"; John W. Meyer, "World Society, Institutional Theories, and the Actor."

[67] But see Colin J. Beck, "The World-Cultural Origins of Revolutionary Waves: Five Centuries of European Contention." *Social Science History* 35.2 (2011): 167–207; Elizabeth Heger Boyle and Sharon E. Preves, "National Politics as International Process: The Case of Anti-Female-Genital-Cutting Laws." *Law & Society Review* 34.3 (2000): 703–737; Frank Dobbin, *Forging Industrial Policy: The United States, Britain, and France in the Railway Age.* New York: Cambridge University Press, 1994; Tim Hallett and Marc J. Ventresca, "Inhabited Institutions: Social Interactions and Organizational Forms in Gouldner's *Patterns of Industrial Bureaucracy.*" *Theory and Society* 35 (2006): 213–236; Marc Schneiberg and Sarah A. Soule, "Institutionalization as a Contested, Multi-Level Process: Rate Regulation in American Fire Insurance." In *Social Movements and Organization Theory*, edited by Jerry Davis, Doug McAdam, Dick Scott, and Mayer Zald, 122–160. Cambridge: Cambridge University Press, 2005.

[68] Wade M. Cole, "Sovereignty Relinquished? Explaining Commitment to the International Human Rights Covenants, 1966–1999." *American Sociological Review* 70 (2005): 472–495; Wade M. Cole, "Human Rights as Myth and Ceremony? Reevaluating the Effectiveness of Human Rights Treaties, 1981–2007." *American Journal of Sociology* 117 (2012): 1131–1171; Wade M. Cole and Francisco O. Ramirez, "Conditional Decoupling: Assessing the Impact of National Human Rights Institutions, 1981 to 2004." *American Sociological Review* 78 (2013): 702–725; David John Frank and Jay Gabler, *Reconstructing the University: Worldwide Shifts in Academia in the 20th Century.* Stanford: Stanford University Press, 2006; Emilie M. Hafner-Burton and Kiyoteru Tsutsui, "Human Rights in a Globalizing World: The Paradox of Empty Promises." *American Journal of Sociology* 110 (2005): 1373–1411; Alwyn Lim and Kiyoteru Tsutsui, "Globalization and Commitment in Corporate Social Responsibility: Cross-National Analyses of Institutional and Political-Economy Effects." *American Sociological Review* 77 (2012): 69–98.

society. In such a world, there is much potential for conflict.[69] The result is not the Hobbesian conflict imagined by realists, but rather something akin to a set of jousts among the Great Powers played out in front of a global audience.

THE OBSOLESCENCE OF GREAT POWER WAR?

War has dominated the international affairs of Europe and has fundamentally "shaped the evolution of the modern international system," as Levy and Thompson observe.[70] Conventional scholarship interprets European history as a centuries-long competition for survival. This book seeks to recast this history as a series of duels within a society of nations over arbitrary tokens of power – tokens that are costly to acquire and often have little intrinsic value in the end.

While it is no small matter to reinterpret Great Power conflict, one may nevertheless ask: Is this study relevant for the present day, where Great Power wars appear to be few and far between? Recent scholarship attests to the unprecedented period of calm among the Great Powers.[71] Perhaps Great Power war has become relegated to the dustbin of history, along with other barbaric practices that our civilization has outgrown.

Scholars have pointed to several factors that might contribute to the decline or even obsolescence of interstate war.[72] Mueller proposes that a growing aversion to war throughout the international community is responsible for the current period of peace among the industrialized states.[73] Goldstein emphasizes the increasing effectiveness of the UN peacekeeping forces and the role of international organizations.[74] Pinker notes the rise of political and economic institutions that allow the exercise

[69] Boli and Thomas, *Constructing World Culture*.
[70] Jack S. Levy and William R. Thompson, *Causes of War*. Malden: Wiley-Blackwell, 2010: 3.
[71] John Lewis Gaddis, *The Long Peace: Inquiries into the History of the Cold War*. Oxford: Oxford University Press, 1987; Randolph M. Siverson and Michael D. Ward, "The Long Peace: A Reconsideration." *International Organization* 56 (2002): 679–691. Siverson and Ward show that individual Great Power dyads have gone even longer without a war.
[72] Nils Petter Gleditsch, Steven Pinker, Bradley A. Thayer, Jack S. Levy, and William R. Thompson, "The Decline of War." *International Studies Review* 15 (2013): 396–419; Azar Gat, *War in Human Civilization*. Oxford: Oxford University Press, 2006.
[73] John Mueller, *The Remnants of War*. Ithaca: Cornell University Press, 2004; John Mueller, *Retreat from Doomsday: The Obsolescence of Major War*. New York: Basic Books, 1989.
[74] Joshua S. Goldstein, *Winning the War on War: The Decline of Armed Conflict Worldwide*. New York: Dutton, 2011.

of more pacific human capacities for empathy, self-control, morality, and reason.[75] Yet critics note the absence of consideration of the power dynamics of the international system in these accounts.[76] Scholars in previous eras also pointed to the existence of similar factors in their time; nevertheless, major wars followed. Can we be sure that our own era will be different?

This book argues that Great Power wars have historically been motivated largely by the quest for status in the Great Power hierarchy, spurring competitions over symbolic "tokens" of power. Defeating a rival boosts the status of the victor within the hierarchy of Great Power states. For the current peace to continue indefinitely into the future, states must either cease competing generally, which is hard to imagine, or the tokens of power must shift away from military prowess toward some less destructive form of state activity. Optimists might suggest that economic competition is replacing military victory as the basis for the international hierarchy. The rise in status of Japan and Germany, despite their withdrawal from military competition, seems encouraging. And international institutions may ultimately shepherd such a transition, as suggested by Mueller, Goldstein, and other scholars.

However, I suggest that military prowess still remains central to the global status order. While the Cold War did not turn hot, the last major Great Power rivalry between the United States and the Soviet Union is only a quarter century in the past. And Great Powers continue to flex their muscles, in ways that suggests military power continues to bear symbolic weight. This seems most true of the United States, which has had its finger in most contemporary conflicts, but one can also interpret conflicts in the Falklands or Crimea as similar efforts to sustain status.[77] Nations such as China continue to develop military capability as part of a broader effort to stand at the center of the international stage as a Great Power.

The point is not to say that military competition is inevitable or rational. Indeed, a central theme of this book is that the power and security afforded by military competition is illusory. The issue is that military prowess remains one of the key currencies of the international

---

[75] Steven Pinker, *The Better Angels of Our Nature: Why Violence Has Declined*. New York: Viking, 2011.

[76] Bradley A. Thayer, "Humans, Not Angels: Reasons to Doubt the Decline of War Thesis." *International Studies Review* 15 (2013): 405–411; Jack S. Levy and William R. Thompson, "The Decline of War? Multiple Trajectories and Diverging Trends." *International Studies Review* (2013): 16–24.

[77] Sarkees and Wayman, *Resort to War*.

realm, perhaps now joined by other status markers such as economic success, in a very competitive community of states.

What would it take to fully dispel military competition as a source of status? One theme developed later in this book is that nations take object lessons from history. If the United States – currently the undisputed military hegemon – were to spectacularly implode for some nonmilitary reason (economic, environmental, or otherwise), the international community might draw new "lessons" and shift attention and energies away from military affairs. Instead, the continued dominance of the United States currently reinforces the notion that the global leader is necessarily a *military* power. The lengthy history of military conflict in the West has deeply enshrined war as a primary state activity, a point taken up again in Chapter 9. Replacing military capability as the primary measure of state power may require substantial reshaping of the international system.

Thus it may be premature to expect the obsolescence of rivalry and one-upmanship among the Great Powers. The community of nations is rife with status competition, whether military, economic, or over numbers of Olympic medals and Nobel prizes. This may not be an inevitable state of affairs, but the historical roots of this pattern are long and deep. At best, over the medium term, we can hope that the underlying dynamics motivating Great Power competition discussed in this book will be expressed in a less deadly form than war. And even if we are fortunate enough to see Great Power wars becoming a relic of the past, the arguments of this book have relevance in other arenas. Patterns of competition over symbolic tokens of power can be seen in regional rivalries and even forms of nonmilitary state competition, topics that are addressed more fully in the conclusion.

OVERVIEW OF THE BOOK

This book characterizes military competition as a deeply social process operating within an international community of states. The book reframes key concepts: (1) Power – how states come to understand and evaluate power; (2) Strategy – how states distill "lessons" from major wars and how that affects subsequent military competition; and (3) Competition and interests – how states identify rivals and compete in the international community. Chapters 2, 3, and 4 develop these theoretical points, in turn, each illustrated by a brief historical case.

Chapters 5 through 8 apply the theoretical arguments to major cases of Great Power competition in the past 150 years: the Franco-Prussian War, the world wars, and the Cold War. The empirical cases are broad and sweeping, seeking to convey the full breadth of the book's arguments, rather than delving into fine-grained historical detail. While the cases focus on Great Power wars, the arguments could be applied to a range of interstate wars, such as conflicts in the Indian subcontinent or the Middle East. They might also be extended, with some caveats, to asymmetric conflicts between the Great Powers and weaker states. Such applications will be discussed in the conclusion.

Theoretical Chapters

Chapter 2 examines the Great Power hierarchy of states. While academics continue to debate abstract definitions of power, political decision-makers are forced to make pragmatic assessments of military capability, based on the understandings of their era. This chapter examines the construction of the rubrics that have been used to evaluate power historically. I argue that evaluations of power largely reduce to post hoc characterizations of the existing Great Power states, with little predictive power for future conflicts. The chapter also argues that becoming a Great Power is partly a matter of social identity, not simply the result of material capability. Arguments are illustrated via a discussion of the changing Great Power hierarchy over the last four centuries, with particular attention to the emergence of the United States as a Great Power.

Chapter 3 examines the development of military strategy and points to the difficulties of learning from history. Between wars, militaries engage in close study of the most recent Great Power war. In practice, the lessons learned from history often reduce to post hoc descriptions of the recent victors. From a social science perspective, it is not surprising that such lessons are flawed, given the difficulties of learning from a single case. However, the lessons gleaned from Great Power wars are highly consequential because they provide the basis for future military plans and calculations. This chapter illustrates these arguments by looking at the military use of cavalry in the late nineteenth century.

Chapter 4 examines national interests and the causes of war. War is the most consequential form of Great Power competition, although other competitions such as arms races and diplomatic negotiations also matter. These competitions among the Great Powers often take on a life of their own, far beyond the original value of the stake of contention. This chapter briefly discusses the origins of the Franco-Prussian War of 1870 as an example of Great Power competition.

Empirical Cases

Chapter 5 describes the late nineteenth-century paradigm of warfare, as exemplified in the military planning for the First World War. World War I represents a particularly vexing case for conventional theories, because all the participants were caught flat-footed by the unexpected course of the war. In short, the European militaries experienced the massive ambiguity that underlies wars. Since France had fought Prussia/Germany only forty years previously, both sides believed they knew what to expect and prepared for a replay of that war. When history failed to repeat itself, the First World War proved a huge shock for all.

Chapter 6 examines the planning for the Second World War with a focus on the development of tank technology. Technology might be seen as a special case of strategy development, since the objective properties of a technology can be well understood. More ambiguous, however, are the battle conditions under which a military technology will be deployed. In the case of tanks, the development of tank capabilities and strategies depended on assumptions about the conditions of the battlefield. This chapter addresses the academic literature on tanks and their role in technological innovation.

Chapter 7 focuses on the nuclear arms race and the implications for the five Great Powers after the Second World War. As typical in Great Power competitions, the frenzy to acquire the atomic bomb and the subsequent superpower arms race was driven by the competitive context of the Great Power system. Nuclear weapons became an essential symbol of Great Power status. This chapter argues that the arms race was driven primarily by the Great Power value in one-upmanship rather than by the military utility of nuclear weapons.

Chapter 8 examines the onset of the Korean War in 1950 within the general context of the Cold War. The Korean War was one of the largest interstate conflicts of the Cold War, eventually involving all of the Great Power states. The involvement of the United States on the Korean peninsula clearly reveals the competitive nature of Great Power dynamics. This chapter also discusses the enmity between the Soviet Union and the United States as a social construction that emerged from ambiguous conditions at the end of the Second World War.

Chapter 9 concludes with a discussion of the book's implications. The alternative framework of war presented in this book does not easily adapt to speculations of how military learning might be made more efficient. Military planners work with imperfect data under conditions of substantial ambiguity. This problem cannot be easily remedied. Instead, recognizing the tenuous foundations on which military theories are based might encourage greater caution among states, which have historically been all too eager to engage in military competition and vie for tokens of power.

2

The Measurement of Military Power

"The concept of power is one of the most troublesome in the field of international relations and, more generally, political science."[1]

Power is a central concept in the study of war. Military calculations are fundamentally based on the evaluation of the relative military power of potential enemies and allies. Those states with the most power – the Great Powers – have substantial impact on the international affairs of the day. As Copeland notes, "For realists, there is one factor that cuts across all these wars, one factor that drives states regardless of their particular characteristics: in a word, *power*."[2]

Yet traditional scholarship has had considerable difficulty pinning down a satisfactory empirical measure of power. In particular, scholars have been vexed by the mismatch between the outcome of wars and the standard indicators of military power, as will be discussed. Standard indicators of power have been surprisingly poor at predicting war outcomes a priori. In a startling number of cases, the seemingly more powerful state suffered unexpected catastrophic losses, while the ostensibly weaker state ended up victorious.[3]

---

[1] Robert Gilpin, *War and Change in World Politics*. Cambridge: Cambridge University Press, 1981, 13.

[2] Dale C. Copeland, *The Origins of Major War*. Ithaca: Cornell University Press, 2000, 1.

[3] General Rupert Smith, *The Utility of Force: The Art of War in the Modern World*. New York: Knopf, 2007; William C. Martel, *Victory in War: Foundations of Modern Strategy*, revised second edition. Cambridge: Cambridge University Press, 2011; Patricia L. Sullivan, *Who Wins: Predicting Strategic Success and Failure in Armed Conflict*. Oxford: Oxford University Press, 2012; Patricia L. Sullivan, "War Aims and War Outcomes: Why Powerful States Lose Limited Wars." *The Journal of Conflict Resolution* 51 (2007): 496–524.

This chapter highlights recent scholarship as well as classic work by Robert Jervis that suggests power might be better understood as multidimensional and contingent rather than as a single global attribute.[4] In contrast to the conventional belief that military power can be measured by a fairly straightforward and broadly generalizable index, the work of these scholars suggests that military power may be fundamentally dependent on context. The type of power necessary to have prevailed in the Second World War may be very different from the power needed for the Cold War conflicts in the global South, for instance. Different types of power might be needed for political goals such as changing the political structure of a country, in contrast to the classic military goal of occupying territory.[5] Instead, as these scholars have argued, military power can better be understood as a multifaceted construct.

Yet this multifaceted definition of power, while intellectually more satisfying, leads to another puzzle. Practically speaking, there is strong consensus in the international system on which states have the greatest military power in each era.[6] Throughout history, the states known as the Great Powers carry the preponderance of diplomatic and political weight in the international affairs of each era. If power is complex and contingent, what is the basis for the simple one-dimensional hierarchy that is broadly recognized throughout the international community?

The answer developed in this chapter is that Great Power status in the international system is rooted in a tautological interpretation of past events. Great Power status derives principally from the record of a

---

[4] Stephen Biddle, *Military Power: Explaining Victory and Defeat in Modern Battle*. Princeton: Princeton University Press, 2004; Emily O. Goldman, *Power in Uncertain Times: Strategy in the Fog of Peace*. Stanford: Stanford University Press, 2011; Robert Jervis, *Perception and Misperception in International Politics*. Princeton: Princeton University Press, 1976; Simon Reich and Richard Ned Lebow, *Good-Bye Hegemony! Power and Influence in the Global System*. Princeton: Princeton University Press, 2014; Patricia L. Sullivan, *Who Wins: Predicting Strategic Success and Failure in Armed Conflict*. Oxford: Oxford University Press, 2012; William Curti Wohlforth, *The Elusive Balance: Power and Perceptions during the Cold War*. Ithaca: Cornell University Press, 1993.

[5] Martel, *Victory in War*; Smith, *The Utility of Force*; Sullivan, *Who Wins*; Sullivan, "War Aims and War Outcomes."

[6] J. David Singer and Melvin Small, *The Wages of War, 1816–1965*. Ann Arbor: Inter-University Consortium for Political Research, 1974; Jack S. Levy, *War in the Modern Great Power System, 1495–1975*. Lexington: University Press of Kentucky, 1983; Gordon A. Craig, *Europe since 1815*. New York: Holt, Rinehart and Winston, 1966; Derek McKay and H. M. Scott, *The Rise of the Great Powers, 1648–1815*. New York: Longman, 1983; A. J. P. Taylor, *The Struggle for Mastery in Europe, 1848–1918*. Oxford: Clarendon Press, 1954; Kenneth N. Waltz, *Theory of International Politics*. Reading: Addison-Wesley, 1979.

state's past military victories against other Powers. Simply put, the victors of recent major wars are recognized as the Great Powers. Military theorists and planners work backwards – aided by the efficient war assumption – to define and measure power in a manner that is congruent with the established Great Power hierarchy. As the Great Power hierarchy shifts in response to the outcomes of wars, understandings of power across the international community tend to change in lockstep. Moreover, Great Power status requires that a Great Power participate in international military competition in order to maintain its Great Power status, increasing the competition and likelihood of war for the Great Powers.

In other words, Great Power status, as well as widely held beliefs about the sources of power in a given era, can best be understood as social constructions. The socially constructed understanding of power is extremely consequential for both great and small powers. Perceived power yields real deference. The attributes and resources believed to generate power become the primary foci of military competition, an argument developed further in Chapter 4. However, to the extent that power is actually highly contextual and multifaceted, the socially constructed understandings of power in any particular era are likely to prove an unreliable basis for predicting the future. Consequently, there is a frequent mismatch between perceptions of state military power and the outcomes of subsequent Great Power wars.

This chapter begins with a short history of two Great Power states, France and Prussia/Germany, over the past four centuries. The brief sketch illustrates how Great Power victory affected the status of nations and also reshaped military thought across Europe, changing beliefs about the basis of military power. Next, the traditional literature on power is reviewed. Third, the chapter develops the idea that power is merely a retrospective label drawn from the outcome of past events. Military scholars in the international community generate frameworks for evaluating power in order to explain why the victorious state won. In turn, these theories about power are highly consequential, driving Great Power states to expand their interests and engage in competition with rivals. Finally, these dynamics are illustrated by a brief history of the rise of the United States from peripheral status to post–Second World War superpower. The example of the United States also shows that power involves identity: to be a Great Power, a state must not only win wars but also embrace the Great Power role by participating in international affairs.

HISTORICAL GREAT POWER SHIFTS

This section presents a brief history of the back-and-forth passing of power between two Great Powers, France and Prussia/Germany, who vied for position at or near the top of the Great Power hierarchy over the course of several centuries. Shifts in relative position between France and Prussia-Germany prompted successive reevaluations of the fundamental bases of military power across the system as a whole. After each reversal, European militaries looked to the new victor as embodying the ideal principles of military power, and revised their theories of power to match. Meanwhile, the defeated state was castigated as foolishly slow to recognize new military opportunities.

In this section I draw on criticisms of the efficient war hypothesis developed in Chapter 1 to recast the competition between France and Prussia/Germany. I suggest that the shifting tides of war can be understood as illustrating the probabilistic outcomes of interactions highly complex and contingent interactions, as discussed in greater detail in Chapter 3. Superiority in the Great Power hierarchy might more readily be likened to a coin toss between top contenders, dependent on the details of circumstance and chance rather than an objective indication of generalized military power. Small differences of terrain, weather, or particular command decisions might have yielded a different victor. Overall differences in power, if such a thing exists, might be made manifest were the war refought hundreds of times. But the result of a single war is likely to be statistical noise rather than a reliable signal indicating national military power. Nevertheless, shifts in the Great Power hierarchy have historically been taken as extremely salient social facts that prompted European-wide changes in military planning and strategy.

This brief historical sketch begins in 1648, when France was considered one of the leading Great Powers in Europe due to its strong showing in the Thirty Years War. Contemporaries assumed French victories were indicative of the preeminence of its military. Indeed, the France of Louis XIV was widely regarded as having the best army in Europe. "At the beginning of the century, under Louis XIV, the French army was by common consent the most perfect military instrument in Europe."[7] In recognition of French power, the rest of Europe modeled their militaries after the French throughout the seventeenth and

---

[7] Walter Louis Dorn, *Competition for Empire, 1740–1763.* New York: Harper Brothers, 1940, p. 85.

eighteenth centuries. "The [French] military institutions ... were copied with local variants by all the other states of Western Europe, Britain not excepted, in much the same way as was French architecture, French art, French fashions, French court protocol, and French cuisine."[8] France, given its superiority on the indicators of the day of territorial size, genius of commanders, and wealth of treasury, appeared to be militarily indomitable. Louis XIV further solidified the power of France through successful wars against Spain, Dutch Netherlands, England, Sweden, Austria, Denmark, Brandenberg-Prussia, and the Holy Roman Empire.[9]

A century later, however, the tiny city-state of Prussia astonished Europe with its victory over the combined Great Power armies of France, Austria, and Russia. Triumphing in the Seven Years War with the aid of England, the previously inconsequential Prussia was suddenly viewed as a serious contender among the Great Powers. Prussia was very different from France, and had none of the attributes of territorial size, population, or state wealth that had been assumed to be essential sources of power according to the military theories of the day.[10] Nevertheless, the indisputable fact of Prussian victory suggested to military practitioners that a new way of war had emerged.

Following Prussia's surprising victory, eighteenth-century military theorists scrambled to develop new theories of war that would explain Prussian military might.[11] In hopes of replicating Prussian success, a "wave of Prussian imitation" overtook the continent after 1763.[12] "In Europe generally military men sought to express their admiration for things Prussian by imitating every conceivable external of [Prussian King] Frederick's army, rather as a savage might adorn himself with the feathers of an eagle in an attempt to endow himself with the creature's qualities."[13] The militaries of Europe copied virtually everything Prussian, down to the style of the Prussian military hats and coats. International observers turned out to watch the Prussian training maneuvers, and

[8] Michael Howard, *War in European History*. Oxford: Oxford University Press, 1976, p. 66.
[9] John A. Lynn, *The Wars of Louis XIV, 1667–1714*. New York: Longman, 1999.
[10] Christopher Duffy, *The Army of Frederick the Great*. Vancouver: Douglas David and Charles Limited, 1974.
[11] John Childs, *Armies and Warfare in Europe, 1648–1789*. Manchester: Manchester University Press, 1982, p. vii.
[12] Basil H. Liddell Hart, *The Ghost of Napoleon*. New Haven: Yale University Press, 1935, p. 43.
[13] Duffy, *The Army of Frederick the Great*, 209.

"many disputes were settled by the statement: 'Oh, but I saw it in Prussia.'"[14] For a couple of decades, European understandings of military power were built on abstracted descriptions of the Prussian army, with an emphasis on the discipline and training of the soldiers as the key to success.

However, Prussia's moment in the sun was relatively brief. Despite its fearsome reputation, Prussia had an extraordinarily poor showing in the Napoleonic wars twenty years later. French armies quickly defeated Prussia in two decisive battles in 1806. Military theorists of the nineteenth century, including Scharnhorst, Gneisenau, Blücher, and Clausewitz, interpreted the Prussian defeats as indicating an objective reversal in military superiority. As one historian sagely noted in hindsight, "The impossible conservatism and anachronism of the Prussian style of discipline and tactics were finally revealed on the twin battlefields of Auerstadt and Jena in 1806."[15] Military scholars quickly reversed their adulation of Prussia, claiming instead that "it had been the mentality of the [Prussian] era, with its mindless discipline and its divorce of the people from the government, that was accountable in large measure for Prussia's humiliation by the French."[16] The discipline that had so recently been lauded as the source of Prussia's power was retrospectively constructed as a weakness that led to its defeat.

Although France was eventually defeated in 1815 by the combined strength of the rest of Europe, the impressive military effectiveness of Napoleonic France led to a major rethinking of military theory for the next century. "For the first time in the history of modern Europe a single state had inflicted a crushing defeat over all the other powers of the continent."[17] "The Napoleonic Wars overturned many of the theories of the eighteenth century model of war, including assumptions about the size, spirit, and feasibility of a mass army."[18] Theories based on the Napoleonic war were to dominate military thinking well into the twentieth century.

France was to enjoy its superior position over Prussia in the Great Power hierarchy for much of the nineteenth century, bolstered by military

---

[14] Gunther E. Rothenberg, *The Art of Warfare in the Age of Napoleon.* Bloomington: Indiana University Press, 1978, 19.

[15] Childs, *Armies and Warfare in Europe*, 70.

[16] Duffy, *The Army of Frederick the Great*, 211.

[17] Azar Gat, *The Origins of Military Thought from the Enlightenment to Clausewitz.* Oxford: Clarendon Press, 1989, 200.

[18] Michael Howard, *The Franco-Prussian War: The German Invasion of France, 1870–1871.* New York: Macmillan, 1962, 9.

victories against Russia, Mexico, Italy, and success in various diplomatic contests. However, in its next war against Prussia, France was shockingly defeated in only two months. As discussed in Chapter 5, the Prussian victory over France in 1870 gave ammunition to a new set of post-Napoleonic military theories that, in perfect hindsight, argued that Prussia alone had understood the evolving nature of war and developed the most powerful army in the world. Military leaders scrambled first to understand the quick, effective style of warfare exemplified by the Prussian military, and second to emulate it. These lessons were to have a substantial effect on the preparations for the First World War.

Prussia, now known as Germany, maintained its position at the top of the Great Power hierarchy only until the First World War. After the Allied victory in 1919, Prussia lost its luster and military theorists turned their attention elsewhere. In the interwar period, states often looked to France instead, emulating French tank strategy, for instance, as described in Chapter 6.

Nevertheless, the French way of war was thoroughly rejected following its ignominious defeat and occupation by Germany in 1940. Germany was also defeated in the Second World War, and postwar German leadership decided against making a bid for rearmament and Great Power status.[19] After 1945, Germany dropped out of the Great Power hierarchy. Although France remained a Great Power, its stunning defeat by Germany in the Second World War allowed only a tenuous foothold in the eyes of the international community (see Chapters 6 and 7).

Ultimately, both France and Germany were displaced in the Great Power hierarchy in favor of two new top Great Powers, the United States and the Soviet Union. Russia had been a long-standing member of the Great Powers, but toward the bottom of the hierarchy.[20] At the turn of the twentieth century, the United States had barely made the slate of Great Powers, by virtue of its victory in the Spanish-American war. By the end of the Second World War, however, both the Soviet Union and the United States had become the leading states in the Great Power hierarchy. Their position in the hierarchy was the result of their role in the Allied victory and success in postwar competitions such as the acquisition of nuclear capability (discussed in Chapter 7). The rise of the United States to Great

[19] John S. Duffield, *World Power Forsaken: Political Culture, International Institutions, and German Security Policy After Unification.* Stanford: Stanford University Press, 1998.

[20] Levy, *War in the Modern Great Power System*; McKay and Scott, *The Rise of the Great Powers*.

Power status is discussed in a short case study at the end of this chapter. The rise of the Soviet Union is discussed, even more briefly, in Chapter 8, which examines the origins of the Cold War.

There is strong agreement on this basic chronology of Great Power competition between France and Prussia/Germany. It is the interpretation of events that this chapter seeks to overturn. The conventional assumption, rooted in the efficient war hypothesis, is that the changing positions of France and Germany in the Great Power hierarchy signaled true differences in the extent of their military power, and more importantly implied changes in the fundamental basis of military power of particular historical eras.

By contrast, this chapter argues that Great Power history might better be understood as an essentially random outcome between closely matched militaries rather than as a series of decisive shifts in objective power or the means to obtain it. This is not to suggest that military power is imaginary, or that there is *no* objective basis for the measurement of military capability. France and Prussia/Germany did reliably defeat other states throughout their histories, especially those with minimal military forces. However, the alternating outcomes for the conflicts between France and Prussia/Germany may not have been the result of large objective shifts in actual military power, but rather the workings of contingency and chance on two closely matched militaries.

SCHOLARLY CONCEPTIONS OF POWER

Traditionally, scholars have defined military power in two ways. The first is a relational definition, in which the more powerful state is revealed through battle outcomes. This definition is implied in the efficient war hypothesis and has an intuitive appeal, since military power should meaningfully correspond with victory in war. Yet scholars have identified several problems with this approach, in particular that power can only be recognized in hindsight. Consequently, scholars have largely abandoned the relational definition in favor of a second approach: a material definition that is based on a list of objective material (and sometimes intangible) indicators such as military size and economic resources. However, the material approach has problems as well; perhaps the most distressing is the consistent failure of material attributes to correspond with military outcomes.

More recently, scholars have begun to articulate a multifaceted, contextual definition of power. From this perspective, the military power of a state is not a generalized property, but instead can only be measured relative to a specific opponent in a particular context. Hypothetically, a small state with favorable terrain might be more powerful in a military showdown than a Great Power bristling with an unusable nuclear arsenal. This nuanced definition of power might be more gratifying from an academic point of view. Its main drawback, however, is that it does not seem to explain power politics in practice. Each of these scholarly conceptions of power, therefore, suffers from serious disadvantages. This section unpacks these scholarly conceptions and their shortcomings.

Relational Definition of Power

Robert A. Dahl provided the classic statement of relational power as "A's ability to get B to do something it would not otherwise do."[21] And, in the case of Great Power competition, war is the most important and dramatic way that states force compliance on others. An instance of power, from this point of view, might be a war in which Germany defeated France and acquired territory that France would not otherwise have ceded.

The advantage of the relational definition is that it fits with the intuition that power should correlate with victory. After all, if military power does not correspond with victory, the concept of power seems rather useless. Battlefield outcomes are widely assumed to provide the ultimate test of military power. As Reiter remarks, "[C]ombat bears unavoidable truth ... As horrible as combat is, it does serve the critical function of providing real information to the belligerents."[22] It is assumed that errors in the evaluation of power will be corrected by the iron realities of the battlefield.

However, the relational definition has frequently been criticized by scholars because of the considerable difficulty of identifying the critical relationships in the equation. As James G. March has pointed out, it is challenging to know what A and B want in any given historical moment, much less whether B's actions were due to A's coercion or to wholly unrelated reasons.[23] For instance, in the France vs. Germany scenario, it is difficult to tell what aspect of Germany's military or political power led to French capitulation. Perhaps German victory was due to a domestic

[21] Robert A. Dahl, "The Concept of Power." *Behavioural Science* 2 (1957): 201–215.
[22] Dan Reiter, *How Wars End*. Princeton: Princeton University Press, 2009, 20.
[23] James G. March, "The Power of Power." In *Varieties of Political Theory*, edited by David Easton, 39–70. Englewood Cliffs: Prentice Hall, 1966.

French political crisis rather than any attribute of the German military. Or, more likely, a constellation of factors, some German and some French, affected the outcome. These and other ambiguities discussed in Chapter 3 suggest that the sources of power that led to victory are rarely clear-cut.

Another difficulty for the relational definition is the logical inability to generalize the outcomes of one particular incident to different issues between A and B, or to relations between A and B at a later period in time, or, even more problematically, to power relations between A and another state, C. Implicit in the efficient war hypothesis is the assumption that the victorious state is more powerful in a generalized sense, not only in a single instance. Logically however, even if Germany defeats France, it does not necessarily follow that Germany would be able to defeat Russia, or Spain, or Mexico – states that France had previously defeated. Additional assumptions are required to generalize beyond the event, such as the assumption that military capability is a global (rather than specific) trait and that military capability is strongly determinative of victory (rather than highly contingent and probabilistic). These supplementary assumptions are needed in order to construct a hierarchy of military power in which the Great Powers have reliably more military power than small states do.

A third, even more vexing problem with the relational definition of power is its lack of correspondence with real-world perceptions. From this perspective, Vietnam should be considered a superpower, having defeated both France and the United States in the postwar period, while Afghanistan ought to be viewed as at least more powerful than the Soviet Union. In recent years, ostensibly powerful states such as the United States have been unable to force states such as Iraq or Afghanistan to do a number of things they would not otherwise do.[24] As Sechser points out, "States typically issue compellent threats against considerably weaker adversaries, yet their threats often fail."[25] Sullivan notes, "Despite their immense war-fighting capacity, major power states have failed to attain their primary political objective in almost 40 percent of their military operations against weak state and nonstate targets since 1945."[26] Lyall

---

[24] Simon Reich and Richard Ned Lebow, *Good-Bye Hegemony! Power and Influence in the Global System*. Princeton: Princeton University Press, 2014.
[25] Todd S. Sechser, "Goliath's Curse: Coercive Threats and Asymmetric Power." *International Organization* 64 (2010): 627–660; 627.
[26] Sullivan, "War Aims and War Outcomes."

and Wilson observe that Great Powers often fare poorly against counter-insurgencies.[27] Despite their apparent power, the Great Power states often face odds little better than a coin toss in getting other states to do their bidding.

According to the relational definition, those defiant states that have successfully resisted Great Power military pressure ought to be viewed as more powerful than the Great Powers that failed to force compliance. Yet this putative power has not been recognized by the international system, nor have these states been accorded the Great Power status they seem owed. Perhaps the problem lies in the relational conception of power. Due to the plethora of problems – logical and empirical – scholars have advanced an alternative definition of power based on material attributes.

Material Definition of Power

A second conception of power is based on the material attributes of the military and the state. Wohlforth refers to this conception as "the capabilities or resources, mainly military, with which states can influence one another."[28] For instance, in 1948, Hans J. Morgenthau listed geography, resources, industrial capacity, military capability, population, national character and morale, and diplomacy as key attributes of power.[29] Fifty years later, John J. Mearsheimer provided a somewhat different list, including population size, economic wealth, sea power, air power, land power, and nuclear weapons.[30] These lists seem to correspond gratifyingly with intuitions about which states are powerful and which attributes provide the mainstays for that power.

The material definition appears to avert the problem of generalizability by theorizing the abstract resources and capabilities by which military power can be evaluated. All states, including the Great Powers, could be ranked according to these objective measurements of their attributes and resources. The definition recognizes that the Great Powers have larger arsenals, more sophisticated weaponry, and bigger standing armies than small powers do. These attributes are inferred to be essential components

---

[27] Jason Lyall and Isaiah Wilson III, "Rage against the Machines: Explaining Outcomes in Counterinsurgency Wars." *International Organization* 63 (2009): 67–106.

[28] William Curti Wohlforth, *The Elusive Balance: Power and Perceptions during the Cold War*. Ithaca: Cornell University Press, 1993, 4.

[29] Hans J. Morgenthau, *Politics among Nations*. New York: Alfred A. Knopf, 1973 [1948].

[30] John J. Mearsheimer, *The Tragedy of Great Power Politics*. New York: W.W. Norton and Company, 2001.

of military power and can be generalized to other states and various military contexts.

However, it is the lists of attributes themselves that are of questionable utility. The differing lists of the resources of military power by Morgenthau and Mearsheimer, mentioned earlier, illustrate this problem. While scholars can develop arbitrary lists of resources and capabilities, no means is provided to evaluate the validity of these lists. As Wohlforth has pointed out, if one cannot objectively evaluate the lists, nearly any ranking of states is possible.[31] Even if the list is accurate at one historical moment, the relative importance of these attributes may change over time; yet there is no way to assess such change. For instance, national character appears on Morgenthau's list of indicators of military power but is absent from Mearsheimer's list. Neither scholar gives a basis for evaluating when his list will become outdated. Logically, in order for the lists of attributes to provide an objective measure of military power, there must be a reliable way to identify the underlying basis for the lists.

Even more troubling, however, is the frustrating disparity between the material attributes of military power and the outcomes of wars.[32] The simple relationship posited between power and victory does not fit with real-world examples. As Biddle observes, "[T]he standard capability measures ... are actually no better than coin flips at predicting real military outcomes. An enormous scholarly edifice thus rests on very shaky foundations."[33] Biddle finds that four standard indicators of military power – gross national product, population, military personnel, and military expenditure – failed to predict outcomes more than 60 percent of the time, while pure chance would have predicted 50 percent.[34] As Sullivan summarizes, "The vast majority of military doctrine is predicated on the assumption that troop strength, firepower, and military effectiveness determine war outcomes ... But none of these factors can fully explain why powerful states frequently fail to prevail in the armed conflicts they initiate against materially weak targets."[35]

Scholars have found ways post hoc to predict the outcome of a war based on the initial distribution of material capabilities. One way is to include factors that were not considered at the time but can be seen as

[31] Wohlforth, *The Elusive Balance*, 7.
[32] Wohlforth, *The Elusive Balance*; March, "The Power of Power"; James N. Rosenau, *The Scientific Study of Foreign Policy*. New York: Free Press, 1971, 244–245.
[33] Stephen Biddle, *Military Power: Explaining Victory and Defeat in Modern Battle*. Princeton: Princeton University Press, 2004, 2.
[34] Biddle, *Military Power*, 25.   [35] Sullivan, *Who Wins*, 7.

important in retrospect. Paul M. Kennedy, for instance, examined the antebellum distribution of industrial economic resources coupled with military attributes between the two sides in the First World War.[36] According to his analysis, the military resources of Britain and France materially outweighed those of Germany and Austria, even before the resources of the United States are considered. Such an analysis may be intellectually pleasing, but it only serves to show that hindsight is more powerful than foresight. Kennedy fails to explain why German and Austrian decision-makers at the time did not recognize their relative disadvantages in military power. Instead, the pre–First World War militaries did not correctly predict which attributes would be most important in the war to come. They focused on indicators such as army size and mobilization speed – indicators learned from history, as discussed in Chapter 3 – which gave different answers as to the relative weighting of military power.

Another effort has been to include intangible factors, such as resolve or skill, into the list of material attributes. As Biddle convincingly argues, "Capability is not primarily a matter of materiel. It is chiefly a product of how states *use* their material resources."[37] Others, such as Goldman and Eliason, have similarly pointed out that "it is the way militaries take raw technologies and use them that creates military force," not the acquisition of technology in itself.[38] These claims are supported by historical evidence of the importance of these intangibles for predicting victory in various wars.

However, the inclusion of intangibles only exacerbates the difficulty of measurement. Tangible material factors, such as the size of the enemy army or numbers of nuclear weapons, are challenging enough to estimate. On numerous historical occasions, egregious errors have been made in these estimates. Intangible factors, such as enemy resolve or skill, are vastly more challenging to measure. Indeed, since Goldman has pointed out that "states may be uncertain about their own intentions and capabilities;" the difficulties of ascertaining the intentions and capabilities of

---

[36] Paul Kennedy, *The Rise and Fall of the Great Powers: Economic Change and Military Conflict from 1500 to 2000.* New York: Random House, 1986.

[37] Biddle, *Military Power*, 192.

[38] Michael C. Horowitz, *The Diffusion of Military Power: Causes and Consequences for International Relations.* Princeton: Princeton University Press, 2010, 5; Emily O. Goldman and Leslie C. Eliason (eds.), *The Diffusion of Military Technology and Ideas.* Stanford: Stanford University Press, 2003.

other states seem insurmountably greater.[39] The difficulty of measuring intangible factors gives an advantage to scholars in hindsight, who can show in retrospect that the resolve of the victor was – perhaps by definition – greater than that of the defeated state.

This difficulty of measuring intangible factors may be the source of the false optimism that often leads states to go to war. As Van Evera has noted, states often indulge in false optimism in their evaluations of relative military power prior to a conflict. He argues that "Unduly rosy estimates of relative military power infect the belligerents before the vast majority of wars."[40] Adding intangible factors to the list of material attributes may create as many problems as it solves.

The material definition of war does solve some of the problems offered by the relational definition. In particular, it explains why Vietnam and Afghanistan are not counted as Great Powers, and why the United States continues to be perceived as powerful despite its inability to get weaker states to accede to its will. Nevertheless, if key material attributes can only be identified after a war is over, the lists of material attributes have far less utility for military planning than is desirable.

Multidimensional Contextualized Power

Scholars have suggested a third possibility, in which military power is multidimensional and contextual. As Biddle puts it, "The whole notion of a simple, unitary 'capability' fundamentally misrepresents military potential, which is inherently multidimensional."[41] Militaries recognize that different sorts of capabilities might be necessary for a land war in Asia than for a naval war in the Caribbean. Moreover, states fight wars for a variety of political ends, affecting the strategies involved and the capabilities needed. In practice, military decision-makers utilize complex and nuanced assessments contingently based on the context of the situation, rather than blanket calculations applied irrespective of the enemy.

First of all, military capability is multidimensional. As Biddle notes, militaries are expected to accomplish a wide range of tasks, "ranging from defending national territory to invading other states, hunting down

[39] Emily O. Goldman, *Power in Uncertain Times: Strategy in the Fog of Peace*. Stanford: Stanford University Press, 2011.

[40] Stephen Van Evera, *Causes of War: Power and the Roots of Conflict*. Ithaca: Cornell University Press, 1999, 16. Interestingly, Van Evera (p. 24) writes: "The false optimism observed in the run-ups to these wars exceeds what we see in typical peacetime. Even odd examples of such false optimism are uncommon when war is not imminent."

[41] Biddle, *Military Power*, 192.

terrorists, coercing concessions, countering insurgencies, keeping the peace, enforcing economic sanctions, showing the flag, or maintaining domestic order."[42] The ability to do one task well does not necessarily imply that a military is configured to do them all. Biddle concludes: "Different military tasks are very dissimilar ... There is thus no single, underlying quality of generic "capability" to which all specific mission capacities are epiphenomenal."[43] Similarly, Press points out: "[D]ecision makers are not interested in abstract measures of national power ... they ask themselves: Can the adversary do what he threatens to do and achieve his objectives at reasonable cost? To answer this question, they evaluate the specific instruments of military and economic power that will determine whether the threats can be carried out successfully, and at what cost."[44] Depending on the task and the capabilities of the opponent, militaries fine-tune their assessments of relative capabilities.

Second, the assessments of military power should also vary depending on the war aims of the state. Scholars such as Sullivan, Martel, and Smith have argued that victory should also be conceptualized as multidimensional. In particular, military dimensions of victory might not correspond with political dimensions.[45] Martel further distinguishes between victory on the tactical level, the strategic level, and the political level.[46] Levy also differentiates types of threats, arguing that France in the 1930s was most concerned about the threat of German land power, while Britain worried about German air power. Germany, on the other hand, feared long-term demographic and economic power, and Japan was preoccupied with short-term economic issues.[47] These different dimensions of power call for "a more detailed and nuanced analysis of the impact of shifting power among states."[48]

Third, a wide variety of conditions may affect the military effectiveness of a state.[49] Brooks, Stanley, and their colleagues have found that a

[42] Biddle, *Military Power*, 5.   [43] Biddle, *Military Power*, 192.

[44] Daryl G. Press, *Calculating Credibility: How Leaders Assess Military Threats*. Ithaca: Cornell University Press, 2005, 24.

[45] Martel, *Victory in War*; Smith, *The Utility of Force*; Sullivan, *Who Wins*; Sullivan, "War Aims and War Outcomes."

[46] Martel, *Victory in War*. Martel calls it the political "grand strategy."

[47] Jack S. Levy and John A. Vasquez (eds.), *The Outbreak of the First World War: Structure, Politics and Decision-Making*. Cambridge: Cambridge University Press, 2014, 146.

[48] Levy and Vasquez, *The Outbreak of the First World War*, 146.

[49] Risa A. Brooks, "Introduction: The Impact of Culture, Society, Institutions, and International Forces on Military Effectiveness." In *Creating Military Power: The Sources of Military Effectiveness*, edited by Risa A. Brooks and Elizabeth A. Stanley, 1–26. Stanford:

diverse array of factors, including political culture, social structures, institutions, and the global environment, contribute to military power. They find that "military power only partially depends on states' material and human resources"; organizational and political effectiveness may be equally important.[50] Domestic political conditions, such as democracy or civil-military relations, can have a significant effect on military effectiveness.[51] Even more broadly, cultural and national differences and global norms can affect military effectiveness and action.[52]

In response, scholars have proposed multidimensional measures of power. Levy distinguishes among military, economic, and demographic power.[53] Barnett and Duvall consider compulsory, institutional, structural, and productive aspects of power.[54] Van Evera posits distinctions between offensive and defensive power, first-strike capability, and second-strike retaliation. He also differentiates rising power, waning power, and "the power to parlay gains into further gains."[55] These complex and nuanced conceptions of power allow a country such as Vietnam to be considered more militarily effective than the United States in certain

Stanford University Press, 2007; Theo Farrell, "Culture and Military Power," *Review of International Studies* 24 (1998): 407–416.

[50] Risa A. Brooks, "Introduction: The Impact of Culture, Society, Institutions, and International Forces on Military Effectiveness." In *Creating Military Power: The Sources of Military Effectiveness*, edited by Risa A. Brooks and Elizabeth A. Stanley, 1–26. Stanford: Stanford University Press, 2007.

[51] Dan Reiter and Allen C. Stam, *Democracies at War*. Princeton: Princeton University Press, 2002; Deborah Avant, "Political Institutions and Military Effectiveness: Contemporary United States and United Kingdom." In *Creating Military Power: The Sources of Military Effectiveness*, edited by Risa A. Brooks and Elizabeth A. Stanley, 80–105. Stanford: Stanford University Press, 2007; Barry R. Posen, *The Sources of Military Doctrine: France, Britain, and Germany between the World Wars*. Ithaca: Cornell University Press, 1984; Jack Snyder, *The Ideology of the Offensive: Military Decision Making and the Disasters of 1914*. Ithaca: Cornell University Press, 1984; Van Evera, *Causes of War*.

[52] Reiter, *How Wars End*; Goldman, "International Competition and Military Effectiveness"; Theo Farrell, "Global Norms and Military Effectiveness: The Army in Early Twentieth-Century Ireland." In *Creating Military Power: The Sources of Military Effectiveness*, edited by Risa A. Brooks and Elizabeth A. Stanley, 136–157. Stanford: Stanford University Press, 2007; Peter J. Katzenstein (ed.), *The Culture of National Security: Norms and Identity in World Politics*. New York: Columbia University Press, 1996.

[53] Jack S. Levy and John A. Vasquez (eds.), *The Outbreak of the First World War: Structure, Politics and Decision-Making*. Cambridge: Cambridge University Press, 2014, 146.

[54] Michael Barnett and Raymond Duvall, "Power in International Politics." *International Organization* 59 (Winter 2005): 39–75.

[55] Van Evera *Causes of War*, 8.

contexts, such as when fighting an overseas power for control of its homeland. In other contexts, Vietnam might not be able to militarily prevail when fighting over another set of political goals or under different conditions. These multidimensional measures may also provide a better description of how militaries evaluate an enemy in practice.

However, the contextual conception of power suffers from one major drawback: it does not correspond to conceptions of military power as broadly perceived in the international system. The academic literature on definitions and indicators of power suggests that one can hardly assess military power without reams of data and a supercomputer. In practice, however, these nuanced evaluations of military power do not drive international relations. Instead it is a simple, one-dimensional evaluation of power, the hierarchical ranking of the Great Powers, which provides the fundamental underpinnings of war and international diplomacy. This is the topic of discussion in the next section.

POWER FROM TAUTOLOGY

In every era, a handful of states are recognized as the most powerful militaries in the world – colloquially known as the Great Powers. After the Second World War, for instance, there was general agreement that the United States, the Soviet Union, Britain, France, and China comprised the Great Powers of the era.[56] Great Power status is not a complex academic construct that is conditional on battlefield context or political nuances. It is a simple hierarchy in which a handful of states are recognized at the top, and where one or two states sometimes stand out as preeminent.

This strong consensus belies the confusion of scholars. While scholars debate among themselves over appropriate measures of power, the international community takes the composition of the Great Power hierarchy as a fact. There is widespread agreement on the Great Power states of the day.[57] As Waltz has noted, in practice the identification of the Great Powers can be answered by common sense and that "one finds general

---

[56] J. David Singer and Melvin Small, *The Wages of War, 1816–1965*. Ann Arbor: Inter-University Consortium for Political Research, 1974; Jack S. Levy, *War in the Modern Great Power System, 1495–1975*. Lexington: University Press of Kentucky, 1983; Kenneth N. Waltz, *Theory of International Politics*. Reading: Addison-Wesley, 1979.

[57] Gordon A. Craig, *Europe since 1815*. New York: Holt, Rinehart and Winston, 1966; Derek McKay and H. M. Scott. *The Rise of the Great Powers, 1648–1815*. New York: Longman, 1983; A. J. P. Taylor, *The Struggle for Mastery in Europe, 1848–1918*. Oxford: Clarendon Press, 1954.

agreement about who the great powers of a period are, with occasional doubt about marginal cases."[58] Little debate or disagreement is suggested by compilations of the Great Power states of different historical eras.[59] Such lists also tend to agree with the perceptions of statesmen and military leaders in those periods. This divergence between the academic and the practical leads to the question: What provides the basis for this common-sense recognition of military power?

In this section I argue that the recognition of military power in the Great Power hierarchy is tied to both the relational and material defin-itions outlined earlier, despite their logical and empirical flaws. These definitions allow the widespread consensus on the identification of the Great Powers within the international community. However, the evalu-ation of power is fundamentally retrospective. The Great Powers are, by and large, simply those states that were victors in the last Great Power war, supplemented by material indicators that retrospectively account for their victories.

The Relational Aspect: Great Power Victory

The starting point for understanding Great Power status is the relational definition of power: the Great Powers are those states that were victorious in recent Great Power wars. This requirement fits with the commonsense intuition that powerful states should be able to defeat weaker states. Simply put, a state that defeats a Great Power becomes a candidate for Great Power status itself; conversely, Great Powers that are defeated are likely to be demoted from Great Power status. This requirement of victory in a Great Power war is no small achievement. Bragging alone, or highly inflated national egotism, does not make a Great Power. States must prove themselves in battle against another Great Power. However as the scholarly criticisms mentioned earlier imply, past victory does not logic-ally imply successful military outcomes in the future.

According to the relational definition, war is perceived to be the ultimate test of military power. As historian Ernest R. May notes, "Between wars judgments are entirely subjective; war is the only objective test."[60] Thompson points out that seven out of eight Great Powers

---

[58] Waltz, *Theory of International Politics*, 131.

[59] Singer and Small, *The Wages of War*; Levy, *War in the Modern Great Power System*.

[60] Ernest R. May, *Imperial Democracy: The Emergence of America as a Great Power*. New York: Harcourt, Brace and World, 1961, 6.

achieved their status through "martial prowess on the battlefield."[61] Even China, Thompson's sole exception, actually fits the pattern, since China acquired its Great Power status after fighting the United States to a draw in the Korean War (the war ended in an armstice). China's Great Power status was also supplemented by the acquisition of nuclear weapons in the 1950s, which fits the material definition discussed later in the chapter. In short, war outcomes provide the primary mechanism for the promotion and demotion of the Great Powers. In peacetime, other contests such as arms races, colonial acquisitions, or diplomatic arm-wrestling may provide secondary support for relative ranking among the Great Powers, as discussed in Chapter 4.

Victory in war is not the only requirement to become a Great Power. Vietnam defeated two postwar Great Powers – France and the United States – but was not considered a contender for Great Power status. Similarly, Afghanistan fought off Great Britain in the nineteenth century and the Soviet Union in the twentieth century, yet was still considered a minor power.[62] Victory in a recent Great Power conflict is a necessary component of Great Power status, but it is not sufficient.

Scholars have frequently criticized the relational definition of power as tautological, as noted earlier. This indicator of power simply reflects history rather than providing an independent measure of intrinsic military superiority. For instance, as Wohlforth remarks, the relational definition "leads almost inexorably to tautology," since one cannot know which country is more powerful except in retrospect.[63] Consequently, the tautological provenance of the relational definition raises questions about its utility for predicting the outcome of future wars. Victory in a particular Great Power conflict may not indicate a fundamental superiority among militaries. As suggested by the brief history at the beginning of the chapter, subsequent wars between the same two militaries may yield different outcomes if military outcomes are probabilistic rather than inevitable. Hypothetically, if the underlying distribution of power granted France victory 55 percent of the time while Prussia/Germany won 45 percent of the encounters, victory by either side should imply very little, and

[61] William R. Thompson, "Status Conflict, Hierarchies, and Interpretation Dilemmas." In *Status in World Politics*, edited by T. V. Paul, Deborah Welch Larson, and William C. Wohlforth. Cambridge: Cambridge University Press, 2014, 219.

[62] Douglas A. Borer, *Superpowers Defeated: Vietnam and Afghanistan Compared*. London: Frank Cass, 1999.

[63] Wohlforth, *The Elusive Balance*, 4.

should not prompt nations to rethink military planning and strategy as they often do.[64]

Even more importantly, however, the relational definition logically undermines the validity of the hierarchical assumptions of the Great Power hierarchy. Even Dahl's relational definition of the power of A and B described earlier in the chapter does not try to generalize to conflicts against other competitors. Even if Germany did defeat France, the relational definition does not necessarily permit the extension that Germany would defeat other states that had been defeated by France. As Maoz and Mor have pointed out, less than 1 percent of all dyads account for nearly 80 percent of interstate wars.[65] Thus, any hierarchical ranking of power based on past events is filled with holes, since most states have not fought each other recently or ever.

The slender empirical basis for the Great Power hierarchy can be seen historically as well as theoretically. As Biddle and other scholars have pointed out, the Great Powers have frequently been defeated throughout history by states believed to be militarily weaker.[66] These defeats have been especially likely in wars fought under conditions that diverged from those on the European continent. In the past two centuries, the European Great Powers were defeated by indigenous militaries in Afghanistan, Algeria, Ethiopia, India, Sudan, and a host of other places. The postwar Great Powers were also defeated by militaries held in low esteem, such as Vietnam, Afghanistan, and Algeria. These outcomes suggest the limitations of the relational definition of military power, which cannot logically be generalized into a global hierarchy of military power.

In practice however, the relational requirement of victory in a Great Power war is the primary basis for the recognition of military power in the international community. To supplement this, however, a state must acquire the material trappings of a Great Power and also enact the role of a Great Power, as discussed in the next two sections.

Material Definition: Learning from History

The victorious Great Power states also provide the basis for the material lists of factors that are widely accepted as providing the foundation of

---

[64] Daniel Kahneman, Paul Slovic, and Amos Tversky, *Judgment under Uncertainty: Heuristics and Biases*. Cambridge: Cambridge University Press, 1982.

[65] Zeev Maoz and Ben D. Mor, *Bound by Struggle: The Strategic Evolution of Enduring International Rivalries*. Ann Arbor: University of Michigan Press, 2002, 3.

[66] Biddle, *Military Power*; Reich and Lebow, *Good-Bye Hegemony!*; Sullivan, *Who Wins*.

military power. Those factors theorized as decisive in the last major Great Power war – or that generally reflect the common attributes of the Great Powers in a given era – become institutionalized as critical material attributes used to evaluate power generally. Consequently, material understandings of power are rooted in the same problematic tautology as relational understandings of power. Chapter 3 unpacks this point further: material attributes that are believed to form the essential basis for power are presented as abstract and generalizable, but they are in essence reified descriptions of recent history and often do not predict future success in war.

The indicators of Great Power status typically reflect resources "learned" from history such as battleships, military manpower, or nuclear arsenals. Although these definitions pretend to be objective, they are actually founded on historical descriptions of the factors theorized to have led to victory in the last Great Power war. These resources may have been critical in wars of the past, yet this historical utility does not ensure their relevance to future conflicts, as argued in Chapter 3. Thus Mearsheimer's list of military factors provides an abstract summary of the military attributes of the superpowers during the Cold War, while Morgenthau's list generalizes attributes of the Allies in the Second World War.

History suggests that the attributes on these lists may have little influence on the outcome of subsequent wars. However, the broad international agreement on these lists has several important implications. For one, the agreed-on material indicators are used to evaluate states that have not recently been involved in a Great Power competition or to settle rankings among the Great Powers. The seeming impartiality of the rubric allows all militaries to be ranked, regardless of whether they have fought each other. This explains cases such as Vietnam and Afghanistan, which were not viewed as militarily powerful in part due to their low ranking on other military attributes such as standing army size and lack of a nuclear arsenal. Despite defeating Great Power militaries, Vietnam and Afghanistan failed to meet these material criteria for Great Power status.

Related to this, material attributes provide a means to rank the Great Powers against each other. For instance the post–Second World War Great Power hierarchy can be approximated by using the size and sophistication of the nuclear arsenal as a means of ranking states.[67] Supporting indicators are also used, including measures such as the numbers of high-

[67] Barry O'Neill, "Nuclear Weapons and National Prestige." Cowles Foundation Discussion Paper No. 1560, 2006.

tech bombers and aircraft carriers and the size of the standing army. These indicators were arguably quite important during the Second World War. However, even if these factors were critical in the past, that is little assurance that they will be essential for subsequent conflicts, as will be discussed in Chapter 3. Indeed, the U.S. experience in Vietnam emphasizes the point that the size and sophistication of the technological arsenal does not necessarily provide the critical edge for victory in all situations.

Secondly, the international consensus over the key material attributes of military power provides a basis for Great Power competition, as discussed in Chapter 4. The Great Powers compete to acquire the specific resources deemed essential for military power in a given era, such as nuclear weapons or huge armies. Consequently, interwar periods are often filled with arms races, territorial grabs, and other forms of competition among the Great Powers for the material resources that have been theorized as augmenting military power.

Third, the material definition of power appears to reduce the ambiguities of military planning. However, the reduction of ambiguity is an illusion. Although presented as abstract and universal indicators of power, these lists tend to be simple post hoc descriptions of the Great Powers of each era, with an emphasis on the attributes of the victor of the last Great Power war. As Wohlforth criticizes, "[T]his approach still begs the question how the analyst measures 'real power,' if not by reference to the outcomes he is explaining. What, if not hindsight, gives the scholar remote in place and time from the events she analyzes a special insight into the distribution of capabilities, not possessed by the participants themselves?"[68]

Sadly, history frequently reveals that these lists of material resources were based on idiosyncratic historical circumstances rather than enduring military truths. The material attributes that were important in one particular war often have little relevance in the next. For instance, speedy military mobilization was theorized as essential in the late nineteenth century based on the outcomes of the Franco-Prussian war, but proved irrelevant in the First World War – or worse, may have actually helped precipitate the conflict. Moreover, the material attributes that were critical in a European war are often unimportant for wars fought under quite different conditions on other continents.

---

[68] Wohlforth, *The Elusive Balance*, 6.

In sum, retrospective tautology provides the basis for the material indicators of military power that hold sway in a given historical period. Despite claims of objectivity, the lists of material attributes are actually founded on historical descriptions of the factors theorized to have led to victory in the last Great Power war. These resources may have been essential in wars of the past, but as Chapter 3 points out, they may not be relevant to future conflicts. However, competition to acquire these indicators of military capability has substantial implications for position in the Great Power hierarchy, and focuses military competition between major wars.

Enacting a Great Power Identity

A third element for the recognition of Great Power status is that a state must act like a Great Power. To be a Great Power requires the willingness of a state to be involved in the political and diplomatic crises and competitions of the era.[69] This involvement in international diplomacy forces Great Powers to develop a much wider range of interests than those of regional powers. These wider interests in turn involve a broader scope of action, increasing the likelihood that a Great Power will come into conflict with another Great Power. As Jervis has noted, "The expansion of power usually brings with it an expansion of responsibilities and commitments; to meet them, still greater power is required."[70] This requirement of involvement for Great Power status is illustrated in the brief history of the United States discussed at the end of the chapter.

To be a Great Power, a state must be recognized as one by its peers. As Lebow puts it, "Great powership is a status conferred by other states."[71] A state cannot simply declare itself to be a Great Power and expect to be taken seriously. Nor is Great Power status a passive condition or a latent attribute of a state. Instead, it is an active role that requires Great Powers to embroil themselves in the conflicts and diplomatic affairs of the era.

Enacting the Great Power identity requires the development of an expanded set of interests and action. Larson and colleagues note that major power status requires the willingness to "conduct an expansive, largely

---

[69] Taylor, *The Struggle for Mastery in Europe*; Waltz, *Theory of International Politics*.

[70] Robert Jervis, "Cooperation under the Security Dilemma." *World Politics* 30 (1978): 167–214, 169.

[71] Richard Ned Lebow, *A Cultural Theory of International Relations*. Cambridge: Cambridge University Press, 2008, 484.

independent policy outside the region."[72] Previously, scholars have viewed this expansion of interests as a natural law. As Martin Wight argued, "It is the nature of powers to expand. The energies of their members radiate culturally, economically, and politically, and unless there are strong obstacles these tendencies will be summed up in territorial growth."[73] Schweller similarly claims: "[S]tates expand when they can; that is, when they perceive relative increases in their own state power and when changes in the relative costs and benefits of expansion make it profitable for them to do so."[74] A constructivist perspective might argue instead that Great Powers develop these interests in order to enact the role of a Great Power. Regardless, these expanded interests are a fundamental part of the package of a Great Power state.

A Great Power must be willing to engage in competitions against other Great Power states in order to maintain its status. As noted earlier, the relational definition of power requires that Great Powers be victorious in wars and competitions with other Great Powers. The consequence is that the Great Powers are engaged in interstate conflicts against both great and small powers at a much higher rate than other states are.[75] Far from shying away with conflicts against other Great Powers – those states deemed the most militarily dangerous in the world – the Great Powers seek out opportunities to challenge their Great Power rivals in matters large and small. While even Great Powers may avoid outright war, they are often willing to go to the brink with surprising readiness.

Conversely, states that frequently opt out of Great Power competitions are likely to be demoted from Great Power status. Empirically, many states with sufficient material resources have chosen against the pursuit of Great Power status, including, in the postwar era, Canada, Sweden, Japan, and Germany, among others.[76] Dropping out of Great Power

[72] Deborah Welch Larson, T. V. Paul, and William C. Wohlforth, "Status and World Order." In *Status in World Politics*, edited by T. V. Paul, Deborah Welch Larson, and William C. Wohlforth, 3–32. Cambridge: Cambridge University Press, 2014, 21.

[73] Martin Wight, *Power Politics*, edited by Hedley Bull and Carsten Holbraad. London: Leicester University Press, 1978, 144.

[74] Randall L. Schweller, *Unanswered Threats: Political Constraints on the Balance of Power*. Princeton: Princeton University Press, 2006, 24.

[75] Maoz and Mor, *Bound by Struggle*; Michael P. Colaresi, Karen Rasler, and William R. Thompson, *Strategic Rivalries in World Politics: Position, Space and Conflict Escalation*. Cambridge: Cambridge University Press, 2007; Karen Rasler, William R. Thompson, and Sumit Ganguly, *How Rivalries End*. Philadelphia: University of Pennsylvania Press, 2013, 2–3.

[76] Mitchell Reiss, *Bridled Ambition: Why Countries Constrain Their Nuclear Capabilities*. Baltimore: Johns Hopkins Press, 1995, 322–323.

competitions conserves resources that might be directed profitably toward economic or welfare ends. However, the danger of disengagement in Great Power competitions is that states risk being militarily evaluated as weak. Assessments of military weakness may be costly, leading to calculations of easy invasion as historically experienced by states such as Belgium, Luxembourg, and Poland.

Nevertheless, it is important to note that the costs of competition may be even higher for the Great Powers. The Great Powers expend considerable resources acquiring the attributes believed to yield military power (determined retrospectively, as described earlier in the chapter). These competitions are likely to entail considerable costs, both economically and in risks to national security. Following the Second World War, for instance, the acquisition and expansion of nuclear arsenals proved a huge economic cost for the Great Powers. The security risks of being a Great Power may prove even more damaging. In pursuit of Great Power status, the Great Powers regularly hurl themselves into war against other Great Powers, often with devastating results for all involved.

In short, Great Powers maintain their status by successfully competing against other Great Powers in a variety of venues. This dynamic addresses several arguments in the scholarly literature. One is the tendency of Great Powers to overextend themselves in pursuit of interests beyond their military capabilities. Paul M. Kennedy has argued that Great Powers at the peak of their power are likely to overextend themselves by protecting interests of only secondary value, which in turn causes their downfall.[77] Kennedy argues that hubris leads Great Powers to make this foolish mistake. In contrast, my argument suggests the tendency of Great Powers to overextend is simply the workings of the Great Power identity, which demands expanded interests, coupled with ambiguity in the measurement of military power, which encourages the appearance of hubris. After all, hubris can only be identified tautologically once a Great Power has been defeated – if the Great Power wins, it is labeled as power.

The Great Power identity that states must adopt to gain Great Power status in the international community also contributes to the security dilemma and the conflict spiral theorized by Robert Jervis. The security dilemma holds that states working to ensure their own security may

---

[77] Paul Kennedy, *The Rise and Fall of the Great Powers: Economic Change and Military Conflict from 1500 to 2000*. New York: Random House, 1986; Jack Snyder, *Myths of Empire: Domestic Empire and International Ambition*. Ithaca: Cornell University Press, 1991.

appear threatening to other states. As Jervis noted, "This is especially true of the great powers. Any state that has interests throughout the world cannot avoid possessing the power to menace others."[78] Press agrees: "The rise of new great powers ... will likely engender security dilemmas or intensify existing ones."[79] Some scholars differentiate between aggressive Great Powers and security-seeking ones.[80] However, I would suggest that the identity needed to gain Great Power status all but ensures that Great Powers will have expanded interests and competitive tendencies that might be viewed as threateningly aggressive by others.

The following brief history of the United States emphasizes the importance of identity as a requirement for Great Power status. Throughout its history, the United States had many of the material attributes – territory, industrial power, and technological sophistication – that contemporaries viewed as important bases for military power. Yet the United States was not recognized as a potential Great Power until 1898, and the United States did not make a serious bid for Great Power status until after the Second World War. In order to be perceived as a Great Power, the United States needed (1) victory in recent Great Power conflicts, (2) material indicators of power, themselves retrospectively inferred from recent conflicts, and (3) the willingness to enact a Great Power identity by entering competitions against the European Great Powers.

THE HISTORICAL RISE OF THE UNITED STATES

American historians have at times idealized the military abilities of the United States, with images of American colonial patriots sniping at British redcoats.[81] Yet the United States was also notable for its historical isolationist policy, refusing to become involved in Great Power competitions in Europe for its first century and a half. The lack of U.S. involvement in Great Power competitions led to low evaluations of U.S. military capabilities by all members of the international community, including the United States itself. It was not until after the Second World War that the United States chose to enter into Great Power politics, and even that required some prodding from Britain. As one historian notes, "The United States

---

[78] Jervis, *Perception and Misperception*, 64.   [79] Press, *Calculating Credibility*, 25.

[80] For instance, see Charles L. Glaser, *Rational Theory of International Politics: The Logic of Competition and Cooperation*. Princeton: Princeton University Press, 2010.

[81] Russell Frank Weigley, *The American Way of War: A History of United States Military Strategy and Policy*. New York: Macmillan, 1973.

thus did not aimlessly wander into world power status; the American people deliberately chose to seek it."[82] According to the argument outlined earlier in the chapter, this epigraph might be applied to all Great Powers.

The United States actively chose against entering competitions with the European Great Powers through the first century of its statehood.[83] The United States briefly declared war against Britain in the War of 1812 and scuffled with the European powers in its Latin American and Caribbean backyard. Yet besides these involvements, the United States consciously chose to stand apart from European conflicts. As the Monroe Doctrine self-consciously proclaimed, the United States would remain uninvolved in the Great Power competitions of Europe.[84]

The Spanish-American war of 1898 altered the perception of the United States by the European Great Powers. As argued earlier, the first requirement for Great Power status is military victory against a Great Power. The United States entered the Spanish-American war to support Cuban revolutionaries in their struggle against Spain.[85] Somewhat to its surprise, the United States won the war and ended up with the colonial spoils of Cuba, Puerto Rico, and the Philippines. Although Spain was a second-tier Great Power, the European states began to view the United States as a nascent military power. "[T]he United States' effortless dispatch of Spain immediately boosted the American ranking among the powers."[86] "Newspapers and magazines burst out with wide-eyed exclamations that Europe now had to reckon with a seventh great power."[87] An editorial in the London *Times* declared: "This war must in any event effect a profound change in the whole attitude and policy of the United States. In future America will play a part in the general affairs of the world such as she has never played before.'[88] One concrete indicator of the swelling opinion of U.S. perceived power in the international community was the upgrade of the European legations to full-fledged embassies in Washington, DC.[89]

---

[82] John M. Dobson, *America's Ascent: The United States Becomes a Great Power, 1880–1914*. DeKalb: Northern Illinois University Press, 1978, 4.

[83] Robert E. Hannigan, 2002. *The New World Power: American Foreign Policy, 1898–1917*. Philadelphia: University of Pennsylvania Press, 2002; Howard Jones, *Crucible of Power: A History of American Foreign Relations from 1897*, second edition. Lanham: Rowman and Littlefield, 2008.

[84] Robert D. Schulzinger, *U.S. Diplomacy since 1900*. Oxford: Oxford University Press, 2002.

[85] Hannigan, *The New World Power*.   [86] Dobson, *America's Ascent*, 3.

[87] May, *Imperial Democracy*, 221.   [88] Quoted in May, *Imperial Democracy*, 221.

[89] May, *Imperial Democracy*, 5, with the exception of Austria.

A second dimension of Great Power status is the possession of material attributes of power. According to the dominant military theories of the nineteenth century, the United States possessed them in spades. The theories of the day focused on territorial size and population, and the United States was second only to Russia on these factors.[90] U.S. agricultural and industrial output was staggering, and the United States was the world leader in wheat production as well as coal, iron, and steel. By 1892, the "ponderous *Dictionary of Statistics* of 1892 showed the United States overtaking or surpassing Europe by nearly every measurable standard."[91] In retrospect, historians have underscored this potential military capacity for the United States.[92]

But the United States failed on the third component of Great Power status due to its conscious refusal to enter any further Great Power competitions. As May wrote about the Spanish-American war, "From first to last, the makers of American policy and the presumed leaders of American opinion ... scarcely thought of proclaiming to the world that America was a power."[93] Instead at the beginning of the twentieth century, American leadership "showed more intense preoccupation with matters at home than even the most isolationist advocate of national solipsism [would] in the 1920's and 1930's."[94]

Although the United States had defeated a Great Power and amassed the material attributes of a Great Power, it declined to enact the identity of a Great Power. Consequently, the European militaries discounted the military power of the United States in the early twentieth century. The United States discounted itself as well. At a time when the European states were amassing conscript armies of unprecedented size, the United States maintained a modest standing army that was too small to impact European conflicts. The standing U.S. army numbered only 133,000 men and was a "constabulary force" compared to the French and German pre-1914 armies of nearly a million men each.[95] European planners estimated – correctly, as it turned out – that the United States would take

[90] Paul M. Kennedy, "The First World War and the International Power System." *International Security* 9 (1984): 7–40.
[91] May, *Imperial Democracy*, 6.
[92] Kennedy, "The First World War and the International Power System."
[93] May, *Imperial Democracy*, 269.   [94] May, *Imperial Democracy*, 270.
[95] Timothy K. Nenniger, "American Military Effectiveness in the First World War." In *Military Effectiveness: Volume I, The First World War*, edited by Allan R. Millett and Williamson Murray, 116–156. Boston: Allen and Unwin, 1988, 116; Theodore Ropp, *War in the Modern World*. Durham: Duke University Press, 1959, 240.

nearly a year to mobilize an army sizable enough to weigh in on a European conflict.[96]

Nor did the United States plan to be involved in a European war. Even by 1913, the military preparations of the United States were for a war on the wrong continent. American planners assumed that any military action in which the United States was involved would take place on the North American side of the Atlantic. U.S. military planners did imagine the possibility of war against Germany, but one based on economic rivalry rather than a German bid for political and territorial dominance in Europe. In this hypothetical war, Britain would ally with Germany, and the rest of Europe would remain neutral.[97] U.S. military planners envisioned a German fleet of forty-one ships assembling at Puerto Rico. The paper plan called for this hypothetical force to be met by a smaller American fleet of thirty-three ships, which U.S. planners believed would nonetheless be adequate to repel the Germans and win the hypothetical war.[98]

Even once European war had been declared in 1914, American military planners did not redesign their plans for involvement on the European continent. Instead, it was assumed that any U.S. military action in the war would be "limited to meeting any hostile German cruisers in the Atlantic."[99] Yet as events turned out, the United States was to fight the war on the European continent rather than in the Americas. The problem of transporting and supplying troops across the Atlantic would become an American headache rather than a German one. Instead of manning a fleet of 33 ships, the United States scrambled to call up and equip a fleet of 147 ships and submarines. Prewar planning was rendered essentially worthless.

The United States was not the only military to have failed to plan correctly. The prewar Great Powers had also dismissed the military power of the United States, an ocean away and dominated by an isolationist political stance. Based on these calculations, German decision-makers were unconcerned with the possibility of the United States entering the

---

[96] Ropp, *War in the Modern World.*

[97] Holger H. Herwig and D. F. Trask, "Naval Operations Plans between Germany and the USA, 1898–1913." In *The War Plans of the Great Powers, 1880–1914*, edited by Paul M. Kennedy, 39–74. London: George Allen and Unwin, 1979 [1970], 62.

[98] Herwig and Trask, "Naval Operations Plans between Germany and the USA," 63.

[99] J. A. S. Grenville, "Diplomacy and War Plans in the United States, 1890–1917." In *The War Plans of the Great Powers, 1880–1914*, edited by Paul M. Kennedy, 23–28. London: George Allen and Unwin, 1979 [1961], 35.

First World War.[100] German Chancellor Bethmann stated, "Although America, because of its lack of military forces, can hardly declare war on us ... still it is capable of proclaiming a trade boycott against us."[101] German General Ludendorff commented in 1916 that "The United States does not bother me ... in the least; I look upon a declaration of war by the United States with indifference."[102] Germany was not alone; all the major combatants evaluated the United States as a minor power in the prewar calculations for the First World War.

Nevertheless, the entry of the United States into the First World War has generally been seen as pivotal for the eventual Allied victory.[103] The prominent role of the United States in the Allied victory in the First World War gave the United States another opportunity to compete in Great Power politics. Again, however, the United States consciously chose to retire to its side of the Atlantic and bow out of Great Power competitions. The U.S. Senate refused to ratify the Versailles Treaty and did not participate in the League of Nations. As Dobson writes, "[T]he nation was seeking to retreat to the status it had held between 1880 and 1914, a status in which its relative freedom from external responsibilities had enabled it to predominate within its chosen spheres of interest."[104]

Even at the onset of the Second World War, the United States planned to be involved only peripherally on the western side of the Atlantic. The United States seemed to have no inkling that it was about to be engaged in the costliest war of its history. In the interwar period, U.S. military planners had developed the Color Plans, a set of plans for potential future wars. U.S. planners put the greatest amount of effort into the Red and the White plans, which detailed the possibility of civil uprisings in Cuba. The Orange plan did consider a war with Japan, although this plan had not yet been drawn up at the time of the Second World War. More fully developed was the Blue plan, which envisaged an Atlantic war against Great Britain. By 1938, the United States had not developed even a paper

---

[100] Ernest R. May, "The U-Boat Campaign." In *The Use of Force: International Politics and Foreign Policy*, edited by Robert J. Art and Kenneth N. Waltz, 298–315. Boston: Little, Brown and Company, 1971 [1959], 305, 302.

[101] Quoted in May, "The U-Boat Campaign," 302.

[102] Quoted in Holger H. Herwig, *The First World War: Germany and Austria-Hungary 1914–1918*. New York: Bloomsbury Academic, 1996, 229 n5.

[103] Ropp, *War in the Modern World*; Schulzinger, *U.S. Diplomacy since 1900*.

[104] Dobson, *America's Ascent*, 225.

plan in the event of war against Germany, despite the fact that Germany had been its enemy in the most recent war.[105]

Again, European military planners were aware of this isolationist position and discounted the United States as a military combatant. Even the United States shared this evaluation. In the 1939 report of the U.S. Secretary of War, for instance, the United States ranked itself "seventeenth in military strength behind Portugal, Yugoslavia, and Belgium."[106] German military planners similarly slighted U.S. military power: "The United States, the money lender and supplier of raw and industrialised materials and troops to Germany's enemies in the Great War, did not seem to enter Hitler's mind as he schemed to make Germany preeminent on the European continent."[107]

However, the United States was forcefully drawn into the Second World War by the Japanese attack on Pearl Harbor. Again, U.S. involvement was pivotal to the Allied victory in Europe and in the Pacific. Yet again, the Great Powers including Britain feared that the United States would withdraw from European politics at the conclusion of the Second World War. Churchill gave his "Iron Curtain" speech in part to encourage the United States to stay involved in European politics.[108] The question of whether the United States would retreat to its historical isolationist policies hung in the balance for a moment.

In the end, the United States chose to plunge into the role of a Great Power following the Second World War. It became deeply involved in European politics, played a prominent role in the design of the United Nations, and oversaw postwar arrangements. Even more, the United States self-consciously took on the role of policeman of the world, protecting the West from Communist incursions (see Chapter 8). It also began to enter, and win, a series of Great Power competitions including the nuclear arms race (see Chapter 7).

[105] Maurice Matloff, "The American Approach to War, 1919–1945." In *The Theory and Practice of War*, edited by Michael Howard, 218–219. Bloomington: Indiana University Press, 1975.

[106] Steven Ross, "American War Plans." In *Military Planning and the Origins of the Second World War in Europe*, edited by B. J. C. McKercher and Roch Legault, 145–166. Westport: Praeger, 2001, 147.

[107] B.J.C. McKercher and Roch Legault, "Introduction." In *Military Planning and the Origins of the Second World War in Europe*, edited by B. J. C. McKercher and Roch Legault, 1–10. Westport: Praeger, 2001, 5.

[108] Jones, *Crucible of Power*, 247.

In retrospect, many scholars have viewed the historical rise of the United States as inevitable. Based on Mearsheimer's list of military power, the United States excelled on indicators such as population size, economic wealth, sea power, air power, land power, and nuclear weapons. These high scores are not coincidental, since Mearsheimer doubtless based his list largely on the attributes of the United States and the other victors of the Second World War. However, the "power" of the United States was not recognized until it began to be regularly involved and victorious in Great Power competitions. The United States self-consciously chose to reconstruct its interests to fit the broader mantle of a Great Power rather than the narrow scope of a regional power that it had played through the nineteenth century. The U.S. rise to Great Power status required active intention to take up the identity of a Great Power, in addition to recent victories and material resources.

THE CONSEQUENCES OF POWER

The Great Power states have paid dearly, in money and blood, for their predominant military position in the world. Does this power matter?[109] Samuel P. Huntington responds that "the answer can only be: of course ... it obviously matters in national and international affairs."[110] Powerful states can influence the international system to favor their interests and values, promote their interests, and pressure small powers without needing recourse to war. Above all, states seek power in order to ensure their survival and security. Powerful states should find themselves with greater protection from the dangers of war than their militarily weaker neighbors.

In recent decades, however, the dismal political and military failures of top Great Powers have confounded conventional definitions of power. While the United States is generally recognized as being the leading Great Power in the world, Reich and Lebow have pointed out that "one of the principal anomalies of contemporary international relations" is "*the extraordinary military and economic power of the United States and its increasing inability to get other states to do what it wants.*"[111] In the case

---

[109] Daniel W. Drezner, "Military Primacy Doesn't Pay (Nearly As Much As You Think)." *International Security* 38.1 (2013): 52–79; Samuel P. Huntington, "Why International Primacy Matters." *International Security* 17 (1993): 68–83; Robert Jervis, "International Primacy: Is the Game Worth the Candle?" *International Security* 17 (1993): 52–67.

[110] Huntington, "Why International Primacy Matters," 68.

[111] Reich and Lebow, *Good-Bye Hegemony!*, 3.

of the second war with Iraq, "Raw power was ineffective ... It eroded, not enhanced, American influence."[112] While the United States has been perceived as militarily victorious in the wars against Iraq and Afghanistan, these victories have been politically unsatisfying in multiple ways.[113]

The Soviet Union offers another dramatic example. Bristling with nuclear weaponry, the Soviet Union was undeniably a superpower, even though in retrospect, "[t]hese weapons and their delivery systems were expensive and all but unusable in any scenario." Engaging in an arms race with the United States proved costly, however, as "[e]xtravagant expenditure on the military in the context of a stagnating economy is generally understood to have been one of the causes of the Soviet collapse," Reich and Lebow note.[114] Again, with the perfection of hindsight, scholars have been able to foresee (in retrospect) that competition to increase its Great Power status would lead to the demise of the Soviet Union.

These examples are but the most recent examples of the historical inability of relational and material indicators to predict the outcome of wars or the prosperity of societies. Recent scholarship suggests instead that we might simply give up the belief that power can be reliably measured or that it even exists as a single generalizable property of states. Instead, Great Power status can be seen as a label given to those states that have won wars against Great Powers in the past. The perception of military power is essentially a tautological label drawn from historical events that should not be expected to reliably predict future military outcomes.

In the following chapters, this perspective on power informs three aspects of the argument. First, the composition of the Great Power hierarchy affects the lessons learned from history. As argued in Chapter 3, the lessons taken from history – and thus the basis of future military planning – are disproportionately weighted toward the experiences of the Great Power at the top of the hierarchy as well as the practices of the Great Power states generally. These effects of the Great Power hierarchy can be seen in empirical chapters in the latter half of the book. In Chapter 5, the European Great Powers "learned" a particular set of indicators of power from the 1870 Franco-Prussian war. In Chapter 6, the First World War led to the identification of a different set of indicators

---

[112] Reich and Lebow, *Good-Bye Hegemony!*, 6.
[113] Biddle, *Military Power*; Martel, *Victory in War*; Smith, *The Utility of Force*.
[114] Reich and Lebow, *Good-Bye Hegemony*, 5.

of power. Still another set of indicators was gleaned post hoc from the Second World War, as described in Chapters 7 and 8.

Second, the set of Great Power states defines the identification of potential enemies and allies, as argued in Chapter 4. The Great Power states engage in the majority of wars in each era, and carefully monitor the actions of rival Great Powers. States that are estimated as weak, such as Belgium or Poland, are perceived as easy targets for invasion. States that are evaluated as powerful may be sought as allies or identified as potential enemies. Chapter 5 shows that the war plans of the European militaries depended fundamentally on evaluations of relative military capability among the states. In Chapter 8, the enmity between the United States and the Soviet Union depended in part of estimates of relative power among the Great Powers. These estimates of power – and thus potential threat – may become a self-fulfilling prophecy leading to the brink of war and beyond.

Third, the Great Powers engage in the majority of conflicts and competitions in each era. These competitions are fueled by the Great Power identity, and the requirement of victory to gain and maintain Great Power status, as will be argued in Chapter 4. These conflicts among the Great Powers shape the politics of each historical period. Following the Second World War, the Great Powers entered into the competition to acquire nuclear capability, as will be argued in Chapter 7. The competition between the new rivals of the United States and the Soviet Union also drove the Cold War, discussed in Chapter 8. In the end, however, the tautological basis of Great Power status implies that these competitions were at best irrelevant – and at worst, disastrous – for the Great Power states.

3

Military Strategy and the Lessons of History

"The past is infinitely various, an inexhaustible storehouse of events from which we can prove anything or its contrary."[1]

Ambiguity is the starting point for all the arguments developed in this book. War is so complex and rapidly changing as to be, for all intents and purposes, unplannable. Militaries can and do plan, but the results are often disastrous. This is a difficult pill to swallow. Militaries create fearsome weapons and deploy forces on immense scales. Obviously, militaries are capable of impressive feats of learning, innovation, and preparation. How could it be that military planning is fundamentally ambiguous?

The answer, developed in this chapter, is that militaries excel at some kinds of learning and planning, but often fail when it comes to grand strategy and the big picture. Specifically, militaries are extremely good at addressing concrete problems under consistent conditions for which they have sufficient information. As a result, militaries are very successful at some kinds of preparations, such as the development and refinement of specific technologies.[2] In the 1960s, for example, the United States not only put a man on the moon but also developed strategic ballistic missile guidance systems and honed scores of other technologies as well.[3]

---

[1] Michael Howard, *The Lessons of History*. New Haven: Yale University Press, 1991, 11.
[2] Stephen Peter Rosen, *Winning the Next War: Innovation and the Modern Military*. Ithaca: Cornell University Press, 1991; Allan Millett and Williamson Murray (eds.), *Military Effectiveness*. Boston: Allen & Unwin, 1988.
[3] Donald Mackenzie, *Inventing Accuracy: A Historical Sociology of Nuclear Missile Guidance*. Cambridge, MA: MIT Press, 1993.

Militaries have tremendous resources, manpower, and the best minds of the generation to put toward planning. The results can be impressive. Each year seems to bring technological capabilities that were merely science fiction a decade earlier.[4]

These many successes of military planning ironically encourage the belief that militaries can be equally good at macro-level planning for war. However, the big-picture questions of military planning – expectations about the fundamental parameters of a war – are far more challenging.[5] History demonstrates that even the most prepared militaries fail, time and again, to correctly foretell the likely enemies, strategies, and battlefield conditions of future conflicts. Should militaries pursue offensive or defensive strategies? Which technologies will prove decisive? How firm is the enemy's resolve? Like social scientists, militaries collect data on previous wars and develop theories about likely future battle conditions. Unfortunately, wars are simply too complex, and comparable wars are too scarce, to allow effective learning and planning. As Lebow observes, "Our presumed ability to make sense of the past – to discover patterns that allow us to explain social behavior in terms of its enduring regularities – makes us unreasonably confident of our ability to predict, or at least to cope with the future."[6]

This chapter unpacks the challenges of military planning, and in particular the difficulties of learning from history.[7] The chapter begins by discussing how militaries can learn and plan effectively when dealing with simple problems, consistent conditions, and plentiful data. However, even small shifts in context may disrupt planning or render lessons of prior wars irrelevant. Next, the chapter explores the profound ambiguity when it comes to the big picture, involving complex questions and limited data. The chapter draws on the skepticism of Robert Jervis, Richard Betts,

---

[4] Although see Theo Farrell, *Weapons without a Cause: The Politics of Weapons Acquisition in the United States.* New York: Palgrave Macmillan, 1996.

[5] Richard K. Betts, "Is Strategy an Illusion?" *International Security* 25 (2003): 5–50; Stephen Biddle, *Military Power: Explaining Victory and Defeat in Modern Battle.* Princeton: Princeton University Press, 2004; Robert Jervis, *Perception and Misperception in International Politics.* Princeton: Princeton University Press, 1976; Patricia L. Sullivan, *Who Wins: Predicting Strategic Success and Failure in Armed Conflict.* Oxford: Oxford University Press, 2012.

[6] Richard Ned Lebow, *Forbidden Fruit: Counterfactuals and International Relations.* Princeton: Princeton University Press, 2010, 14.

[7] See Jack S. Levy, "Learning and Foreign Policy: Sweeping a Conceptual Minefield." *International Organization* 48.2 (1994): 279–312, for a particularly useful analysis of the concept of learning.

Stephen Biddle, and other scholars who suggest that the empirical basis for selecting military strategies and technologies is quite precarious.

Third, the chapter examines how militaries typically confront the ambiguity regarding big questions of military strategy and technology. Essentially, militaries try to learn from prior wars. Sullivan summarizes the observation of many scholars when she notes: "[D]ecision-makers 'reason by analogy,' applying the lessons of the last war, or a prominent case considered to be similar to the current situation."[8] Militaries look to recent wars, especially those fought by Great Powers, to gain information about the likely conditions under which the next set of military battles will be fought. The hope is to distill essentials that may pertain even if specific knowledge about upcoming wars is missing. Unfortunately, when the next war occurs the lessons of prior wars are frequently overturned. Military planners usually find in hindsight that they have planned for the wrong war.

The process of "learning from history" is illustrated by a short case example of the military debates over the utility of cavalry that occurred in the late nineteenth century. One of the big lessons that European militaries "learned" from the battles of the Franco-Prussian war of 1870 was that cavalry would be essential in future continental conflicts. The cavalry debates illustrate the difficulty of learning from even a single battle in a particular war. The broader consequences of learning from the Franco-Prussian War are developed in Chapter 5.

THE DIFFICULTY OF APPLYING LESSONS OF WAR

Militaries excel at learning, improving, and planning when they are dealing with straightforward problems, consistent conditions, and ample data. Learning is most effective when dealing with specific tasks, concrete outcomes and when repeated events occur under highly similar conditions. This might include optimizing military technologies, improving logistics of troop mobilization, or training soldiers to perform specific tasks on the battlefield. With numerous opportunities for trial and error coupled with close observation, effective learning and adaptation can

---

[8] Sullivan, *Who Wins*, 6; see also Jervis, *Perception and Misperception*; Yuen Foong Khong, *Analogies at War: Korea, Munich, Dien Bien Phu, and the Vietnam Decisions of 1965*. Princeton: Princeton University Press, 1992; Ernest R. May, *"Lessons" of the Past: The Use and Misuse of History in American Foreign Policy*. London: Oxford University Press, 1979 [1973].

occur rapidly. In the interwar period, for example, the British Royal Air Force effectively developed an early version of radar and swiftly learned how to identify incoming German planes by day and by night. These preparations, which paid off in the Battle of Britain, were greatly aided by the continuity of conditions, since German planes necessarily followed a fairly set course from German airfields to the British coast. Impressively, in only a few years, "Britain possessed a technically efficient and fully operational early warning system all along the greater part of its vulnerable south and east coast."[9] Farrell provides a similar but more recent example of adaptive learning by the British military in Afghanistan.[10]

However, effective learning depends on a high degree of consistency in the conditions. Those strategies that were successful in 1940 might not extrapolate well to different aircraft, different targets, or different terrain. The Royal Air Force experienced a substantially different situation in Greece in 1944, for instance, where the lessons and strategies that worked brilliantly in the Battle of Britain did not translate straightforwardly. Conversely, when militaries are fighting an enemy encountered recently, on the same terrain, and with similar weaponry, there may be greater utility to the lessons learned from the last war.

Military planning hinges profoundly on assumptions about future battle conditions. Elizabeth Kier makes this point vividly in her study of tanks in the interwar period, in which there was considerable ambiguity and disagreement about the conditions under which tanks would operate.[11] British and German tank designers envisioned different battle conditions and designed different kinds of tanks accordingly, a topic further discussed in Chapter 6.

These shifting conditions of war are the bane of military planners. Militaries design their technology based on the conditions they expect to find on the battlefield. Given the complexity of contemporary military technology, technological design decisions must be made years, even decades before the technology will be used. For instance, in the 1980s, the United States worked on the development of technologically advanced

---

[9] M. Kirby and R. Capey, "The Air Defence of Great Britain, 1920–1940: An Operational Research Perspective." *The Journal of the Operational Research Society* 48 (1997): 555–568, 562.

[10] Theo Farrell, "Improving in War: Military Adaptation and the British in Helmand Province, Afghanistan, 2006–2009." *Journal of Strategic Studies* 33 (4): 567–594, 2010.

[11] Elizabeth Kier, *Imagining War: French and British Military Doctrine between the Wars.* Princeton: Princeton University Press, 1997.

nuclear submarines, based on predictions regarding likely battle conditions that would be faced in the 1990s.[12] By the time the submarines were
ready, however, the Cold War was over and the United States was
fighting a war in the deserts of the Middle East.

For instance, scholars have sought to develop generalizations about the
impact of technological change on offensive and defensive military strategies.[13] The rest of this section takes a closer look at these academic
theories. In a nutshell, scholars have argued that the technological capabilities of certain historical eras favored offensive strategies, while at
other times technology favored defense. The invention of the machine
gun and barbed wire are seen as favoring defensive strategies in the early
twentieth century. By the late 1930s, technologies such as the tank and
aircraft favored offensive strategies. The technological bias toward
offense or defense is argued to ultimately shape the way in which wars
are fought as well as the likelihood of war.[14]

In its basic form, the offensive-defensive nature of military technology
provides an elegant rubric for the planning of future wars. Unfortunately,
such efforts inevitably succumb to the complexities and shifting conditions of war. One complexity, as Jervis has noted, is the terrain.
A technology such as the tank may be advantageous to offensive strategies
in the limited and shallow frontiers of Western Europe but might be less
optimal in the open landscape of the Soviet Union.[15] Scholars have
addressed additional confounding factors as well. Van Evera considers
domestic social and political factors and the nature of diplomacy, while
Sagan and Snyder consider civil-military relations and the organizational
culture of the military as factors influencing the effectiveness of offensive
and defensive strategies.[16] Going further, Shimshoni argues that canny

---

[12] James Fallows, *National Defense*. New York: Random House, 1981.

[13] Michael E. Brown, Owen R. Coté Jr., Sean M. Lynn-Jones, and Steven E. Miller (eds.),
Offense, Defense, and War. Cambridge, MA: MIT Press, 2004.

[14] Stephen Van Evera, *Causes of War: Power and the Roots of Conflict*. Ithaca: Cornell
University Press, 1999; Barry R. Posen, *The Sources of Military Doctrine: France, Britain,
and Germany between the World Wars*. Ithaca: Cornell University Press, 1984; Stephen
Peter Rosen, *Winning the Next War: Innovation and the Modern Military*. Ithaca:
Cornell University Press, 1991; Stephen Van Evera, "The Cult of the Offensive and the
Origins of the First World War." *International Security* 9 (1984): 58–107; Brown, Coté,
Lynn-Jones, and Miller, *Offense, Defense and War*.

[15] Robert Jervis, "Cooperation Under the Security Dilemma." *World Politics* 30 (1978):
167–214.

[16] Van Evera, *Causes of War*; Scott D. Sagan, "1914 Revisited: Allies, Offense, and Instability." *International Security* 11 (1986): 151–175; Jack Snyder, "Civil-Military Relations
and the Cult of the Offensive, 1914 and 1984." *International Security* 9 (1984): 108–146.

strategists actively construct their own opportunities by cleverly combining available technologies with the battle conditions that give an offensive or defensive advantage.[17] Each of these complexities makes it more difficult for the military planner to know whether offensive or defensive strategies are more appropriate in any given situation. The elegant notion that optimal strategy can be easily inferred from existing technology collapses in a morass of complicating factors.

Even more problematically, military planners have done a disastrous job of assessing the offensive-defensive balance of the period as a practical matter. For the First World War, which provides the central case for the offensive-defensive theory, scholars have claimed that the technology of the period was well suited to defensive strategies. But "elites mistakenly believed the opposite," Van Evera notes, and militaries utilized offensive strategies during the First World War instead.[18] In contrast, the technologies of the Second World War favored offensive strategies according to theory, but "[t]his offensive innovation was unrecognized outside Germany and doubted by many within."[19] Instead, the major combatants utilized defensive strategies in the Second World War. One resolution to this propensity for misinterpretation might lie in the specific situations of the battle rather than in the fundamental characteristics of the technology. Machine guns and barbed wire might be favorable for defensive strategies under some conditions, such as the fields of Western Europe, but might be appropriate for offensive strategies under different conditions. Yet as the complexity of the factors increases, the simplicity of the offensive-defensive technological balance becomes hopelessly muddled.

In short, learning and planning are most effective when battle conditions can be accurately identified. The greater the ambiguity of those battle conditions, the less applicable learning and planning will be. Unfortunately, military planners rarely know the important details of the next war, as discussed in the next section. Consequently, militaries often find out too late that they have planned for the wrong war.

THE AMBIGUITY OF MILITARY PLANNING

Chapters 1 and 2 pointed out that military power is fundamentally ambiguous, but argued that the outcome of recent Great Power wars generates a

---

[17] Jonathan Shimshoni, "Technology, Military Advantage and World War I: A Case of Military Entrepreneurship." *International Security* 15 (1990–1991): 187–215.
[18] Van Evera, *Causes of War*, 174. [19] Van Evera, *Causes of War*, 175.

social consensus regarding the power hierarchy. This section develops a parallel argument for the case of military learning and planning. War is hopelessly complex, but militaries resolve ambiguity by drawing lessons from recent wars, creating consensus within the international military community regarding the strategies and technologies needed for future wars.

Scholars have increasingly begun to appreciate that military planning takes place in a sea of ambiguity.[20] Wars may begin with only a week's notice. Thus important decisions must be made long beforehand – battle plans sketched out, military technology designed and developed, and military personnel trained. How do militaries know what to plan for? The short answer is: they usually do not. It is common for militaries to plan for the wrong war – against the wrong enemy, using different technologies, and in support of different political goals. These errors are usually condemned as indicating the foolishness or stodgy inertia of the military. Afterwards, the next generation of military planners sets out to make the same mistakes over again.

As Jervis pointed out decades ago: military planners are bedeviled by "the complexity of the subject matter, the small and biased sample of cases available for study, [and] the conditions under which learning takes place."[21] More recently, proponents of bargaining theory have emphasized the role of uncertainty in explaining the misestimates of military decision-making.[22] Uncertainty over the intentions and capabilities of the enemy commonly leads to miscalculation. As Goldman writes, "Uncertainty about the identity of potential threats is central to international relations theory."[23] These types of uncertainty lead militaries to make grievous errors in their planning.

In this section, I unpack three main challenges of trying to learn lessons from war as the basis for future planning. The first is the difficulty of comparison: wars are highly dissimilar and difficult to compare with

---

[20] Scott Sigmund Gartner, *Strategic Assessment in War*. New Haven: Yale University Press, 1997; Emily O. Goldman, *Power in Uncertain Times: Strategy in the Fog of Peace*. Stanford: Stanford University Press, 2011; Jervis, *Perception and Misperception*; Dan Reiter, *Crucible of Beliefs: Learning, Alliances, and World Wars*. Ithaca: Cornell University Press, 1996; Talbot C. Imlay and Monica Duffy Toft (eds.), *The Fog of Peace and War Planning*. New York: Routledge, 2006.

[21] Jervis *Perception and Misperception*, 235.

[22] James D. Fearon, "Rationalist Explanations for War." *International Organization* 49 (1995): 379–414; Robert Powell, *In the Shadow of Power: States and Strategies in International Politics*. Princeton: Princeton University Press, 1999; Reiter, *Crucible of Beliefs*.

[23] Goldman, *Power in Uncertain Times*, 16.

each other. The second is the ambiguity of explanation. Even if one side prevails in a conflict, it is often difficult to understand why, making it difficult to draw the correct lessons. The third is the ambiguity of contingency: one must assume that generalized lessons can be learned from war – yet the outcome may have been driven by chance or highly contingent circumstances that are unlikely to be repeated in the future. These ambiguities bedevil those who would learn from war.

Ambiguity of Comparison

Social scientists are quite familiar with the difficulties of working with real-world events, in all their harrowing complexity, rather than the laboratory conditions enjoyed by physical scientists.[24] One solution to the problem is to look at a large number of similar events in the hopes of being able to infer the dynamics of an "average" war under these conditions. This approach requires large amounts of comparable data.

Unfortunately for military strategists – but beneficial for humanity – there tends to be only a handful of battles or wars in each historical period that can provide grist for empirical analyses. Although interstate warfare seems like an endemic condition of humanity, there has been an average of only five wars per decade since 1816.[25] For Great Powers seeking to prepare for a conflict against their peers, there are even fewer relevant wars to analyze. As Jervis notes, "With only a few cases available, it is difficult to make the numerous comparisons that are necessary to develop the complex and abstract explanations that would help the decision-maker cope with contemporary problems."[26] Reiter similarly observes that "[military] organizations have to make the best from information sources that are very limited in number."[27] Even the most diligent theorist has surprisingly few relevant wars available to answer a given question.

Posing an even greater challenge is the difficulty of comparing one war with another.[28] Even among the small set of recent wars, each war is

---

[24] Gary King, Robert O. Keohane, and Sidney Verba, *Designing Social Inquiry: Scientific Inference in Qualitative Research*. Princeton: Princeton University Press, 1994.

[25] Meredith Reid Sarkees and Frank Wayman, *Resort to War: 1816–2007*. Washington, DC: CQ Press, 2010.

[26] Jervis, *Perception and Misperception*, 235.   [27] Reiter, *Crucible of Beliefs*, 35.

[28] James G. March, "Exploration and Exploitation in Organizational Learning." *Organization Science* 2 (1991): 71–87; James G. March and Johan P. Olsen, "The New Institutionalism: Organizational Factors in Political Life." *The American Political Science Review* 78 (1984): 734–749.

likely to have been fought between different states, with different military configurations, different technologies, and on varying terrain and weather conditions. The capabilities of the leadership matter significantly, as even the best army can be brought to disaster by incompetent generals. The difficulty of comparison is exacerbated the further back in history the comparison goes. Military students may still study the Napoleonic Wars or the battles of Julius Caesar, but applying those lessons in the contemporary world is intellectually perilous given the vast differences in technology, economy, political context, composition of the armies, and logistical capabilities.

Due to these difficulties of comparison, military analyses tend to focus primarily on one recent war. Consequently, the selection of that single war for analysis is critical.[29] The lessons of a single case are most generalizable if the war under scrutiny is representative of the modal war of the period. Unfortunately, the representativeness of a war cannot be assessed without the advantage of hindsight.

The Ambiguity of Explanation

Another challenge for militaries hoping to learn lessons from the past is the difficulty of *explanation*, due to the complexity of the causal relations among empirical facts.[30] What are the important lessons to be inferred? As Jervis summarizes, "The detrimental effect of complexity on scholars' understanding of international relations has been discussed at length, and we will only add that there is no reason to expect decision-makers to do much better."[31] Complex events provide bread and butter for social scientists, whose livelihood consists of the adjudication of competing explanations. For instance, Allison "explains" the causes of the Cuban

---

[29] James G. March, Lee S. Sproull, and Michal Tamuz, "Learning from Samples of One or Fewer." *Organization Science* 2 (1991): 1–13.

[30] Betts, "Is Strategy an Illusion?"; Robert Jervis, *System Effects: Complexity in Political and Social Life*. Princeton: Princeton University Press, 1997; Jack Snyder and Robert Jervis (eds.), *Coping with Complexity in the International System*. Boulder: Westview Press, 1993; Charles Perrow, *The Next Catastrophe: Reducing our Vulnerabilities to Natural, Industrial, and Terrorist Disasters*. Princeton: Princeton University Press, 2011; Charles Perrow, *Complex Organizations: A Critical Essay*, third edition. New York: Random House, 1986; Scott D. Sagan, *The Limits of Safety: Organizations, Accidents, and Nuclear Weapons*. Princeton: Princeton University Press, 1993; Diane Vaughan, *The Challenger Launch Decision: Risky Technology, Culture, and Deviance at War*. Chicago: University of Chicago Press, 1996.

[31] Jervis, *Perception and Misperception*, 235.

Missile Crisis in three very different ways.[32] Each explanation is plausible, and is supported by agreed-on empirical facts. Such situations, in which multiple plausible explanations can be broached for a single event, are ubiquitous for theorists of interstate war.

Complex events, such as a war, tend to be subject to an even greater multiplicity of plausible explanations than simpler events. As Gray has noted, "[T]echnology, generalship, economic strength, logistic competence, [and] political popularity" are "but a few of the dimensions ... [that] have all been promoted as the golden key to strategic success."[33] In addition, the particulars of a battle, including weather, terrain, morale, and, above all, luck have long been regarded as playing an important role in the outcome of a battle or even a war. For such a complex event, a wide variety of explanations for the outcome are plausible. Gartner argues: "[Militaries] do not misperceive situations; rather, because of the variety of information sources available and the random factors involved in warfare, the results of combat can support diverse perceptions of the performance of a strategy."[34] Betts agrees: "Some strategies seem to 'work' in some cases and not others; evidence about efficacy is too mixed to command enough consensus on a verdict to qualify as proof."[35]

Moreover, organizational scholars such as Perrow have noted that *complex interactions*, which involve "branching paths, feedback loops, [and] jumps from one linear sequence to another," are particularly difficult for humans to comprehend.[36] Snyder has pointed out that one barrier to understanding "is the sheer difficulty of tracing all the multifarious causal chains, including their complex feedback effects, that a hypothetical action might set in motion."[37] Studies have shown that major disasters may result from a series of small and seemingly trivial events that interact with each other in complex systems, such as nuclear power plants, space shuttles, or weapons systems that are too intricate to be comprehended in their entirety.[38] Rasler and Thompson suggest that

[32] Graham T. Allison, *Essence of Decision: Explaining the Cuban Missile Crisis*. Boston: Little, Brown, 1971.

[33] Colin S. Gray, *Modern Strategy*. Oxford: Oxford University Press, 1999, 7.

[34] Scott Sigmund Gartner, *Strategic Assessment in War*. New Haven: Yale University Press, 1997, 26.

[35] Betts, "Is Strategy an Illusion?"   [36] Perrow, *Complex Organizations*, 75.

[37] Jack Snyder, "Introduction." In *Dominoes and Bandwagon: Strategic Beliefs and Great Power Competition in the Eurasian Rimland*, edited by Robert Jervis and Jack Snyder, 3–19. Oxford: Oxford University Press, 1991, 18.

[38] Perrow, *Complex Organizations*; Sagan, *The Limits of Safety*; Vaughan, *The Challenger Launch Decision*.

"it may not be possible for any decision-maker to foresee, or even track the implications of a change in one part of a tightly connected network of interstate hostilities."[39]

However, even if a consensus is reached on a satisfying explanation for one war, the key factors of that war cannot easily be extrapolated into the basis for a general theory. Social scientists are extremely wary of the dangers of overgeneralizing the factors of one war to the outcomes of future wars, against other armies under different conditions with updated technologies. As Betts argues, "effective strategy is often an illusion" because the causal relationships are "too complex and unpredictable to be manipulated to a specified end."[40] Scholars might agree with Lebow that "[r]adical skepticism about prediction of any but the most short-term outcomes is fully warranted."[41] These dangers of overgeneralization are generally recognized by social scientists but must be set aside by military planners in practice, due to the urgency of the pressure to prepare for war.

The Ambiguity of Contingency

A third aspect of ambiguity, related to the previous two, derives from the contingent nature of events. Specific outcomes such as military victory are probabilistic in that they represent only one of a range of possible outcomes that might have occurred. Random factors are often highly influential in the outcome of a battle. Military outcomes may hinge on the fact that a general started the march in the afternoon rather than the morning, or camped on one bank of a river rather than the other. Indeed, military scholars and practitioners from Clausewitz to the present have given much respect to the "the unholy trinity of friction, chance, and uncertainty."[42] Betts notes: "War turned out better for Churchill than for Hitler not because Churchill's strategic choices were wiser, but because of events and influences that . . . simply turned up on the roll of the dice."[43]

---

[39] Karen Rasler and William R. Thompson, "Strategic Rivalries and Complex Causality in 1914." In *The Outbreak of the First World War: Structure, Politics and Decision-Making*, edited by Jack S. Levy and John A. Vasquez, 65–86. New York: Cambridge University Press, 2014, 67.

[40] Betts, "Is Strategy an Illusion?," 5.

[41] Richard Ned Lebow, *Forbidden Fruit: Counterfactuals and International Relations*. Princeton: Princeton University Press, 2010, 11.

[42] Gray, *Modern Strategy*, 41.   [43] Betts, "Is Strategy an Illusion?," 19.

An entire range of possible wars could have been fought in a given place and time, presumably with varying outcomes. Nevertheless, military and political decision-makers tend to fall into the trap of hindsight bias – the assumption that the outcome of a war was determined at the start. As defined by Lebow, hindsight bias occurs when "we upgrade the probability of events once they have occurred and come to regard the past as overdetermined – but the future as highly contingent."[44] Similarly, March has noted: "[P]articipants seem to exaggerate the necessity of historical events. They overestimate the likelihood of events that actually occur and underestimate the likelihood of events that do not occur but might very easily have occurred."[45]

Ignoring the probabilistic nature of the outcome is even more seductive in cases such as war where the outcome is dichotomous – one side wins while the other is defeated. Victory and defeat are outcomes that are too blunt to allow the analysis of the multiple factors at play in so complex an event as a war. Even a single battle evinces myriad complexities that cannot be summarized in the simple outcome of victory. Some academics have also pointed out that victory itself is a social construction. As Mandel, Johnson, and Tierney have argued, subjective components contribute to the perception of victory, beyond the material gains and losses experienced on the battlefield.[46] Nevertheless, military planners – and the rest of the nonacademic world – take victory and defeat as solid empirical facts that provide an important basis for military planning.

The study of counterfactuals has attracted serious theoretical attention in social science, and even armchair generals dabble in "what if "scenarios.[47] Scholars have provided useful rules to think about the construction of counterfactuals and their utility in advancing theory. However, it is not clear that counterfactual methods have gained widespread use even among academics. Lebow notes that although political scientists are

[44] Lebow, *Forbidden Fruit*, 8.
[45] James G. March, "Decisions in Organizations and Theories of Choice." In *Perspectives on Organization Design and Behavior*, edited by Andrew H. Van de Ven and William F. Joyce, 205–244. New York: John Wiley and Sons, 1981, 227.
[46] Robert Mandel, *The Meaning of Military Victory*. London: Lynne Rienner, 2006; Dominic D. P. Johnson and Dominic Tierney, *Failing to Win: Perceptions of Victory and Defeat in International Politics*. Cambridge, MA: Harvard University Press, 2006.
[47] Lebow, *Forbidden Fruit*; Philip E. Tetlock, and Aaron Belkin (eds.), *Counterfactual Thought Experiments in World Politics: Logical, Methodological, and Psychological Perspectives*. Princeton: Princeton University Press, 1996; Gary Goertz and Jack S. Levy (eds.), *Explaining War and Peace: Case Studies and Necessary Condition Counterfactuals*. New York: Routledge, 2007; Biddle, *Military Power*, 195.

interested in counterfactuals, they simultaneously display "widespread confidence in the high probability, if not near inevitability, of major twentieth-century international outcomes."[48] In practice, military accounts often contain "strong elements of determinism," as Overy points out, "We now know the story [of Allied victory in the Second World War] so well that we do not consider the uncomfortable prospect that other outcomes might have been possible."[49]

Military planners, even more than academic scholars, are constrained in their ability to use counterfactuals as the basis for planning.[50] Of course military decision-makers do make allowances for contingencies and build alternatives into their plans. And contingent events during the course of a war are likely to change the decisions made, as states learn more about the military capabilities of their enemy. Nevertheless, the consideration of counterfactuals is difficult to incorporate into long-range military plans. Excessive contingency is useless for military planners, who must move forward with these plans. Allowing significant consideration of contingency introduces intolerable ambiguity into military analyses. Military theorists are driven by hindsight bias because full consideration of the probabilistic aspect of victory, in addition to the ambiguity of explanation and the lack of cases for comparison, would make planning impossible.

The magnitude of the error of hindsight bias depends on the underlying probability of the outcome. If the outcome of a war can be seen as analogous to a coin toss, it would be a grave error to attribute the ability to win the next coin toss to the winner. Yet the erroneousness of the assumption is only apparent because we know the fifty-fifty probability distribution of coin outcomes. On the other extreme, a war might be based on a different set of probabilities, such as a free-throw competition between a professional basketball player and an amateur fan. In this case the underlying odds might so greatly favor the professional that the outcome might be taken as reasonably certain. The problem is that without knowing the underlying probability distribution, we cannot know whether it is reasonable to assume that the winner is essentially inevitable or whether the odds were fifty-fifty.

Consequently, planners frequently disregard the probabilistic nature of military outcomes. In particular, military analysts typically cast the losing

[48] Lebow, *Forbidden Fruit*, 9.   [49] Cited in Gartner, *Strategic Assessment in War*, 24–25.
[50] Robert Jervis, *Why Intelligence Fails: Lessons from the Iranian Revolution and the Iraq War*. Ithaca: Cornell University Press, 2010, 9.

state as having done many things incorrectly, while the winning state is presented as having been correct in every detail of military preparation. As Gartner notes, "Most of the literature fails to account for the *ex post* problem we have as observers: we know which side lost and so wonder why the loser did not do something different. Determining which strategy failed is always easier after the fact than while combat is going on."[51] This assumption biases the resulting analyses. Under the lens of hindsight bias, it becomes nearly impossible to "learn" any valuable strategies from the defeated state or to counter any ineffective practices of the victor. This often boils down to the assumption that the outcome of the war was largely determined from the initial military capabilities of each side at the beginning of the war, or at least that the outcome had a high probability of occurring.

Some of the lessons that militaries "learn" will turn out to be appropriate for the future battles that are fought. Some standard operating procedures may be generically useful under a variety of conditions; others might require specific conditions that happily coincided with the actual battle conditions encountered. In a probabilistic world, however, militaries cannot know in advance which of the lessons will turn out to have been appropriate and which were in error. Militaries must make their best guesses in an ambiguous reality, aware that some of those guesses will be right and others disastrously wrong.

SCHOLARLY EXPLANATIONS

Two major scholarly perspectives from the academic literature are discussed in this section: realism and domestic politics. Realist explanations of military planning view the planning of wars as a reasonable endeavor. Military theorists observe empirical events and learn from history. The objective analysis of the utility of resources and technologies can be derived from their physical properties or from battlefield experiences. While optimal strategies are not always identified, in principle it is possible to deduce the correct lessons from history. These assumptions allow the rational planning of war to occur. This view has been contested, however, by the domestic politics perspective, which examines the effects of bureaucratic interests, economic elites, or military culture on strategic decision-making.

---

[51] Gartner, *Strategic Assessment in War*, 24–25.

Realism

Studies of war tend to depict militaries as rationally making preparations for war in an orderly environment.[52] Military leaders are expected to learn lessons from past events and to straightforwardly apply those lessons to their military preparations. Those who fail to take heed of history will find themselves chastised by the ironclad rules of war.[53] The realist perspective assumes that empirical facts are sufficient in themselves to identify the indicators of military capability.[54] Embedded in this perspective is the assumption that astute military leaders should be able to accurately predict and plan for future wars. Three assumptions of realism enable accurate learning from history.

First, militaries seek to identify the "best practices" in the military domain by studying the full set of historical wars. In principle, any war might demonstrate these best practices, although it is more likely that contemporary wars will provide the primary basis for insights. It is also unsurprising that recent Great Power conflicts will receive the greatest attention, since the Great Powers have tested their strategies in battle and emerged victorious. Drawing on the efficient war assumption that victorious battle practices must have been the best, militaries look to recent Great Power wars.

The second assumption is that the lessons of history can be straightforwardly gleaned from empirical facts alone. An astute survey of the military facts should be sufficient to point decision-makers toward a reliable analysis. Since independent observers should draw the same conclusions under conditions of minimal ambiguity, no involved explanation is needed as to why states tend to come to the same interpretation of military events. Moreover, since states draw on a common body of past wars, they are likely to "learn" the same lessons from the data. As a result, multiple evaluations of the factors leading to military capability should tend to converge.

---

[52] Posen, *The Sources of Military Doctrine*; Rosen, *Winning the Next War*; Van Evera, "The Cult of the Offensive."

[53] Kenneth N. Waltz, *Theory of International Politics*. Reading, MA: Addison-Wesley, 1979.

[54] Robert Gilpin, *War and Change in World Politics*. Cambridge: Cambridge University Press, 1981; Hans J. Morgenthau, *Politics Among Nations*. New York: Alfred A. Knopf, 1973 [1948]; John J. Mearsheimer, *The Tragedy of Great Power Politics*. New York: W. W. Norton and Company, 2001; William Curti Wohlforth, *The Elusive Balance: Power and Perceptions during the Cold War*. Ithaca: Cornell University Press, 1993.

Third, battlefield outcomes are assumed to be the ultimate arbiter of capability. This assumption implies that the outcome of the war is largely determined from the initial military capabilities of each side at the beginning of the war, or at least that the outcome had a high probability of occurring. Although the combatants may have been unaware of the initial probabilities, superior military capability might have been recognized before the war with sufficient insight. Irrespective of insight, military superiority will be revealed by battlefield performance. Implicit in this assumption is the expectation that mistakes in evaluation will be corrected by the outcomes of historical events.

To the extent that these assumptions are reasonable, the conclusions of military theorists will be reliable as well. These arguments are most applicable when repeated events occur under highly similar conditions. With numerous opportunities for trial and error coupled with close observation, effective learning can occur incrementally. Unfortunately, wars as a whole do not generally fit these parameters under which realist learning is most effective.

Domestic Politics

A second perspective focuses on the influence of domestic politics and culture on military planning. In contrast to the realists, domestic politics scholars recognize the ambiguity inherent in history.[55] Since the historical facts can support various interpretations, proponents argue that different military cultures each support their own interpretations. Domestic politics scholars emphasize the variations in the lessons "learned" by different militaries, which serve to question the realist assumptions. Problematically, however, these domestic politics accounts have failed to explain the

---

[55] Deborah D. Avant, *Political Institutions and Military Change: Lessons from Peripheral Wars*. Ithaca: Cornell University Press, 1994; Deborah Avant, "Political Institutions and Military Effectiveness: Contemporary United States and United Kingdom." In *Creating Military Power: The Sources of Military Effectiveness*, edited by Risa A. Brooks and Elizabeth A. Stanley, 80–105. Stanford: Stanford University Press, 2007; Lynn Eden, *Whole World on Fire: Organizations, Knowledge, and Nuclear Weapons Devastation*. Ithaca: Cornell University Press, 2004; Matthew Evangelista, *Innovation and the Arms Race: How the United States and the Soviet Union Develop New Military Technologies*. Ithaca: Cornell University Press, 1988; Elizabeth Kier, *Imagining War: French and British Military Doctrine between the Wars*. Princeton: Princeton University Press, 1997; Scott D. Sagan, "1914 Revisited: Allies, Offense, and Instability." *International Security* 11 (1986): 151–175; Kimberly Marten Zisk, *Engaging the Enemy: Organization Theory and Soviet Military Innovation, 1955–1991*. Princeton: Princeton University Press, 1993.

historical convergence of the European militaries on similar military strategies, evaluations of capability, and issues of conflict.

From the domestic politics perspective, it is not surprising that history does not provide clear and straightforward lessons.[56] Instead, the ambiguity of history suggests that reasonable people can independently come to quite different interpretations of a single event. From this perspective, the difficulty lies in the selection of the appropriate interpretation, a challenge enhanced by the gravity of military affairs. Selection cannot be arbitrary or whimsical, since thousands of lives may be at stake. While there is no shortage of Cassandras in any era, picking out the one correct voice among hundreds is no straightforward task. Domestic politics scholars argue that selection occurs through the influence of local powerful groups, rather than driven by the empirical facts posited by the realists.

The ambiguity of military affairs implies that multiple plausible interpretations can be generated for any event. This multiplicity is evidenced in the debates that fill the pages of military journals and the floors of parliaments. The importance and urgency of finding the right answer to military questions brings even greater virulence to these controversies. Yet the necessity to act implies that debates cannot linger indefinitely. Unlike academics who can luxuriate in infinite debate, militaries are under strong pressure to resolve debates with reasonable speed. Militaries must choose a course of action as a basis for military preparations and decision-making.

Scholars have shown that domestic structural arrangements, local cultures, or strong personalities can bend military policies toward local interests. One school of thought argues that local elites take advantage of the ambiguity of military planning by pushing the interpretation that advantages their own interests. Whether these powerful elites are capitalists,[57]

---

[56] Peter J. Katzenstein (ed.), *The Culture of National Security: Norms and Identity in World Politics*. New York: Columbia University Press, 1996; Jutta Weldes, Mark Lafffey, Hugh Gusterson, and Raymond Duvall (eds.), *Cultures of Insecurity: States, Communities and the Production of Danger*. Minneapolis: University of Minnesota Press, 1999; Alexander Wendt, *Social Theory of International Politics*. Cambridge: Cambridge University Press, 1999; Alexander Wendt, "Anarchy Is What States Make of It: The Social Construction of Power Politics." *International Organization* 46 (1992): 391–425.

[57] Paul A. Baran and Paul M. Sweezy, *Monopoly Capital: An Essay on the American Economic and Social Order*. New York: Monthly Review Press, 1968; Larry J. Griffin, Joel A. Devine, and Michael Wallace, "Monopoly Capital, Organized Labor, and Military Expenditures in the United States, 1949–1976." *The American Journal of Sociology* 88 (1982): S113–S153; Charles C. Moskos, Jr., "The Concept of the Military-Industrial Complex: Radical Critique or Liberal Bogey?" *Social Problems* 21 (1974): 498–512; Maurice Zeitlin, "Military Spending and Economic Stagnation." *The American Journal of Sociology* 79 (1974): 1452–1456.

bureaucratic wonks,[58] or military generals varies according to the particular theoretical stripe of the theorist. Alternately, scholars have argued that domestic institutional cultures and structural arrangements prefer certain interpretations to others.[59] Stodgy military cultures or backward-looking bureaucratic attitudes may be resistant to technological and strategic innovations. In any case, domestic institutions resolve ambiguity in favor of powerful local groups. In the absence of an unambiguous method for victory, decision-makers select the alternative that gives them the greatest advantage in local or bureaucratic politics.

The evidence in support of these perspectives is the variation that is empirically evident in military practices. Arguing against the realist perspective, scholars in this tradition have shown that empirical facts alone do not lead to the selection of optimal strategies and policies. Instead, the debates and variation in practice in military planning, such as the utility of cavalry in the late nineteenth century, discussed later, are used to illustrate that political and cultural processes supplement empirical facts. These studies clearly show that local processes and decision-makers are influential in the setting of military policies and strategies.

The question is whether domestic arguments can explain the whole story. Domestic politics scholars have convincingly argued against the realist claim that empirical facts should lead straightforwardly to a single conclusion. Taken to their logical conclusion, however, the domestic politics perspective suggests that each military would idiosyncratically reflect purely local influences. Yet the European militaries have historically utilized similar strategies and technologies. For instance, the European militaries converged on a similar outlook on cavalry in the late nineteenth century. Domestic politics scholars have failed to explain these commonalities of military planning that give credence to realist perspectives. Thus the challenge for scholars in the domestic perspective is to explain why militaries often arrive at broadly the same conclusions on military goals and tactics despite domestic differences.

These two scholarly perspectives, realism and domestic politics, have a long tradition in the academic literature. Yet both fail to explain how militaries learn in the real world. Realists posit that the lessons of

[58] Allison, *Essence of Decision*; Graham T. Allison and Morton H. Halperin, "Bureaucratic Politics: A Paradigm and Some Policy Implications." *World Politics* 24 (1972): 40–79; Morton H. Halperin, *Bureaucratic Politics and Foreign Policy*. Washington, DC: Brookings Institution, 1974.

[59] Eden, *Whole World on Fire*; Kier, *Imagining War*; Sagan, "1914 Revisited."

history are overly determined, overlooking the massive amounts of ambiguity in historical events. Domestic politics scholars, on the other hand, admit too much ambiguity. From their perspective, two militaries with different domestic configurations are unlikely to agree sufficiently on interests and strategies for war to be possible in the first place. Drawing on the work of Jervis, Reiter, and others, a third solution to the puzzle of how militaries reach broad agreement on the lessons of history despite massive levels of ambiguity is developed in the following section.

LEARNING FROM HISTORY

The ambiguities discussed in the previous section make life difficult for both scholars and military planners alike. However, military planners are under an onus to act that is absent for intellectuals. Academic scholars can debate endlessly, reanalyzing historical events and pondering complex counterfactuals. For military planners, the urgent need for action is an overriding concern. Conclusions must be drawn even if the data is insufficient.

Under pressure to plan, militaries fall back on the limited information that is available: they seek to learn from past wars. Consequently, scholars have repeatedly observed militaries drawing on faulty history, emulating each other's flawed designs, and imprudently planning for the last war.[60] As Reiter notes, "History dominates both the actions and the rhetoric of international politics ... [which are] haunted by the ghosts of Sarajevo, Munich, and Vietnam."[61] Pointing to the recent U.S. wars in the Persian Gulf, Reiter continues: "Foreign policy on all sides seemed to be conducted straight out of history books, and many of the actors in the crisis drew lessons from past experiences to guide their decisions."[62]

---

[60] Deborah Avant, "From Mercenary to Citizen Armies: Explaining Change in the Practice of War." *International Organization* 54 (2000): 41–72; Robert Jervis, *Perception and Misperception in International Politics*. Princeton: Princeton University Press, 1976; Dan Reiter, *Crucible of Beliefs: Learning, Alliances, and World Wars*. Ithaca: Cornell University Press, 1996; João Resende-Santos, *Neorealism, States, and the Modern Mass Army*. Cambridge: Cambridge University Press, 2007.

[61] Dan Reiter, *Crucible of Beliefs: Learning, Alliances, and World Wars*. Ithaca: Cornell University Press, 1996, 1.

[62] Reiter, 1996, 1.

A wide array of scholars has noted that militaries develop strategy based on analogies from the past.[63] Militaries "learn" in the sense that they alter their behavior as a result of interpretations of past events. However, these inductive "lessons" learned from history are likely to be biased in predictable ways. As Reiter notes, "[T]hese tools favor cognitive economy but tend to incur certain systematic biases."[64] In particular, military theorists tend to focus on one war, usually the last major Great Power conflict. Explanations for victory in this war are developed into supposedly generalized rules of war that only rarely prove applicable for subsequent events. Moreover, a tendency toward teleology limits the positive lessons that might be learned from the defeated state. These biases may be sufficient to alleviate anxiety, allowing militaries to carry out planning. However, the biases cannot erase the essential underlying ambiguity. Jervis writes: "The world is ambiguous, and indicators of success are likely to be elusive."[65] In the end, military planning is likely to be deeply flawed.

Overemphasis on Great Power Wars

First, military thinkers sidestep the ambiguity of comparison by narrowing their gaze, often focusing on the last Great Power war. Since the complexity of wars makes detailed comparison nearly impossible, military planners usually select one war to provide the primary basis for theorizing. Reiter argues that militaries tend to "rely on a single, representative event – often an analogy from past experience – to guide their decisions."[66] However, the dangers of generalizing from a single case are well known to social scientists. Moreover, military thinkers do not attempt to identify the most representative war of an era (which would be an intellectually impossible task anyway, except in hindsight). Military analyses tend to emphasize the last Great Power war, particularly one in which the previous leading Great Power was defeated. As Reiter notes, "An important implication ... is that individuals will tend to focus on individual, representative events more than they 'should,' that is, more

---

[63] Deborah Avant, "From Mercenary to Citizen Armies: Explaining Change in the Practice of War." *International Organization* 54 (2000): 41–72; Betts, "Is Strategy an Illusion?"; Biddle, *Military Power*; Jervis, *Perception and Misperception*; Lebow, *Forbidden Fruit*; Reiter, *Crucible of Beliefs*.

[64] Reiter, *Crucible of Beliefs*, 21. [65] Jervis, *Why Intelligence Fails*, 164.

[66] Reiter, *Crucible of Beliefs*, 25.

than might be dictated by laws of scientific inference."[67] This war provides the empirical starting point for the "lessons" of history.

In principle, military scholars might begin with a study of several wars of the period. Yet these wars are often so disparate that they are essentially incommensurable. For instance, a number of wars were fought in the interwar period between the First and Second World Wars, including wars between the Soviet Union, China, and Japan, a war between Greece and Turkey, and a war between Bolivia and Paraguay.[68] These wars, which were fought on different continents between armies with quite different strategies and for different political purposes, were so varied that it was impossible to develop a common set of rules that explained them all.

Instead, the Great Power status hierarchy – presumed to identify the "best" militaries – strongly influences which war becomes the focus of analysis. In particular, the last major Great Power war – in which two or more Great Powers fought against each other – is often the centerpiece of military analyses. Such a war is given even greater weight if a new Great Power ascended to the top of the hierarchy. Thus in the interwar period, military scholars focused on the First World War as the basis for their theory of war. While the wars in East Asia and elsewhere may have attracted some slight academic attention, it was the events of the First World War that were given the greatest weight in military planning by the European militaries.

Although this selection may appear reasonable at first glance, its selection depends on several tacit assumptions that were addressed in Chapters 1 and 2. One assumption is that the Great Powers exemplify the state of the military art. This assumption is based on the belief that military power is a global trait – thus a Great Power military that is victorious in Europe will similarly triumph over militaries on other continents and conditions, and over other European armies at other times. In practice, however, even Great Power armies are likely to be well suited for some types of battles but ill-equipped to fight on different terrains or under different weather conditions. Depending on the conditions, an army viewed as weaker might defeat a Great Power, as history has clearly demonstrated. Thus when examined closely, the underpinnings for the belief that the Great Powers are universally powerful appear evanescent, as discussed in Chapter 2.

---

[67] Reiter, *Crucible of Beliefs*, 25.   [68] Sarkees and Wayman, *Resort to War*.

Second, the selection of the last Great Power war is warranted only to the extent that the next war will be fought under very similar conditions. Since few wars replicate the conditions of any particular historical war, reliance on the lessons of any particular war might be considered dubious. When different militaries are involved, on different terrains and under different conditions, there is no assurance that the past practices of one army will be effective under quite different circumstances. Instead, it is more likely to bet on ambiguity; whichever war is selected for analysis will be substantially different from subsequent wars.

A third assumption is that the outcomes of the war were determined rather than probabilistic. If the victorious Great Power had only a 30 percent chance of winning the war, for instance, it might be less useful to study its military practices. In actuality, however, the baseline probabilities cannot be known, given the limited number of wars that are fought between any two militaries. Assuming that military outcomes are determined reduces the ambiguity in analysis. However, the convenience of this assumption does not necessarily mean that it is logically supported.

One implication of this argument is that changes in the Great Power pecking order of the international system ultimately propel shifts in strategy. Work by scholars such as Avant and Wohlforth suggests that changes in military strategy may not simply be a response to exogenous factors such as new technologies or innovation. Instead, shifts in the status hierarchy of the Great Power system produce rapid transformations in military strategy for reasons that are principally social. The prevailing knowledge and paradigms of an era are rooted in post hoc analysis of the dominant powers. When an upstart power defeats the current hegemon, the conventionally accepted military paradigm is called into question. The rise of a new Great Power ultimately prompts a Kuhnian paradigm shift that can make sense of the "anomalous" new social hierarchy. The changed hierarchy and a corresponding new conventional wisdom form a new social foundation for competition – one that may be very different from the previously accepted social reality.

Overgeneralization of History

Under pressure to plan, military thinkers are forced to distill lessons from the complex miasma of events that transpire in every war. Generally, a consensus emerges on the major aspects of optimal military strategy, which is subsequently adopted widely within the international military community. The model for optimal military strategy is generally the victor of the last Great Power war. As Avant argues, "Institutions that have met with success (even by sheer luck or accident) become a 'past practice' and are thus more likely to become models for reformers in other countries."[69]

In the case of military planning, this tendency toward overgeneralization often manifests as the invocation of historical analogies. As many scholars such as Jervis, May, Reiter, Khong, and Larson have noted, decision-makers tend to rely on historical analogies, despite the obvious logical flaws in this method.[70] As Reiter notes, "[A]nalogies are generally kept simple to facilitate generalization; the more complex the analogy, the more difficult is its application to a different context."[71] In order to plan, military decision-makers draw on historical analogies, that are ultimately "superficial, overgeneralized, and based on post hoc ergo propter hoc reasoning," Jervis notes.[72]

Despite these academic cautions, a simplified interpretation thus emerges that purports to explain the outcome of important Great Power wars. This interpretation becomes the basis for future military planning. Different militaries may develop variations of the dominant interpretation, or even develop idiosyncratic explanations of their own, as Chapter 6 discusses. However, European military theorists are immersed in a common community and draw on a common body of past wars, so militaries tend to "learn" similar lessons. Consequently, as scholars have frequently observed, military theories and preparations of different states tend to converge.

In some cases, militaries attempt to learn the negative lesson – the avoidance of the repetition of historical military disasters. For example, as discussed in Chapter 6, the European Great Powers sought to avoid the stalemate of the Western front, and, as discussed in Chapter 8, the United States sought to avoid the causes of the Second World War. However, as these cases suggest, there is greater ambiguity in learning a negative lesson. A lengthier list can be generated for the plausible things that were *not* done than for actions that were taken. For instance, during the interwar period, various theories were put forth on how to avoid trench warfare deadlock in future wars. Nevertheless, planning did not move

---

[69] Avant, "From Mercenary to Citizen Armies."

[70] Jervis, *Perception and Misperception*; May, *"Lessons" of the Past*; Khong, *Analogies at War*.

[71] Reiter, *Crucible of Beliefs*; Deborah Welch Larson, *Anatomy of Mistrust: U.S.-Soviet Relations during the Cold War*. Ithaca: Cornell University Press, 1997.

[72] Jervis, *Perception and Misperception*, 228.

forward until some degree of consensus was developed for the negative lessons as well as for the positive ones.

Overemphasis on Victorious Outcomes

Militaries must prepare for wars rather than indulge in endless academic speculation about the past. A military cannot optimize all possible factors that might be important in the next war. Resources must be allocated; men must be trained; plans must be developed. Spreading organizational attention too thinly can be as great an error as focusing too narrowly on the wrong issues. While academics may put forth a variety of reasons why the past might not predict the future, military planners have little choice but to assume that it does. Otherwise militaries are left adrift, without any basis from which to develop plans.

Scholars use the term "hedging" to describe an organizational strategy in which an organization attempts to buffer itself against uncertainty by planning for as many avenues of action as possible. Militaries, with their vast material and organizational resources, are able to hedge more than other kinds of organizations can. However, as Goldman writes, "Hedging . . . turns out to be very expensive, even for the wealthiest states." Even militaries must "invest" in a particular grand strategy, as Ikenberry notes, given "a world of multiple threats and uncertainty about their relative significance in the decades to come."[73] For instance, militaries must not only design technologies on paper but must invest resources in building the technologies, laying in adequate supplies, and training personnel in the new strategies and technologies. These investments in men and resources must be made years before an actual war might be declared.

Consequently, militaries must disregard the ambiguity of contingency to some degree simply in order to prepare for war. A social scientist can entertain the notion that a range of possible wars could hypothetically be fought in a given place and time, expanding the ambiguity of analyzing wars. Militaries do not have that option. As Colin Powell, the former chairman of the Joint Chiefs of Staff, writes, "We do not have the luxury of collecting information indefinitely. At some point, before we can have every possible fact in hand, we have to decide."[74] Viewing victory as

[73] G. John Ikenberry, "Liberal Order Building." In *To Lead the World: American Strategy after the Bush Doctrine*, edited by Melvyn P. Leffler and Jeffrey W. Legro. New York: Oxford University Press, 2008, 91.

[74] Gartner, *Strategic Assessment in War*, 7.

probabilistic, with many conditional factors, simply increases the ambiguity of analysis until action becomes impossible.

Instead, there is nearly universal agreement that in military matters, war among the Great Powers is the ultimate mechanism to resolve debate. Victory on the battlefield – especially swift or decisive victory – is collectively perceived as resolving debates and identifying the best of military practice. As Resende-Santos has noted, "In the area of military emulation, states use battlefield performance, especially victory in war, as the truest observable measure of effectiveness."[75] The dichotomous win/loss outcome of wars creates the perception that the results of this test were particularly indisputable. The clear definition of winners and losers makes it nearly impossible to support emulation of the defeated state or any weaker states. In peacetime, disagreements and debates may proliferate, particularly over new technologies or strategies that had not been previously tested in battle. However, such debates tend to be perceived as resolved by the outcome of the next Great Power war.

Militaries tend to emulate the victor in as many respects as possible. As Resende-Santos asserts, "[M]ilitary emulation is the quickest and most dependable way to increase power and bolster security."[76] Jervis warns, however: "With a successful outcome, relatively little attention is paid to . . . the possibility that success was largely attributable to luck and that the policy might just as easily have failed . . . . The result is that . . . policies that were followed by success will be too quickly repeated in the future."[77] Proponents face an uphill battle to argue for alternative formulations in which noncombatant states – or even more unthinkably the defeated state – might serve as a model for military practice. As Avant notes in the case of the citizen army of the nineteenth century, "Advocates for reform in Prussia could use the French success with a citizen army to bolster their interpretation . . . reformers argued that the French won (and the Prussians lost) because of the commitment of citizen soldiers."[78] Reiter also notes: "States are continually preparing for the next war by copying the best practices of the previous war."[79] However, he also notes: "This appears irrational, since these practices often turn out to be inappropriate or obsolete for the next war."[80]

---

[75] João Resende-Santos, *Neorealism, States, and the Modern Mass Army.* Cambridge: Cambridge University Press, 2007, 7.

[76] Resende-Santos, *Neorealism*, 5.   [77] Jervis, *Perception and Misperception*, 232–233.

[78] Avant, "From Mercenary to Citizen Armies," 51.   [79] Resende-Santos, *Neorealism*, 7.

[80] Resende-Santos, *Neorealism*, 7.

Consequently, it is common for the formulae to prove to be wrong in military domains – not because theorists are dim-witted, but because of the complexity of history. Academic caution renders history essentially useless for the military planner. Yet the danger of overgeneralization is that the lessons learned from the case may not apply if the case is not representative of future conflicts. Errors are the expected outcome of reckless oversimplification and overgeneralization. Instead of effective learning, militaries haphazardly blunder from one set of strategies and technologies to another, without the promise of incremental improvement.

THE HISTORICAL LESSONS OF CAVALRY

The challenges of learning from history are illustrated in debates surrounding the role of the cavalry in the decades preceding the First World War.[81] One might imagine that cavalry were obviously anachronistic in the era of machine guns. Yet when examined closely, the evidence on the utility of cavalry was quite ambiguous. Bond notes: "A study of British cavalry doctrine and training in the era before 1914 illustrates just how difficult it is to learn from war."[82]

The following account briefly describes the academic literature on cavalry. The account focuses on the Franco-Prussian War of 1870, which provided the "lessons" that yielded a continent-wide consensus on the value of cavalry. These analyses were biased by (1) the analytical dependence on a single war, (2) the complexity of events, and (3) disregard for the probabilistic nature of battle outcomes. These biases encouraged the militaries of Europe to converge on the idea that cavalry would be important for subsequent wars. Unfortunately, the lessons of the past yielded erroneous predictions regarding the role cavalry would play in the First World War.

Historical Context

With the benefit of hindsight, it seems incredible that serious military thinkers were still debating the merits and drawbacks of cavalry even as

---

[81] Edward L. Katzenbach, Jr., "The Horse Cavalry in the Twentieth Century." In *The Use of Force: International Politics and Foreign Policy*, edited by Robert J. Art and Kenneth N. Waltz, 277–297. Boston: Little, Brown and Company, 1971 [1958].

[82] Brian Bond, "Doctrine and Training in the British Cavalry, 1870–1914." In *The Theory and Practice of War*, edited by Michael Howard, 95–128. Bloomington: Indiana University Press, 1965, 118.

late as the 1930s. As one historian exclaims, "What is astonishing is that in ... the years immediately preceding the outbreak of the 1914 war – an issue so clearly settled and dead as the role of heavy cavalry in modern war should have become the subject of embittered controversy among the senior generals and the historians at the staff colleges and in the military periodicals of western Europe."[83]

In retrospect, scholars today attribute the demise of cavalry to major advances in the technology of firearms that occurred during the late nineteenth century. Infantry weapons were capable of greater accuracy and range and could be loaded much quicker than previous generations of firearms – as we know, these weapons would develop into the machine guns of the First World War. Armed with modern weaponry, the infantry could mow down the cavalry before the horses could close the distance.

The capabilities of the horse, by contrast, had not improved much from previous centuries. European cavalry had developed at a time when infantry were armed principally with handheld swords, bayonets, and pikes. With these weapons, infantry could only wait in dread until the line of cavalry horses reached them, and the infantry was usually bowled over by sheer momentum. Yet once guns – or even longbows – became available, the advantage of cavalry over infantry diminished. This suggested that the comparative advantage lay with modern firepower to the detriment of the horse.[84]

However, the apparently straightforward interpretation – that the machine gun rendered cavalry obsolete – was not apparent to nineteenth-century military planners. Instead, virulent debate ensued. Even more surprisingly from a contemporary vantage point, the debate ended with the conclusion that cavalry would be even more essential in the First World War than in previous wars.

Ambiguity and Lessons of History

In order to resolve ambiguity, military theorists narrowed their gaze and made simplifying assumptions, leading to a biased interpretation of history. In the case of cavalry, these biases began with the analysis of a single war – the Franco-Prussian war of 1870. The Prussian victory was explained by factors including speed and the importance of offensive

---

[83] William McElwee, *The Art of War: Waterloo to Mons*. Bloomington: Indiana University Press, 1974, 314.

[84] McElwee, *The Art of War*, 315.

spirit, as discussed more generally in Chapter 5. Importantly for the cavalry debates, speed and offensive attack had long been associated with cavalry. This theory of Prussian victory was extrapolated into a general theory of the utility of cavalry, rendered seemingly irrefutable by the decisive the Prussian victory.

Overemphasis on Great Power War. In the case of cavalry, the influence of a single Great Power war can clearly be seen. During the nineteenth century, France was considered one of the leading Great Power states, while Prussia (Germany) was barely on the ledger as a member of the Great Power hierarchy. The dramatic Prussian victory over France in 1870 astounded Europe and placed Prussia as a leading Great Power, as mentioned in Chapter 2 and discussed in Chapter 5. Consequently, the cavalry debates of the late nineteenth century were focused on the successes of the Prussian cavalry in the Franco-Prussian war rather than on several other cavalry battles that were available for analysis.

Cavalry theorists in the late nineteenth century studied other battles that had taken place in Europe in the past half-century. However, cavalry did not play a key role in every battle, and there were relatively few European wars during this period. Although cavalry had been a core component of armies for centuries, comparison was hampered by the greater ineffectiveness of infantry weaponry in earlier eras. While some claimed that cavalry had basically been useless since the invention of the longbow, comparisons to the far past were not generally seen as relevant in the debate.[85]

Even more problematic, the limited number of cavalry battles varied so greatly that it was difficult to evaluate the universal utility of cavalry. For instance, proponents of cavalry pointed to battles of the 1878 Russo-Turkish war, in which both Russian and Turkish cavalry acquitted themselves admirably against each other.[86] Opponents of cavalry instead drew the conclusion that the open terrain of Eastern Europe was better suited to cavalry than the more densely forested terrain of western Europe.[87] The 1905 Russo-Japanese War also provided ambiguous evidence on the utility of cavalry. The poor performance of cavalry on both sides was attributed either to the "the horse soldier's vulnerability to machine gun and artillery fire" or to the weaker military abilities of non-European

---

[85] McElwee, *The Art of War.*

[86] McElwee, *The Art of War,* 198; Antulio J. Echevarria, II, *After Clausewitz: German Military Thinkers before the Great War.* Lawrence: University of Kansas Press, 2000, 216.

[87] McElwee, *The Art of War,* 198.

cavalry and the Russian lack of offensive spirit.[88] These examples provided the bulk of recent cavalry battles available to analysts in the late nineteenth century.

Although a range of cavalry battles were studied, the cavalry theorists of the late nineteenth century gave the greatest weight to the cavalry engagements of the Franco-Prussian War of 1870. In particular, a single battle became the focus of these efforts to learn from the history of cavalry. During the battle of Vionville-Mars-la-Tour, a successful Prussian cavalry charge turned the tide of battle in favor of the Prussians. Interestingly, a different cavalry charge by the French during that same battle failed to achieve its military objective. Consequently, the successful ride of the Prussian cavalry in this battle became the centerpiece of the nineteenth-century debates.

Over-Generalization of History. Even the single battle of Vionville-Mars-la-Tour was sufficiently complex to support multiple interpretations of the effectiveness of cavalry. Proponents of cavalry pointed to the Prussian cavalry charge as evidence that cavalry could still play a critical role in demoralizing infantry despite technological improvements in firearms. During the battle, the Prussian cavalry had charged well-established French batteries. Initially, the approach of the Prussian horses was hidden by a depression in the terrain, yet the Prussians still took high casualties as they crossed the final few hundred yards and were exposed to French fire. The French infantry were so surprised by the sudden onset of the cavalry charge that they scattered, allowing the Prussians to occupy the position, which proved critical for the eventual Prussian victory in this battle. The Prussian success was cited "to prove that cavalry was not an anachronism in battle," but rather the norm.[89]

Opponents of cavalry dismissed the Prussian victory as due to luck rather than the inherent utility of cavalry. Instead, cavalry pessimists pointed to the failure of a French cavalry charge in the same battle. Unlike the Prussians, the French cavalry commander had attempted a direct frontal attack. Charging the prepared Prussian line, "A few volleys reduced each splendid [French cavalry] unit in turn to a line of kicking, bloodstained heaps."[90] The French cavalry regiment was wiped out by

---

[88] Echevarria, *After Clausewitz*, 216; Michael Howard, *The Lessons of History*. New Haven: Yale University Press, 1991, 108.

[89] Michael Howard, *The Franco-Prussian War: The German Invasion of France, 1870–1871*. New York: Macmillan, 1962, 157.

[90] Howard, *The Franco-Prussian War*, 156.

Prussian infantry fire. Proponents of cavalry dismissed the poor showing of the French cavalry as a result of bad tactics and questionable command decisions.

Even in this relatively simple event – two cavalry charges in a single battle – complexities are glaring. In order to evaluate the effectiveness of cavalry, an analyst would prefer cases in which the commanders were competent, since any battle can be lost by bumbling command decisions. Similarly, luck and random chance can be seen in both battles. Ideally, analysts would be able to draw on a large body of cavalry charges among comparably trained militaries, to assess the utility of cavalry apart from the vagaries of the skill of the commander, terrain, weather, and luck. However, military analysts rarely enjoy such an abundance of data. Instead, the nineteenth-century debaters overgeneralized the single Prussian charge in the battle of Vionville-Mars-la-Tour to the broader principle that cavalry was essential for the strategic goal of overpowering infantry with modern firepower.

These ambiguous episodes gave rise to two opposing theories about the utility of cavalry. The first, which is now dominant in the post–Second World War period, proposed that horse cavalry was useless in the face of modern firearms. For instance, McElwee scornfully claimed that cavalry was only barely useful even during the seventeenth and eighteenth centuries. He placed the end of cavalry in 1854 at the battle of Balaclava during the Crimean War and disregarded the successes of cavalry in the Franco-Austrian and Franco-Prussian wars as mere flukes.[91]

Although the obsolescence of cavalry seems obvious to modern eyes, the opposing point of view was widely accepted by militaries in preparations for the First World War. From this perspective, the mobility of the cavalry would be a necessary asset on a battlefield in which the range of firearms had greatly increased. Military theorists of the nineteenth century argued that rifled weapons and prepared positions made it critical for the soldier to cross the field as quickly as possible so that hand-to-hand fighting could take place.[92] Men on horseback could obviously cover ground more rapidly than men on foot. Thus, cavalry advocates claimed, the increased range of firearms meant that the ability of cavalry to cover ground quickly was even more essential than in previous eras. In addition, a line of galloping horses, riders arrayed in bright dress and armed with sabers, would provide "shock value," overwhelming the

---

[91] McElwee, *The Art of War*, 315.   [92] Howard, *The Franco-Prussian War*, 6.

defenders and preventing them from thinking or aiming straight. Drawing on the battle of Vionville-Mars-la-Tour and other empirical data available at the time, military thinkers of the late nineteenth century found this logic persuasive.

Overemphasis on Victorious Outcomes. In the cavalry debates of the late nineteenth century, debate focused on explaining the successes of the Prussian cavalry. Although the anti-cavalry position was represented, it was greatly disadvantaged in the debate by the undeniable fact of the Prussian victory. The fact that the Prussians had won both the cavalry battle and the war in 1870 was widely taken as support for the pro-cavalry position. Assuming that victory was determined by the superiority of the Prussian army, the battle was taken as proof that offensive spirit was more essential than technological superiority. Despite lively debate on the utility of cavalry, by 1905 "a consensus developed among European strategic thinkers ... cavalry would now develop their own firepower ... and exploit opportunities on a scale undreamed of since the days of the American Civil War."[93]

In hindsight, merits might have been discerned in the French tactics. The French army boasted better firearms than the Prussians and had adopted a defensive strategy that utilized the capabilities of their long-range weapons. Prussian cavalry and troops, employing offensive tactics (which would later be criticized in the First World War), attacked these well-defended French positions and were slaughtered.[94] Yet the French had lost the war. In the face of French defeat, no European army could countenance adopting the defensive tactics of the French or overlook the potential value of cavalry. Even the French sought to emulate the qualities of the Prussians.

Militaries did vary somewhat in their reliance on the horse, depending on the predominant institutional culture of the military. Domestic politics scholars have pointed out that the British and American armies favored the horse primarily as transportation, and trained their soldiers to fight dismounted. The French and German armies, on the other hand, clung to their horses and believed that the awe-inspiring sight of a massed cavalry charge was still of great importance in battle. Although there were differences in military culture, there was still a great deal of consensus. As one British theorist wrote at the time, "It must be accepted as a principle that

---

[93] Howard, *The Lessons of History*, 102. This case is discussed in greater detail in Chapter 2.
[94] Echevarria, *After Clausewitz*, 25.

the rifle, effective as it is, cannot replace the effect produced by the speed of the horse, the magnetism of the charge, and the terror of cold steel."[95]

As a result of these "lessons" of history, each of the major European armies fortified their cavalries before the First World War. Military thinkers believed that the First World War would open, and practically be decided, with an initial clash of opposing cavalries. As Michael Howard claims, "1914 saw all the armies of Europe still equipped with full establishments of cavalry armed with lances and sabers, trained to charge on the battlefield and exploit a breakthrough."[96] While alternate interpretations were possible, the seemingly decisive Prussian victory in the Franco-Prussian war led nearly all armies to adopt the dominant view that the offensive spirit manifested in the cavalry charge was an enduring and universal military asset.

CONSEQUENCES OF LEARNING

Military planners have often been accused of planning for the last war. This chapter explains why. Militaries base their preparations for the next war on the lessons "learned" from past wars. These preparations critically influence calculations about wars, often leading to surprises on all sides. The lessons of history also theorize the resources that were critical to military power in the last Great Power conflict. These theorized resources become the measure of Great Power military strength (discussed in Chapter 2) and the focal point of Great Power competitions (discussed in Chapter 4), fundamentally affecting Great Power politics of the era.

Militaries must lay their plans years, even decades in advance of an actual war. Recruiting and training an army, developing strategies, and developing technological weaponry cannot wait until war is declared. Lack of knowledge of the particulars of the enemy, the likely terrain of the battlefield, and the composition, tactics, and weaponry of the army they will be facing mean that the development of accurate plans becomes a pipe dream. Militaries are given the nearly impossible task of equipping for a war without knowing the key elements of that war.

Consequently, militaries typically prepare for the wrong war, as the following chapters will show. Chapter 5 discusses the preparations for the

[95] Quoted in Jay Luvaas, *The Military Legacy of the Civil War: The European Inheritance.* Chicago: University of Chicago Press, 1959, 89.
[96] Michael Howard, *War in European History.* Oxford: Oxford University Press, 1976, 104.

First World War, which drew on erroneous conclusions from the Franco-Prussian War of 1870. Chapter 6 focuses on the interwar period, in which the European militaries were determined to learn from the errors that had occurred during the First World War. Chapter 7 argues that states "learned" from the Second World War that the acquisition of nuclear capability would separate the Great Powers from the lesser ones, based on the dramatic unleashing of the first atomic bomb as the denouement. The application of the lessons to the Cold War is discussed in Chapter 8, especially the plans of the United States to refight the Second World War more effectively.

4

Great Power Competition and the Causes of War

"[One] may be surprised by how small a role ... considerations of practical utility and material gain, and even ambition for power itself, play in bringing on wars, and how often some aspect of honor is decisive."[1]

Another puzzle for scholars is the seemingly trivial stakes that trigger major wars. States go to war over tiny pieces of territory, or to overthrow the regime of minor peripheral countries, or even over minor diplomatic insults. Sometimes Great Powers enter a war without any instrumental goals at all beyond the simple desire to oppose the other participants. The First World War is surely the winner in this category. A war that caused the death of 15 million people in battles on nearly every continent was initiated by the assassination of an Austrian archduke by a handful of Serbian nationalists.[2] When first learning this, students of history typically react with perplexity. Nor is the First World War the only contender. The Franco-Prussian War of 1870, which cost France the provinces of Alsace-Lorraine and Strasbourg, was triggered by a diplomatic incident involving the candidacy of a Prussian prince to the Spanish monarchy. Many other wars, such as the Vietnam War, the Boer War, and the Spanish-American War, have similarly puzzled scholars and the public throughout history in regards to their respective casus belli.

Classic military scholarship presumes that wars are fought over objectively valuable military interests or critical resources that warrant the cost

---

[1] Donald Kagan, *On the Origins of War and the Preservation of Peace.* New York: Doubleday, 1995, 8.
[2] Michael Howard, *The First World War.* Oxford: Oxford University Press, 2002.

and risk of war.[3] Scholars argue that states have historically shed blood to acquire territory.[4] More recently, states have come into conflict over water rights or natural resources.[5] Intuitively this makes sense: costly wars should be fought over valuable objectives. Surprisingly, however, conflicts over valuable resources seem the exception rather than the rule, and so the academic literature has been forced to consider other possibilities.

Some conflicts, such as the Boer and Vietnam wars, were so puzzling that scholars developed domestic conspiracy theories to make sense of them. This has led to a general tendency to explain puzzling conflicts purely in terms of idiosyncratic domestic interests. However, such explanations have not gained much academic traction, and are not systematically addressed in this chapter for a couple of reasons. First, Great Power conflicts typically emerge in the context of long-term international rivalries – often developing over decades – as well as complex international crises, which are not easily attributed to local interests. In addition, idiosyncratic domestic explanations, while potentially contributing to the understanding of individual cases, cannot easily explain the systematic patterns of conflict in the Great Power system that is the goal of this book.

The dominant explanation in the scholarly literature for the seemingly trivial triggers of war is that wars are fundamentally power struggles between states.[6] From this perspective, the trigger or proximate justification for war is unimportant; the actual stakes are power dominance

[3] Paul D. Senese and John A. Vasquez, *The Steps to War: An Empirical Study*. Princeton: Princeton University Press, 2008; John A. Vasquez, *The War Puzzle Revisited*. New York: Cambridge University Press, 2009; John A. Vasquez, *The War Puzzle*. New York: Cambridge University Press, 1993; Paul K. Huth, *Standing your Ground: Territorial Disputes and International Conflict*. Ann Arbor: University of Michigan Press, 1996.

[4] Kalevi J. Holsti, *Peace and War: Armed Conflicts and International Order, 1648–1989*. Cambridge: Cambridge University Press, 1991.

[5] Thomas F. Homer-Dixon and Marc A. Levy, "Environment and Security." *International Security* 20 (1995–1996): 189–198.

[6] Jonathan M. DiCicco and Jack S. Levy, "Power Shifts and Problem Shifts: The Evolution of the Power Transition Research Program." *The Journal of Conflict Resolution* 43 (1999): 675–704; Robert Gilpin, "The Theory of Hegemonic War." *The Journal of Interdisciplinary History* 18 (1988): 591–613; A. F. K. Organski, *World Politics*. New York: Alfred A. Knopf, 1958; A. F. K. Organski and Jacek Kugler, *The War Ledger*. Chicago: University of Chicago Press, 1980; Jacek Kugler and Douglas Lemke (eds.), *Parity and War: Evaluations and Extensions of 'The War Ledger.'* Ann Arbor: University of Michigan Press, 1996; Jeffrey S. Morton and Harvey Starr, "Uncertainty, Change, and War: Power Fluctuations in the Modern Elite Power System." *Journal of Peace Research* 38 (2001): 49–66; William Moul, "Power Parity, Preponderance, and War between Great Powers, 1816–1989." *The Journal of Conflict Resolution* 47 (2003): 468–489.

between two states. For instance, preventive wars occur when a state foresees that a rival will have overmatching power in the near future. The dominant state may initiate war against the rival to prevent its predicted rise in power. Or the rival may declare war to reorder the international system to its advantage.

These claims are questioned by the proponents of bargaining theory, who point to the inability to measure relative differences in power as the central cause of war.[7] If states could accurately assess power, the weak would concede to the powerful. Costly wars would be avoided to mutual benefit. Instead, states misestimate the military power of opponents, which may encourage an unwise decision to go to war. Moreover, as discussed in Chapter 2, states do not simply misestimate power on rare occasions. Rather, objective power is fundamentally ambiguous and only resolved through reference to the social reality of the hierarchy of the Great Power system. Yet bargaining theory does not explain why political decision-makers are blind to their repeated tendency to misestimate.

This chapter offers a more radical response to the puzzle of why states leap into war over seemingly minor issues: Great Powers are fighting primarily over status and prestige. Objective power is fundamentally ambiguous (as argued in Chapter 2), but broad consensus exists on the ranking of the Great Power hierarchy. Wars are thus motivated by the desire to increase standing within the Great Power hierarchy. Moreover, to be a Great Power is to take on a particular identity that requires opting into the grand competitions of the interstate system. Great Powers are

---

[7] James D. Fearon, "Rationalist Explanations for War." *International Organization* 49 (1995): 380; Darren Filson and Suzanne Werner, "A Bargaining Model of War and Peace." *American Journal of Political Science* 46 (2002): 819–838; Andrew Kydd, "Which Side Are You On? Bias, Credibility and Mediation." *American Journal of Political Science* 47 (2003): 597–611; Robert Powell, "Uncertainty, Shifting Power, and Appeasement." *The American Political Science Review* 90 (1996): 749–764; Robert Powell, "War as a Commitment Problem." *International Organization* 60 (2006): 169–203; Robert Powell, "The Inefficient Use of Power: Costly Conflict with Complete Information." *American Political Science Review* 98 (2004): 231–241; Robert Powell, *In the Shadow of Power: States and Strategies in International Politics*. Princeton: Princeton University Press, 1999; Alastair Smith and Allan C. Stam, "Bargaining and the Nature of War." *The Journal of Conflict Resolution* 48 (2004): 783–813; R. Harrison Wagner, "Bargaining and War." *American Journal of Political Science* 44 (2000): 469–484; Alex Weisiger, *Logics of War: Explanations for Limited and Unlimited Conflicts*. Ithaca: Cornell University Press, 2013; Suzanne Werner, "Deterring Intervention: The Stakes of War and Third Party Involvement." *American Journal of Political Science* 44 (2000): 720–732; Scott Wolford, Dan Reiter, and Clifford J. Carrubba, "Information, Commitment, and War." *The Journal of Conflict Resolution* 55 (2011): 556–579.

primed to continually seek out their rivals and compete over tokens of power. These tokens may be resources believed to yield future power and success, based on socially constructed "lessons" of prior wars (discussed in Chapter 3). Great Power states often refuse to back down and choose instead to fight to redress insults as a matter of prestige. Not every tiff or diplomatic crisis leads to war, as cooler heads sometimes prevail or decision-makers consider the circumstances to be unfavorable. But since rivalry is endemic to the Great Power system, the potential for brinks-manship is never far off.

Another way to put it: the seemingly trivial causes of war are tokens of Great Power one-upmanship in a system that is fundamentally based on competition for status. In the context of geopolitical rivalry, seemingly minor concerns – such as who sits on the Spanish throne or the ideological underpinnings in Vietnam – may nevertheless have potent symbolic importance in the eyes of Great Powers and the wider international audience. These situations create the potential for states to lose face or engage in one-upmanship, which sometimes escalates to war.

This chapter brings together scholarly work by Lebow, Mercer, Jervis, Wohlforth, and O'Neill to develop an answer that invokes status in its various forms – prestige, honor, credibility, and reputation – as the funda-mental root of Great Power competition and war.[8] Ambiguity is central to this perspective. Since the measurement of actual power is unclear, states end up fighting about position in the Great Power hierarchy. Actual changes in the distribution of power are murky, yet states can clearly anticipate the effect of victory or defeat – or backing down and losing face – on their status in the international community. In the absence of reliable indicators of military power, status and symbolic tokens become the de facto motivators of Great Power rivalry.

---

[8] Michael P. Colaresi, *Scare Tactics: The Politics of International Rivalry*. Syracuse: Syra-cuse University Press, 2005; Michael P. Colaresi, Karen Rasler, and William R. Thompson, *Strategic Rivalries in World Politics: Position, Space and Conflict Escal-ation*. Cambridge: Cambridge University Press, 2007; Richard Ned Lebow, *Why Nations Fight: Past and Future Motives for War*. Cambridge: Cambridge University Press, 2010; Jonathan Mercer, *Reputation and International Politics*. Ithaca: Cornell University Press, 1996; Barry O'Neill, *Honor, Symbols, and War*. Ann Arbor: University of Michigan Press, 1999; T. V. Paul, Deborah Welch Larson, and William C. Wohlforth (eds.), *Status in World Politics*. New York: Cambridge University Press, 2014; Karen A. Rasler and Wil-liam R. Thompson, *The Great Powers and Global Struggle, 1490–1990*. Lexington: University of Kentucky Press, 1994; William R.Thompson (ed.), *Great Power Rivalries*. Columbia: University of South Carolina Press, 1999; William C. Wohlforth, "Unipolarity, Status Competition, and Great Power War." *World Politics* 61 (2009): 28–57.

There are three parts to this argument. First, the instrumental perspective claims that states fight over valuable resources, but it fails to explain how states recognize which resources are valuable. Drawing on Chapter 3, I argue that the material factors believed to contribute to state power in a given era are social constructions that are "learned" from history. These material factors become the focus of military competition in particular historical periods.[9] Great Power squabbles over tangible material issues quickly devolve into competitions of symbolic status and one-upmanship among rivals.

Second, the chapter unpacks the nature of Great Power rivalry. Realist theory presumes that states can straightforwardly evaluate power and identify rivals that might be a threat. However, history suggests that the identification of an enemy rival is fraught with ambiguity.[10] Drawing on the work of Thompson and his colleagues Rasler and Colaresi, as well as scholarship by Jervis and Larson, I argue that Great Power rivalries are constructed from dubious evaluations of military capability and even more dubious evaluations of hostility (see Chapter 8 for a more detailed treatment).[11] Rivalries bias the interpretation of future events, which reinforces hostilities, and quickly become self-fulfilling prophecies.

Third, the chapter argues that status and one-upmanship in the Great Power hierarchy become the primary motive for war among the Great Powers.[12] Rivals often begin by competing over resources, but competition quickly moves beyond the instrumental value of the material prize under contention. As the rivalry between two Great Power states grows, the belligerent motives ascribed to each other become a self-fulfilling prophecy. The maintenance of Great Power status and the gains to reputation of outdoing a rival Power become the primary motivations

[9] Holsti, *Peace and War.*

[10] Emily O. Goldman, *Power in Uncertain Times: Strategy in the Fog of Peace.* Stanford: Stanford University Press, 2011; Talbot C. Imlay and Monica Duffy Toft (eds.), *The Fog of Peace and War Planning.* New York: Routledge, 2006.

[11] Colaresi, *Scare Tactics*; Colaresi, Rasler, and Thompson, *Strategic Rivalries in World Politics*; Rasler and Thompson. *The Great Powers and Global Struggle*; Thompson, *Great Power Rivalries*; Deborah Welch Larson, *Anatomy of Mistrust: U.S.-Soviet Relations during the Cold War.* Ithaca: Cornell University Press, 1997; Robert Jervis, "Cooperation Under the Security Dilemma." *World Politics* 30 (1978): 167–214.

[12] Mercer, *Reputation and International Politics*; O'Neill, *Honor, Symbols, and War*; Richard Ned Lebow, *A Cultural Theory of International Relations.* Cambridge: Cambridge University Press, 2008; Paul, Larson, and Wohlforth, *Status in World Politics*; William C. Wohlforth, "Unipolarity, Status Competition, and Great Power War." *World Politics* 61 (2009): 28–57.

for war. Under these conditions, trivial events can easily trigger major wars between Great Power rivals.

This chapter first reviews the major traditional scholarly accounts. The rest of the chapter is devoted to developing an explanation that highlights Great Power reputation and status as the primary motivators of war. These arguments are illustrated via a short discussion of the origins of the Franco-Prussian war of 1870. This line of reasoning is also central to understanding the nuclear arms race and the onset of the Korean War, discussed in Chapters 7 and 8, respectively.

TRADITIONAL EXPLANATIONS ON THE CAUSES OF WAR

Three major perspectives have been developed to explain the onset of war. The instrumental perspective argues that tangible state interests, such as valuable territory, merit the costs of war. Realism provides a second major explanation: states are fighting over the distribution of power in the interstate system, not necessarily the nominal issue that triggered a conflict. Third, bargaining theory scholars have argued that misperception in the measurement of power is a common cause of war. I review these perspectives and then develop the alternative argument that states are competing over symbolic tokens of power and status in the Great Power hierarchy.

Instrumentalist Perspective

According to the instrumental perspective, Great Power competitions are fueled by the desire to acquire strategically valuable resources. Classic theories posit that competition and conflict may occur when actor A and actor B both have an interest in the same scarce resource.[13] Given the magnitude of the costs of war, especially wars involving Great Power rivals, one would expect to see conflicts only when the stakes are very high indeed.

Scholars in this tradition have pointed to territory as one of the primary historical causes of conflict in Europe, but natural resources or the composition of a national government might also be at stake.[14] Johnson and Toft, for instance, claim there is an "iron law of global

---

[13] Robert Axelrod, *Conflict of Interest: A Theory of Divergent Goals with Applications to Politics*. Chicago: Markham Publishing Company, 1970.
[14] Dan Reiter, *How Wars End*. Princeton: Princeton University Press, 2009.

politics: human territoriality."[15] Likewise, Vasquez has argued: "[I]t is *territoriality*, the tendency for humans to occupy and, if necessary, defend territory, rather than the struggle for power, that is the key to understanding interstate war."[16] Vasquez and his colleagues outline a model in which a core territorial dispute provides the impetus for war.[17] Following on the territorial disagreement, a predictable sequence of "steps to war" occurs, leading to a series of political crises that encourage disputatious neighbors to build up their military power. In turn, these buildups promote further crises that may eventually result in war.

There are two main problems with the instrumentalist argument. First, scholars have frequently had difficulty identifying the a priori material interests that ostensibly motivated states to go to war. Scholars who have examined war termination have found that interests are rarely specified clearly at the outset.[18] Instead, the war aims of states appear ambiguous, or even wrongheaded in hindsight. Bond has observed, "[A]ll students of history must be struck by the ambivalence, irony, or transience of most military victories, however spectacular and 'decisive' they appear at the time."[19] Mandel similarly notes: "Historical cases abound where the identified war aims of victors have appeared, with the benefit of hindsight, to be misguided."[20] The instrumentalist perspective has difficulty explaining the puzzle mentioned at the outset of the chapter – why states go to war over issues that end up being of minimal importance.

A second challenge for the instrumentalist perspective is that resource disputes often develop broader symbolic overtones, which then become the basis for war. Even Senese and Vasquez note that "concrete and tangible stakes" become "infused with first symbolic and later transcendent qualities."[21] In many cases, the symbolic aspects outweigh the importance of

---

[15] Dominic D. P. Johnson and Monica Duffy Toft, "Grounds for War: The Evolution of Territorial Conflict." *International Security* 38 (2013–2014): 7–38.

[16] John A. Vasquez, *The War Puzzle Revisited*. New York: Cambridge University Press, 2009; Peter Liberman, *Does Conquest Pay?* Princeton: Princeton University Press, 1996. For counterarguments, see Mark W. Zacher, "The Territorial Integrity Norm: International Boundaries and the Use of Force." *International Organization* 55 (2001): 215–250.

[17] Senese and Vasquez, *The Steps to War*.

[18] Robert Mandel, *The Meaning of Military Victory*. London: Lynne Rienner, 2006; Fred Ikle, *Every War Must End*. New York: Columbia University Press, 1991.

[19] Brian Bond, *The Pursuit of Victory: From Napoleon to Saddam Hussein*. New York: Oxford University Press, 1996, 1.

[20] Mandel, *The Meaning of Military Victory*, 6.

[21] Senese and Vasquez, *The Steps to War*, 17.

the original material issues that began the conflict. Indeed, these symbolic stakes "involve reputational effects and costs beyond the intrinsic value of the concrete stake under question, and therefore give rise to a commitment by the defending party to expend more costs than would seem warranted by a superficial examination of the concrete stake itself," as Senese and Vasquez note.[22] Recent scholarship by Hassner and Goddard has also demonstrated that objects of dispute frequently take on symbolic overtones that prevent the stakes from being divided among the parties.[23] As Wohlforth has argued, "[I]ssues that are physically divisible can become socially indivisible, depending on how they relate to the identities of decision makers."[24]

These complexities belie the straightforward instrumentalist account. If war aims are often vague, and if the calculable value of a tangible stake is augmented by intangible factors such as reputation, status, or honor, the instrumentalist perspective falls apart. Empirically, history bears this out: the origins of major wars are typically located in inconsequential disputes that are of minor importance to either party. To explain this peculiar yet common occurrence, realists have developed an alternate explanation for war that focuses on the shifting balance of power among states.

Realism

Realist scholars argue that power dynamics underlie the onset of wars, rendering the proximate triggers or stakes to be irrelevant. According to this perspective, Great Power wars are driven by shifts in the relative power between states and the overall balance of power in the international system.[25] As Gilpin writes, "the fundamental cause of wars

---

[22] Senese and Vasquez, *The Steps to War*, 17.

[23] Ron E. Hassner, *War on Sacred Grounds*. Ithaca: Cornell University Press, 2009; Ron E. Hassner, "The Path to Intractability Time and the Entrenchment of Territorial Disputes." *International Security* 31 (2006): 107–138; Stacie E. Goddard, *Indivisible Territory and the Politics of Legitimacy: Jerusalem and Northern Ireland*. New York: Cambridge University Press, 2010; Monica Duffy Toft, "Indivisible Territory, Geographic Concentration, and Ethnic War." *Security Studies* 12 (2002): 82–119.

[24] Wohlforth, "Unipolarity, Status Competition, and Great Power War."

[25] Kenneth N. Waltz, *Theory of International Politics*. Reading, MA: Addison-Wesley, 1979; John J. Mearsheimer, *The Tragedy of Great Power Politics*. New York: W. W. Norton and Company, 2001; Arnold Wolfers, *Discord and Collaboration: Essays on International Politics*. Baltimore: Johns Hopkins Press, 1962; Inis L. Claude, Jr., *Power and International Relations*. New York: Random House, 1962; Jonathan M. DiCicco and Jack S. Levy, "Power Shifts and Problem Shifts: The Evolution of the Power Transition Research Program." *The Journal of Conflict Resolution* 43 (1999): 675–704; Robert

among states and changes in international systems is the uneven growth of power among states."[26] Van Evera finds that preventive logic "is a ubiquitous motive for war."[27] A. J. P. Taylor has claimed that "every war between Great Powers [in the 1848–1918 period] started out as a preventive war."[28] Strong states may fight wars to maintain their dominant position, or subordinate states growing in power may fight wars to reorder the interstate system in a way that supports their interests.

According to the realist tradition, preventive war is one of the major forms of interstate war. As Levy defines it, "Preventive war is a strategy designed to forestall an adverse shift in the balance of power and driven by better-now-than-later logic."[29] In a preventive war, the state declining in power fears that a rising adversary will soon equal it in strength. The adversary growing in power has an interest in pouncing as soon as it gains the upper hand. To prevent this, the declining state is impelled to declare war before the adversary grows so powerful that defeat is inevitable. Based on these assumptions, the logic of preemption seems unassailable – strike before the enemy amasses sufficient resources to strike themselves.[30]

Yet these calculations require a high degree of accuracy in the measurement of relative military power. If any one of the major variables is significantly in error – the power of the declining state, the power of the rising state, or the inevitability of war – what appears to be prudence may be suicidal foolhardiness. Copeland, for instance, demands a great deal of

Gilpin, "The Theory of Hegemonic War." *The Journal of Interdisciplinary History* 18 (1988): 591–613; A. F. K. Organski, *World Politics*. New York: Alfred A. Knopf, 1958; A. F. K. Organski and Jacek Kugler, *The War Ledger*. Chicago: University of Chicago Press, 1980; Jacek Kugler and Douglas Lemke (eds.), *Parity and War: Evaluations and Extensions of 'The War Ledger.'* Ann Arbor: University of Michigan Press, 1996; Jeffrey S. Morton and Harvey Starr, "Uncertainty, Change, and War: Power Fluctuations in the Modern Elite Power System." *Journal of Peace Research* 38 (2001): 49–66; William Moul, "Power Parity, Preponderance, and War between Great Powers, 1816–1989." *The Journal of Conflict Resolution* 47 (2003): 468–489.

[26] Gilpin, *War and Change*, 94.

[27] Stephen Van Evera, *Causes of War: Power and the Roots of Conflict*. Ithaca: Cornell University Press, 1999, 76.

[28] A. J. P. Taylor, *The Struggle for Mastery in Europe, 1848–1918*. Oxford: Clarendon Press, 1954, p. 66; Van Evera, *Causes of War*.

[29] Jack S. Levy, "Preventive War and Democratic Politics." *International Studies Quarterly* 52 (2008): 1–24, 1.

[30] Dale C. Copeland, *The Origins of Major War*. Ithaca: Cornell University Press, 2000; Levy, "Preventive War and Democratic Politics"; Jack S. Levy and William R. Thompson, *Causes of War*. Malden: Wiley-Blackwell, 2010, 46; Van Evera, *Causes of War*.

information for a preventive war: for instance, the state should know "the depth of decline – how far the state will fall before it bottoms out; and the inevitability of decline – the degree of certainty that the state will fall if it sticks with current policies."[31] Copeland also requires consideration of multiple dimensions of power, including economic, technological, social, military and potential power, for the assessments of rising and falling power between the state and its adversary."[32]

Chapter 2 fundamentally questions the ability of states to effectively evaluate relative power differences between two states, implying even greater dubiousness over calculations of the rate of change in sources of potential power. While Copeland and other scholars provide their own rubrics, these suffer from a common problem: no means is provided to assess the rubrics. Instead, as Jervis has noted, "The world is ambiguous, and indicators of success are likely to be elusive. If it were easy to tell who would win a political or military struggle, it would soon come to an end (or would not start at all)."[33] Betts agrees: "In many wars, it is not clear before the fact that one side has superiority. Indeed, if it were, there would be fewer wars, because the weaker would more often capitulate without a fight."[34] States may go to war for preventive motives, but history suggests they will be based on highly unreliable estimates of power.

Even greater difficulties are evident in assessing the balance of power in the international system broadly. Press has argued that the European states historically failed to recognize shifts in the international distribution of power, thus in many instances "threatened countries have failed to recognize a clear and present danger or, more typically ... have responded in paltry and imprudent ways."[35] Powell notes that Great Britain's uncertainty over German political aims in the interwar period encouraged appeasement rather than standing firm.[36] States may believe their side has the preponderance of power and mistakenly instigate war when power is actually evenly distributed between the two sides. At other times, states may believe that power is evenly balanced, yet recognize their side is weaker only once fighting begins.

---

[31] Copeland, *The Origins of Major War*, 5.   [32] Copeland, *The Origins of Major War*, 6.

[33] Jervis, *Why Intelligence Fails*, 164.

[34] Richard K. Betts, "Is Strategy an Illusion?" *International Security* 25 (2003): 5–50, 21.

[35] Daryl G. Press, *Calculating Credibility: How Leaders Assess Military Threats*. Ithaca: Cornell University Press, 2005, 1.

[36] Powell, "Uncertainty, Shifting Power, and Appeasement."

In short, the flaw in the realist argument is the presumption that an accurate assessment of the relative military capabilities of states is possible. If misperception and error are common in international politics as Chapter 2 asserts, the standard realist account is undermined. In practice, scholars are relying on post hoc assessments of previous wars in which the victorious state is assumed to have been more powerful. If military capability can only be assessed in hindsight, it cannot satisfactorily provide the basis for concepts such the balance of power or preemptive logics. As Biddle notes, "[M]uch of the empirical and theoretical literature will need to be revised in light of a more meaningful measure of real capability."[37] Instead, as German Chancellor Otto von Bismarck once remarked, "[P]reventive war is like [committing] suicide from fear of death."[38]

Bargaining Theory

Scholars in the bargaining theory perspective recognize the initial ambiguity in the measurement of power as central to the onset of war.[39] In his seminal article, James Fearon posited that uncertainty and incomplete information are one of the major causes of war.[40] As Levy argues, "Mutual preventive motivations could occur because of a faulty assessment, by at least one state, of existing military capabilities and their trends in the near future."[41] Reiter also claims: "[W]hen two states in dispute disagree about the balance of power or the relative steadfastness of each side to prevail, war may result, especially if each side is confident it can prevail in a clash of arms."[42] Compounding the problem, Reiter notes, "There is, of course, no central clearinghouse of information on warmaking capacity and resolve. Making matters worse, states have incentives to misrepresent their capabilities and resolve to each other."[43]

---

[37] Stephen Biddle, *Military Power: Explaining Victory and Defeat in Modern Battle*. Princeton: Princeton University Press, 2006, 4.

[38] Cited in Jack S. Levy, "Declining Power and the Preventive Motivation for War." *World Politics* 40 (1987): 82–107, 103.

[39] Fearon, "Rationalist Explanations for War"; Filson and Werner, "A Bargaining Model of War and Peace"; Kydd, "Which Side Are You On?"; Powell, *In the Shadow of Power*; Smith and Stam, "Bargaining and the Nature of War"; Wagner, "Bargaining and War"; Weisiger, *Logics of War*.

[40] Fearon, "Rationalist Explanations for War."

[41] Levy, "Declining Power and the Preventive Motivation for War," 93.

[42] Reiter, *How Wars End*, 2.   [43] Reiter, *How Wars End*, 14.

This asymmetric information argument builds on the inherent ambiguity in the measurement of power.[44] In this case, one side is posited as having more information and less uncertainty, leading the two opponents to arrive at different estimates of the costs of war and the odds of victory. Perhaps one side has a secret weapon, and thus has more accurate information about its own military capabilities than its opponent.[45] Or there may be a secret alliance that will only be revealed when the enemy attacks.

However, bargaining theory assumes that ambiguity decreases once battle begins. War is posited as providing information on the capabilities of the two combatants. In this neat formulation, the war will end when sufficient information has been gathered on the relative military capabilities of each party.[46] As Reiter summarizes, "In short, uncertainty causes war, combat provides information and reduces uncertainty, and war ends when enough information has been provided."[47]

However, the assumption that war provides high-quality information may itself be open to doubt. As Reiter himself notes, "[C]ombat is a relatively inefficient means of hastening war termination through information transmission ... The fog of war makes combat outcomes often quite ambiguous."[48] Studies have found that wars do not become more likely to end the longer they continue. Instead, stronger states may shift their expectations to more difficult goals.[49] Even if the war did provide accurate information on which state had greater military power in that particular encounter, there would be the limitations of overgeneralizing the outcome to future conflicts, as discussed in Chapter 2.

[44] Fearon, "Rationalist Explanations for War"; Filson and Werner, "A Bargaining Model of War and Peace"; Kydd, "Which Side Are You On?"; Powell, *In the Shadow of Power*; Smith and Stam. "Bargaining and the Nature of War"; Wagner, "Bargaining and War"; Weisiger, *Logics of War*.

[45] Levy and Thompson, *Causes of War*; Alexandre Debs and Nuno P. Monteiro, "Known Unknowns: Power Shifts, Uncertainty, and War." *International Organization* 68 (2014): 1–31.

[46] Filson and Werner, "A Bargaining Model of War and Peace"; Reiter, *How Wars End*; Branislav Slantchev, "The Principle of Convergence in Wartime Negotiations." *American Political Science Review* 47 (2003): 621–632; Hein E. Goemans, *War and Punishment: The Causes of War Termination and the First World War*. Princeton: Princeton University Press, 2000. Interestingly, Goemans argues that if the domestic costs of continuing the war are lower than the costs of surrender, states may continue to fight even when new information suggests they will lose.

[47] Reiter, *How Wars End*, 3.   [48] Reiter, *How Wars End*, 220–221.

[49] Robert Powell, "Persistent Fighting and Shifting Power." *American Journal of Political Science* 56 (2012): 620–637.

Furthermore, if the calculations that underlie wars, preventive or otherwise, are unreliable, then a rational decision-maker should be extremely cautious about initiating wars. Without reliable assessments of power, military calculations are likely to be of questionable utility. Yet if every war must be explained as a mistake by one or both sides, the puzzle remains – why don't states recognize that military calculations are so prone to error?[50] Bargaining theory scholars have failed to explain why states are unable to recognize the propensity for error in estimates of power. Once the magnitude of ambiguity in military planning is admitted, the puzzle becomes: Why do states fight wars at all?

COMPETITION FOR STATUS AND PRESTIGE

Scholars have increasingly come to appreciate the idea that warmaking may be driven by status and prestige. Even realist scholars observed that prestige plays some role in Great Power behavior.[51] As E. H. Carr noted, "[P]restige ... is enormously important, because if your strength is recognized, you can generally achieve your aims without having to use it."[52] Similarly, Gilpin wrote: "Prestige, rather than power, is the everyday currency of international relations."[53] Generally speaking, however, realists have viewed prestige, honor, and status as subsidiary to the more fundamental contest over power among states. But if power is fundamentally evanescent, as discussed in Chapter 2, contests among the Great Powers devolve de facto into struggles over status.

This section develops the argument that status and prestige provide the primary motivation for Great Power competition and war. First, competition tends to focus initially on resources, the value of which has been socially constructed from the "lessons" of prior wars. Second, ambiguity in the assessment of power provides space for the construction of rivalry.

---

[50] Jervis, *Perception and Misperception*; Jack S. Levy, "Misperception and the Causes of War: Theoretical Linkages and Analytical Problems." *World Politics* 36 (1983): 76–99; Barbara W. Tuchman, *The March of Folly: From Troy to Vietnam*. London: Abacus, 1984.

[51] Hans J. Morgenthau, *Politics Among Nations*. New York: Alfred A. Knopf, 1973 [1948]; Edward Hallett Carr, *The Twenty Years' Crisis, 1919–1939: An Introduction to the Study of International Relations*. New York: Palgrave, 2001 [1939]; Gilpin, *War and Change*.

[52] E. H. Carr, *Great Britain as a Mediterranean Power*, Cust Foundation Lecture, University College, Nottingham, 1937, 10.

[53] Gilpin, *War and Change*, 31.

Finally, Great Power competitions quickly escalate into contests over status – that is, relative position in the Great Power hierarchy. Victory over a Great Power is the primary mechanism by which states move up the Great Power hierarchy. The sweetness of one-upping a rival, coupled with the opportunity to rise in the Great Power hierarchy, swiftly outweighs any material stake. These dynamics combine to encourage the Great Powers to fight costly wars over the wildest variety of issues, including quite trivial ones.

Instrumental Interests "Learned" from History

In each era, states tend to compete over a common set of issues. Scholars from the instrumentalist perspective tend to presume these interests – in territorial gain, dynastic succession, or communist ideology – were self-evident. For instance, the deadly intent with which Cold War statesmen pursued alliances with Third World countries has been taken as implying – tautologically – the essential value of these alliances for national interests (see Chapter 8).

Chapter 3, by contrast, argued that statesmen draw on "lessons" from the last major war in order to identify the resources that will be of importance in the next Great Power war. The collective nature of learning from history, described in Chapter 3, leads to a general consensus on the value of particular resources. Since states are drawing on common discourses, historical data, and interpretations from the international military community, they tend to impute similar value to the theorized resources. These theorized resources become the basis for national interests, broadly construed.

These interests "learned" from history become important sources of contention in interstate competition. The Great Powers focus much of their attention on acquiring these resources, under the assumption that they will prove as necessary for the next war as they were for the last. Competition does not always take the form of war, but may also include arms races, bids for territory, or diplomatic negotiation.

Nevertheless, broad national interests do not always translate into the specific disputes that provide the focus for particular wars. Even when states agree on the importance of territory, dynastic politics, or political ideology, uncertainty remains about whether any particular issue is worth the cost of war. The initiation of specific competitions and conflicts are filled in by the identification of a Great Power rival coupled with the desire for one-upmanship.

The Construction of Rivalry

Great Power rivalries are usually acknowledged by both states long before any war occurs. The Cold War rivalry between the United States and the Soviet Union, for instance, fundamentally shaped interstate politics for a half-century. Yet the origin of the Cold War rivalry is another one of the puzzles of the historical literature, and the subject of Chapter 8. Realist scholarship on preventive wars tends to assume that the identification of Great Power rivals is self-evident. By contrast, Chapter 8 suggests that ambiguity reigns, and that social construction processes explain how Great Power rivals identify each other in the first place.

Thompson and his colleagues Rasler and Colaresi have shown that in each historical period, the Great Powers have historically tended to construct both rivals and allies.[54] These rivalries have been highly consequential, playing a critical role in the construction of the interests and wars of the Great Powers. The tendency for the Great Powers to identify rivals is, in part, due to the challenges of military planning, in which the identification of the enemy is a necessary first step. As Goldman has pointed out, having no ostensible enemy can be paralyzing.[55]

From this perspective, the identification of the enemy is based on two major pieces of information.[56] The first is estimates of relative military power. Rasler and colleagues note: "States view other states as competitive when they are roughly in the same capability league."[57] Frequently, the state that is estimated to be nearest in military capability is identified as the rival Great Power. Chapter 2 points out that such estimations are

---

[54] William R. Thompson (ed.), *Great Power Rivalries.* Columbia: University of South Carolina Press, 1999. Paul F. Diehl and Gary Goertz, *War and Peace in International Rivalry.* Ann Arbor: University of Michigan Press, 2000; Michael P. Colaresi, *Scare Tactics: The Politics of International Rivalry.* Syracuse: Syracuse University Press, 2005; Karen A. Rasler and William R. Thompson. *The Great Powers and Global Struggle, 1490–1990.* Lexington: University of Kentucky, 1994; Michael P. Colaresi, Karen Rasler, and William R. Thompson, *Strategic Rivalries in World Politics: Position, Space and Conflict Escalation.* Cambridge: Cambridge University Press, 2007; Karen Rasler and William R. Thompson, "Explaining Rivalry Escalation to War: Space, Position, and Contiguity in the Major Power Subsystem." *International Studies Quarterly* 44 (2000): 503–530; Paul Poast, "Can Issue Linkage Improve Treaty Credibility?" *Journal of Conflict Resolution* 57 (2013): 739–764.

[55] Goldman, *Power in Uncertain Times.*

[56] Randall L. Schweller, *Unanswered Threats: Political Constraints on the Balance of Power.* Princeton: Princeton University Press, 2006.

[57] Karen Rasler, William R. Thompson, and Sumit Ganguly. *How Rivalries End.* Philadelphia: University of Pennsylvania Press, 2013, 3.

fundamentally problematic and, in practice, often resolved through reference to the social hierarchy. In other words, Great Powers tend to identify enemies based on their relative status position in the Great Power hierarchy.

Secondly, the identification of a Great Power enemy is moderated by another factor: estimates of hostility. Hostility is even more difficult to ascertain than military capability is, and necessarily has a subjective character depending on the personalities involved. As Jervis notes, "Judging others' intentions is notoriously difficult. Any number of methods of inference can be used, all of them fallible."[58] Unfortunately, this implies that "decision-makers, and especially military leaders, worry about the most implausible threats."[59] Regardless, the Great Powers draw on past actions and predicted military capability in order to construct enmities and alliances among themselves.

Third, once a state has been categorized as a rival and potential enemy, subsequent interpretations tend to be biased in ways that reinforce the initial perceptions.[60] As Larson notes, "Distrust of another state is apt to be self-fulfilling."[61] The actions of an identified rival can easily be perceived as inimical, lending further (illusory) support to the prophecy. Indeed, a state may view any action of a rival as disadvantageous to its own interests. Drawing on this logic, it can seem to be in the interest of a state to oppose whatever its rival is doing. As Thompson writes, "One round of hostility then reinforces the expectation of future hostility – and rivalry – and leads to some likelihood of a further exchange of hostile behavior in cyclical fashion."[62]

These perceptions of rivalry and enmity can translate into hostile actions by either or both states, until the prophecy is fulfilled. At this point, the perceptions of enmity are no longer illusory; the rival state is actively a hostile threat. Jervis writes: "If the prophecy of hostility is thoroughly self-fulfilling, the belief that there is a high degree of real conflict will create a conflict that is no longer illusory."[63] Consequently,

---

[58] Robert Jervis, Richard Ned Lebow, and Janice Gross Stein, *Psychology and Deterrence.* Baltimore: Johns Hopkins Press, 1985, 14.

[59] Jervis, *Perception and Misperception*, 62.

[60] Jervis, *Perception and Misperception*; Deborah Welch Larson, *Anatomy of Mistrust: U.S.-Soviet Relations during the Cold War.* Ithaca: Cornell University Press, 1997.

[61] Larson, *Anatomy of Mistrust*, 245.

[62] William R. Thompson, "Identifying Rivals and Rivalries in World Politics." *International Studies Quarterly* 45 (2001): 557–586, 562.

[63] Jervis, *Perception and Misperception*, 76–77.

a state may declare a preemptive war against a Great Power rival. However, the ambiguity of measuring power implies that there may not have been an objective empirical basis for the rivalry in the first place. Instead, preemptive war may be purely the result of a self-fulfilling prophecy, bringing about war between two states that originally had no objective reason to fight each other.

Status Competition

Scholars, both classic and contemporary, have noted the uncertainty involved in the onset of Great Power war, as discussed earlier. According to realist balance of power theory, states are motivated to go to war in order to reduce uncertainty over the distribution of power. In contrast, bargaining theory scholars argue that states fail to recognize the consistent tendency toward misinformation and error in the decision to go to war. Yet both perspectives fail to explain why states engage in costly wars when the magnitude of ambiguity is so great.

A growing set of scholars have argued that status, and related concepts of prestige, honor, will, resolve, and credibility, provide a primary motivation for Great Power war.[64] O'Neill writes that states "worry about intangible goals like saving face and preserving national honor and prestige."[65] Rasler and Thompson also note that "decision makers worry about national status, whether their state's prestige and ranking in the system's (or some subsystem's) hierarchy is being threatened."[66] Wohlforth finds that "efforts to attain recognition in order to secure actors' own estimates of their status" led to wars such as the Crimean

---

[64] Colaresi, Rasler, and Thompson, *Strategic Rivalries in World Politics*; Allen Dafoe, Jonathan Renshon, and Paul Huth, "Reputation and Status as Motives for War." *Annual Review of Political Science* 17 (2014): 371–393; David A. Lake, *Hierarchy in International Relations*. Ithaca: Cornell University Press, 2009; David A. Lake, "Escape from the State of Nature: Authority and Hierarchy in World Politics." *International Security* 32 (2007): 47–79; Deborah Welch Larson, T. V. Paul, and William C. Wohlforth, "Status and World Order." In *Status in World Politics*, edited by T. V. Paul, Deborah Welch Larson, and William C. Wohlforth, 3–32. Cambridge: Cambridge University Press, 2014, 7–8; Jonathan Mercer, *Reputation and International Politics*. Ithaca: Cornell University Press, 1996, 19; Michael Tomz, *Reputation and International Cooperation: Sovereign Debt across Three Centuries*. Princeton: Princeton University Press, 2007. For an opposing perspective, see Benjamin Miller, *States, Nations, and the Great Powers: The Sources of Regional War and Peace*. Cambridge: Cambridge University Press, 2007.

[65] O'Neill, *Honor, Symbols, and War*, xi.

[66] Rasler and Thompson, "Explaining Rivalry Escalation to War," 505.

War and the Cold War,[67] finding that Great Power competitions can escalate due to one-upmanship and competitive behavior among rivals. As Wohlforth concludes, "The historical record surrounding major wars is rich with evidence suggesting that positional concerns over status frustrate bargaining."[68]

I argue that the rules of the Great Power hierarchy motivate the Great Powers to go to war. Since the actual measurement of power is ambiguous, status in the Great Power hierarchy becomes both the primary underlying cause and the main positive outcome of Great Power war. As Rasler and Thompson point out, "[S]tates fight because they are, or wish to be, moving up or down in status."[69] This becomes the fundamental dynamic that drives Great Power warfare.

Great Power competition enhances the instrumental value of the object of contention, at times far disproportionate to any intrinsic value. At the heart of the matter is the desire for one-upmanship against a rival Great Power. The object of competition becomes secondary to the goal of winning the competition. In many cases, decision-makers have previously assessed a resource as relatively low in value, yet that value changes after a rival Great Power desires the resource. Once Great Powers enter the competition for an object, the object gains additional value as a trophy – a marker of victory in a Great Power competition (Chapters 7 and 8 describe examples). Taking this dynamic into account, it is not surprising that minor issues can trigger major wars. The value of triumphing over a rival justifies the costs of competition, regardless of the value of the resource being competed over. Victory in a Great Power war substantially enhances the status of a state; conversely, defeat causes significant demotion.

The Great Powers compete over issues large and small, as O'Neill has noted for a variety of contests, some of which develop into full-fledged wars.[70] Between two rival Powers, nearly any issue can provide opportunities

---

[67] William C. Wohlforth, "Status Dilemmas and Interstate Conflict." In *Status in World Politics*, edited by T. V. Paul, Deborah Welch Larson, and William C. Wohlforth, 115–140. Cambridge: Cambridge University Press, 2014, 138; for an opposing viewpoint, see William R. Thompson, "Status Conflict, Hierarchies, and Interpretation Dilemmas." In *Status in World Politics*, edited by T. V. Paul, Deborah Welch Larson, and William C. Wohlforth, 219–245. Cambridge: Cambridge University Press, 2014.

[68] Wohlforth, "Unipolarity, Status Competition, and Great Power War," 33.

[69] Karen A. Rasler and William R. Thompson, *The Great Powers and Global Struggle, 1490–1990*. Lexington: University of Kentucky, 1994, 1.

[70] O'Neill, *Honor, Symbols, and War*, xii; Toby J. Rider, Michael G. Findley, and Paul Diehl, "Just Part of the Game? Arms Races, Rivalry, and War." *Journal of Peace Research* 48 (2011): 85–100.

for competition. For instance in 1957, the Soviets initiated a "space race" with their success in putting the first satellite into space.[71] Immediately thereafter, the United States developed an interest in space capability, upping the ante with the goal of putting a man on the moon by the end of the 1960s. The United States gave various rationales for the utility of having satellite capabilities, including potential security or economic advantages – although these advantages were not mentioned until after the initial Soviet success. Rather, one-upmanship can be seen as a predominant motivation for the U.S. space program in the Kennedy era. Being the first state to put a man on the moon did not give obvious military advantages to the United States. Yet to obtain a symbolic triumph over the Soviet Union in this matter the United States invested billions of dollars, which might have otherwise been spent on weapons or other forms of military capability.

In short, Great Power competition typically takes on a life of its own that goes far beyond the initially estimated value of the object of contention. The desire to triumph in a Great Power competition becomes the primary motivation for the competitors, regardless of the value of the object. Although these competitions appear urgent and compelling to the participants, the quest for superiority often trumps more prosaic calculations of cost and benefit. The simple fact that a rival Great Power state vies for an object often proves sufficient to construct the object as a token of power.

THE ORIGINS OF THE FRANCO-PRUSSIAN WAR

The origins of the Franco-Prussian War of 1870 show how dynamics of Great Power competition bring importance to an issue that would otherwise have had insufficient value to prompt a costly war. The war between France and Prussia (Germany) in 1870–1871 constituted the most significant European war between 1815 and 1914. The outcomes of the war were far-reaching, leading to the French loss of the provinces of Alsace-Lorraine and Strasbourg and the rise of Prussia as a leading Great Power in Europe. The events of the war also had a substantial impact on the military planning of the late nineteenth century, which is the subject of Chapter 5.

---

[71] John M. Logsdon, *The Decision to Go to the Moon: Project Apollo and the National Interest.* Cambridge, MA: MIT Press, 1970; Sir Bernard Lovell, *The Origins and International Economics of Space Exploration.* Edinburgh: Edinburgh University Press, 1973.

Yet given the magnitude of the outcomes of the war, scholars have been confounded by the seemingly trivial incidents that triggered the war.

There is little disagreement about the basic facts. Historians agree that the Franco-Prussian War erupted following dynastic contention over the throne of Spain. The Spanish queen Isabella II had been overthrown in 1868 and a replacement monarch was needed. After a series of negotiations, Prince Leopold accepted the offer of the Spanish monarchy in May 1870. Prince Leopold was a member of the Hohenzollern family, a dynasty that was headed by Wilhelm I, King of Prussia. France took strong exception to a Prussian prince for Spain, given Spain's strategic location on the southern border of France. Following a number of diplomatic missteps, France declared war two months later.

The puzzle arises over how these basic facts can be translated into a reasonable account. As one historian writes, "The origin and development of the Hohenzollern Candidacy were long one of the great mysteries of nineteenth-century history."[72] Three explanations are described in what follows. The instrumental account focuses on the value of the Spanish throne in European geopolitical strategy, the second focuses on preventive war between a declining France and a rising Prussia. Yet neither provides a fully convincing account that explains the historical facts.

However, the puzzle disappears when status in the Great Power hierarchy is viewed as the predominant stake. From this perspective, Great Power reputation and the value of triumphing over a rival provide the primary impetus for war. This value of Great Power reputation was no secret to the diplomats involved. Indeed, the diplomats and publics of the period immediately recognized that a diplomatic insult that wounded French pride was a likely cause for war. As Holsti claims, "As in a duel, France declared war in 1870 as much to vindicate honor as to achieve any specific political or security objective."[73] This was reasonable only in a world where Great Power status mattered more than the issue that initially triggered the confrontation.

Instrumentalist Explanation

The instrumentalist argument posits that the issue that triggered the Franco-Prussian War was of sufficient political importance as to warrant

---

[72] Robert Howard Lord, *The Origins of the War of 1870.* New York: Russell and Russell, 1966, 16.

[73] Holsti, *Peace and War*, 150.

the cost of war. Instrumentalist scholars have argued that the geopolitical threat of a member of the Prussian family on the Spanish throne was so grave a risk to France that the risk of war was justified.[74] Spain's strategic position on the border of southern France provided security in friendly hands but created vulnerability if Spain was an enemy.

The Bourbon monarchy had been overthrown in Spain in 1868, ousting Queen Isabella II. Yet the dynastic families of Europe showed little interest in providing the next ruler of Spain, since the Spanish throne was known as "the most unstable throne in Europe."[75] Several candidates were brought forth, including one Portuguese and two Italian princes.[76] All three declined. In desperate need of a ruler, the Spanish turned to a fourth candidate, Prince Leopold von Hohenzollern-Sigmaringen. By September 1869, an emissary of the Spanish government had formally offered Prince Leopold the throne of Spain.[77]

Like the other candidates, Prince Leopold was unenthusiastic about the prospect of becoming the Spanish king. Nevertheless, Prince Leopold and his father Karl Anton considered the offer and consulted with the family head of the Hohenzollern dynasty, King Wilhelm I of Prussia.[78] King Wilhelm I was strongly opposed to the investiture of Prince Leopold and Hohenzollern involvement in Spain. He advised Prince Leopold and Karl Anton against accepting the Spanish offer. As Wawro writes, "[N]either Leopold nor the senior Hohenzollern, King Wilhelm I of Prussia, expressed much interest in the project."[79]

Nevertheless, Bismarck, the Prussian Chancellor and mastermind, was working behind the scenes to get Leopold on the Spanish throne. Historians have gone to great lengths to explain Bismarck's covert maneuvering. The instrumental explanation is that the strategic value of Spain in European geopolitics was sufficiently important to warrant Prussian interference. Spain lies directly on the southern border of France. If Prussia were to attack from the east in league with a Spanish attack from the south, France would be caught in a difficult two-front war. However, if Spain were a reliable French ally, she might aid France in the event of war with Prussia. As Lord writes, "[I]n case of a war in Central Europe it was highly

---

[74] Lord, *The Origins of the War of 1870*; Geoffrey Wawro, *The Franco-Prussian War: The German Conquest of France in 1870–1871*. Cambridge: Cambridge University Press, 2003.

[75] Howard, *The Origins of the War of 1870*, 48.

[76] Lord, *The Origins of the War of 1870*, 14.

[77] Howard, *The Origins of the War of 1870*, 48.

[78] Lord, *The Origins of the War of 1870*, 14.   [79] Wawro, *The Franco-Prussian War*, 34.

important for France not to be exposed to an attack from the rear, and to be able to throw the whole of her forces to the eastern front."[80]

From the instrumentalist perspective, the intrinsic strategic value of Spain, mediated by the Hohenzollern Candidacy, was of sufficient import to trigger the war. Lord claims: "That candidacy, if successful, promised very real advantages to Prussia: a great increase in the prestige of the dynasty, commercial benefits, and, above all, the raising up of a new enemy for [the French king] Napoleon at the rear."[81] Howard concurs that Bismarck "saw not only the advantages of a dynastic link with Spain, advantages both commercial and military, but the disadvantages which would arise if the throne were to fall into the hands of a party inimical to Prussia."[82] Lord adds tautologically, "The candidacy was a menace to the security of France ... When Bismarck attached so much importance to the candidacy as to declare it 'a political necessity' and 'politically invaluable' to Prussia, surely the French cannot be accused of becoming alarmed over shadows."[83]

In any event, Bismarck eventually got his way. "Bismarck wrote Leopold's father in May 1870 and pressed him to accept the throne for his son on patriotic grounds."[84] By June 21, 1870, Prince Leopold, perhaps feeling guilty for waffling on his princely obligations, indicated that he would accept the Spanish offer. King Wilhelm still disapproved but did not formally forbid the Prince to accept the offer.

Bismarck was happy. The French were not. The announcement that Prince Leopold had accepted the Spanish throne created a huge furor. "At court, in the cabinet, in the newspapers [of Paris], there was but one opinion. The candidacy was a menace to the security of France, and the secrecy with which it had been enveloped was an insult."[85] Numerous diplomatic missives were telegrammed back and forth. So great was the commotion that the withdrawal of Prince Leopold seemed to be the only way that war could be averted. As Lord writes, "[H]alf the courts and diplomats of Europe had simultaneously discovered that the voluntary withdrawal of the candidate would offer the one means of avoiding war between France and Prussia without compromising the dignity of either power."[86]

---

[80] Lord, *The Origins of the War of 1870*, 12.
[81] Lord, *The Origins of the War of 1870*, 8.
[82] Howard, *The Origins of the War of 1870*, 49.
[83] Lord, *The Origins of the War of 1870*, 27.   [84] Wawro, *The Franco-Prussian War*, 34.
[85] Lord, *The Origins of the War of 1870*, 27.
[86] Lord, *The Origins of the War of 1870*, 64.

The events that followed prove fatal to the instrumentalist account. On July 12, 1870, Karl Anton withdrew his son's candidacy for the Spanish monarchy. In light of the French reaction, the Spanish emissary had visited Karl Anton and asked the father to renounce the candidacy on behalf of his son. In one of the humorous twists of history, Prince Leopold had left on a hiking trip in the Austrian Alps during this crisis, and could not be contacted until after the whole crisis had been resolved. After some conferencing with King Wilhelm of Prussia, Karl Anton agreed to end the candidacy. "[O]n 12th July Charles Antony, besieged by envoys from Madrid, Paris and Ems [King Wilhelm's residence] and by letters from Queen Victoria and the King of the Belgians, renounced the throne on his son's behalf."[87]

The issue that originally caused the crisis was resolved. France had achieved her political aims. So why did France declare war a week later?

Preventive War

The empirical fact of the withdrawal of Prince Leopold's candidacy presents an insurmountable obstacle for the instrumental account. If the main cause of the war was the strategic importance of Spain, it is inexplicable that France declared war after achieving its political goals without bloodshed. In response, scholars have devised a host of other arguments to explain the puzzle of the Franco-Prussian war. The realist account focuses on preventive war: France was declining and feared the rising power of its Prussian rival. From this perspective, the details of the original diplomatic crisis are unimportant.

According to preventive war theory, war was likely or even inevitable given the shifting balance of power between France and Prussia. As Prussia gained military power, it sought to expand its territory. Yet such expansion would upset the status quo, endangering French interests as well as France's dominant position in the Great Power hierarchy. According to realists, this unstable situation was bound to deteriorate into war eventually. The actual events leading to war were unimportant; the real cause was the growing threat Prussia posed to French interests.

Since the conclusion of the Napoleonic Wars, France had been one of the leading Great Powers, and was generally viewed as having the best land army in the world. Yet Prussian military victories in the mid-nineteenth

---

[87] Howard, *The Origins of the War of 1870*, 52.

century had closed the gap, upping European estimates of Prussian power. From the preventive war perspective, France sought to crush Prussia before Prussia grew too powerful to oppose. Prussia, on the other hand, desired to expand its territory and incorporate the independent South German states, threatening the balance of power. Realists argue that sooner or later these Great Powers would fight in order to determine which state was the most powerful.

This argument sidesteps the incongruity of the events leading up to the war, since the particular events triggering the Franco-Prussian War are theoretically unimportant to the realists. Diplomatic crises between France and Prussia had occurred in 1867, 1868, and 1869, and the circumstances of the crisis in 1870 that initiated the war mattered little. As Wawro suggests, from the realist perspective, the Hohenzollern Candidacy was merely one of several thorns that Bismarck was sticking into France's side: "Though Bismarck had initially ascribed the Spanish crown question no more importance than the St. Gotthard tunnel project or the "Kaiser title" ... it rather surprisingly became the trigger for the Franco-Prussian War."[88] In the event, France declared war but was quickly defeated.

But the realist approach requires that states can accurately evaluate their own military power and the power of others. From a realist perspective, the conditions of inevitable war between opponents of near-parity should encourage each side to seek the maximum amount of advantage possible. The initiator of the war should calculate when conditions create the most advantageous window of opportunity for its military. The country caught at a disadvantageous moment would be penalized at the outset and should face a greater likelihood of being defeated. In this case, both France and Prussia believed the strategic window of opportunity was in their favor in 1870. As Van Evera notes, "In 1870 leaders in both France and Prussia advised war for preventive reasons."[89] This misidentification of the window of opportunity, at least by one side, substantially weakens the realist argument and opens the door to arguments emphasizing misconception, misinformation, and error.[90]

The French military believed that the window of opportunity was favorable to them in the summer of 1870. French rifles were superior to Prussian weapons, having greater range and accuracy. These technological advantages were so great that, as Howard notes, "The effect on

---

[88] Wawro, *The Franco-Prussian War*, 34.   [89] Van Evera, *Causes of War*, 77.
[90] Fearon, "Rationalist Explanations for War"; Jervis, *Perception and Misperception*.

the battlefield could only be revolutionary."[91] In addition, the French had a secret weapon, the *mitrailleuse*, which was a forerunner of the machine guns of the next century. These technological advantages were supported by evidence in the field, as discussed in Chapter 5. In light of these advantages, the French Minister of War "Leboeuf stoutly assured them the army was ready. Better war now, he said … than in a few years' time when the Prussians would have improved their rifles and copied the *mitrailleuse*."[92]

Yet Prussian Commander in Chief Moltke believed that conditions favored the Prussian military. "By July 1870 Moltke knew that he had under his hand one of the greatest engines of war the world had ever known; and he was openly impatient to use it."[93] The Prussian army had completed six railroads and a major mobilization plan for the transportation of troops to the French border of the Rhineland.[94] Moreover, Moltke was aware that the French were in the middle of a major military renovation, which would not be completed for several years. As Howard notes, "The social and economic developments of the past fifty years had brought about a military as well as an industrial revolution. The Prussians had kept abreast of it and France had not. Therein lay the basic cause of her defeat."[95]

Both sides could not logically have had a strategic window of opportunity. One side (or possibly both) must have misjudged the relative capabilities. The weakness in the preventive war argument is the presumption that military power can be correctly evaluated. The fact that France declared war only to be quickly defeated highlights the issue. It may be that the outcome in this particular war may be a fluke. However, it is the history of constant errors, described in Chapter 2, which undermines the realist explanation of preventive war.

The Bargaining Theory Solution

France's ill-fated decision to go to war – to the extent that it is historically representative rather than an anomaly – raises questions about the realist preventive war theory. In response, scholars have displayed considerable

[91] Howard, *The Origins of the War of 1870*, 5.
[92] Howard, *The Origins of the War of 1870*, 56.
[93] Howard, *The Origins of the War of 1870*, 44.
[94] Howard, *The Origins of the War of 1870*, 44.
[95] Howard, *The Origins of the War of 1870*, 1.

ingenuity, contriving accounts to maneuver around this historical obstacle. Bismarck has been ascribed almost supernatural cunning, single-handedly discerning the true balance of power and goading France to a war that served Germany's interests. Napoleon III and his French ministers are portrayed as dupes of irrational emotions and shortsighted political ambitions. Yet, it is far simpler to just accept that countries have great difficulty evaluating military power accurately.

Bargaining theory seeks to address this failing of conventional realist scholarship. From this perspective, wars result from errors of perception by otherwise rational states. From this perspective, France was simply wrong to believe that it could defeat Germany and paid a big price for her mistake.

Bargaining theory's emphasis on uncertainty fits well with arguments in this book, and certainly does a better job than realism of explaining the Franco-Prussian war. However, the arguments in this book go much further, claiming that ambiguity regarding power is omnipresent rather than exceptional. For instance, bargaining scholars might be tempted to interpret the German victory as providing accurate information about the relative power between Germany and France – a point that is strongly disputed in Chapter 5. Even if this information were correct in 1871, there is every reason to question its continued accuracy forty years later in 1914. Moreover, identifying the source of that power – the explanation for the German victory – might reasonably be attributed to a wide range of factors from treason by French generals to extensive railroad time-tables by the Germans. More generally, the fundamental ambiguity of power leads Great Powers to struggle over status and prestige. This insight leads toward a deeper understanding of the Franco-Prussian conflict, rather than merely ascribing it to miscalculation by the French.

Status, Great Power Competition, and War

This chapter develops the idea that Great Power competitions such as the Franco-Prussian War are motivated by the desire to triumph over a rival as a matter of prestige more than anything else. As in the realist account, the particular events that triggered a crisis quickly become unimportant. War between France and Prussia might easily have occurred over diplomatic crises in other years. Yet in pursuit of Great Power reputation, a diplomatic insult easily became the pretext for war. Coupled with the ambiguity of the evaluation of military power, France declared war in an effort of one-upmanship over Prussia. This section briefly discusses the construction of broad historical interests in dynastic control and the co-construction of France and Prussia as mutual enemies. Against this background, the recognized historical fact that the French sought to humble Prussia either diplomatically or militarily makes sense as the basis for the Franco-Prussian War.

Interests Drawn from History. Dynastic succession had long-standing political importance in Europe. Over the course of the seventeenth and eighteenth centuries, dynastic concerns figured at the center of many European wars. Drawing on experiences of the Thirty Years War in the seventeenth century, dynastic connections were theorized as creating alliances that could bring important military resources to bear – although even in dynastic families, siblings did not always get along. Since statesmen in the seventeenth and eighteenth centuries viewed dynastic connections as important military resources, it seems unsurprising – even necessary – that dynastic issues formed the basis for many European wars. However, the Napoleonic Wars overturned the theoretical importance of the dynasty in favor of the newly theorized importance of the nation-at-arms. The Franco-Prussian war was the last breath of dynastic logic as a national interest.

Construction of Rivalry. Historical evidence suggests that both France and Prussia had viewed each other as chief Great Power rivals since the late 1860s. This view was based largely on estimations of the closing gap in military capability, as expected by realists. France was acknowledged as one of the leaders of the Great Powers in the late nineteenth century. Prussia was the upstart challenger, the surprise victor in her recent war against the Great Power of Austria. As the nearest rivals in military capability, France and Prussia eyed each other suspiciously.

These estimations of military power were based on "lessons of history" – specifically, the factors that were thought to have been critical in the Napoleonic Wars. In the nineteenth century, focus on the size of the military as a major indicator of military power was drawn from theories of the Napoleonic Wars. Napoleon had been able to mobilize armies on a much grander scale than previously imaginable. After the Napoleonic Wars, prior military theories were quickly discarded in favor of ones that could explain Napoleon's successes.[96] Over the next few decades, military thinkers worked out a new model that emphasized the size and spirit of the mass army. As Clausewitz wrote in *On War*, "An unbiased

---

[96] Deborah Avant, "From Mercenary to Citizen Armies: Explaining Change in the Practice of War." *International Organization* 54 (2000): 41–72.

examination of modern military history leads to the conviction that *superiority in numbers becomes every day more decisive*; the principle of assembling the greatest possible numbers may therefore be regarded as more important than ever."[97]

According to these indicators, Prussia was rapidly becoming a formidable adversary for France. By 1870, the Prussian army was one-third larger than the French army, by virtue of the addition of military units from its recent victory against Austria as well as contributions from the Southern German states. Population size was also seen as an important indicator of military capability, since the practice of conscription forged a link between the national population and the size of the military. In the 1820s, the Prussian population had been only one-third the size of France, and by 1860 the Prussian population was still less than half of France.[98] By the 1860s, France had a population of 38 million, but population growth was declining. Ominously, the population of Prussia was nearing that of France, having recently doubled to 30 million as a result of territorial annexations following the Austro-Prussian war of 1866.[99]

Hostility was also evident between these two countries. Historical evidence indicates that both France and Prussia believed that war was inescapable. Howard reports, "In all ranks of French society war with Prussia was considered inevitable," and "In Germany war was also recognised as being sooner or later inevitable."[100] Lord similarly reports, "From the time of the Luxemburg crisis [in 1867] onward, the relations between France and Prussia were as cold and strained as possible, and all Europe lived in constant fear of the 'inevitable' conflict."[101]

Of course, the sense of inevitability was very much a social construction. It was largely driven by the social consensus around the "lessons" of the Napoleonic wars. This yielded a sense of threat that paved the way to rivalry. Once rivals see war as likely or inevitable, it quickly becomes a self-fulfilling prophecy. As Lord muses, "[U]nless one accepts the view that a Franco-Prussian war was under any circumstances inevitable, it is difficult not to accuse both governments in 1870 of criminally playing with fire."[102]

[97] Carl von Clausewitz, *On War*, edited and translated by Michael Howard and Peter Paret. Princeton: Princeton University Press, 1989, 265.
[98] Wawro, *The Franco-Prussian War*, 19.   [99] Wawro, *The Franco-Prussian War*, 19.
[100] Howard, *The Origins of the War of 1870*, 40–41.
[101] Lord, *The Origins of the War of 1870*, 12.
[102] Lord, *The Origins of the War of 1870*, 9.

Great Power Reputation and One-Upmanship. Against the background of dynastic interests and the construction of rivalry between France and Prussia, the events of the Hohenzollern Candidacy provided the spark that lit the Franco-Prussian War. Yet the issue quickly escalated beyond the dispute of the Hohenzollern Candidacy, which, after all, had been withdrawn. Instead, the affair swiftly developed into an issue of one-upmanship between rivals. A diplomatic insult became the ultimate trigger for the Franco-Prussian War.

Although the crisis of the Hohenzollern Candidacy appeared to be settled to French satisfaction, the French were not satisfied. The French claimed that the affair had been conducted inappropriately. Various pieces of evidence had surfaced about Bismarck's illicit meddling in this issue, which all recognized ought to have been a private affair of the Hohenzollern family. The French were incensed over the denials of the Prussian Minister of State that he had no knowledge of the affair. The issue rapidly escalated into an issue of French honor. "In [French foreign minister] Gramont's eyes, and those of his supporters, the question of the Candidature itself had thus become secondary to the more vital point of obtaining 'satisfaction' from Prussia."[103]

In pursuit of honor, the French revived the crisis, despite the news of Prince Leopold's withdrawal from candidacy. The French ministers directed the French ambassador Benedetti "to see the King [of Prussia] at once and demand a promise that he would not again permit Leopold to renew his candidacy."[104] Both the King of Prussia and the French ministers recognized that such an apology would be a blow to the dignity of Prussia. "[King] Wilhelm now understood that Napoleon III was after something more than security; he sought to humble Prussia in the eyes of Europe."[105]

Prussian King Wilhelm politely refused to offer an apology to France during his meeting with the French ambassador. Bismarck, still maneuvering to bring about war, saw the opportunity to create a diplomatic incident. In a key move, Bismarck revised the telegram from Ems, King Wilhelm's residence, that carried the news of the meeting between the King and the French ambassador. Without falsifying the events, Bismarck rewrote the telegram to imply a diplomatic insult. Where the original telegram had depicted acceptable diplomatic behavior, "Bismarck's rewritten version had the king gruffly canceling the audience [with the French ambassador]

[103] Howard, *The Origins of the War of 1870,* 52.
[104] Lord, *The Origins of the War of 1870,* 80.
[105] Wawro, *The Franco-Prussian War,* 36–37.

without explanation."[106] "All the various incidents in [the original] despatch were reduced to two: (1) Count Benedetti had presented a demand for guarantees 'for all future time,' and (2) 'His Majesty thereupon refused to receive the French ambassador again, and sent word to him through the adjutant on duty that His Majesty had nothing further to communicate to the ambassador.'"[107] The implied omission of the usual flowery diplomatic phrases was all it took to start the war.

Knowing the rules of the game and the stakes of Great Power reputation, all parties recognized this diplomatic insult as a sufficient cause for war. Howard reports that Bismarck "assured his friends" that the telegram "would have the effect of a red rag on the Gallic bull."[108] Wawro writes: "Because the French were seeking nothing less than 'satisfaction' in the increasingly abstract dispute, Bismarck's insolent wording alone would be interpreted as a *casus belli*."[109] Lord notes: "That a conflict was henceforth inevitable, all Germany seems to have recognized, and the rest of Europe too, as fast as the news of the Ems Telegram travelled. As soon as he saw the newspaper on the night of the 13th, the Dutch minister reported home, 'War henceforth certain.'"[110] The French minister, Ollivier, also interpreted the telegram as being an insult tantamount to war: "Both in Berlin and in Paris excited crowds gathered shouting 'to the Rhine!' William I cried, on reading the telegram, 'This is war!' So did the French ministers Ollivier and Gramont."[111]

War followed straight away, in a manner detailed in Chapter 5. Although France had won the substantive issue without a war, the value of that victory paled in comparison to the desire to humble its Great Power rival. The value of reputation quickly exceeded the value of the initial issue under contention. Given the ambiguity of evaluating military power, France declared war on Prussia – foolishly, as events were to show. Lord quotes the memoirs of French minister of war Emile Ollivier himself, who wrote: "[T]he French ministers ... by their too persistent efforts to achieve a complete and spectacular diplomatic victory, did much to bring on the conflict and to drag their country into 'the most imprudent war that ever was.'"[112]

---

[106] Wawro, *The Franco-Prussian War*, 37.
[107] Lord, *The Origins of the War of 1870*, 101.
[108] Howard, *The Origins of the War of 1870*, 55.
[109] Wawro, *The Franco-Prussian War*, 37.
[110] Lord, *The Origins of the War of 1870*, 107.
[111] Howard, *The Origins of the War of 1870*, 55.
[112] Lord, *The Origins of the War of 1870*, 4, quoting Emile Ollivier.

The Franco-Prussian War has provided a challenge to generations of scholars seeking to provide a rational explanation for how a diplomatic insult rendered in a routine telegram could trigger this major conflict. Yet the puzzle is easily solved if one ceases to look for deep underlying motivations and takes events at face value: when Great Power reputations are involved and power is ambiguous, the need to one-up a rival provides sufficient incentive for the initiation of war. The symbolic victory becomes the primary value of a conflict, while the original object of contention becomes nearly irrelevant. The dynamics of Great Power one-upmanship makes sense of the seeming triviality of the events that have led to many Great Power wars.

CONSEQUENCES OF GREAT POWER COMPETITION

Power – or at least the perception of power – is directly related to the onset of wars. Simplistically, one might expect that states are more likely to go to war when they believe they are more powerful than their opponent is. Alternately, scholars have hypothesized that wars may occur due to uncertainty over which state has the greater power. States might fight preemptive wars when they calculate a window of opportunity, or preventive wars to forestall their opponent from gaining even more power. Although various permutations have been theorized, military power and war are fundamentally connected. Underlying these theories of war is the belief that power can be accurately measured in some fundamental objective sense.

In contrast, if power is recognized as tautologically discerned in a post-hoc fashion, rather than as objectively based and accurately measurable, the causes of war must be reconceptualized as well. Instead, war might be understood as stemming from the requirement that Great Powers must successfully compete against rival Great Powers in order to maintain their status, as argued in Chapter 2. Under these circumstances, victory in a Great Power competition becomes the primary goal, regardless of costs that may far exceed the economic or strategic value of the bone of contention. Consequently, Great Power conflicts frequently escalate into one-upmanship competitions against rivals. These wars are often triggered by seemingly trivial events because the real stake is the reputation of the Great Power.

The following chapters illustrate several aspects of Great Power competition. Chapter 5 examines the role of "lessons" of history in providing the issues over which Great Power competition becomes focused. In the years preceding the First World War, mobilization speed and offensive spirit played a critical role in the calculations for the War. In hindsight, however, these factors turned out to be inconsequential for the outcomes of the First World War. Similarly, Chapter 7 showcases the Great Power competition over the acquisition of nuclear weapons during the Cold War. The costs of nuclear weapons were considerable, in terms of economic and security considerations. While the benefits may be debatable, the clearest value of the nuclear arsenals has been the conferral of Great Power status.

A second consequence of competition is that it resolves military debates within the broad international community. This resolution is based on the assumption that Great Power wars provide a true test of military technologies and strategies. Yet these competitions deviate extravagantly from a rigorous scientific experiment. Thus when Great Power competition closes a debate, its conclusion is not necessarily incontrovertible. Chapter 6 analyzes the decisive German defeat of France in 1940, which was broadly perceived as resolving the interwar tank debates in favor of the German position. More broadly, the outcomes of the Second World War were taken as resolving the interwar debates over the value of technology and mechanization more broadly, leading to the shift to the technological way of war.

Finally, competition among the Great Powers leads to war. Chapter 8 focuses on the events leading to the onset of the Korean War (1950–1953) between the United States and North Korea. Although the Soviet Union was involved only secondarily in the war, interpretations of Soviet interests played a fundamental role in the minds of U.S. decision-makers. The events leading up to the Korean War, played against the backdrop of the Cold War, are an excellent example of the arguments in this chapter, in which Great Power competition leads to the valuation of territories that were otherwise calculated to be of little interest to the United States.

5

Planning for the First World War

"The Great War is one of the most depressing episodes in modern history. Born in a muddle of diplomacy, its operations became a byword for military incompetence, lack of imagination and inhumanity which entombed the best of a generation in a furrowed, splintered landscape of mud and utter desolation."[1]

The First World War has provided a formidable academic challenge for several generations of scholars.[2] As one scholar has despaired, "Many alternative interpretations are possible, and all are speculative."[3] The only point that scholars agree on is that the war did not go as planned.[4] Military historian Luvaas queries: "What happened? Why did so few military thinkers anticipate what the machine-gun and trench would do

[1] Douglas Porch, *The March to the Marne: The French Army 1871–1914*. Cambridge: Cambridge University Press, 1981, 246.

[2] Niall Ferguson, *The Pity of War*. New York: Basic Books, 2000; Fritz Fischer, *Germany's Aims in the First World War*. New York: W. W. Norton, 1967; Sean McMeekin, The Russian Origins of the First World War. Cambridge, MA: Belknap Press, 2011; Annika Mombauer, *The Origins of the First World War: Controversies and Consensus*. New York: Longman 2002; Samuel R. Williamson, Jr., *Austria-Hungary and the Origins of the First World War*. New York: Palgrave Macmillan, 1991.

[3] Max Hastings, *Catastrophe 1914: Europe Goes to War*. New York: Knopf, 2013, xx–xxi.

[4] Michael Howard, "Men against Fire: Expectations of War in 1914." In *Military Strategy and the Origins of the First World War*, edited by Sean M. Lynn-Jones and Stephen Van Evera, 3–19. Princeton: Princeton University Press, 1991 [1984]; Jack Snyder, *The Ideology of the Offensive: Military Decision Making and the Disasters of 1914*. Ithaca: Cornell University Press, 1984; Stephen Van Evera, "The Cult of the Offensive and the Origins of the First World War." *International Security* 9 (1984): 58–107; Scott D. Sagan, "1914 Revisited: Allies, Offense, and Instability." *International Security* 11 (1986): 151–175.

to war?"[5] Van Evera puts it more bluntly: "Why so many blunders?"[6] Military planners had prepared massive cavalry offensives and expected the war to be over in a matter of weeks. Instead, the grinding war of attrition lasted four years. All sides suffered shockingly high casualties, as the European armies experienced the effects of nearly a half-century of weapons innovation.

Generations of scholars have offered withering criticism of the nineteenth-century military planners who failed to anticipate changes in warfare. Apparently, these military planners had been blinded by an irrational obsession with offensive tactics and were oblivious to the effects of trench warfare and machine guns. As a result, countless numbers of troops were sent charging across open fields toward almost certain death.[7]

This chapter seeks to understand military planning for the First World War, both to explain the focus on rapid mobilization and offensive tactics and to shed light on the origins of the war. Rather than criticize the architects of the First World War with the benefit of hindsight, this chapter emphasizes the vast ambiguities that confronted military planners. States must plan for the future, and prior wars provide the main body of evidence on which to base those plans. However, warfare is exceedingly complex, and the outcomes of past wars are heavily contingent on the specifics of the situation. Consequently, it is difficult to discern which lessons of the past are important and generalizable to future conflicts.

This chapter applies insights from Chapter 3 to understand how the European militaries distilled lessons from history as the basis for their ill-fated plans for the First World War. In particular, the Great Power hierarchy powerfully influenced the attention of military thinkers at the time. The surprising Prussian victory in the Franco-Prussian war of 1870 focused attention on Prussian/German military strategies. With the Franco-Prussian war as their primary reference point, European military theorists worked to distill abstract lessons that permitted planning for the future. Explaining the Prussian victory through a teleological lens, military planners at the time focused on rapid mobilization and offense while downplaying the importance of military technologies. These views

[5] Jay Luvaas, "European Military Thought and Doctrine, 1870–1914." In *The Theory and Practice of War*, edited by Michael Howard. 69–94. Bloomington: Indiana University Press, 1965, 91.
[6] Van Evera, "The Cult of the Offensive and the Origins of the First World War," 101.
[7] Jay Luvaas, *The Military Legacy of the Civil War: The European Inheritance*. Chicago: University of Chicago Press, 1959.

became the established consensus among military theorists of Europe, shaping military planning across the continent and beyond.

Great Power competition over specific indicators or tokens of power leads to the construction of rivalry and patterns of one-upmanship, sometimes producing wars over the most trivial of issues, as described in Chapter 4. The Franco-Prussian War encouraged the measurement of military power in terms of military size and mobilization speed. States began to compete over these indicators, amassing larger forces and devising the fastest possible mobilization plans. The Great Powers used these particular indicators to evaluate their own power and that of potential allies and competitors – affecting alliances and war plans (drawing on the arguments in Chapter 2). Ultimately, the resulting power calculations, hair-trigger mobilization schemes, and rivalries help explain the onset of the First World War.

In short, the lessons from the Franco-Prussian War provided the foundation for military plans and calculations leading to the First World War. Given the difficulties of predicting the future from the past, it should not be surprising that the First World War deviated substantially from expectations. European militaries planned for different enemies and a very different type of conflict than they actually faced. Rather than a short offensive war, the First World War developed into a lengthy war of attrition. The lessons from the Franco-Prussian War, so eagerly adopted across Europe, led to one of the greatest blunders of military history.

TRADITIONAL EXPLANATIONS OF THE FIRST WORLD WAR

The First World War has been the subject of extensive analysis, much of it focused on the mystery of why the major European militaries were completely blindsided by the effects of machine guns. The failures of the First World War are most often blamed on the conservatism or incompetence of political and military leaders who stubbornly refused to see or adapt to the reality of new military technologies. As McNeill suggests gloomily, "The irrationality of rational, professionalized planning could not have been made more patently manifest."[8]

One problem was the stubborn focus of nineteenth-century military thinkers on the wrong war as the source of lessons. Scholars have heavily

[8] William H. McNeill, *The Pursuit of Power: Technology, Armed Force, and Society since A.D. 1000.* Chicago: University of Chicago Press, 1982, 306.

criticized the European military planners for their reliance on the Franco-Prussian War of 1870 as the basis for planning the First World War. As Sagan summarizes, "The popular explanation is that European soldiers and statesmen blithely ignored the demonstrations of defensive firepower in the American Civil War and the Russo-Japanese War and simply believed that the next European war would be like the [Franco-Prussian War]."[9] The late nineteenth century saw several interstate and civil wars, ranging from the American Civil War of 1860 to the colonial Boer War of 1880 to the war between Russia and Japan in 1905.[10] In hindsight, scholars have argued that any of these wars would have provided a more prophetic window into the experiences of the First World War than did the Franco-Prussian War.[11]

Secondly, planners drew lessons from the Franco-Prussian war that seemingly ignored the improvements that had occurred in military technology. Analyses of the Franco-Prussian war suggested that military speed and offensive strategies had been the critical factors that had won the day for Prussia. Consequently, military planners focused on these factors as critical variables in their plans for the First World War. However, the speed of military mobilization that had been critical in the brief Franco-Prussian conflict turned out to be irrelevant in the First World War, which immediately bogged down and eventually lasted for years.

Similarly, the focus on offensive strategies was particularly ill suited to conditions in the First World War. Arrays of disciplined troops charging fixed machine gun emplacements presented nothing so much as an opportunity for target practice. The resulting casualties shocked the continent. An entire scholarly literature has arisen to explain this mistake – to understand why the military planners of the First World War insisted on pursuing offensive strategies when (in hindsight) the technology of the age demanded a defensive approach. The literature concludes that the

---

[9] Sagan, "1914 Revisited," 110.

[10] Scholars have shown that militaries did consider these peripheral wars, with some impact on policies. Nevertheless, these became amendments or modifications of the lessons of the Franco-Prussian War rather than the primary basis for military planning. See, for instance, Michael Howard, *The Lessons of History*. New Haven: Yale University Press, 1991; Sagan, "1914 Revisited" and J. McDermott, "The Revolution in British Military Thinking from the War to the Moroccan Crisis." In *The War Plans of the Great Powers, 1880–1914*, edited by Paul M. Kennedy, 99–117. London: George Allen and Unwin, 1979 [1974].

[11] J. F. C. Fuller, *The Conduct of War, 1789–1961*. New Brunswick: Rutgers University Press, 1961; Sagan, "1914 Revisited"; McNeill, *The Pursuit of Power*.

focus on offensive strategies represented an irrational commitment, an ingrained tradition among military men, which led to blindness among all the militaries of Europe.[12] As one historian claims, "The reckless attacks of 1914 were not the result of a rational doctrine but of a 'mystique,' an irrational cult."[13]

Third, scholars have despaired over the failure of nineteenth-century thinkers to foresee the devastating effect that new military technologies would have on the battlefields of the First World War. With the physical properties of the technology available, "accurate repeating rifles, the machine gun, barbed wire, elaborate entrenchments, and railroads," post hoc scholars contend that military advantage clearly belonged to defense.[14] Since the lesson of technological superiority is retrospectively assumed to have been obvious, modern-day historians summarize nineteenth-century analyses of the Franco-Prussian war as "a grand illusion," foreseeing (in hindsight) that "the Great War would rip away the honorific shrouds hiding the true nature and dimensions of the death machine."[15] As Herrera and Mahnken lament, "none learned ... the central tactical lesson" that "increased firepower made the tactical defensive a necessity."[16] Instead, the emphasis on offensive strategies by all of the major militaries has been widely criticized as resulting in the trench deadlock and high casualties of the First World War. Scholars have struggled to explain away these failures but have failed to acknowledge the magnitude of ambiguity involved.

---

[12] On the other hand, Trachtenberg and Snyder argue that specific historical and political contexts led the major European armies to favor offensive strategies at the particular moment when war broke out, but that the dominance of offensive strategies was not foreordained. Shimshoni goes even further, arguing that technology alone does not determine the value of offensive or defensive strategies, but that they are also influenced by doctrine, war plans, and geopolitical position. Marc Trachtenberg, "The Meaning of Mobilization in 1914." *International Security* 15 (1990–1991): 120–150; Jack Snyder, *The Ideology of the Offensive: Military Decision Making and the Disasters of 1914.* Ithaca: Cornell University Press, 1984; Jonathan Shimshoni, "Technology, Military Advantage, and World War I." *International Security* 15 (1990–1991): 134–162.

[13] Porch, *The March to the Marne*, 216.

[14] Stephen Van Evera, *Causes of War: Power and the Roots of Conflict.* Ithaca: Cornell University Press, 1999, 194.

[15] Robert L. O'Connell, *Of Arms and Men: A History of War, Weapons, and Aggression.* Oxford: Oxford University Press, 1989, 210.

[16] Geoffrey L. Herrera and Thomas G. Mahnken. "Military Diffusion in Nineteenth-Century Europe: The Napoleonic and Prussian Military Systems." In *The Diffusion of Military Technology and Ideas*, edited by Emily O. Goldman and Leslie C. Eliason, 205–242. Stanford: Stanford University Press, 2003, 226.

This chapter seeks to explain why nineteenth-century military theorists developed the theories that they did, rather than decrying their failures with the perfection of hindsight. Applying arguments from Chapter 3, I argue that military thinkers drew on the social realities of the Great Power system and the efficient war assumption in order to simplify the world sufficiently enough for planning to move forward. First, military thinkers tended to focus on the experiences of the Great Powers, presumed to reflect the "state of the art," rather than drawing lessons from minor militaries. Second, the European military community spun interpretations of recent Great Power wars into universal lessons applicable across the international system. To cut through the incredible complexity of warfare, military theories depended on the teleological assumption that victory reflected true military capability rather than circumstance or luck. This assumption introduced obvious biases, making it especially difficult to draw positive lessons from the defeated Powers. Nevertheless, reliance on a post hoc explanation of recent Great Power wars allowed planning to go forward.

In short, military theorists developed an interpretation that reasonably explained the Prussian victory in 1870, and used it to devise military strategies and plans at the turn of the century. However the next major conflict, the First World War, would prove crucially different from the Franco-Prussian war.

The Nineteenth-Century Great Power Hierarchy

As argued in previous chapters, military theory is fundamentally based on the Great Power status hierarchy. Not all wars are treated as equivalent data points. Since wars are incredibly complex and difficult to compare, military planners tend to focus their attention on a single war. Wars that upset the Great Power hierarchy are particularly noteworthy for military scholars, since they raise questions about the presumed "best practices" of the day (see Chapter 3). In the late nineteenth century, the Franco-Prussian War propelled reflection and rethinking across Europe. In this war, lower-ranked Prussia shockingly defeated France, which had rested comfortably near the top of the Great Power hierarchy during the previous century. Other interstate wars of the period, fought by lesser-ranked Powers or non–Great Powers, merited far less attention by military analysts at the time. In other words, military planners bypassed the study of little league baseball in favor of analyses of the World Series championship.

Since the Napoleonic Wars, France had been considered to have one of the best militaries in Europe. Although Napoleon had eventually been defeated, this defeat had taken a quarter of a century to accomplish and involved the efforts of nearly the entire continent of Europe. More recently, France had defeated other Great Powers such as Austria (in 1859) and Russia (in the Crimean War of 1853–1856), and was victorious in non-European wars in Algeria, Mexico, and Indochina.[17] Thus France was considered near the top of the Great Power hierarchy and presumed likely to defeat any other state. As a direct consequence, the rest of Europe sought to emulate the practices of the French Army.[18]

Prussia, by contrast, was barely considered to rank among the Great Powers. The French "hardly thought of the Prussian forces as an army at all," after Napoleon's defeat of Prussia in 1806.[19] The military reputation of Prussia began to revive slowly with its victory over Denmark in 1864. Two years later, Prussia pulled off an even more surprising defeat of Austria, a Great Power, in only seven weeks.[20] Despite Prussia's recent military successes, however, European opinion was confident that the French would handily overpower the Prussian army once war was declared in 1870.

Instead, the French army was defeated in an astonishing two months.[21] As McNeill sums up, "Prussian planning defeated French élan ... to the amazement of all the world."[22] The French defeat shocked Europe and immediately elevated Prussia above France in the Great Power hierarchy. International attention was riveted on Prussia as the new exemplar of best military practices. The battles of the Franco-Prussian War became the primary source of empirical material for European military thought in the late nineteenth century.[23]

By contrast, nineteenth-century military theorists generally downplayed the other wars of the period, such as the American Civil War and other wars involving minor powers. Given the difficulties of comparing wars

[17] Michael Howard, *The Franco-Prussian War: The German Invasion of France, 1870–1871*. New York: Macmillan, 1962, 18.
[18] Richard Holmes, *The Road to Sedan: The French Army 1866–70*. London: Royal Historical Society, 1984, 236.
[19] Howard, *The Franco-Prussian War*, 18.
[20] Geoffrey Wawro, *The Franco-Prussian War: The German Conquest of France in 1870–1871*. Cambridge: Cambridge University Press, 2003.
[21] Although the war continued for another year, its continuance had everything to do with the citizens of Paris and nothing to do with the French army, which had surrendered and allowed the king, Napoleon Bonaparte III, to be taken prisoner.
[22] McNeill, *The Pursuit of Power*, 251.   [23] Howard, *The Franco-Prussian War*, xi.

fought under such different conditions, military theorists tended to discount wars in the periphery. At the time, the United States was not even recognized as a Great Power and had never participated in a continental European war. While contemporary scholars see the lengthy American Civil War as foreshadowing twentieth-century wars of attrition, European observers dismissed it as "a clumsy failure to achieve a professionally efficient management of war." Indeed, the experiences of the new Prussian Great Power suggested that quick offensive wars conducted by professional militaries were the state of the art, unlike the bumbling of the American Civil War or the clumsy British and Russian episodes in the Crimean War.[24]

The Great Power status hierarchy also led military scholars to discount the Russo-Turkish War of 1877, the Boer War of 1880, and the Russo-Japanese War of 1905. Retrospectively, British theorist J. F. C. Fuller claims that the Russo-Turkish War should have taught "the crippling cost of attempting to storm entrenchments."[25] Yet Russia and the Ottoman Empire fell near the bottom of the Great Power hierarchy, and were not viewed as militarily equal to France. Although the Great Power states of Britain and Russia had been defeated by the Boers and by Japan, respectively, European militaries could hardly imagine emulating the military example of non-European states. Furthermore, the Russian defeat of the Ottoman Empire in the Russo-Turkish war was widely expected given the existing Great Power hierarchy, and so occasioned little scrutiny. In light of the European status hierarchy, the Franco-Prussian war was the only war that really mattered, and consequently it provided the primary basis for the military planning in the decades leading up to the First World War.

Overgeneralizations from History

In retrospect, all of the European militaries on the eve of the Great War were focused on aspects of military capability that proved to be irrelevant. Greatest weight was given to the size of the standing army and the speed with which it could be mobilized. American Civil War general Nathan Bedford Forrest summarized this strategic doctrine as getting to the front "fustest with the mostest."[26] Also believed to be important was the quality of the army, particularly its spiritedness and vigor of offensive

---

[24] McNeill, *The Pursuit of Power*, 243, 253.   [25] Fuller, *The Conduct of War*, 121.
[26] Theodore Ropp, *War in the Modern World*. Durham: Duke University Press, 1959, xii.

attack. These views directly followed from analyses of the Prussian victory in 1870. Yet even if these analyses provided a satisfying explanation for the Franco-Prussian war, the "lessons" were overgeneralized by nineteenth-century decision-makers into a general rubric or paradigm for the planning future wars.

Military thinkers of the late nineteenth century learned two principal lessons from the Franco-Prussian war. The surprising victory of the Prussians seemed to result from the combined effectiveness of speedy mobilization and the utilization of offensive tactics. The efficiency of the Prussian mobilization compared to the ineptness of the French mobilization meant that the French were unable to carry out their planned invasion of Prussia. A second factor was the seemingly mistaken reliance of the French on defensive tactics, compared to the offensive tactics of the Prussians.

The Lesson of Mobilization and Conscription. The First World War was to see the mobilization of armies on a much vaster scale than the world had ever seen before. Moreover, these enormous armies were mobilized with unprecedented speed. Rather than taking months to raise, equip, and transport men, as had historically been the case, the French and German armies met on the border within days of the initial declaration of war in 1914.

This emphasis on mobilization was a direct result of lessons drawn from the Franco-Prussian War. European thinkers were already predisposed to see mobilization as critical to victory, following the Napoleonic Wars. Napoleon had raised bigger armies than had historically been common, and indeed, larger than were thought possible by eighteenth-century military thinkers. Although the standing armies in the post-Napoleonic period had generally reverted to smaller professional armies, the lesson of the mass army was embedded in the nineteenth-century model of war. As a result, European military thinkers were primed to conclude that the surprising outcome of the Franco-Prussian War was due largely to the quick mobilization of the Prussian army and, secondarily, to the Prussian conscription of sizeable numbers of the population for short-term service.

In the Franco-Prussian War of 1870, expert opinion recognized that France's main hope was to mobilize before the much larger Prussian force could be brought to bear.[27] As Michael Howard notes, "Every day that passed without a French attack tilted the balance still further in the

---

[27] Wawro, *The Franco-Prussian War*, 65.

German favour."[28] Once both armies were fully mobilized, the Prussian army, estimated at a million men, would greatly outnumber the French, who "would be lucky" to amass an army of 400,000.[29] Although European opinion was that the seasoned French soldiers would perform better than the young, hastily trained Prussian infantry, sheer numbers would necessarily matter. Moreover, a quick French deployment and early success might persuade Austria, Denmark, and Italy to enter the war on the side of France.[30]

Prewar calculations supported the belief that France held the upper hand when it came to mobilization. The French Minister of War estimated that a French army of 300,000 could be mobilized in three weeks, while, according to the ministry's best estimate, the Prussian mobilization would take seven weeks.[31] However, these optimistic French estimates were not borne out. Although the European militaries had used railroads for mobilization and supply since the 1850s, the French had not put much thought into the coordination of railroad schedules that would be needed to ensure the speedy transport of men to the front, complete with their supplies, weapons, and uniforms. This lapse had been noted in the earlier French wars with Austria and Italy, but France had prevailed against these even more disorganized opponents. This was not the case with Prussia.

Not only had the French failed to give sufficient attention to the mundane logistics of mobilization; the French army faced a particularly complicated circumstance. Fearing domestic revolution more than interstate war, French policymakers had stationed troops as far from their native provinces as possible. With the outbreak of war on the Prussian border, the French high command decided to combine mobilization with concentration. Regiments had to travel from their peacetime stations to their distant home depot to pick up reserves and equipment before traveling to the front.[32] Unfortunately, the train schedules had not been planned out in advance, and as a result these complicated maneuvers quickly overburdened the railway system, causing utter confusion. As one historian comments, "the French army's management of trains in 1870–1 touches such heights of absurdity as to suggest fantasy."[33]

---

[28] Howard, *The Franco-Prussian War*, 77.   [29] Wawro, *The Franco-Prussian War*, 41.

[30] Wawro, *The Franco-Prussian War*, 73.

[31] Howard, *The Franco-Prussian War*, 66; Wawro, *The Franco-Prussian War*, 73.

[32] Howard, *The Franco-Prussian War*; William McElwee, *The Art of War: Waterloo to Mons*. Bloomington: Indiana University Press, 1974, 45.

[33] Hew Strachan, *European Armies and the Conduct of War*. London: George Allen and Unwin, 1983, 122.

By contrast, the Prussian mobilization occurred with great efficiency, even though Prussian Chancellor Bismarck had just sent many of his officers on vacation, and was himself on vacation right before the French declaration of war.[34] Half a million Prussian troops assembled on the French frontier in only two weeks, whereas the French mobilization order had still not been fully implemented nineteen days after it went out.[35] As a result, the French were unable to carry out an invasion of Prussia and were forced to fight battles in which they were frequently outnumbered three to two.

After the war, the swift Prussian mobilization was credited to the German General Staff. Each member of the German General Staff had practiced working out train schedules and infantry march tables for each unit as an exercise in preparation for war.[36] In contrast, the French General Staff were "mere popinjays and clerks."[37] Thus the Prussian mobilization proceeded like clockwork, while the French army became a hopeless jumble of trains, horses, men, and supplies.

Following the Prussian victory in a mere six weeks, the European military community quickly came to a consensus that a General Staff was a critical requirement for rapid mobilization and thus military success.[38] France, Austria, Italy, Russia, and Japan created their own versions of the General Staff, and many other countries sent observers to Prussia, including Greece, Turkey, China, Chile, and Argentina.[39] The Prussian system of universal conscription, which had previously been resisted by many European militaries, was also widely adopted. Even France, which had long opposed conscription on the grounds that it was incompatible with French values of democracy and freedom, quickly converted to the new faith.[40] By the time of the First World War, all of the combatants except Great Britain and the United States had implemented mass conscription.

More importantly, mobilization speed was extrapolated beyond the particular events of 1870 to a universal tenet of military theory. The

---

[34] Wawro, *The Franco-Prussian War*, 83.   [35] Wawro, *The Franco-Prussian War*.
[36] Wawro, *The Franco-Prussian War*, 82.
[37] J. F. C. Fuller, *A Military History of the Western World, Volume III*. New York: Funk and Wagnalls, 1956, 106.
[38] McNeill, *The Pursuit of Power*, 251; Ropp, *War in the Modern World*, 177.
[39] Herrera and Mahnken, "Military Diffusion in Nineteenth-Century Europe," 225; Trevor N. Dupuy, *A Genius for War: The German Army and General Staff, 1807–1945*. Englewood Cliffs: Prentice-Hall, 1977.
[40] Richard D. Challener, *The French Theory of the Nation in Arms, 1866–1939*. New York: Columbia University Press, 1952.

newly created General Staffs across Europe were put to work calculating railroad schedules and logistical schemes. As military planners honed ever-faster mobilization schemes, they came to believe that the next major European war would be settled in a manner of weeks. Any army that could not assemble quickly enough was likely to be left out of the fight. As it turned out, however, mobilization speed proved to be much less important in the First World War, which would last for four years.

The Lesson of Offensive Strategy. In the preparations for the First World War, military planners drew on the Prussian victory, as well as previous successes of the offensively minded Napoleon, to conclude that offensive strategies were particularly essential against the new technologies of the day. The problems of military leadership and strategy were to engage French military theorists for decades, leading to the school of thought characterized by later historians as the "cult of the offensive." Not only the French but also other European militaries including the Germans were to conclude from the Franco-Prussian War that offensive tactics were overwhelmingly effective.

The French defeat in 1870 was a shock to all of Europe, and prompted a great deal of reflection. Blame was attributed to defects in the French political and military leadership. In particular, historians have not viewed kindly the French Emperor Louis Napoleon Bonaparte III. As Howard has summed up, "[B]y a tragic combination of ill-luck, stupidity, and ignorance France blundered into war with the greatest military power that Europe had yet seen, in a bad cause, with her army unready and without allies."[41] Napoleon III's hopes of bolstering his image as the successor of Napoleon I evaporated as the French army lost battle after battle, finally surrendering ignominiously after the defeat at Sedan. With the emperor taken prisoner by the Prussians, the French masses were quick to take to the streets and announce a revolutionary, post-Napoleonic government. If the cause of the French defeat lay with poor political leadership, a change in government would be the remedy.[42]

The French postmortem also included an indictment of its military leadership. Marshal Bazaine, the commander of the main French army, was court-martialed after the surrender. Military leaders are commonly blamed following a defeat. Yet in the case of Bazaine, some decisions seemed truly inexplicable, such as his retreat from Metz at a moment

---

[41] Howard, *The Franco-Prussian War*, 57.
[42] Allan Mitchell, *Victors and Vanquished: The German Influence on Army and Church in France after 1870*. Chapel Hill: University of North Carolina Press, 1984, 22.

when the French army appeared on the verge of winning. So puzzling was his ineptness that it was widely believed that he had actually committed treason by colluding with the enemy during the war.[43] A sympathetic historian acknowledged, "Bazaine had actually won the decisive battle of Gravelotte at the moment when he conceded it to the enemy."[44] Likewise, at the battle of Mars-la-Tour, Bazaine "snatched defeat from the jaws of certain victory." Even the farsighted German Chancellor Bismarck admitted that he had not expected such incompetence among the French high command.[45]

Beyond the specifics of the French leadership, however, the international military community debated the failure of French military strategies. European military thinkers deduced a general lesson from the Franco-Prussian War: French strategies had overemphasized the defensive. Interestingly, the French had utilized defensive tactics during the Franco-Prussian War in deference to the perceived characteristics of the new battlefield technologies, in a manner that was quite prescient of the First World War. Since both French rifles and artillery greatly outranged Prussian weapons, the French planned to entrench themselves in strong defensive positions. The attacking waves of Prussians "would be mowed down by the accurate, rolling fire of entire [French] battalions."[46] Had the French been victorious in the Franco-Prussian War, these defensive tactics might have been adopted across Europe, considerably altering the battlefield experiences of the First World War.

Instead, the defensive tactics of the French were maligned as one of the causes of their defeat. French General Ferdinand Foch was one of the principle creators of the new offensive tactics, which would become the tenets of the "cult of the offensive." Foch argued that the Prussian victory resulted from their "single-minded devotion to the capital idea: Hit, and hit hard."[47] Foch and other French military theorists "rediscovered" the Napoleonic lesson of rapid offensive strikes, which they argued was the embodiment of the true French spirit.[48] In contrast to French Marshal

---

[43] Holmes, *The Road to Sedan*, 2.

[44] Paddy Griffith, *Military Thought in the French Army, 1815–51*. Manchester: Manchester University Press, 1989, 5.

[45] Wawro, *The Franco-Prussian War*, 161, 300.

[46] Wawro, *The Franco-Prussian War*, 54.

[47] Quoted in Wawro, *The Franco-Prussian War*, 307–308.

[48] Although the strategy of the offensive was the official doctrine of the French army, in practice there was a "mass of conflicting tactical theories." Porch, *The March to the Marne*, 221.

Bazaine, who had thought he was defeated when he was actually winning, "[Prussian] General von Zastrow was half-defeated, but refused to be and so was not. This was the secret of the Prussian victory."[49] French General Foch believed that the offensive spirit was the true expression of the French national character. The lesson that modern warfare favored offensive strategies was quickly taken up by militaries across Europe. By 1914, all of the Continental General Staffs had plans for strategic offensives.[50] German military leaders believed that digging foxholes "damaged the offensive spirit of our infantry."[51] British military leaders also focused on offensive strategies, despite experiences in the First Boer war that might have suggested the contrary.[52]

Consequently, the plans for the First World War were for all parties to mobilize quickly and fight with offensive strikes, refusing to believe in the possibility of defeat. As one historian summarizes: "All of the 1914 war plans of the Continental General Staffs were offensive. All of them were to fail."[53] Indeed, it was the spectacular failure of these offensive strategies in the First World War that prompted the next set of "lessons" in the interwar period. By the Second World War, all of the European militaries, even the invading Germans, focused on defensive strategies.[54] The historical shift from offensive to defensive strategies simply reflected the lessons drawn reflexively from the most recent Great Power war.

The Franco-Prussian War illustrates the main theme of Chapter 3: war is sufficiently complex and changes are so rapid that lessons of the past cannot easily be extrapolated to the future. The lessons "learned" in the late nineteenth century represented post hoc descriptions of one war, not necessarily a generalizable guide to subsequent wars. This was to be even more the case in the lesson learned about technology.

Teleology and the Lesson Not Learned. The importance of technological advantage was the big lesson that was not learned from the Franco-Prussian War. Contemporary scholars are incredulous that European military planners were so thoroughly unable to anticipate the effects of the machine gun. Yet this blind spot makes sense given the biases that

[49] Quoted in Howard, *The Franco-Prussian War*, 98.
[50] Ropp, *War in the Modern World*, 200.
[51] Eric Dorn Brose, *The Kaiser's Army: The Politics of Military Technology in Germany during the Machine Age, 1870–1918*. Oxford: Oxford University Press, 2001, 24.
[52] Van Evera, "The Cult of the Offensive and the Origins of the First World War."
[53] Ropp, *War in the Modern World*, 204.
[54] Barry R. Posen, *The Sources of Military Doctrine: France, Britain, and Germany between the World Wars*. Ithaca: Cornell University Press, 1984.

affect military learning. In the Franco-Prussian war, the French were widely acknowledged as having better firearms. This superiority was evident not only in the observable technical characteristics of the weapons but also in the high casualty rates of the Prussians in nearly every battle. Nevertheless, the Prussians won anyway. The indisputable reality of the Prussian victory – and the subsequent consensus that Prussia ranked above France in the Great Power hierarchy – made it difficult for militaries to appreciate the French military's insights regarding technological innovation and the importance of defensive strategies.

Military scholars in the nineteenth century had generally considered technology as one of several important considerations in military planning. In particular, Europe had been impressed by the Prussian defeat of another Great Power army – that of Austria in 1866. While multiple explanations were propounded, much credit for the victory was attributed to the Prussian needle gun.[55] The Prussian needle gun fired six shots for every one shot from an Austrian gun, had greater accuracy, and moreover, enabled the soldier to lie down to reload.[56] In hindsight, these attributes seemed obviously advantageous – especially given the knowledge that the Prussians had been victorious. Before the Austro-Prussian war, however, it had been hotly debated whether these features were assets or deficits. For instance, an Austrian commission studied the needle-gun before the war and concluded that the rapid rate of fire would merely exhaust ammunition supplies more quickly.[57] The ease of loading, which could even be done while lying down, might also prove detrimental, since "what could persuade men lying upon the ground under enemy fire to get up on their feet again and move about the field of battle?"[58]

As with many military debates, however, the matter was settled by the fact of Prussian victory.[59] After the Austro-Prussian War, European militaries hastened to rearm their troops with breech-loading weapons – and the French were among the first.[60] Significantly, the French firearm, known as the chassepot, was a better weapon in several respects than the Prussian needle gun. The range of the chassepot was effectively 1,000 yards, which was more than double that of the Prussian firearms.

[55] Herrera and Mahnken, "Military Diffusion in Nineteenth-Century Europe," 221.

[56] Howard, *The Franco-Prussian War*, 5.

[57] Regan, Geoffrey. *Someone Had Blundered: A Historical Survey of Military Incompetence.* London: B.T. Batsford, 1987, 103.

[58] McNeill, *The Pursuit of Power*, 245–246.

[59] Howard, *The Franco-Prussian War*, 29.   [60] McNeill, *The Pursuit of Power*, 250.

The superiority of the French firearm was widely acknowledged both at the time and today. One historian noted: "[N]ervous Prussian infantrymen ... had constantly to be reassured (fraudulently), that 'the [Prussian] needle rifle is *not* outranged by the [French] Chassepot.'"[61]

In addition to the chassepot, the French had a "secret weapon" – the *mitrailleuse*, a forerunner of the machine-gun that was mounted on an artillery carriage.[62] The weapon was so secret that it was not issued to the armies until just before the Franco-Prussian war, so few French commanders had been trained in its use. Since little thought had been put into the tactical use of the *mitrailleuse*, it was used "in a perfectly idiotic fashion" and had relatively little impact on battlefield outcomes.[63]

The high casualties suffered by the Prussians in nearly every battle suggest that the superior French firearms did make a difference. In most military battles, the victor has equivalent or fewer casualties than the defeated army. Yet the Prussians had higher casualties than the French even in the battles the Prussians won. For instance, at the battle of Spicheren, the victorious Prussian army lost 4,500 men compared to 2,000 French casualties.[64] Other battles had similarly high Prussian losses. At Gravelotte, the victorious Prussians had 20,000 casualties compared to the French 12,000.[65] In one battle, the Prussian First Guard Division lost more than half its men – 8,000 casualties – in twenty minutes due to the disadvantage of mounting an offensive attack against an enemy entrenched with accurate long-range firearms.[66] Despite these high casualties, however, the Prussians still won these battles, and the war itself.

This outcome – the army with superior technology being defeated – has been uncomfortable for post–Second World War military scholars who have tended to favor explanations with technological determinism. Indeed, technological determinist scholars have worked hard to advance the counterintuitive claim that the victorious Prussian actually had superior technology. For instance, one military historian argued that the Prussian gun, while inferior in range and accuracy, "jammed less often, had a simpler construction, and had a better sighting system than the [French]

---

[61] Wawro, *The Franco-Prussian War*, 52, 56–57.
[62] Larry H. Addington, *The Patterns of War since the Eighteenth Century*. Bloomington: Indiana University Press, 1994 [1984], 98.
[63] Fuller, *A Military History of the Western World*, 106.
[64] McElwee, *The Art of War*, 140.   [65] McElwee, *The Art of War*, 141.
[66] Antulio J. Echevarria, II, *After Clausewitz: German Military Thinkers before the Great War*. Lawrence: University of Kansas Press, 2000, 19.

chassepot."[67] Yet most historians simply accept that the French chassepot was a technological improvement over the Prussian firearms in 1870.

Others have tried to argue that superior Prussian artillery was the key to victory.[68] For instance, scholars have argued for the importance of the breech-loading steel Prussian Krupp cannon.[69] At times this technological advantage appeared decisive, and the German generals began to hold back the infantry in favor of the field artillery.[70] Thus, O'Connell concludes that the Prussian army "blew the French apart with concentrated artillery fire. This was how [the final battle of] Sedan was won."[71] J. F. C. Fuller argues that the Franco-Prussian war clearly showed "the growing preponderance of artillery over infantry,"[72] and that "the superiority in handling of the Prussian breech-loading rifled guns over the French bronze muzzle-loading rifled cannon which was the decisive battle."[73]

Contemporary debates about the importance of Prussian artillery are not yet resolved, and may never be. Importantly, however, the European military theorists in the late nineteenth century did not recognize or attribute significance to Prussian artillery technology. Such conclusions have been made only by scholars who could draw on the experiences of both the First and the Second World Wars, which focused attention on technology as a critical aspect of military capability. Military thinkers of the late nineteenth century drew the opposite lesson from the Franco-Prussian War: between two closely matched armies, superior weaponry does not win the war. This conclusion seemed indisputable, given the fact that the better-armed French had been defeated.

The bias of teleology resulted in a negative lesson regarding technology. Observers in the international community as well as the French and Prussians concluded that the rapid Prussian mobilization coupled with offensive tactics greatly outweighed the technological advantages of the French army. While the role of improved firearms and artillery was recognized and discussed, these discussions occurred within the cognitive framework of nineteenth-century military thought rather than with the hindsight of twentieth-century views. Thus the solution to the increased

---

[67] Echevarria, *After Clausewitz*, 18.
[68] O'Connell, *Of Arms and Men*, 208; Snyder, *The Ideology of the Offensive*, 199; Fuller, *A Military History of the Western World*, 133.
[69] Wawro, *The Franco-Prussian War*, 56–57.
[70] Howard, *The Franco-Prussian War*, 118.   [71] O'Connell, *Of Arms and Men*, 208.
[72] Fuller, *A Military History of the Western World*, 133.
[73] J. F. C. Fuller, *Armament and History*. New York: Charles Scribner's Sons, 1945, 118.

power of firearms followed the standard nineteenth-century recipe for military victory – bigger armies, mobilized more quickly. As Michael Howard sums up, European military leaders concluded that the increased power of firearms meant that "the army with the greatest resources in man-power would enjoy a decisive advantage"; consequently, "between 1871 and 1914 General Staffs vied with one another in demanding ever larger forces as the solution to their problems."[74]

CALCULATIONS FOR WAR

Scholars have been puzzled over how the relatively minor event of the assassination of an Austrian archduke in Serbia could lead to the First World War in which millions of men were to lose their lives. A wide variety of explanations have been offered, from the war as a long-planned German bid for dominance,[75] to war as a result of an arms race,[76] to war as an inadvertent result of "lockstep" mobilization.[77]

This chapter explains the First World War in terms of the socially constructed features of Great Power competition, drawing on arguments from Chapter 4. The lessons from recent Great Power wars not only shape evaluations of power but also serve to focus competition in a fundamentally ambiguous world. Power is discerned through reference to the social hierarchy of the Great Power system and indicators of power theorized to have been salient in prior conflicts. As argued in Chapter 4, Great Powers experience great pressure to identify rivals, compete, and one-up each other, allowing wars to begin over even the most trivial of issues.

As this section will show, in the early twentieth century each state based its calculations on the same indicators of Great Power military strength that were being made by all the other European militaries. Across

---

[74] Michael Howard, *War in European History*. Oxford: Oxford University Press, 1976, 105.

[75] Fritz Fischer, *War of Illusions: German Policies from 1911 to 1914*. London: Chatto and Windus, 1975; Fritz Fischer, *Germany's Aims in the First World War*. New York: W. W. Norton, 1967.

[76] David G. Herrmann, *The Arming of Europe and the Making of the First World War*. Princeton: Princeton University Press, 1996; David Stevenson, *Armaments and the Coming of War*. Oxford: Clarendon Press, 1996.

[77] Alan J. P. Taylor, *War by Time-Table: How the First World War Began*. London: MacDonald and Company, 1969; Barbara W. Tuchman, *The Guns of August*. New York: Macmillan, 1962.

the continent, decision-makers agreed on the relative capabilities of states, which also led to similar calculations on the capabilities of potential enemies and allies. These military calculations informed political decisions on which states were candidates for alliances and which should be viewed with wariness as potential enemies. The focus on mobilization and offensive strategies led to an inflexibility that increased the pace of the political decisions that led to the onset of the war. These collective agreements on the lessons of the Franco-Prussian war were to be highly consequential in the planning and initiation of the First World War.

Definition of the Enemy

One of the common explanations for the onset of the First World War was that the Great Powers were pulled into war by pre-agreed interlocking alliances.[78] Germany had agreed to support Austria-Hungary in a war. Russia had signed on to support France in the case of conflict with Germany, while Britain was pledged to aid Belgium in the event of invasion. Underlying these alliances was consensus on the measures by which state military power was to be measured. Like picking players for a sports team, each military hoped to recruit powerful allies while correctly identifying the potential enemies in the struggle that lay ahead.

Traditional scholarly accounts assume that objective assessments of military power should have been clear to the decision-makers at the time. For instance, Paul M. Kennedy points to indicators such as industrial production, steel manufacturing, energy production, and manufacturing output to show that the alliance between France, Russia, and Britain had greater aggregate military capability than that of Germany and Austria-Hungary in 1914.[79] The advantage of the Allies became even more overwhelming when the industrial capacity of the United States was added. Yet economic indicators became meaningful measures of military capability only in retrospect, with the sure knowledge that the First World War would become a war of economic stamina lasting four years. European decision-makers did not focus on these factors because they had not proven important in their historical experience.

---

[78] James Joll, *The Origins of the First World War*. New York: Longman, 1992. This is a classic argument of realist theory; see Stephen M. Walt, *The Origins of Alliances*. Ithaca: Cornell University Press, 1987.

[79] Paul M. Kennedy, "The First World War and the International Power System." *International Security* 9 (1984): 7–40.

In the decades leading up to the First World War, Germany (formerly Prussia) was regarded as being the most powerful country in the world. With an army of a million men, Germany was estimated to have the fastest mobilization capabilities and the most effective offensive strategies. The other Great Powers were recognized as comparatively lacking on these indicators of power. Britain could mobilize quickly but had a small army. Russia had a huge army, but would mobilize slowly. The United States was dismissed from consideration due to its small standing army and the estimated length of its mobilization time of a year or more. France was the nearest rival to Germany in terms of army size, offensive tactics, and mobilization speed, but had been defeated conclusively by Germany in the Franco-Prussian War four decades earlier.

Calculations of enmity followed these measures of military capability. Germany feared the combined strength of France and Russia, but had much less concern for either opponent taken singly. France feared taking on Germany alone. Great Britain and Russia also worried about Germany as an enemy. Calculations of allies followed correspondingly. Germany sought to ally itself with Austria and Italy, which ranked as second-tier Great Powers according to the indicators of the day. France sought alliances with Russia and Britain. Belgium counted on Britain and France as powerful allies. Decision-makers took into account a variety of factors in these diplomatic maneuvers, including personalities, history, and political sensibilities. Nevertheless, the foreign policy fluctuations of the moment were fundamentally based on consensus on estimates of the relative military capability, focusing on the specific rubric of military size, speed of mobilization, and offensive spirit.

States ranked as militarily weak on those key indicators, by contrast, were dismissed. German planners, as well as the rest of Europe, considered Belgium and Luxembourg to be inconsequential from a military standpoint (as did the leaders of these countries themselves). Although the German invasion of France would be initiated by the overrunning of the borders of Belgium and Luxembourg, the German war plans assumed these militaries would prove capable of little resistance, based on the prevailing indicators. More importantly, the military capabilities of Britain and the United States were also discounted. Not only did German decision-makers misjudge the political likelihood of British and American entry into the war; their military capabilities were also written off.

As to be expected, some of these judgments proved accurate in retrospect while others have been criticized as foolish mistakes. Russia and Britain turned out to be weighty allies for France, while Austria proved a weaker ally for Germany than its apparent score on the indicators of military capability of the day suggested. Belgium and Luxembourg provided little obstacle to the German timetable, as had been generally predicted. However, the United States ended up playing a considerable role in the outcome of the war, to the surprise of all (including itself). While scholars have argued that better indicators of military power should have been used, these calculations of alliance and hostility seemed reasonable to decision-makers at the time, based on continent-wide consensus on the indicators of military capability.

Planning for War

The European militaries developed mobilization plans that were to prove highly significant in the unfolding of the First World War. These plans assumed that the war would transpire similarly to the Franco-Prussian war, thus all plans emphasized quick mobilization along the most probable front. Drawing on these assumptions, planners forecast the likely location of the front and developed complex schedules to arrange for the timely arrival of their armies. However, these plans did not foresee the possibility of a world war in which each state would face multiple enemies. The post-Napoleonic wars of the nineteenth century had featured two or at most three combatant states, with the rest of Europe playing minor or neutral roles. Thus each military planned for a full mobilization against its most likely enemy.

The German military plan, infamously known as the Schlieffen Plan, was based on fundamental assumptions about which states would be the enemy. German military thinkers had been obsessed for decades with the logistical problems of carrying out a two-front war against France and Russia – the two Great Powers estimated as its most likely enemies. The plan was fundamentally based on the assumption of the importance of mobilization speed. Originally formulated in 1905, the Schlieffen Plan did not allow for basic changes in the strength of other European armies or alterations in the political and diplomatic context in which war might occur.[80]

According to the Schlieffen Plan, the entire German army would first be mobilized against France, then be transported to the eastern border to

---

[80] Holger H. Herwig, *The First World War: Germany and Austria-Hungary 1914–1918.* New York: Bloomsbury Academic, 1996; Gerhard Ritter, *The Schlieffen Plan: Critique of a Myth.* New York: Frederick A. Praeger, 1958; Terence Zubin, *Inventing the Schlieffen Plan: German War Planning, 1871–1914.* Oxford: Oxford University Press, 2002.

fight against Russia. The French army would, according to German calculations, be defeated in six weeks. Not coincidentally, six weeks was the time it had taken the Germans to defeat the French army in 1870. More importantly, six weeks was the estimated time for the Russian army to mobilize on the German border. With France safely subdued, the German army would be quickly transferred to the Eastern front in time to meet the second Great Power army. The German plan would fail if the estimates of mobilization time for France, Russia, or Germany were substantially in error. As historian Ritter noted, "The enormous pressure of time is an essential feature of the whole Schlieffen Plan."[81]

The other European militaries also had developed plans against the states they assumed would be their enemies. Prewar Austria planned to mobilize its army along the Russian border, assuming that its back would be protected by Germany. Russia planned a more complex mobilization, in which half its army would be mobilized along the Austrian border while the other half was sent to the German border. France planned for a mobilization along its short border with Germany, neglecting the possibility that Germany would violate Belgian neutrality. Britain assumed that its role in a continental war would be primarily naval, if it were to have a role at all. British plans for army mobilization assumed an alliance with France against Germany, planning for a British landing at Mauberge on the French coast.

As events turned out, different mobilizations were needed to respond to actual events. Austria found it lacked the capacity to mobilize against Serbia while still retaining the potential for mobilization against Russia. The Russian General Staff contended that partial mobilization against Austria alone was "impracticable, and urge[d] that only a general mobilization can avoid upsetting the machine."[82] The French scrambled to mobilize along the Belgian border rather than the German one. And the British were forced to land at Mauberge due to prearranged plans, although in hindsight scholars have pointed to more fortuitous spots for contesting the German occupation of Belgium.

As Ropp notes, "Since each side could estimate the carrying power of the other's railways, strategy became a fairly exact guessing game."[83] The flaw lay not in the calculations but in the assumptions. Unfortunately for

---

[81] Ritter, *The Schlieffen Plan*, x.
[82] Basil H. Liddell Hart, *The Real War, 1914–1918*. Boston: Little, Brown and Company, 1930, 29.
[83] Ropp, *War in the Modern World*, 182–183.

the Europeans, the plans assumed enemies that did not fit with the political context of the day. Subsequent generations of scholars have criticized the shortsightedness of European military planners, since events suggested different locations at different strengths that might have been more effective.

In particular, the failure of the European Great Powers to plan for partial mobilization appears foolish. Yet given the assumption of pre–First World War planners that wars would be intense but short, the need for partial mobilizations seemed obscure in the plans that had been laid decades or years in advance. Nor could mobilization plans easily be changed midstream, given the number of men and supplies and the need for coordination of railway schedules. Partial mobilizations could not be undertaken without fouling up the plans for full mobilization. Changing the plans midstream would create confusion and dismay, creating maximum vulnerability to an attack by another state. Thus the Great Power armies found themselves mobilized at their prearranged destinations, despite political events that called for different arrangements.

Competition Leads to War

The unfolding of the First World War illustrates the competitiveness of Great Power dynamics outlined in Chapter 4. The eagerness of the Great Powers to enter the mobilization competition may have turned the possibility of war into a certainty. As one historian commented, "The lesson of 1870 was burnt into the mind of every staff officer in Europe: the nation which loses the mobilization-race is likely to lose the war."[84] Each Great Power military mobilized according to its prearranged plan, against the states predicted to be its enemies. In some cases, those plans called for mobilization against the wrong states – yet mobilization had to occur anyway. The vastness of the armies and the complexity of the mobilization plans of the day meant that, "once mobilization was begun, it could not be stopped or altered extensively without risking chaos."[85]

Scholars have developed a wide range of explanations for the onset of the First World War. Prominent in these explanations is the seemingly foolish rush to mobilize according to an interlocking timetable that

---

[84] Michael Howard, "Reflections on the First World War," *Studies in War and Peace*. New York: Viking Press, 1970, 105.
[85] Addington, *The Patterns of War since the Eighteenth Century*, 102.

was a consequence of previous alliances.[86,87] Van Evera remarks, "The spreading of World War I outward from the Balkans is often ascribed to the scope and rigidity of the Russian and German plans for mobilization."[88] As the European armies rushed to mobilize quickly, the initial Russian mobilization led to an "uncanny, somnambulant lockstep" in which the other Great Power militaries mobilized for war.[89] Liddell Hart laments, "In constructing their huge and cumbrous machines the general staffs of Europe had forgotten the first principle of war – elasticity."[90]

The European-wide consensus on the importance of mobilization speed coupled with the competitive tendencies of the Great Powers encouraged the rush to war. Once one Great Power mobilized, the other Great Powers hastened to mobilize before carefully thought out war aims could be formulated, or even before it was clear what was happening. As Turner notes, "The urgent need of both France and Germany for rapid mobilization and early offensive action by their eastern allies accelerated the whole tempo of the crisis of July 1914."[91]

In hindsight, scholars have argued that a pause for diplomatic communication might have avoided the Great War entirely.[92] Turner claims that "none of the rulers of the Great Powers really knew what they were fighting about in August 1914 … the crisis gathered momentum and the calculations of statesmen were overwhelmed by the rapid succession of events, the tide of emotion in the various capitals, and the inexorable demands of military planning."[93] However, the competitive dynamics of Great Power rivalries make it unsurprising that such a pause did not occur.

---

[86] Tuchman, *The Guns of August*; Taylor, *War by Time-Table*; Miles Kahler, "Rumors of War: The 1914 Analogy." *Foreign Affairs* 58 (1979–1980): 374–396; Luigi Albertini, *The Origins of the War of 1914*, volume 2. Oxford: Oxford University Press, 1952, 479–483.

[87] Trachtenberg, Levy, and Stevenson argue against the claim that mobilization led to an inadvertent slide into war. Instead, they argue that political decision-makers actively sought war. In any case, mobilization was seen as the first step toward war. Trachtenberg, "The Meaning of Mobilization in 1914"; Jack S. Levy, "Preferences, Constraints, and Choices in July 1914." *International Security* 15 (1990–1991): 151–186; David Stevenson, "Militarization and Diplomacy in Europe before 1914." *International Security* 22 (1997):125–161.

[88] Van Evera, "The Cult of the Offensive and the Origins of the First World War," 85.

[89] McNeill, *The Pursuit of Power*, 306.   [90] Liddell Hart, *The Real War*, 28.

[91] Leonard C. F. Turner, *Origins of the First World War*. New York: W. W. Norton and Company, 1970, 77.

[92] Snyder, "Civil-Military Relations and the Cult of the Offensive."

[93] Turner, *Origins of the First World War*, 112.

Other scholars have disputed the inadvertency of war, making the even stronger claim that all the European states understood that mobilization was a signal for the onset of war.[94] "A decision for general mobilization was quite consciously a decision for war," argues Trachtenberg.[95] This claim contrasts with historical experience, in which mobilization has frequently occurred as a diplomatic maneuver rather than serving as a practical declaration of war. Nor are all wars preceded by immediate mobilization – in the Second World War, the declarations of war by France and Britain preceded mobilization by several weeks.[96] Only in the First World War would mobilization be given such priority in decision-making. This priority was the result of the preceding decades of continent-wide agreement on the importance of mobilization speed as the critical factor for victory. Only given the consensus on the meaningfulness of mobilization, based on collective "lessons" learned from the Franco-Prussian War, could mobilization itself been read as a practical declaration of war.

Thus the "lockstep" mobilizations unfolded. Russia began mobilizing against Austria, as a diplomatic maneuver in support of Serbia. In response, Austria mobilized against Russia. This produced a dilemma for Germany: Germany could not support Austria by mobilizing against Russia without first defeating France, according to the Schlieffen Plan. Thus Germany went forward with its plan by invading Luxembourg and Belgium on its way to the French border. The violation of Belgian neutrality brought Britain into the war on the side of France, although prewar British plans required landing on the French coast rather than more usefully in Belgium. The French, who had waited with complacency while the diplomats bickered over the Austrian-Serbian conflict, hastened to mobilize on the Belgian rather the German border.

Historians have suggested a variety of alternate ways in which events might have turned out. For instance, Barbara Tuchman has argued that the need to keep mobilization schedules on track prevented German leaders from drawing back from the brink of war.[97] At the last moment, German leaders received diplomatic signals that France might countenance

---

[94] Trachtenberg, "The Meaning of Mobilization in 1914"; David Stevenson, "Militarization and Diplomacy in Europe before 1914." *International Security*, 22 (1997): 125–161.

[95] Trachtenberg, "The Meaning of Mobilization in 1914," 148.

[96] Basil H. Liddell Hart, *History of the Second World War*. New York: G. P. Putnam's Sons, 1970, 18, 32.

[97] Tuchman, *The Guns of August*.

a conflict between Russia and Germany without becoming involved.[98] This would have overturned the decades-long German assumption that a declaration of war against Russia would necessarily bring in France and create the feared two-front war. Instead, Germany would be left to fight a much simpler one-front war with Russia alone. However, German military commanders had only a few hours to abort their planned invasion of Luxembourg, which all realized would necessarily bring France into the war. According to Tuchman, German General Moltke argued strenuously against the recall of the army, on the grounds that once the mobilization had begun, altering it would cause chaos.[99] As a result of the need to stick to the mobilization schedule, the two-front war proceeded as planned, to Germany's ultimate detriment.

Scholars have also argued that alternate mobilization plans might have led to better outcomes. Had Austria mobilized against Serbia alone, the essentially domestic affair of the assassination of the Archduke might not have led to a world war. If the Russians had enacted a partial mobilization against Austria alone, a Russian mobilization against Austria would not have threatened Germany and might have forced Austria to back down. Had Germany been able to mobilize against Russia without involving France, conflict might have been confined to Eastern Europe. Yet the need for these partial mobilizations had not been foreseen in prewar plans, which had been based on the calculations of military power derived from the Franco-Prussian War.

In the end, these attempts to second-guess European decision-makers are fruitless; plans can always be improved with the advantage of hindsight. Regardless, the broad agreement on the critical value of mobilization was fundamental in the planning and onset of the First World War for all of the European militaries. Assumptions about the indicators of military capability led each state to make similar evaluations of the power of other states, influencing the diplomatic alliances of the age. Military plans for mobilization depended on the identification of a destination for the armies, so assumptions of the enemy were built into mobilization plans and could not be overturned at the last minute. Thus conformity to the dominant indicators led to the "lockstep" mobilization that characterized the First World War – although not in wars before or since. Subsequently, as militaries "learned" the lessons of the First World War, the importance of mobilization was downgraded in

---

[98] Taylor, *War by Time-Table*, disagrees with this claim.
[99] Trachtenberg, "The Meaning of Mobilization in 1914."

military planning, which turned toward defensive rather than offensive strategies for the Second World War.

CONCLUSION

To nineteenth-century theorists, the Franco-Prussian war seemed to uphold the principles of Napoleonic warfare. Even though the Prussians had won the war, they appeared to have done so using the time-honored tools of Napoleon: the rapid mobilization of a mass army using aggressive tactics to seize the offense. As a result, military scholars perceived the Franco-Prussian war as "short, offensive, and beneficial."[100] Military planners of the late nineteenth and early twentieth centuries drew on these "lessons" in their planning for the First World War. As Ropp comments

> [T]he theorists' picture of the next war was surprisingly like that of the wars of 1866 and 1870, which had been decided by a series of initial shocks from which the defeated armies had never recovered. Then, arguing from these historical examples, these theorists had built mass armies which seemed capable, to their builders, only of fighting the kind of war which had been posited by these historical examples.[101]

As argued in Chapter 3, this tendency to "learn" and take to heart the wrong lessons from past wars is normal rather than exceptional.

Following the experiences of both world wars, the nineteenth-century model of war was discarded. Scholars strongly criticized both French and German militaries for relying on the experiences of the Franco-Prussian War as the basis for their analyses. Instead, military thinkers in the interwar period took the First World War as the prototype of the new model of war. Michael Howard writes: "By the end of [1915] it was clear that the Napoleonic principles on which soldiers had been raised for a hundred years ... were no longer valid."[102] Military analysis and discussion after the First World War developed new and improved lessons that would be learned.

But as the following chapter will show, the lessons of the First World War were by no means as clear to interwar military theorists as they would be to later generations of scholars. Instead, the utility of recent technological innovations such as the tank, the airplane, and the U-boat would be hotly debated. Drawing on the often-ambiguous experiences of

[100] Snyder, "Civil-Military Relations and the Cult of the Offensive," 199.
[101] Ropp, *War in the Modern World*, 186.
[102] Howard, *War in European History*, 113.

the First World War, military theorists again planned for the wrong war in their preparations for the Second World War. This seeming inability of early twentieth-century thinkers to see what appears so obvious to twenty-first century eyes merely emphasizes the ambiguity of military planning. From the vantage point of the twentieth century model of war, technology obviously held the key to all military dilemmas – just as a sufficiently large concentration of men seemed to be the solution to military thinkers in the nineteenth century.

6

Tanks in the Second World War

Asking the cavalry to give up horses for trucks "was like asking a great musical performer to throw away his violin and devote himself in the future to the gramophone."[1]

Alfred Duff Cooper, British Secretary of State for War, in a speech to the House of Commons in 1935

This chapter extends arguments regarding ambiguity and the "lessons" of war to the more challenging case of military technology. Technology plays a central role in historical accounts of military affairs, and is often characterized as a material reality that compels the evolution of strategy and warfare. It is harder to see how ambiguity affects the adoption and use of technology. While some aspects of strategy, such as the "cult of the offensive," seem subjective and might be the product of national culture, the utility of guns and bombs and tanks appear obvious and inevitable. It seems evident, for instance, that the machine gun would trump horse cavalry. However, this supposedly clear technological reality had been debated for decades, fueled by counterexamples and ambiguity (see Chapter 3). This chapter draws on the case of tanks in the interwar period to further explore the ambiguities of military technology.

It is conventional to argue that technology shapes warfare. Scholars often point to technological innovation as an important exogenous factor that leads to the development of new military strategies, as well as new

---

[1] Quoted in Brian Bond and Williamson Murray, "The British Armed Forces, 1918–39." In *Military Effectiveness: Volume II: The Interwar Period*, edited by Allan R. Millett and Williamson Murray, 98–130. Boston: Allen and Unwin, 1988, 111.

technological countermeasures.[2] Battlefield experience with new technology provides an empirical basis for the development of optimal strategies. In the case of tanks, scholars have claimed that the initial impetus to develop the tank was driven by prior technological innovations such as the machine gun. As one historian puts it, "It was the trenches, and the need to destroy machine gun nests and to crush wire, that impelled the tank's subsequent development."[3]

This chapter questions this seemingly simple relationship between technological innovation and warfare. Just as planners have to make huge assumptions about the circumstances of future wars in order to devise plans and strategy, one must make similarly strong assumptions to develop and incorporate new technologies. Battlefield conditions vary enormously across wars. Military technologies that have optimal utility in the battlefields of northern France might prove useless in the jungles of southeast Asia. Technologies and strategies must be developed to work in a given terrain, against a specific type of enemy, and in the face of particular countermeasures. While technologies are objectively based on physical laws, the battlefield conditions in which a technology will be used can be quite variable. As described in Chapter 3, this variability creates ambiguity that is often resolved by reference to the Great Power hierarchy and through teleological lessons drawn from recent Great Power wars.

The tank debates of the interwar period exemplify the difficulties of learning from history even when it comes to technology. Tanks today have become such a part of the military landscape that it is hard to believe that their utility was ever questioned. Thus, it may come as a surprise that a virulent interwar debate erupted over tanks, which was only one part of the broader controversy over the role of technology in warfare in this period. In the end, the events of the Second World War resolved the debates not only on the tank but also on the importance of military technology generally.

Retracing the themes of Chapter 3, the development of tank strategy was hampered by tremendous ambiguity arising from: (1) the small number of comparable empirical cases to draw on, (2) the difficulty of generalizing

---

[2] William H. McNeill, *The Pursuit of Power: Technology, Armed Force, and Society since A.D. 1000.* Chicago: University of Chicago Press, 1982; J. F. C. Fuller, *Armament and History.* New York: Charles Scribner's Sons, 1945; Barry R. Posen, *The Sources of Military Doctrine: France, Britain, and Germany between the World Wars.* Ithaca: Cornell University Press, 1984.

[3] Hew Strachan, *European Armies and the Conduct of War.* London: George Allen and Unwin, 1983, 143.

from past events, and (3) the biases of teleology. Experiences with the tank were quite limited in the First World War. Amid this ambiguity, each Great Power "learned" somewhat different lessons regarding the uses and overall strategic importance of the tank.

The presence of multiple interpretations underscores the contingent nature of the lessons learned from history. As argued in Chapter 3, it is not difficult to develop a score of plausible interpretations for any particular military event. Thus it is not surprising that each of the major Great Powers – Britain, France, and Germany – developed their own interpretation of tanks despite drawing from the same set of empirical facts. Variants were also developed by the militaries of the United States, Soviet Union, Poland, Belgium, and others. Domestic politics scholars have partly explained this heterogeneity as arising from the various political and military cultures within each country.[4]

However, there was abrupt convergence and closure on the debate with the stunning German victory over France in 1940. The debate was immediately perceived as resolved in favor of German tank strategy. This battlefield success – itself a complex historical event, subject to many possible interpretations (as will be discussed) – was nevertheless universally seen as "proving" the merits of both the tank and German tank doctrine. The militaries of Europe immediately scrambled to reconfigure their tanks and strategy in the German mode. Interestingly, later difficulties of German tank strategy in Russia were largely ignored, since the tank debates had been "resolved" and the attention of military planners and theorists had moved to other issues.

The case of tanks during the interwar period highlights the ambiguities of military planning when applied to technology. The objective features of military technology may be empirically verifiable and stable, but there is a great deal of flexibility in the ways that technology is incorporated into military plans and tremendous variability in how technology performs under heterogeneous battle conditions.

---

[4] Deborah D. Avant, *Political Institutions and Military Change: Lessons from Peripheral Wars*. Ithaca: Cornell University Press, 1994; Elizabeth Kier, *Imagining War: French and British Military Doctrine between the Wars*. Princeton: Princeton University Press, 1997; Stephen Peter Rosen, *Winning the Next War: Innovation and the Modern Military*. Ithaca: Cornell University Press, 1991; Matthew Evangelista, *Innovation and the Arms Race; How the United States and the Soviet Union Develop New Military Technologies*. Ithaca: Cornell University Press, 1988; Kimberly Marten Zisk, *Engaging the Enemy: Organization Theory and Soviet Military Innovation, 1955–1991*. Princeton: Princeton University Press, 1993.

There is also substantial variation in the extent to which militaries focus on technology versus other military issues such as training and supply. Military planners have always paid some attention to technology. No general would go into battle with weapons that were a century out of date. But historically, military hardware was a secondary consideration. The Franco-Prussian War was widely seen as "proving" that strategy and resolve can trump even fairly significant differences in technology, as discussed in Chapter 5.

In contrast, the ultimate lesson taken from the Second World War would be that technology reigns as the supreme military factor, a lesson discussed in greater detail in Chapter 7. The sophistication of a country's technological arsenal has become enshrined as a key indicator of military power and the primary focus of postwar competition. As a result, technological determinism has come strongly into fashion, and military history books have been rewritten to stress the ways that technology drives the evolution of war. This chapter is intended as a corrective, unpacking the ambiguities of military technology and its strategic uses.

AMBIGUITY IN TECHNOLOGY

Retrospectively, the invention of the tank has been viewed as a necessary and utilitarian response to trench warfare. Yet during the interwar period, the merits of the tank were not nearly so apparent to military planners. Instead, debate among military planners on the most effective way to utilize tanks became quite heated, driven by the ambiguous and limited experiences of tanks under battlefield conditions. For tank opponents, the military and strategic vulnerabilities of tanks, as well as their dismal performance in the First World War, suggested that the tank was already outdated in the interwar period. For advocates, the speed and armor of tanks – potentially, if not yet in actuality – promised a new way of warfare.

Scholars have sought to identify the conditions under which optimal adoption of technological and organizational innovations takes place. Millett and Murray have edited volumes of case studies that attempt to ferret out the ideal conditions for effective innovation. Rosen claims that innovation depends on the efforts and support of senior officers within the military, while Posen argues that military mavericks supported by civilian politicians are responsible for innovation.[5] Other scholars,

---

[5] Rosen, *Winning the Next War.*

such as Evangelista and Roxborough, have focused on aspects of the organizational structures of the military such as decentralization, complexity, informality, interconnectedness, and autonomy that may promote innovation.[6]

However, history suggests that military innovation has rarely occurred in an optimal manner. Typically, military adoption of major technological innovations has been slow and fumbling. In the case of the tank, for instance, a storm of debate arose in the interwar period regarding the role tanks could play in modern war. The failure of militaries to straightforwardly and efficiently recognize the best uses of new technologies has often been explained away by pointing to military inertia or interservice rivalries in particular cases that prevented military minds from appreciating the value of new technologies.[7] By contrast, this chapter argues that the omnipresent ambiguity of military planning, described in prior chapters, helps explain the difficulties of adopting new technologies.

This section discusses the empirical facts that underlay the ambiguous utility of tanks that fueled the debates during the interwar period. In the First World War, the British, French, and German armies found themselves on the opposing sides of trenches that stretched for miles. Prewar plans for quick offensive strikes had failed to prepare for this situation, leaving commanders at a loss as to how to resolve the stalemate. Post hoc, scholars have claimed that tanks were a necessary solution to the problem of the trenches, allowing infantry to move forward in the face of machine gun fire. As Strachan argues, tanks were "the obvious technological novelty to recombine fire with movement."[8] Citino remarks that by the end of the First World War, "war without [tanks] was virtually inconceivable."[9]

Thus it may seem surprising that such a seemingly valuable piece of military hardware was bitterly controversial during the years that followed the First World War. Although there was general agreement following the First World War that tanks were a potentially useful part of the arsenal, there was little agreement on "how armies should organize,

---

[6] Evangelista, *Innovation and the Arms Race.*

[7] Rosen, *Winning the Next War*; Evangelista, *Innovation and the Arms Race*; Ian Roxborough, "Organizational Innovation: Lessons from Military Organizations." *Sociological Forum* 15 (2000): 367–372.

[8] Hew Strachan, *European Armies and the Conduct of War*, 143.

[9] Robert M. Citino, *Armored Forces: History and Sourcebook.* Westport: Greenwood Press, 1994, 25–26.

train, and equip themselves to best exploit the potential of the tank."[10] Opponents argued that the tank, only a few years old, was already obsolete. On the other hand, radical advocates of the tank envisioned entire mechanized armies roving the landscape. While the experiences of the First World War seemed to show that tanks were an important piece of military hardware, their ambiguous performance led to multiple plausible positions on tank strategy.

Skepticism about the utility of the tank was fueled by abundant empirical evidence of the tank's multiple vulnerabilities. In many respects, the drawbacks of the tank seemed insurmountable. During the First World War, tanks had frequently broken down, capsized, or required fuel, parts, and maintenance that were difficult to obtain under wartime conditions. During the Anschluss in 1938, for instance, the German tank commander had to telephone ahead to request that Austrian garages stay open so that the tanks would be able to refuel.[11] In early tests, prototype British tanks were unable to cross even a four-foot trench – "the tracks ... came off their frames, totally disabling the vehicle."[12] During the First World War, British tanks were incapable of crossing a sunken road during one battle, and caused "unnecessary infantry casualties" by following, rather than leading, the infantry advance.[13] French tanks in 1937 required at least six hours of daily maintenance, and tread durability was so low that "the machines were to be transported by train whenever possible."[14] Although tanks may have promised to bring mobility to the battlefield in theory, they frequently failed in practice.

An even more critical problem from the military standpoint was the vulnerability of tanks to defensive weapons. Tanks were easily disabled by artillery, mines, or bombs dropped from airplanes. Even in a period when tanks were a novelty and antitank weapons were primitive, "tank

---

[10] Thomas G. Mahnken, "Beyond Blitzkrieg: Allied Responses to Combined-Arms Armored Warfare during World War II." In *The Diffusion of Military Technology and Ideas*, edited by Emily O. Goldman and Leslie C. Eliason, 243–266. Stanford: Stanford University Press, 2003, 245.

[11] Strachan, *European Armies and the Conduct of War*, 164.

[12] J.P. Harris, *Men, Ideas and Tank: British Military Thought and Armoured Forces, 1903–1939*. Manchester: Manchester University Press, 1995, 29.

[13] Tim Travers, *How the War Was Won: Command and Technology in the British Army on the Western Front, 1917–1918*. London: Routledge, 1992, 114.

[14] Eugenia C. Kiesling, "Resting Uncomfortably on Its Laurels: The Army of Interwar France." In *The Challenge of Change: Military Institutions and New Realities, 1918–1941*, edited by Harold R. Winton and David R. Mets, 1–34. Lincoln: University of Nebraska Press, 2000, 21.

casualties rose as high as 50 per cent in battles toward the end of the [First World] war."[15] Early British tank theorists argued that the value of tanks lay in surprise, and "once the first tactical surprise was over it was not too difficult to find means of countering them."[16] During the Spanish Civil War in the late 1930s, for instance, "the tank fared badly: the terrain proved unfavourable, the tanks outstripped their support and they were then broken on the fire of anti-tank guns."[17] Critics of the tank claimed that it was simply "one of those times, periodic in the history of armor, in which ... antitank weapons had eclipsed the power of the tank."[18]

These weaknesses of the tank led to questions about appropriate tank strategy. While visions of tank-only mechanized regiments were "exhilarating," Howard noted, "they left a large number of questions unanswered."[19] Traditional military problems of communication and supply were aggravated by the hypothesized speed with which tank-only units might progress, outpacing the main body of the army. Another strategic problem was coordination between tank units and the rest of the army. Military planners had traditionally worried over the formation of a salient – a bulge in the front line that could be surrounded by enemy forces and cut off. Strategies in which tank units sped off leaving infantry behind foolishly seemed to create a salient on purpose, inviting enemy attack. Howard wonders, "Why should [tanks] not be surrounded and cut off? If tanks could make a breach in a front, could not tanks used in a counter-attack just as effectively seal it?"[20] Military historian Luttwak agrees, "the long, thin columns of armor would be exceedingly vulnerable to counter-attack from either side as they advanced inside enemy-held territory."[21]

Actual battle experience with tanks in the First World War was scanty, and the results were mixed at best. In the immediate postwar analysis, it was not obvious that tanks had been the savior of the battlefield in the First World War, as later histories would portray. Instead, "the performance of those ungainly vehicles in World War I was spotty ... the armored

---

[15] Brian Bond, *British Military Policy between the Two World Wars*. Oxford: Clarendon Press, 1980, 128.
[16] Michael Howard, *War in European History*. London: Oxford University Press, 1976, 131.
[17] Strachan, *European Armies and the Conduct of War*, 159.
[18] Citino, *Armored Forces*, 48.   [19] Howard, *War in European History*, 131.
[20] Howard, *War in European History*, 131.
[21] Edward N. Luttwak, *Strategy and Politics*. New Brunswick: Transaction Books, 1980, 301–302.

fighting vehicle of 1917 and 1918 offered its crews minimum vision, maximum discomfort, and general mechanical unreliability."[22] As Lieber notes, "The use of tanks in World War I provides little guidance as to their eventual impact on warfare."[23]

For instance, in the Battle of the Somme in 1917, the first battle in which tanks were used, the British sent in forty-nine tanks, but only eighteen – just over a third – actually made it to the front line.[24] Of the rest, "some broke down, or sank into craters and collapsing dugouts."[25] At the battle of Passchendaele, the terrain was a swampy morass, which proved disastrous "as tank after tank sank down into the horrible mud."[26]

The battle of Cambrai is typically cited as an example where tanks proved their utility, but even there the evidence was hardly clear. On the first day of the battle, over half the British tanks were "put out of action ... by fire, ditching, and mechanical failure."[27] Although 414 tanks began the battle, just over a third were still in action on the second day, and only 6 tanks – about 1 percent – were still functioning on the fifth day of a battle that continued for weeks.[28] Thus, there is justice in Howard's summation that the "most spectacular breakthrough of the war ... was not the work of tanks at all, but of infantry."[29] In the end, the utility of the tank was questionable to military analysts in the interwar period given its ambiguous performance in battles in the First World War.

Advocates for the tank could point to few successes. Instead, they had to rely partially on science fiction stories of the era, in which entire armored and motorized armies were pictured speeding off to battle. Tanks with the features specified in these scenarios did not actually exist. Interwar tank theorists such as Liddell Hart had to speculate on

---

[22] Williamson Murray, "Armored Warfare: The British, French, and German Experiences." In *Military Innovation in the Interwar Period*, edited by Williamson Murray and Allan R. Millett, 6–49. Cambridge: Cambridge University Press, 1996, 6.

[23] Keir A. Lieber, *War and the Engineers: The Primacy of Politics over Technology*. Ithaca: Cornell University Press, 2005, 101.

[24] David H. Zook, Jr. and Robin Higham. *A Short History of Warfare*. New York: Twayne, 1996, 279.

[25] Patrick Wright, *Tank: The Progress of a Monstrous War Machine*. London: Faber and Faber, 2000, 38.

[26] Citino, *Armored Forces*, 17.

[27] Theodore Ropp, *War in the Modern World*. Durham: Duke University Press, 1959, 250.

[28] Shelford Bidwell and Dominick Graham, *Fire-Power: British Army Weapons and Theories of War 1904–1945*. London: George Allen and Unwin, 1982, 137.

[29] Howard, *War in European History*, 131.

imaginary tanks in order to carry out the tank strategies envisioned. Yet deciding which attributes of tanks should be maximized depended on assumptions on the conditions under which they would be used. One of the major trade-offs of tanks was the thickness of the armor versus the speed at which they traveled. The optimal blend of armor versus speed depended on the type of weapons and terrain that planners envisioned the tank would be facing. Thus the British built lightly armored and speedy tanks for desert warfare in their colonies, while the Germans built heavily armored and slow tanks in anticipation of the terrain of the Russian front.

As Citino summarizes, "By 1939, European military doctrine was in a state of intense confusion," and even "twenty years of discussion and debate ... had not been enough to settle the basic questions about the nature of modern warfare."[30] Nevertheless, tank strategy was on the international military agenda, and the myriad views on tank strategy had broadly consolidated into three main positions. This attention to tanks in the interwar period was an important foundation for later interpretations of the German victory in 1940.

LEARNING FROM HISTORY

The ambiguous events of the First World War yielded significant controversy over the proper uses and strategies for the tank. To fill in these gaps in historical experience, militaries imagined different scenarios in which tanks would be utilized. Each Great Power military envisioned different strategies, generalizing different "lessons" from the First World War.

Elizabeth Kier brilliantly argues in her book, *Imagining War*, that the view of war envisioned by the military planners of each country was critical in determining the tank strategies that each adopted. Each Great Power military pictured a different replay of the First World War, drawing different negative lessons. The British imagined refraining from involvement in continental politics and consequently developed tanks primarily for colonial conditions. The French imagined a long war of attrition, in which central coordination would prevent stalemate. The Germans imagined a quick offensive war in which tanks would provide the mobility necessary to avoid stalemate. Each Great Power developed its tank strategy to reflect this broader military vision.[31]

[30] Robert M. Citino, *Quest for Decisive Victory: From Stalemate to Blitzkrieg in Europe, 1899–1940*. Lawrence: University Press of Kansas, 2002, 251.
[31] Luttwak, *Strategy and Politics*, 295.

Britain

Although the British army had invented the tank in 1915 with the aim of breaking the trench stalemate on the Western front, the dominant view in the British military in the interwar period was quite negative. On one hand, the British military culture favored horsemanship and the gentlemanly culture of the cavalry over technological prowess.[32] On the other hand, the war-weary public and government, hoping never to fight another major European war again, slowed tank development by withholding resources from the military. Thus by 1939, the British military had shifted from being the innovator of the tank to holding the most conservative tank strategy among the Great Powers.

The conservative position on the tank in the interwar period regarded the tank as "merely a passing solution for a problem that was now past – that of breaking a trench-deadlock."[33] In Britain, "the tank was seen ... as no more than a specialized trench-crossing vehicle, a piece of siege machinery."[34] The former British Director of Trench Warfare and Supplies claimed in 1919: "The tank proper was a freak. The circumstances which called it into existence were exceptional and not likely to recur. If they do, they can be dealt with by other means."[35]

This view was not due merely to the thick-headedness of the British officers, but first-hand experience with the vulnerability of the tank to antitank defenses. During the First World War, even those who spearheaded the development of the tank considered it primarily useful for a single surprise attack that would break the trench deadlock. Once there was general awareness of the tank, even the most enthusiastic tank proponents feared that antitank defense measures such as land mines and artillery would be relatively easy to contrive.[36] Even British tank theorist Liddell Hart, one of the strongest proponents of tanks, "believed that modern defensive weapons had become sufficiently strong to ward off attacks by tanks, no matter how thick the armor or heavy the vehicle." As a consequence of this line of thought, British development of the tank prioritized its mobility over armor, developing

[32] Kier, *Imagining War*. Also see Elizabeth Kier, "Culture and Military Doctrine: France Between the Wars." *International Security* 19 (1995): 65–93.
[33] Basil H. Liddell Hart, *Tanks, Volume One 1914–1939*. London: Cassell, 1959, 201.
[34] Luttwak, *Strategy and Politics*, 295.
[35] Quoted in Bond, Brian, *British Military Policy between the Two World Wars*, 129–130.
[36] Harris, *Men, Ideas and Tank*, 53.

a line of "light" tanks that, as events turned out, "would prove to be nearly worthless when the shooting started."[37]

This view of the tank fit with the broader British vision for future wars. British decision-makers hoped to avoid trench deadlock by avoiding involvement in European wars entirely. During the interwar period British political leaders did not foresee a major European war in the near future. Indeed, British policy was that the British army "would *never, under any circumstances,* find employment on the continent again."[38] Britain did not begin rearming for a major continental war until 1938 – far behind France and Germany. As a result, at the onset of the Second World War, "the army had not tank in production, its artillery was antiquated, its antitank gun obsolete, and its vehicular support inadequate."[39]

Instead, British tanks were developed for colonial warfare, especially the deserts of northern Africa. These conditions would require light and speedy tanks that would not face the machine guns and trench warfare conditions of European battlefields. Liddell Hart writes: "As soldiers hoped that trench warfare would never return, they were apt to argue that the tank would have no place in a war of the future."[40] Several historians attribute the "palpable weakness" of British tank doctrine "not least because the army had spent the 1930s preparing to fight not in Europe, but in the colonies" where tanks would have "only limited value."[41] As a result, tank development was starved.[42]

Only a limited number of other European militaries subscribed to the British position – notably Poland, in which apocryphal tales claimed that "Polish cavalry, their lances at the ready," were "actually charging German tanks" during the German invasion of Poland in 1939, with unhappy results.[43] Liddell Hart notes that at the outset of the Second World War, "Poland's leaders still pinned their trust to the value of a large mass of horsed cavalry, and cherished a pathetic belief in the possibility of carrying out cavalry charges."[44] As the swift German defeat of Poland seemed to have demonstrated to observers in 1939, cavalry was no match for German blitzkrieg tank tactics. Yet since Poland was not a

---

[37] Citino, *Armored Forces*, 48. [38] Murray, "Armored Warfare," 12, italics in original.
[39] Murray, "Armored Warfare," 11. [40] Liddell Hart, *Tanks*, 201.
[41] Strachan, *European Armies and the Conduct of War*, 157.
[42] Citino, *Armored Forces*, 32. [43] Citino, *Armored Forces*, 68.
[44] Basil H. Liddell Hart, *History of the Second World War*. New York: G.P. Putnam's Sons, 1970, 20–21.

Great Power, its military defeat was not seen as conclusively demonstrating the strength of the German tank strategy.

France

The French doctrine of the interwar period envisaged the tank primarily as support for infantry.[45] Drawing on the lessons "learned" from the First World War, the French believed that tanks could not function without infantry support. Thus French military theorists developed the concept of the methodical battle, in which each component was carefully orchestrated by the high command rather than left to the initiative of local officers. Defensive rather than offensive tactics were favored. According to this model, the tank was worked into the battle plan as a supporting actor rather than the leading star.

The French viewed the tank as an important military technology, but believed tanks should work in conjunction with the infantry and artillery rather than as an independent force.[46] This view arose from a consideration of the strengths and weaknesses of the tank in the interwar period. On the one hand, the lessons of the First World War seemed to suggest that tanks could be used to gain ground but could not hold it.[47] On the other hand, the infantry could occupy ground and destroy antitank weapons, but could not advance in the face of machine guns and emplaced artillery. Considering this, it seemed logical that careful coordination of infantry and tanks could mitigate the weaknesses of each. Tanks were to be closely synchronized with infantry by centralized command. One historian describes the French battle plan as a "step-by-step battle, with units obediently moving between phase lines and adhering to strictly scheduled timetables ... centralized control was necessary to coordinate the actions of numerous subordinate units."[48] According to this plan, tanks "were not to be unshackled from the confines of the methodical battle."[49]

---

[45] Luttwak, *Strategy and Politics*, 296.

[46] Robert A. Doughty, "The French Armed Forces, 1918–40." In *Military Effectiveness: Volume II: The Interwar Period*, edited by Allan R. Millett and Williamson Murray, 39–69. Boston: Allen and Unwin, 1988, 56.

[47] Eugenia C. Kiesling, *Arming against Hitler: France and the Limits of Military Planning*. Lawrence: University Press of Kansas, 1996, 154.

[48] Robert Allan Doughty, *The Seeds of Disaster: The Development of French Army Doctrine, 1919–1939*. Hamden: Archon, 1985, 4.

[49] Kiesling, *Arming Against Hitler*, 166.

The French concept of battle resulted from the lesson that the French had "learned" from the experiences of the First World War that the defensive was stronger than the offensive. The French believed that "as a result of having learned the lessons of the Great War, [France] had mastered the keys to victory in any future war."[50] The trench warfare of the First World War was widely interpreted by the international military community as showing that modern firepower gave the advantage to the defense. French military thinkers blamed the emphasis on offensive doctrines in the First World War for "catastrophic defeat in 1917, a defeat that had almost broken the army and nearly resulted in the defeat of France."[51] As a result, French tank doctrine was conceptualized as primarily defensive, designed to prevent a disastrous breakthrough rather than to win the war.[52]

The French army put great energy into innovation in the wake of its perceived poor performance during the First World War. French preparations for the Second World War were based on expectations of a reprise of the First World War, beginning with a German attack through Belgium and potentially ending in trench deadlock, as before. To prevent this, French military planners had replaced the "cult of the offensive," which had been blamed for the high casualties of the Western Front, for a doctrine that essentially represented a cult of the defensive.[53] During the interwar period, France adopted "a 'long war' strategy designed to bring victory over Germany only after several years of struggle."[54]

As events occurred, however, the blitzkrieg tactics of the German tanks in the Second World War did not follow a reprise of the First World War. Consequently, French preparations proved fruitless. "Unfortunately," wrote one historian, although "France's forces were fairly efficiently tailored for the type of strategy envisaged by the political military leaders ... its chance of success rested completely on the Germans doing

---

[50] Ernest R. May, *Strange Victory: Hitler's Conquest of France*. New York: Hill and Wang, 2000, 462.
[51] Williamson Murray, "Armored Warfare: The British, French, and German Experiences." In *Military Innovation in the Interwar Period*, edited by Williamson Murray and Allan R. Millett, 6–49. Cambridge: Cambridge University Press, 1996, 32.
[52] Eugenia C. Kiesling, "Resting Uncomfortably on Its Laurels: The Army of Interwar France." In *The Challenge of Change: Military Institutions and New Realities, 1918–1941*, edited by Harold R. Winton and David R. Mets, 1–34. Lincoln: University of Nebraska Press, 2000.
[53] Kier, *Imagining War*.　[54] Kiesling, "Resting Uncomfortably on Its Laurels," 5.

as expected."[55] Regrettably for the French, random events led the Germans to diverge from French expectations.

Germany

The German military represented the most radical position on tank strategy.[56] Tanks would form the backbone of a mechanized army, moving swiftly across the battlefield at the speed of motors rather than men. No longer would infantry be the "queen of the battlefield."[57] Instead, military technologies such as the tank or the airplane would dominate. This radical view was as much rhetoric – or even fantasy – than reality. In fact, the actual German army was more similar to the French model than it was different. Nevertheless, as represented in the interwar debates and particularly in the outcome of the Battle of France, German tank strategy has been portrayed as fundamentally opposite that of the French.

The radical view saw the tank as "the weapon of an entirely new branch, and eventually of a new army, entirely mechanized or at least motorized." As Luttwak notes, in their grandest visions, proponents of the radical view envisioned tanks as enabling "a new kind of war ... the war of large-scale maneuver, swift, decisive and much less destructive of life than the European wars of the recent past."[58] The pure-tank perspective, which was not represented by any actual army, envisioned tank-only units in which other arms of the military, "particularly the infantry, were unnecessary encumbrances that would only hinder tank units in the accomplishment of their missions."[59]

In practice, the German panzer units practiced a milder version of tank doctrine in which tanks were combined with motorized infantry, artillery, and strategic air support.[60] These units were able to move across the

---

[55] Doughty, "The French Armed Forces, 1918–40," 53.

[56] James S. Corum, *The Roots of Blitzkrieg: Hans von Seeckt and German Military Reform.* Lawrence: University Press of Kansas, 1992; James S. Corum, "A Comprehensive Approach to Change: Reform in the German Army in the Interwar Period." In *The Challenge of Change: Military Institutions and New Realities, 1918–1941*, edited by Harold R. Winton and David R. Mets, 35–73. Lincoln: University of Nebraska Press, 2000.

[57] Russell F. Weigley, *The Age of Battles: The Quest for Decisive Warfare from Breitenfeld to Waterloo.* Bloomington: Indiana University Press, 1991.

[58] Luttwak, *Strategy and Politics*, 297.

[59] Harold R. Winton, "Tanks, Votes, and Budgets: The Politics of Mechanization and Armored Warfare in Britain, 1919–1939." In *The Challenge of Change: Military Institutions and New Realities, 1918–1941*, edited by Harold R. Winton and David R. Mets, 74–107. Lincoln: University of Nebraska Press, 2000, 93.

[60] Citino, *Armored Forces*, 53.

landscape at motorized speed rather than the traditional speed of a marching army. Nevertheless, they were not the tank-only units of the radical vision. Similar to the French vision, the German military planned to allow tanks to initially take ground, breaking through the enemy front lines. Infantry would follow, holding the territory gained by the tanks. As with the French, "the Germans thought about tanks only in the context of a combined arms force – never alone."[61] However, German tank commanders were granted much greater independence and initiative from infantry than was allowed by the French high command.[62]

The Germans had also prepared for a replay of the First World War. The attraction of the tank from the German point of view lay in its promise of a quick, offensive war. As with the other combatants, the Germans believed that the historical "lessons" on the use of the tank and the airplane from the First World War would prevent a reoccurrence of the trench deadlock.[63] One historian suggests that "the Germans saw mechanization as a way to restore the operational possibilities" of the Franco-Prussian War of 1870.[64] Unlike the French, the German military believed that tanks promised to avert a lengthy war of attrition, making possible more decisive strikes against French and Soviet borders than had occurred in the First World War.

Yet despite extensive preparations, Germany was also surprised by the way the war actually turned out. Based on its prewar plans, Germany was unprepared for a long war.[65] Consequently, Germany did not foresee the need for technological innovation during the war itself – basic research on radar was stopped in 1940 and not renewed until 1942, and Germany was far behind the United States in the development of the atomic bomb.[66] Moreover, German political and military leaders had not expected that the German invasion of Poland would lead to British and French declarations of war, thus the onset of the war itself came as a shock.[67] As Liddell Hart writes, "The last thing that Hitler wanted to

---

[61] Citino, *Quest for Decisive Victory*, 194.   [62] Citino, *Armored Forces*, 54.

[63] Bernard Brodie and Fawn M. Brodie, *From Crossbow to H-bomb*. Bloomington: Indiana University Press, 1973.

[64] Citino, *Quest for Decisive Victory*, 195.

[65] Manfred Messerschmidt, "German Military Effectiveness between 1919 and 1939." In *Military Effectiveness: Volume II: The Interwar Period*, edited by Allan R. Millett and Williamson Murray, 218–255. Boston: Allen and Unwin, 1988, 227.

[66] Brodie, *From Crossbow to H-bomb*, 201.

[67] Basil H. Liddell Hart, *History of the Second World War*. New York: G.P. Putnam's Sons, 1970.

produce was another great war. His people, and particularly his generals, were profoundly fearful of any such risk – the experiences of World War I had scarred their minds."[68]

Other militaries also experimented with radical tank strategies, similar to the German position. Both the United States and the Soviet Union had all-mechanized tank units in the 1930s but disbanded them in favor of the French model. The British had an Experimental Task Force that dabbled with the idea of an all-mechanized force, but the British government only authorized the creation of a tank brigade in 1939, as the Second World War was about to begin. The French also had their "prophets" of the tank, such as General Estienne and Charles de Gaulle (later to become president), who have been credited with holding the radical position within the French military.[69] These prophets had encouraged French interwar experimentation with mechanized units along the lines suggested by the radical position held by British and German theorists.[70] However, even the German tank enthusiasts found de Gaulle's ideas "fantastical."[71] By the end of the interwar period, international consensus was drifting toward the adoption of the moderate French tank doctrine.

The Great Power Hierarchy and Collective Learning

By the end of the interwar period, the international tank debates had not been fully resolved. Nevertheless, militaries cannot live with ambiguity for long. Despite the lack of clear-cut answers, militaries had to draw up plans, build tanks, and train recruits. Floundering in ambiguity would not improve preparations for the next European war. Consequently, the European militaries had gradually moved closer to the tank strategies of France, the leading Great Power military in this era, since Germany had recently been defeated and Britain had stepped back from the continent. In that context, France developed a military force that was quickly becoming the envy of the world.

Attention to the Great Power hierarchy and the process of collective learning within the European military community help explain common trends in tank doctrine. Scholars in the domestic politics tradition have recognized the ambiguity that planners face by focusing on the debates

---

[68] Liddell Hart, *History of the Second World War*, 6.   [69] Citino, *Armored Forces*, 57.
[70] Kier, *Imagining War*, 43.   [71] Kiesling, *Arming against Hitler*, 158.

that underlie the adoption of new technologies.[72] These scholars would not be surprised that controversies arose in tank doctrine, since the available empirical evidence allowed a multiplicity of interpretations. The domestic politics perspective highlights divergence, discrediting the notion that optimal tank strategies were self-evident. Yet the military domain also demonstrated significant convergence on military technologies and strategies. European militaries first shifted toward French tank doctrine, then later hastily switched toward the German model after the defeat of France. Domestic politics scholars have been unable to explain the broader commonalities among the political and strategic postures of European armies.

As argued in previous chapters, debates tend to be resolved within the broader international military community rather than separately within each nation-state. Militaries display a strong tendency to adopt the practices of the leading Great Powers. This tendency toward conformity is driven by the teleological assumption that battle outcomes provide the ultimate test of the quality of military practice. Since the top Great Power is perceived as having proven its worth on the battlefield, militaries flock to follow its example. Thus there tends to be a general shift over time in the direction of the practices of the Great Power at the top of the military hierarchy. Militaries trust that the leading Great Power can peer farther into the ambiguous mists of military planning than their own domestic leaders can. Consequently, states tend to converge around the military practices of the Great Power at the top of the hierarchy.

The tank debates illustrate this process of collective learning in the international military community. The tank debates in the interwar period were a flourishing subject for discussion in international military forums. Tank theorists of all nationalities read the works of key British, French, and German military theorists. Indeed, it is generally recognized that German blitzkrieg tactics were originally based on the ideas of British theorists such as Liddell Hart.[73] German General Guderian, although "not one to give others credit," admitted in his memoirs that the British field manual on tanks was their "basic primer for developing armored warfare." Other intellectual debts were also apparent. For instance, the work of British

---

[72] Avant, *Political Institutions and Military Change*; Kier, *Imagining War*; Rosen, *Winning the Next War*; Evangelista, *Innovation and the Arms Race*; Zisk, *Engaging the Enemy*.

[73] This claim has generated its own controversy among historians; see John J. Mearsheimer, *Liddell Hart and the Weight of History*. Ithaca: Cornell University Press, 1988; Harris, *Men, Ideas and Tank*.

theorist Martel was translated and distributed to German tank officers.[74]
The tank treatise (*Achtung! Panzer!*) by German commander Guderian was
translated by the French military and accompanied French scrutiny of the
German tank units.[75]

Beyond reading the same set of tank theorists, the international community drew from the same body of empirical evidence, including the tank
battles in the First World War, incidents during the Spanish Civil War, and
peacetime tank exercises of the various militaries. The Americans examined Japanese, German, and British military experiments.[76] The French
paid close attention to the British experiment in creating a fully mechanized tank brigade in 1927.[77] The Germans observed Soviet tank maneuvers in 1936.[78] The French also paid attention to German tank workings,
"aware of what was happening across the Rhine and not particularly
alarmed by it." Kiesling claims that French analysis found substantial
similarities between the French and German tank doctrines."[79]

As one of the main victors of the First World War, the position of
the French army at the top of the Great Power hierarchy supported the
widespread perception that it was the best, most prepared army in the
world in the interwar period. The French had "devoted more efforts and
resources to analyzing advanced weapons, such as the tank, than any
other army." The French army placed a high value on the tank in the
interwar period, and "firmly believed that the tank was one of the most
important weapons introduced during World War I."[80] Not only did the
French army boast more tanks than the German army in 1940, the French
tanks were on the whole "superior in speed, armor, and firepower."[81]
Additionally, French antitank weapons "used the best available technology and were capable of extraordinary velocity and penetrating power."[82]
By contrast, both Britain and especially the United States had retreated
from the European stage – to varying degrees eschewing the identity of a
Great Power (see Chapter 2).

[74] Murray, "Armored Warfare: The British, French, and German Experiences," 41, 24.
[75] Kier, *Imagining War*, 47.
[76] Thomas G. Mahnken, *Uncovering Ways of War: U.S. Intelligence and Foreign Military Innovation, 1918–1941*. Ithaca: Cornell University Press, 2002.
[77] Général d'Armée André Beaufre, "Liddell Hart and the French Army, 1919–1939." In *The Theory and Practice of War*, edited by Michael Howard, 129–142. Bloomington: Indiana University Press, 1965, 135.
[78] Citino, *Quest for Decisive Victory*, 212.
[79] Kiesling, *Arming against Hitler*, 167, 170.   [80] Doughty, *The Seeds of Disaster*, 5, 136.
[81] Murray, "Armored Warfare," 32.
[82] Doughty, "The French Armed Forces, 1918–40," 45.

By the end of the interwar period, most states, such as Sweden and Italy, had moved toward adoption of the French model of tank organization.[83] Even countries that had experimented with independent tank corps, such as the United States and the Soviet Union, had moved much closer to the French model by the 1930s.[84] Proponents of the "moderate" French view of the tank were also evident in the British and German militaries. Although heterogeneity was still evident among European tank strategies by 1939, a consensus was emerging.

Indeed, the difference between the Great Power tank strategies may have been more obvious in hindsight than it was to interwar military observers. By 1939, both the British and German militaries were closer to the French than their experimentation in previous years might have predicted. According to Kiesling, the French and German armies "continued to manifest similar views on the use of armor [tanks] even at the end of the decade [1930s]." Interwar French and American analysts, who scrutinized the differences in French and German tank organization, found the differences small. One German officer suggested in 1937 "that Germany could learn from the French because of their greater experience with the tanks." French analysis suggested substantial similarities between the French and German tank doctrines, and that "[o]n the whole, studying German doctrine reinforced French confidence in their own methods."[85] As Kiesling notes, "Hindsight encourages the historian to stress every indication of French stagnation or of German innovation; many contemporaries, however, did not discern Germany's emerging military supremacy over France."[86]

This consensus was to shift dramatically with the German victory over France.

TELEOLOGY LEADS TO CLOSURE

The interwar debates on technology were conclusively settled by interpretations of the events of the Second World War. The Fall of France, the

---

[83] Richard M. Ogorkiewicz, *Armor: A History of Mechanized Forces*. New York: Frederick A. Praeger, 1960.

[84] Ronald Spector, "The Military Effectiveness of the US Armed Forces, 1919–39." In *Military Effectiveness: Volume II: The Interwar Period*, edited by Allan R. Millett and Williamson Murray, 70–97. Boston: Allen and Unwin, 1988, 83; Mary R. Habeck, *Storm of Steel: The Development of Armor Doctrine in Germany and the Soviet Union, 1919–1939*. Ithaca: Cornell University Press, 2003; David. E. Johnson, *Fast Tanks and Heavy Bombers*. Ithaca: Cornell University Press, 1998.

[85] Kiesling, *Arming against Hitler*, 167, 170.

[86] Kiesling, *Arming against Hitler*, 168, 170, 187.

Battle of Britain, and the Pacific War were perceived post hoc as incontrovertible evidence supporting the technological model of war. In the case of tanks, the debate was to be resolved by the stunningly decisive victory of German tank forces over the French army in 1940. As one group of military historians note, "For many students of warfare the success of the blitzkrieg was a vindication of the radical doctrines of the apostles of mobility and of the tank."[87] The outcome of the competition between these two rival Great Powers was seen as self-evidently proclaiming the superiority of German tank doctrine.

Scholarly accounts portray conclusive battles as providing hard evidence supporting the utility of the tank. Such a view might be reasonable to the extent that one battle is quite similar to the next. Yet the battlefield is far from the controlled conditions of a scientific experiment. Conditions vary wildly from one battle to another, and multiple causes for victory might reasonably be posited in each case. The effectiveness of a particular technology is but one variable in any clash between militaries. To the extent that critical conditions vary in other battles, those factors that proved decisive in one encounter may be unimportant or even disabling in another. Thus effective learning cannot reasonably take place through the observation of a single battle.

However, the bias of teleology encourages the illogical conclusion that battle is the ultimate arbiter of debates and the standard of military success. German tank units decisively defeated the French army in 1940. Whether this victory was due to effective tank strategy – versus alternate factors or sheer luck – is very difficult to determine. Indeed, multiple causes, including the personalities of the German and French commanders, the logistics of the terrain, and the classic military virtue of surprise, were likely critical factors in the outcome. From a logical standpoint, the focus on German tank doctrine as the primary explanation for the victory was arbitrary. But, given pressure to plan, militaries routinely make these sorts of overgeneralizations.

Tanks in the Battle of France

According to the standards of the international military community in 1939, France had the best army in the world, as well as the largest and most advanced tank force. The French declaration of 1939 that "we shall

---

[87] Bidwell and Graham, *Fire-Power*, 210.

win because we are stronger" was taken as simple fact, not only by the French but by most of the rest of the world as well.[88] "Churchill himself had described [the French army] as 'the most perfectly trained and faithful mobile force in Europe.'"[89] The expectation of the military community at the onset of the Second World War was that France and her allies would eventually defeat Germany – possibly after a lengthy and indecisive struggle as occurred in the First World War. After Britain and France had declared war against Germany in 1939, the war idled along without major confrontation among the Great Power states, lending support to predictions of a long conflict.

In May 1940, however, seven German panzer (tank) units broke through the French line in the Ardennes in northeastern France – a region that French military planners had previously assessed as impassable to tanks.[90] The main body of the French army was massed on the Belgian border futilely waiting for a replay of German strategy in the First World War. Fooled into believing the attack in the Ardennes was a feint, the French army moved too slowly to seal the initial breach. The German tanks sped to Paris, catching the bulk of the French army and only narrowly failing to prevent the British army from retreating at Dunkirk. Six days after the German attack, "the great French army seemed on the verge of collapse."[91] After a few more weeks of fighting, France was forced to surrender to Germany, to the shock of the entire world.

Following the French surrender, there were no lengthy debates interpreting the implications for tank strategy. Instead, the European militaries immediately began to switch over to German-style tank doctrine, organization, and hardware – a difficult feat in the midst of war. The German victory was seen throughout the international community as proving the value of German tank strategy. Although these "lessons" might seem obvious and inevitable, the rapid rethinking following the Battle of France was actually built on a foundation that in turn was built in the interwar period. Decades of debate about tanks – and the fact that major doctrines were specifically associated with France and Germany – set the stage for new lessons to be drawn. The fall of France thus resolved the tank debates of the interwar period.

---

[88] Doughty, "The French Armed Forces," 39.
[89] Liddell Hart, *History of the Second World War*, 17.
[90] Kiesling, *Arming against Hitler*, 177.
[91] Julian Jackson, *The Fall of France*. Oxford: Oxford University Press, 2003, 10.

Counterfactual History

The tendency to draw lessons from victors often proves irresistible. Yet if one adopts a probabilistic view of the French defeat as reflecting complex contingencies rather than foreordained by German superiority, different interpretations are plausible. In particular, alternative interpretations of the German victory in 1940 have very different implications for the utility of the tank. As one might expect, a diverse array of explanations have been put forth for the French defeat, ranging from military incompetence to public lethargy. If the German invasion of France were to be replayed multiple times, German victory might be recognized as a probabilistic outcome rather than an inevitable one. Had the radical tank strategies of Germany failed in this battle, military theorists would likely have viewed the outcome as vindicating the French vision of the tank instead.

One alternate explanation for the Fall of France interprets German tanks as one important factor but not the sole cause of victory. Instead, as Jackson argues, "The greatest German weapon in 1940 was not overwhelming military superiority but surprise."[92] Bidwell and Graham agree: "[I]n 1940 the German panzers obtained their effect more by moral effect than by fire-power."[93] The surprise was evident for both the Germans and the French: "In his memoirs, even Guderian characterized his panzer corps' success ... as 'almost a miracle,'" pointing to moments in which success balanced on "razor-thin margins and, in some cases, by sheer luck."[94] Moreover, this surprise concentrated German forces at a tactically weak point in the French defense – a classic military goal.[95]

In this account, the key decision was not the German tank strategy, but Hitler's decision to alter the original German war plan, which had initially featured a replay of the invasion of Belgium of the First World War. This change in plans was due in large part to a random chance event. The original German war plans called for the same opening in the Second World War as in the First – an invasion through Belgium – for which the French had also prepared. Postwar accounts have criticized the French for this foolish expectation of a replay, yet it would have been borne out if not for an utterly random occurrence. Until only a few months before the

[92] Jackson, *The Fall of France*, 219.   [93] Bidwell and Graham, *Fire-Power*, 212.
[94] Cited in May, *Strange Victory*, 451.
[95] Strachan, *European Armies and the Conduct of War*, 166; W. Heinemann, "The Development of German Armoured Forces 1918–40." In *Armoured Warfare*, edited by J. P. Harris and F. H. Toase, 51–69. New York: St. Martin's Press, 1990, 68.

invasion of France, German military plans were to commence with a sweep through Belgium into the northern part of France in a modified version of German strategy of the First World War. Strachan summarizes: "[T]o all intents and purposes, the opening days of 1914 were to be re-enacted in a vast wheel through Belgium."[96] British and French planners, drawing on the same assumptions, had made similar calculations and consequently were waiting on the border of Belgium when the German offensive commenced. May speculates that "the most likely outcome would have been a duel of forces in fixed positions not unlike that of the Great War."[97] Liddell Hart also predicts: "[T]he old plan would almost certainly have failed to produce the fall of France."[98]

However, the planned German invasion through Belgium in January 1940 was cancelled because of extremely cold weather.[99] A subsequent accident was to throw German plans into disarray. Later in January, a German plane carrying the full set of war plans was forced down over Belgium. Although there was reason to believe that the pilot had managed to destroy the war plans before capture, Hitler feared that the Allies now knew of his plans.[100] This event gave impetus to his decision to switch to an alternate plan – the Manstein plan – that envisaged German units moving through the Ardennes at the center of France.[101] Under this new plan, the German attack in Belgium became a feint. The main body of the attack, including seven German tank units, was centered on the eastern border of France. The French, with the bulk of their forces on the Belgian border, would hopefully realize too late that the northern attack was a feint, and would be unable to stem the German attack once it had crossed the Meuse River.[102] Liddell Hart argues that "it was only after the air accident of January 10, when Hitler was looking for a new plan, that Manstein's proposal, thus brought back into this mind, began to get a hold. Even then a month passed before he swung definitely in favour of it."[103]

[96] Strachan, *European Armies and the Conduct of War*, 164.
[97] May, *Strange Victory*, 451.   [98] Liddell Hart, *History of the Second World War*, 40.
[99] Ronald E. Powaski, *Lightning War: Blitzkrieg in the West, 1940*. Hoboken: John Wiley and Sons, 2003, 34.
[100] Liddell Hart, *History of the Second World War*, 37.
[101] John J. Mearsheimer, "Hitler and the Blitzkrieg Strategy." In *The Use of Force: Military Power in International Politics*, edited by Robert J. Art and Kenneth N. Waltz, 152–166. Lanham: Rowman and Littlefield, 2009.
[102] Strachan, *European Armies and the Conduct of War*, 166.
[103] Liddell Hart, *History of the Second World War*, 39.

It has been argued that the Fall of France was nearly as much of a surprise to the German High Command as to the French. The success of the German panzer corps was not based on a well-developed strategy endorsed by the German general staff, but rested importantly on the initiative of its commander, Heinz Guderian. Indeed, one plausible explanation for the German victory offered by Kier focuses on the greater independence of commanders in the German military compared to the French, rather than the technological features of the tank.[104] Liddell Hart claims that, in general, "The heads of the German Army had little faith in the prospects of the offensive, which they had unwillingly launched on Hitler's insistence."[105] Instead, the fast pace of the panzers was extremely upsetting to the German High Command – to such an extent that Hitler imposed a two-day halt on the advance of the panzer units, just as the French defense had been nullified.[106] Guderian was even "momentarily" relieved of command, although fortunately for the Germans he was reinstated later that same night.[107] One historian characterizes the French defeat as occurring "partly because the German High Command temporarily lost control of the battle."[108] As Liddell Hart sums up, "Yet but for [Guderian's] 'offence' in driving so fast the invasion would probably have failed."[109]

Nevertheless, the success of the *blitzkrieg* in France led to the enshrinement in German tank doctrine for the rest of the war. It is noteworthy, however, that German tank strategy did not have the same utility in battles on different terrain against well-equipped opposition. Citino points out that in the ensuing years of the Second World War, "when both sides were mechanized, *Blitzkrieg* ground to a halt."[110] In these later battles, the side with the greatest number of tanks – as well as air support – prevailed, since tactical surprise had been lost.

History also shows that the German application of the blitzkrieg tactics that had worked against France failed miserably against the Soviet Union. "[F]or the German army 'the [French] campaign was an improvised but successful Blitzkrieg while that against Russia was a planned but unsuccessful one.'"[111] There are many possible theories of why the German offensive in the Soviet Union failed, ranging from poor weather to poor

---

[104] Kier, *Imagining War.*   [105] Liddell Hart, *History of the Second World War*, 65.
[106] Julian Jackson, *The Fall of France.* Oxford: Oxford University Press, 2003, 215.
[107] Liddell Hart, *History of the Second World War*, 65.
[108] Jackson, *The Fall of France*, 215.
[109] Liddell Hart, *History of the Second World War*, 65–66.
[110] Citino, *Armored Forces*, 92.   [111] Jackson, *The Fall of France*, 215.

strategy to a lack of industrial capacity. Jackson suggests that terrain was a factor: "Such a doctrine and its assumptions proved sound in those areas for which the doctrine was originally developed – Central and Western Europe – and against states with common land frontiers with Germany and with relatively small land areas in which enemy forces could retreat or maneuver," but not insular countries such as Great Britain or huge territories such as the Soviet Union.[112]

Yet once a debate is resolved, these ambiguities tend to be overlooked and the outcome is presented as obvious and inevitable. In the case of tanks, the Fall of France has been widely perceived as "proving" the efficacy of German tank doctrines. As a result, the debate on the utility of tanks has been closed since 1940, and tanks have become a standard feature of nearly all armies around the world. Reflecting this seemingly fundamental utility, one tank historian notes, "Virtually every conflict fought in the world since 1945 has featured the use of armor [tanks]."[113]

Yet opportunities to reopen the debate exist. The utility of tanks was debated, for instance, following the 1973 Arab-Israeli War. Military opponents of the tank pointed to the efficacy of Egyptian antitank weapons as evidence that "the day of the tank was finished." Conversely, tank proponents cited evidence from the same war, describing the penetration of the Golan by Israeli tanks as "nothing short of epic."[114] Lyall and Wilson also argue that battle conditions in contemporary insurgencies affect the effectiveness of mechanized warfare.[115] Thus even today, empirical evidence suggests ambiguity in the military value of tanks. However, without a major shift at the top of the Great Power hierarchy to focus the attention of military planners, views on tanks are unlikely to change dramatically.

CONCLUSION

Once a military debate is resolved and history books get written, the outcome often seems as though it were inevitable. The dichotomy of battlefield outcomes – one army wins and the other loses – makes it difficult to perceive victory as disputable or contingent. Proponents face an uphill battle to argue for alternative formulations in which the defeated

---

[112] Jackson, *The Fall of France,* 216.   [113] Citino, *Armored Forces,* 123.
[114] Citino, *Armored Forces,* 119, 123.
[115] Jason Lyall and Wilson, Isaiah III, "Rage against the Machines: Explaining Outcomes in Counterinsurgency Wars." *International Organization* 63 (2009): 67–106.

state might serve as a model for military practice. Typically, the victorious military is perceived as ideal on all dimensions, while the defeated military is perceived as broadly deficient. In this case, the French military has been criticized for failing to grasp the perfectly obvious tactics for the tank, foolishly allowing defeat by the Germans.

Technological determinist accounts present the physical properties of a weapon as straightforward and obvious. Consequently, the French military has been widely condemned for failing to grasp the appropriate uses of the tank, which was so apparent to the Germans. As Doughty writes, "The French army, in short, had formulated a doctrine, organized and equipped its units, and trained its soldiers for the wrong type of war."[116]

When examined with an eye to ambiguity, however, the functionality of military technologies obviously hinges on assumptions of the conditions under which battle will take place. The properties of a technology that are quite effective in one situation may be useless under different circumstances. The decisive German victory over France provided a simple resolution to the debates, sweeping away the ambiguity that military planners faced and allowing planning to move forward. In practice, the perceived uses of a technology ultimately hinge on the lessons drawn from Great Power wars.

Beyond resolving specific debates about tank doctrine, the Second World War broadly enshrined advanced military technology as the critical component of military strategy. Tanks, bombers, aircraft carriers, submarines, and the atomic bomb were generally perceived as having proven their military value in battle. This "lesson" – that advanced technology is the key to power – dominates military thought in the contemporary era, just as the cult of the offensive dominated military minds at the beginning of the twentieth century. Military theorists have rewritten accounts of past wars to emphasize the "essential" role played by technology, which had often been unnoticed or wholly dismissed by scholars of prior eras. Military technology, along with its handmaidens of science, industrial strength, and the military industrial complex, became the dominant indicators of military prowess and played a foundational role in post–Second World War military affairs

---

[116] Doughty, *The Seeds of Disaster*, 3.

7

The Great Powers and Nuclear Weapons

"Nuclear weapons serve no military purpose whatsoever."[1]
Robert McNamara, U.S. Secretary of Defense

Nuclear weapons are the ultimate symbol of power, and have served as a primary marker of international status since the end of the Second World War. Nuclear weapons defy the imagination, affording a seemingly god-like ability to reduce entire cities to ashes. At first glance, it seems only reasonable that states seeking power would acquire nuclear weapons in large numbers. Yet the complexities and ambiguities of military planning apply here as well. Perhaps surprisingly, the strategic uses of nuclear weapons have not been at all obvious to military planners. As Henry Kissinger noted, "It would have seemed unbelievable even fifty years ago that there could ever be an excess of power ... Yet this is precisely the challenge of the nuclear age."[2]

It is one thing to fantasize about vaporizing an adversary in one fell swoop. It is another thing to effectively integrate the unimaginably destructive power of nuclear weapons into a country's broader portfolio of military strategies and diplomatic plans. Moreover, the acquisition of nuclear weapons presents a host of economic, political, and military problems, as will be discussed. Most importantly, the acquisition of nuclear capability substantially *decreases* national security, since the nascent nuclear state

---

[1] Mitchell Reiss, *Without the Bomb: The Politics of Nuclear Nonproliferation*. New York: Columbia University Press, 1988, 30–31.
[2] Henry A. Kissenger, *Nuclear Weapons and Foreign Policy*. New York: Harper and Brothers, 1957, 3.

immediately becomes a target for the arsenals of hostile Great Powers. This cost to security is taken as part of the price of Great Power status, but not all states have been willing to pay this steep cost.

This chapter turns the nuclear arms race on its head. Contrary to conventional expectations that nuclear weapons confer the military capability necessary to be a Great Power, I argue that the aspiration to compete in the Great Power system drove Great Power candidates to acquire and expand their nuclear arsenals, regardless of utility. Military competition devolved into status competition, as states sought to acquire the tokens of power that held symbolic value, despite ambiguity over the yield in terms of objective security. Indeed, it is hard to imagine anything that could have fundamentally threatened the survival of a superpower such as the United States in the late twentieth century except for a nuclear arms race with another superpower. Yet, in a world where status hinged on one-upmanship, that is exactly what occurred.

NUCLEAR WEAPONS AND GREAT POWER STATUS

Since the Second World War, nuclear weapons have been a key indicator of military power and Great Power status. As Newhouse notes, "Not much of lasting importance in world politics has been unconnected to the bomb."[3] The Great Powers of the late twentieth century were the five states that possessed nuclear capability in 1964. The relative size of the nuclear arsenals, moreover, generally corresponded with the recognized hierarchy of the Great Powers in the Cold War era.

The conventional view is that nuclear arsenals make countries powerful. From this perspective, countries acquire nuclear arsenals to buttress their military capability in response to security threats, just as they develop any other type of weapon. Indeed, it was initially expected that most states would develop nuclear weapons once they had the economic and technological capability.[4] Yet, the history of nuclear weapons defied expectations in multiple ways. First, nuclear weapons did not proliferate to many economically prosperous states. Second, arms acquisition among the superpowers vastly exceeded any plausible expectation. Instead, the nuclear arms race reached such ridiculous heights that the term "overkill"

---

[3] John Newhouse, *War and Peace in the Nuclear Age.* New York: Alfred A. Knopf, 1988, 416.

[4] Sidney D. Drell and James E. Goodby, *The Gravest Danger: Nuclear Weapons.* Stanford: Hoover Institution Press, 2003; Reiss, *Without the Bomb.*

had to be invented for the capacity to kill every human being on the planet not once, but many times over.

This chapter applies insights from prior chapters to rethink nuclear weapons as an object of Great Power competition. First, in Chapter 3, I argued that states "learn" the material attributes of military power by drawing on the lessons from the last Great Power war. In the case of nuclear weapons, the Great Powers learned the value of nuclear weapons from the historical role the atomic bomb had played in the conclusion of the Second World War, yielding a persistent belief that nuclear weapons must be useful – even though strategists continued to puzzle over the issue.

Second, in Chapter 2, I argued that Great Powers must be willing to act as a Great Power and enter into Great Power competitions. One of the major competitions at the end of the Second World War was the acquisition of nuclear capability. Those states that did not choose to enter into the Great Power nuclear competition were not accorded Great Power status. In the postwar era, the willingness to take on the tremendous economic and security costs of a nuclear arsenal has served as a marker of Great Power status. This chapter provides a historical synopsis of the decision of the Great Powers to acquire nuclear capability, as well as an overview of the nonproliferation literature, which has attempted to explain why many states have opted not to obtain nuclear weapons.

Third, competition with rivals is the key mechanism by which Great Powers maintain their status, as argued in Chapter 4. The arms race between the United States and the Soviet Union became one of the primary competitions of the Cold War, costing trillions of dollars and rubles on each side. The military argument for acquiring so many weapons was unclear, even at the time. What was clear was that each side believed it needed to outdo its rival, as a matter of great symbolic importance in the Cold War. As a result, the superpowers managed to pursue a path that truly threatened their survival, and that of the entire planet.

This chapter builds on the work of Jervis, Holloway, O'Neill, and Hymans, who have provided pathbreaking work on the symbolic aspect of nuclear capability.[5] For instance, Hymans examined the role of individual statesmen who chose to pursue a Great Power identity for their

---

[5] Jacques Hymans, *The Psychology of Nuclear Proliferation: Identity, Emotions, and Foreign Policy*. Cambridge: Cambridge University Press, 2006; Robert Jervis, *The Meaning of the Nuclear Revolution: Statecraft and the Prospect of Armageddon*. Ithaca: Cornell University Press, 1989; Robert Jervis, *The Illogic of American Nuclear Strategy*. Ithaca: Cornell University Press, 1984; Barry O'Neill, "Nuclear Weapons and National Prestige." Cowles Foundation Discussion Paper No. 1560, 2006.

state, finding that political leaders are motivated to acquire nuclear weapons as a step on the path toward Great Power status.[6] Emphasizing a different symbolic aspect of nuclear weapons, Tannenwald argued that the nuclear taboo prevented the United States from using nuclear weapons even when it may have made military sense to do so. My argument provides the international half of the picture that dovetails with these accounts: perceptions within the international community equated nuclear weapons with Great Power status, providing the ingredients for the decisions of domestic statesmen for their acquisition and use or nonuse.

LEARNING FROM HISTORY

A huge amount of ink has been spilled on the development of plausible military uses for nuclear weapons.[7] In such a contentious field, with contributions from some of the brightest minds over half a century, many potential military or political uses for nuclear weapons have been proposed.[8] Yet what is striking is the paucity of specific strategies that have emerged from these debates.

As Jervis summarizes, "A rational strategy for the employment of nuclear weapons is a contradiction in terms. The enormous destructive power of these weapons creates insoluble problems."[9] Throughout the Cold War, nuclear strategists struggled to develop scenarios in which

---

[6] Hymans, *The Psychology of Nuclear Proliferation*, 1.

[7] For instance, see the debate by Todd Sechser and Matthew Fuhrmann, "Crisis Bargaining and Nuclear Blackmail." *International Organization* 67 (2013): 173–195 and Matthew Kroenig, "Nuclear Superiority and the Balance of Resolve: Explaining Nuclear Crisis Outcomes." *International Organization* 67 (2013): 141–171, also Scott D. Sagan and Kenneth N. Waltz, *The Spread of Nuclear Weapons: A Debate Renewed*. New York: Norton, 2002.

[8] Barry Blechman and Douglas Hart, "The Political Utility of Nuclear Weapons: The 1973 Middle East Crisis." In *Strategy and Nuclear Deterrence*, edited by Steven E. Miller, 273–297. Princeton: Princeton University Press, 1987; Bernard Brodie, *Strategy in the Missile Age*. Princeton: Princeton University Press, 1959; Alexander L. George and Richard Smoke, *Deterrence in American Foreign Policy: Theory and Practice*. New York: Columbia University Press, 1974; Herman Kahn, *On Thermonuclear War*. Princeton: Princeton University Press, 1961; George H. Quester, *Nuclear Diplomacy: The First Twenty-Five Years*. New York: Dunellen, 1970; Thomas C. Schelling and Morton H. Halperin, *Strategy and Arms Control*. New York: Twentieth Century Fund, 1961; Richard Smoke, *National Security and the Nuclear Dilemma: An Introduction to the American Experience*, second edition. New York: Random House, 1987; Glenn H. Snyder, *Deterrence and Defense: Toward a Theory of National Security*. Princeton: Princeton University Press, 1961.

[9] Jervis, *The Illogic of American Nuclear Strategy*, 19.

nuclear weapons could be used to military advantage, and largely failed.[10] Generally speaking, conventional armaments provide greater precision at a much lower cost and without the horrific side effects of radiation and massive civilian casualties. Simply put, nuclear weapons are so powerful that it is difficult to find real-world scenarios for their use. In many superpower conflicts such as Vietnam and Afghanistan, there were insufficient numbers of targets for which nuclear weapons would be useful. Moreover, the one historical case of a nuclear monopoly by the United States, discussed below, did not produce the military or political advantages that might be expected.

This section does not attempt to adjudicate whether or not there might be some circumstances in which nuclear weapons could serve military or political ends. Instead, it focuses on the more pertinent question: Why did the postwar Great Powers pour enormous resources into weapons for which no specific military use had been identified? Drawing on the argument of Chapter 3, I argue that the international community had "learned" from the events of the Second World War that technology in general, and the atomic bomb in particular, were key components of military power.[11] The value of the tank was inferred from the Fall of France. The importance of bombers was drawn from the Battle of Britain. Newly invented technologies such as radar, submarines, and aircraft carriers had proven essential for the prosecution of the war and seemed to have been the predictors of Allied victory. And, the sine qua non of the postwar technological arsenal was the atomic bomb.

The utility of the atomic bomb seems so obvious that it may seem implausible to argue that its importance was socially constructed. The events of the Second World War led to the widespread perception of the military utility of the atomic bomb. By the summer of 1945, the war in Europe had been concluded but the Pacific War continued, fought principally between the United States and Japan. The United States dropped one atomic bomb on the Japanese city of Hiroshima on August 6, and a second bomb on Nagasaki on August 9, 1945. After fighting for almost four years, the Japanese surrender was announced on August 15, within

---

[10] Nevertheless, these efforts were consequential for U.S. military thinking – for instance, see Scott D. Sagan's account in *Moving Targets: Nuclear Strategy and National Security*. Princeton: Princeton University Press, 1989.

[11] Lynn Eden, *Whole World on Fire: Organizations, Knowledge, and Nuclear Weapons Devastation*. Ithaca: Cornell University Press, 2004, makes a similar argument that the historically contingent aspects of military organization led the United States to "learn" that blast effects of nuclear weapons were more calculable than fire effects.

days of the detonation of the second atomic bomb, and formally signed on September 2. The timing of the surrender clearly seemed to be in response to the horrific destruction caused by the atomic bomb and the implication that more bombs might follow if the war continued. Thus the American use of the atomic bomb on Japan in 1945 was widely understood as providing a dramatic coup de grace to the Pacific War.

Looking closely, however, the dramatic lesson of the Japanese surrender gives way to a more complex reality. There is broad scholarly consensus that the United States would have won the war regardless of the use of the atomic bomb.[12] As Freedman notes, "Even assuming that the bomb was the major source of surrender the lessons that could be drawn from the minimal operational experience were limited. It was like administering poison on the death bed."[13] Military estimates at the time suggested that the United States could have won the war by launching a ground invasion of Japan, although such a move would likely have cost thousands of American lives.[14]

Regardless, such academic commentaries have done little to diminish the impact of this military demonstration of the utility of nuclear weaponry. Even Freedman admits, "[T]he worth of the bomb was taken to have been proven in action."[15] This interpretation, in which the U.S. victory in the Pacific War is attributed to the use of the atomic bomb, catapulted nuclear weapons to the status of one of the primary indicators of military capability in the postwar era.

Thinking counterfactually, it is easy to imagine very different lessons. The point of these counterfactuals is to illustrate the different "obvious" lessons that might have been inferred and to suggest the probabilistic nature of events, not to assert that these counterfactuals were especially likely. For instance, Japan might have continued fighting for some additional months before surrendering. In that case, atomic weapons would not have appeared so decisive. Alternately, the United States may have decided against using its newly invented atomic bomb, yielding a very different lesson. The point is that if events had happened differently,

[12] For a review, see Ward Wilson, "The Winning Weapon? Rethinking Nuclear Weapons in Light of Hiroshima." *International Security* 31 (2007): 162–179.
[13] Lawrence Freedman, *The Evolution of Nuclear Strategy,* third edition. Basingstoke: Palgrave Macmillan, 2003, 19.
[14] Jeremy Bernstein, *Hitler's Uranium Club.* Woodbury: American Institute of Physics, 1996; Basil H. Liddell Hart, *History of the Second World War.* New York: G.P. Putnam's Sons, 1970.
[15] Freedman, *The Evolution of Nuclear Strategy,* 19.

nuclear weapons might easily have been viewed as an expensive curiosity for which battlefield uses were uncertain.

An historical analogy is the use of chemical weapons during the First World War, a technology that failed to gain the symbolic importance of nuclear weapons.[16] Although chlorine gas was first employed as a military weapon in the First World War, it has garnered much less attention – and to this day prompts much less excitement than attends the possible acquisition of nuclear capability by such countries as Iran and North Korea. Scholars today have argued that chemical (and biological) warfare could be more potent than conventional weapons, especially for the destruction of civilian populations. The relatively limited attention to chemical weapons can be traced in large part to their perceived ineffectiveness during initial trials in the First World War.[17] In battles where chlorine gas was first used, the wind blew the gas the wrong way or the gas dissipated prematurely and failed to harm the enemy. Consequently, the concept of chemical warfare was shelved for decades. Again, one could imagine chance events – such as the wind blowing in a different direction – leading to quite different lessons. Had militaries invested heavily in chemical weapons – even a modest fraction of the resources devoted to nuclear weapons – many of their technical limitations might have been addressed. Or, as in the case of nuclear weapons, the Great Powers might have competed over arsenals even without a clear strategic use in mind.

In the end, the dramatic role of the atomic bomb in the conclusion of the Second World War created the worldwide perception of nuclear weapons as the ultimate military technology. The historical importance of the atomic bomb established nuclear weapons as a key precondition for Great Power status in the postwar years. Even today, the acquisition of nuclear capability – especially if openly avowed – serves as a declaration that a state is stepping up its efforts in regional or Great Power competition.

THE GREAT POWERS AND NUCLEAR ACQUISITION

Since the Second World War, there has been direct correlation between the Great Powers and the size of their nuclear arsenals. The five states

[16] Richard M. Price, *The Chemical Weapons Taboo*. Ithaca: Cornell University Press, 1997.
[17] Basil H. Liddell Hart, *The Real War, 1914–1918*. Boston: Little, Brown and Company, 1930; Richard M. Price, *The Chemical Weapons Taboo*. Ithaca: Cornell University Press, 1997.

with nuclear capability in 1964 are still the dominant nuclear powers at the beginning of the twenty-first century.[18] The status of the nuclear Great Powers is further reflected in their permanent membership on the United Nations Security Council, as well as their inclusion in numerous other political organizations and agreements. As Bloomfield notes, "[T]he extraordinary fact is that as of the late 1980s, the *avowed* nuclear weapons powers remain the original five which, by accident or design, happen also to be the five Permanent Members of the UN Security Council already endowed by treaty with special privileges and, presumably, responsibilities."[19] But which came first: Great Power status or nuclear arsenals?

I argue that aspiration to Great Power status drives the acquisition of nuclear arsenals. O'Neill has similarly argued that considerations of prestige were a major factor in the development of nuclear weapons.[20] Larson, Paul and Wohlforth also view the nuclear arms race as an example of status-seeking behavior in international relations, commenting that "[t]here is considerable evidence that leaders of the United Kingdom, France, and India sought nuclear weapons to maintain or acquire great-power status, apart from security calculations."[21] As discussed later in the chapter, historical accounts suggest that Great Powers were principally focused on nuclear capability in order to secure their Great Power status rather than on specific plans for military use.

The histories of the early nuclear programs are filled with references to the perceived need for states to maintain their prestige in competition with other Great Power states. Considerations of potential military or political uses were of secondary importance. In every case, including that of the United States, nuclear development was driven by a sense of competition with Great Power rivals. The fear that a rival might acquire nuclear capability proved a powerful motivator. In turn, this Great Power competition over nuclear weapons reified their importance as a key marker of

---

[18] Kenneth N. Waltz, *Theory of International Politics*. Reading: Addison-Wesley, 1979; J. David Singer and Melvin Small, *The Wages of War, 1816–1965*. Ann Arbor: Interuniversity Consortium for Political Research, 1974; Jack S. Levy, *War in the Modern Great Power System, 1495–1975*. Lexington: University Press of Kentucky, 1983.

[19] Lincoln P. Bloomfield, "Foreword." In Mitchell Reiss, *Without the Bomb: The Politics of Nuclear Nonproliferation*, vii–x. New York: Columbia University Press, 1988, viii.

[20] O'Neill, "Nuclear Weapons and National Prestige."

[21] Deborah Welch Larson, T. V. Paul, and William C. Wohlforth, "Status and World Order." In *Status in World Politics*, edited by T. V. Paul, Deborah Welch Larson, and William C. Wohlforth, 3–32. Cambridge: Cambridge University Press, 2014, 12.

Great Power status. The Great Power states chose to acquire nuclear weapons first in hopes of figuring out their uses later.

The United States

The United States was the first to develop the atomic bomb and the only one to do so under wartime circumstances. Despite its pioneer status, Great Power competition played an essential role in the U.S. drive to develop nuclear capability. Initially, the United States was motivated to acquire the atomic (fission) bomb before Germany, its Great Power enemy.[22] After the conclusion of the Second World War, the United States was spurred to acquire the thermonuclear (fusion) bomb before its new rival, the Soviet Union.

Great Power competition over nuclear weapons did not begin immediately after the Second World War. The United States enjoyed a nuclear monopoly for a time, as the only state with the capability to produce a fission bomb. From the U.S. point of view, there appeared to be no need to develop the far more potent thermonuclear bomb. Indeed, there were only a handful of Soviet cities that were sizable enough to warrant even a small fission bomb. Consequently, there was little motivation to acquire the massive destructive capabilities of a fusion bomb.

Yet in 1949, the Soviet Union tested an atomic device.[23] U.S. government officials had estimated that it would take the Soviet Union five to fifteen more years to develop atomic weapons – President Truman had dourly prophesied that the Soviets would never be able to build an atomic bomb.[24] The Soviet test of a fission device came as a great shock to the United States. As Holloway claims, "The Soviet atomic test transformed this situation."[25] The discovery that the Soviet Union had tested an atomic bomb – coupled with the Communist takeover in China and other world events – led to a sense that its Cold War competitor was gaining on the United States.

In response to this challenge, the United States threw itself into high gear to build a thermonuclear bomb before the Soviets. Great Power competition, rather than specific military need, drove the U.S. agenda.

---

[22] Bernstein, *Hitler's Uranium Club*; Richard Rhodes, *The Making of the Atomic Bomb*. New York: Simon and Schuster, 1986.

[23] Holloway, *Stalin and the Bomb: The Soviet Union and Atomic Energy 1939–1956*. New Haven: Yale University Press, 1994.

[24] Freedman, *The Evolution of Nuclear Strategy*, 26.

[25] Holloway, *Stalin and the Bomb*, 300.

Indeed, at that time no military utility had been identified that fission bombs would not have covered with greater efficiency. Newhouse claims, "It didn't matter that a military use for the Super [the fusion bomb] hadn't been identified or that its feasibility on technical grounds hadn't been established. What mattered was the likelihood of the Soviets adding insult to injury by moving up from the atomic to the hydrogen bomb."[26] Another historian notes, "[I]t was the political and psychological impact of their existence which dominated the debate. The assumption was that the Soviet Union would inevitably advance in this direction, and the United States had to get there first."[27]

Yet this step from fission to fusion greatly increased the destructive potential of nuclear weapons. Nuclear fusion liberates atomic energies that are degrees of magnitude greater than nuclear fission. For example, the ten-megaton fusion bombs in the U.S. arsenal are one thousand times more destructive than the Hiroshima bomb – three degrees of magnitude. As Smoke has described, a fission bomb the size of the Hiroshima bomb that was dropped on the Statue of Liberty, "would do little more than break windowpanes at the distance of Times Square (some seven miles away)." In contrast, a ten-megaton fusion bomb dropped at the same place "would utterly devastate all of Manhattan ... and indeed the entire New York City and harbor area.'"[28]

The decision to build a thermonuclear bomb enabled a major increase in the destructive potential of the American arsenal. Two Nobel laureates in physics, I. I. Rabi and Enrico Fermi, agreed: "[S]uch a weapon goes far beyond any military objective and enters the range of very great natural catastrophes ... It is necessarily an evil thing considered in any light."[29] Nevertheless, the United States made this decision apparently as a knee-jerk reaction to the prospect that the Soviet Union would someday possess a thermonuclear weapon. As Rhodes wryly summarizes, "[T]he United States announced to the world that it intended to make a potentially genocidal weapon of mass destruction that it did not know how to make, did not want to use, but might need for political leverage in international negotiations."[30] Moreover, this decision was to have

---

[26] Newhouse, *War and Peace in the Nuclear Age*, 78.

[27] John Simpson, *The Independent Nuclear State: The United States, Britain and the Military Atom*. New York: St. Martin's Press, 1983, 56.

[28] Smoke, *National Security and the Nuclear Dilemma*, 58–59.

[29] Quoted in Richard Rhodes, *Arsenals of Folly: The Making of the Nuclear Arms Race*. New York: Alfred A. Knopf, 2007, 76.

[30] Rhodes, *Arsenals of Folly*, 78.

enormous significance for the security of the world. As one scholar notes, "The wholesale death of most of a nation's people and the destruction of civilization ... would actually be fairly difficult to accomplish with fission weapons only. With hydrogen [fusion] weapons it becomes all too feasible."[31]

As the Cold War continued, the expansion of the U.S. nuclear arsenal quickly passed beyond foreseeable utility. As U.S. Secretary of State Henry Kissinger noted, "Above all, the nuclear weapons were taken as another indication of our inherent technological superiority."[32] The U.S. nuclear arsenal proved a fundamental indicator of the new role the United States was playing as a Great Power in the postwar world. Moreover, the atomic bomb would become a primary indicator of military capability for the other Great Power states as well. The immediate effect was to galvanize the Soviet Union into developing its own nuclear weapons. "As the most powerful symbol of American economic and technological might, the atomic bomb was *ipso facto* something the Soviet Union had to have too."[33]

The Soviet Union

The Soviet acquisition of nuclear capability was similarly driven by a sense of competition with its recently acquired Great Power rival, the United States. Although Russia had been a Great Power since the eighteenth century, it had consistently sat at the bottom rungs of the Great Power hierarchy. However, the international community was uncertain how to assess Russia in its new Communist incarnation as the Soviet Union. Possessing the largest army in Europe, Soviet leaders did not feel threatened militarily in the early postwar years. Nevertheless, the overwhelming need to be perceived as a Great Power on par with the United States drove the Soviet push to acquire nuclear capability.

The Soviet Union had begun an atomic weapons project during the Second World War, similar to programs in the United States and Britain. The Soviet program was small and underfunded until the spectacular demonstration of the feasibility of atomic weapons by the United States in August 1945. Once Stalin received word that the United States had successfully used an atomic device, the Soviet project was kicked

---

[31] Smoke, *National Security and the Nuclear Dilemma,* 58–59.
[32] Kissenger, *Nuclear Weapons and Foreign Policy,* 32.
[33] Holloway, *Stalin and the Bomb,* 154–155, 133.

into high gear. As Holloway claims, "Stalin had not taken the atomic bomb seriously until Hiroshima had shown in the most dramatic way that it could be built." Despite the end of the Second World War in both Europe and Asia, Soviet leaders found it intolerable that the United States had an atomic bomb while they did not. Holloway notes, "The atomic bomb was not only a powerful weapon; it was also a symbol of American power." Consequently, Stalin "wanted a bomb of his own."[34]

Once the Soviet Union tested an atomic bomb in 1949, ending the U.S. monopoly, the Soviets immediately began work on a thermonuclear bomb as well. The Soviet Union had known about American work on fusion since 1946, and "the work was begun in the context of intense competition with the United States."[35] Newhouse claims, "Almost certainly, Stalin's decision to develop a fusion bomb preceded Truman's ... After a week's pause, [the Soviet program] shifted ... focus to a fusion program, which rapidly acquired top priority."[36] The Soviet decision to develop a thermonuclear bomb appears to have been the result of as little serious thought as the American decision. As Newhouse notes, "No one from Stalin to Sakharov appears to have harbored any doubt at any time that the right course of action was to get a Russian H-bomb just as fast as possible."[37]

There was no specific military need that spurred the Soviet development of the bomb. Holloway claims, "Stalin did not believe that war was likely in the short term." In addition, the massive Soviet army still seemed adequate to ward off any European military threats in the near future. Nevertheless, the Soviet Union felt the need to keep up with the demonstrated military capabilities of the United States. As a Great Power, the Soviet Union believed it must look to the development of military capability in the long term rather than for immediate military needs. And even more overriding was the need to compete against its rival, the United States. Holloway summarizes, "Strategic nuclear power is the clearest symbol of Soviet superpower status, and that claim to strategic parity shades into the assertion that the Soviet Union is the United States' political equal." He concludes, "It was nuclear weapons above all that made the Soviet Union a superpower."[38]

---

[34] Holloway, *Stalin and the Bomb*, 133.   [35] Holloway, *Stalin and the Bomb*, 296.
[36] Newhouse, *War and Peace in the Nuclear Age*, 80.
[37] Newhouse, *War and Peace in the Nuclear Age*, 80.
[38] Holloway, *Stalin and the Bomb*, 180, 364.

Britain

Britain was the third state to acquire nuclear capability. By the 1950s, the Second World War was over and the Cold War had not yet heated enough to become an imminent concern. Moreover, the geographical position and proximity of the British Isles to the Soviet Union created grave doubts about the utility of nuclear weapons. British military theorist Liddell Hart noted that "it seems a trifle muddle-headed, to put it mildly, for anyone to advocate that we should start the throwing of atom bombs if war began." Instead, political concerns were at the forefront of the decision to acquire nuclear weapons. British politicians feared the other Great Powers would not take them seriously unless they also acquired nuclear weapons.

The Soviet atomic test in 1949 came as a "shattering moment of truth for Britain."[39] Like the United States, British politicians had believed that the Soviets were far behind in their development of nuclear capability. The Soviet fission test showed that Britain had been outcompeted by its chief Great Power rival, the Soviet Union. A driving sense of one-upmanship spurred the British perception that in order to be a credible threat to the Soviet Union, Britain needed an independent nuclear force. Again, this competition was not connected to an imminent military need – even after the British had developed nuclear capability, they lacked the means to deliver bombs to the Soviet Union.[40] Instead, the decision was motivated by a vague sense of the need to keep technologically abreast of its Great Power rivals and allies. Although the United States was an ally, the British Air Staff suggested, 'the Americans will only swap drinks at the bar with fellow club members.'"[41] To be taken seriously by the Americans, Britain believed it needed the bomb.

Yet the development of independent British nuclear capability would be costly. As one historian noted, "Britain was going to spend a disproportionate effort in building up a stock of bombs too small to be of military value." Regardless, "[s]uch considerations were tacitly ignored by those members of the Cabinet committee who made the political decision to press ahead with the programme, and the result was that for the first nine years of its existence it was unrelated 'to strategic and

---

[39] Ian Clark and Nicholas J. Wheeler, *The British Origins of Nuclear Strategy, 1945–1955*. Oxford: Clarendon Press, 1989, 11.
[40] *The Independent Nuclear State*, 76.
[41] Clark and Wheeler, *The British Origins of Nuclear Strategy*, 51, 232.

tactical needs and probabilities.'"[42] Margaret Gowing, one of the foremost historians of British atomic policy, agreed: "[I]t had not been a
response to an immediate military threat but rather something fundamen-
talist and almost instinctive that led to the British decision to build the
atomic bomb."[43]

Thus, the British decision to build a bomb was based in large part
on the sense that Britain must acquire a nuclear arsenal in order to be a
Great Power. Clark and Wheeler summarize, "[T]here is an impressive
consensus . . . that the decision on the bomb was less a product of strategic
reasoning than of a set of implicit assumptions: the need for a British
bomb was taken to be so self-evident as to require no compelling strategic
assessment in support of it."[44] As Gowing notes, the British decision was
based on "a feeling that Britain as a great power must acquire all major
new weapons."[45] Bluth agrees that "[t]he British decision after the war to
become a self-sufficient nuclear power was based on the assumption that
it was necessary for a major power to be in possession of the most modern
weapons, recognized to be of possibly decisive military significance in the
future."[46] By the 1950s, Britain had established itself as a Great Power
with the third-largest nuclear arsenal in the world.

France

France was fourth to develop nuclear capability. France had been in the
Great Power club for centuries, and for much of that period had been at
the top of the hierarchy. Yet the humiliating defeat during the Second
World War had raised serious questions about France's status in the
postwar world. In order to regain Great Power status in the eyes of
the international community, France believed it had to acquire nuclear
weapons.[47]

Like the other Great Powers, French policy on nuclear weapons
"centered on considerations of international status and prestige and an

[42] Quoted in Simpson, *The Independent Nuclear State*, 52.
[43] Britain and Atomic Energy, quoted in Clark and Wheeler, *The British Origins of Nuclear Strategy*, 44.
[44] Clark and Wheeler, *The British Origins of Nuclear Strategy*, 43.
[45] Cited in Freedman, *The Evolution of Nuclear Strategy*, 74.
[46] Christoph Bluth, *Britain, Germany, and Western Nuclear Strategy*. Oxford: Clarendon Press, 1995, 42.
[47] Bertrand Goldschmidt, *Atomic Rivals*. Translated by Georges M. Temmer. New Bruns-wick: Rutgers University Press, 1990.

insistence that France's voice be heard and listened to in the councils of the Great Powers of the mid-twentieth century."[48] France believed that it was increasingly being edged out of postwar Great Power politics. Scheinman writes: "More and more Frenchmen came to regard the atomic arsenal as the means to bridge the gap between the real and theoretical status of France in the world. Only with such capability, it was argued, could France exercise substantial influence over her major allies in the Atlantic Alliance, or support diplomatic action outside the purview of the organization and beyond the protective American nuclear umbrella."[49]

When de Gaulle became president in 1958, "the nuclear programme became a key instrument in his endeavors to reassert France's distinctive identity and to enable Europe to become independent from the superpowers. 'A Great State,' explained de Gaulle, which does not possess nuclear weapons while others have them 'does not command its own destiny.'"[50] The acquisition of nuclear weapons played a key part in the French reassertion of Great Power status. Even more than in the British case, historians agree, "it should not be doubted that the *primary* motivating factor behind the nuclear force was a symbolic French place among the world's great powers." "To the French, even outside of its military considerations ... [nuclear weapons] could bring France immediate prestige, demonstrate industrial expertise ... [and] give France a status not shared by its European neighbors." Gordon notes that "the French themselves never tried to hide the fact that they saw their nuclear force, for the present at least, primarily as a key to great power status."[51]

The military rationale for the maintenance of an independent French nuclear arsenal was widely regarded as weak. France could not afford the vast arsenals, the bomber fleets, and the development of second-strike capability that was at the command of the United States and the Soviet Union. In 1968, *Le Monde*'s military correspondent noted, "If we accept the most optimistic hypothesis, France will have a nuclear capacity of about thirty megatons around 1975. In other words ... what one American bomber carries today in its storage tank." Indeed, although France had proven itself as nuclear capable in 1960, it lacked a bomber force that would have allowed it to deliver a bomb until 1964. Even by the early

[48] Lawrence Scheinman, *Atomic Energy Policy in France under the Fourth Republic*. Princeton: Princeton University Press, 1965, 218.

[49] Scheinman, *Atomic Energy Policy in France under the Fourth Republic*, 217–218.

[50] Freedman, *The Evolution of Nuclear Strategy*, 298.

[51] Philip H. Gordon, *A Certain Idea of France: French Security Policy and the Gaullist Legacy*. Princeton: Princeton University Press, 1993, 43, 41, 41–42.

1970s, "the major analysts of French security would still quite naturally see the French nuclear force as a diplomatic instrument rather than a military one." The French nuclear force was so small, compared to the size of American and Soviet arsenals, that "the [French nuclear force] was far more a symbol of independence than a serious enhancement of deterrence in Europe."[52]

Instead, matters of prestige rather than functionality held precedence in the French decision to develop a nuclear arsenal. Scheinman notes, "It does not appear that in reaching the decision to enter the nuclear club, French officials or their advisors gave much serious consideration to the effectiveness or credibility of a French nuclear force. ... There is no evidence that the costs involved in building a sophisticated nuclear arsenal were taken into account."[53] Instead, the French decision to acquire nuclear weapons was driven substantially by a desire to claim Great Power status. As Scheinman concludes: "France's international image was considerably tarnished." Despite "a tradition of first-rank status and prestige ... either France had to relinquish her pretensions, reconsider her goals and reconcile herself to new circumstances, or she had to strive to reassert herself materially in the rank of Great Power nations."[54]

China

China first tested an atomic weapon in 1964, and developed thermonuclear capability in 1968. Long an outsider to Great Power politics, China's claim to Great Power status seemed dubious after the Second World War. By most estimates, it was quite improbable that China would be recognized as a Great Power. It was the attainment of nuclear capability that was essential in marking China as a Great Power in the eyes of the international community. Chinese decision-makers were well aware of the increased status that nuclear capability conferred, and willingly accepted the increased costs. Nuclear development was spurred by competition with France, which was also trying to gain nuclear capability at the same time.

Like the other nuclear powers, China did not have a military need for the bomb: "As the strongest regional power by far, China never

---

[52] Gordon, *A Certain Idea of France*, 40–41, 43, 39.

[53] Scheinman, *Atomic Energy Policy in France under the Fourth Republic*, 219, xvii–xviii,

[54] Scheinman, *Atomic Energy Policy in France under the Fourth Republic*, 219, xvii–xviii, 216.

required nuclear weapons to deal with her immediate neighbors." Instead, "[b]uilding the Bomb was part of a wider drive toward national independence, self-assertion, and scientific progress.[55] China's nuclear forces remained small and "did not move beyond the most modest objectives for its nuclear force, offering no nuclear guarantees to others. It developed suitably modest capabilities, oriented toward the Soviet Union, but it was not, at the end of the 1970s, a force which met the full requirements of a second-strike capability."[56] Nevertheless, the Chinese nuclear force was regarded within the international community as meeting the requirements for Great Power status.

The development of nuclear technology incurred significant costs for China, both economic and political. Scholars have attributed the split between the Soviet Union and China in part to the latter's insistence of having nuclear capability.[57] Moreover, the existence of a Chinese nuclear arsenal was tantamount to announcing itself as a potential target for the other Great Power states. Chinese political decision-makers were well aware that the acquisition of nuclear weapons increased their security risk. The Chinese nuclear arsenal meant foregoing the "nuclear umbrella" of the Soviet Union, while simultaneously declaring itself a target for a nuclear attack by the United States. As Lewis and Xue noted, "In China as elsewhere, the possession of nuclear weapons exposed the country to the nuclear paradox: such power imposes an unprecedented risk." Chinese military planners understood that China would become a more tempting military target to the West, although they believed that "since the United States had already targeted China with nuclear weapons, 'a few more' would not add to the danger."[58]

More than the other Great Power states, most of which had held that status for centuries, China was unlikely to have been taken seriously as a Great Power without the bomb. Lewis and Xue note that China "had concluded very early that an independent nuclear arsenal would add measurable weight to their international position."[59] As Quester muses, "[H]ow much importance [would] the outside world would have attached to Communist China if she had not entered the nuclear club[?] Would we

---

[55] Cited in Martin Van Creveld, *Nuclear Proliferation and the Future of Conflict.* New York: Free Press, 1993, 70.

[56] Freedman, *The Evolution of Nuclear Strategy,* 266.

[57] John Wilson Lewis and Xue Litai, *China Builds the Bomb.* Stanford: Stanford University Press, 1988.

[58] Lewis and Xue, *China Builds the Bomb,* 225–226, 193.

[59] Lewis and Xue, *China Builds the Bomb,* 228–229.

not have passed Peking off . . . as an internationally insignificant conglomeration of feuding factions? Bombs do make a difference."[60]

These histories repeatedly show that decision-makers perceived Great Power status to be one of the primary advantages of the possession of nuclear capability. As Holloway notes, "The disjunction between military capability and political effect can be explained in terms of the bomb's symbolic meaning. It symbolized the immense power – not only the military, but also the economic and technological power."[61] Quester writes: "Closer examination of the policies of France, Britain, and China might lead us to conclude that their status as nuclear powers has helped them gain (or retain) prestige that would not have been obtainable otherwise."[62] In the reconstruction of the post–Second World War order, nuclear capability had become a necessary signifier of Great Power status.

THE PUZZLE OF NONPROLIFERATION

Similarly, the decision of state leaders against the acquisition of nuclear weapons also depended on their symbolic significance as an indicator of Great Power status. Realist scholars in 1960 expected the widespread proliferation of nuclear weapons in the 1960s and 1970s, based simply on the material requirements of nuclear capability.[63] At that time, Canada seemed an anomaly, being the only country "technically and financially capable of achieving nuclear status" that had not done so. The U.S. National Planning Association predicted in 1958 that in twelve years, "most nations with appreciable military strength will have in their arsenals nuclear weapons – strategic, tactical, or both." Yet this did not occur, "contrary to almost all predictions."[64] Drell and Goodby add that "[t]his slow pace of proliferation . . . is all the more impressive when one adds up the number of nations that contemplated and, in some cases, actually started down the path to building nuclear weapons before abandoning them."[65]

---

[60] George H. Quester, *The Politics of Nuclear Proliferation.* Baltimore: Johns Hopkins University Press, 1973, 66.

[61] Holloway, *Stalin and the Bomb,* 154–155.

[62] Quester, *The Politics of Nuclear Proliferation,* 7.

[63] A recent explanation for widespread proliferation is M. Kroenig, "Importing the Bomb: Sensitive Nuclear Assistance and Nuclear Proliferation." *Journal of Conflict Resolution* 53 (2009): 161–180.

[64] Reiss, *Without the Bomb,* 14–15, xxii.

[65] Drell and Goodby, *The Gravest Danger,* 5–6.

The current scholarly literature today seeks to explain why non–Great Power states have chosen against the open development of nuclear capability.[66] There seem to be a plethora of reasons. Domestic politics theorists have pointed to the high costs accompanying the acquisition of nuclear weapons, which deterred politicians.[67] Sweden, Canada, and Japan decided against the development of a nuclear arsenal because of exorbitant economic, political, and military costs. Sagan similarly develops a domestic argument to explain the cases of nuclear restraint by India and South Africa.[68] Hymans points to conflicts between political leaders and scientific professionals.[69] Yet these accounts fail to explain why these same dynamics failed to deter the development of nuclear capability in the Great Power states.

Neither the realist nor the domestic politics literatures have recognized that both sides of the puzzle must be explained: Why did the Great Powers develop nuclear weapons when faced with the same high costs and indeterminate benefits that deterred minor powers? I argue that the same objective costs and benefits were perceived differently by those states hoping to become Great Powers. For an aspiring Great Power, the high military costs were interpreted as simply the price of being a Great Power. A Great Power candidate must be actively willing to pay the costs of Great Power status and engage in the competitions of rival states, even if the costs of these competitions may be inordinately high. The difference between the Great Powers and the nonnuclear powers was not due to differences in the price tags for the economic and security costs. Instead, states with the mettle to be a Great Power accepted the expensive gamble that a use for nuclear weapons would be found at some point, even if those uses were not foreseeable at the time of acquisition.

[66] Some scholars have argued that differences in economic or political position may lead to different calculations. For instance, see Etel Solingen, "The Political Economy of Nuclear Restraint." *International Security* 19 (1994): 126–169.
[67] Lawrence S. Wittner, *Resisting the Bomb: A History of the World Nuclear Disarmament Movement, 1954–1970.* Stanford: Stanford University Press, 1997; John Davey Lewis Moore, *South Africa and Nuclear Proliferation.* New York: St. Martin's Press, 1987; Matthias Küntzel, *Bonn and the Bomb: German Politics and the Nuclear Option.* London: Pluto Press, 1995.
[68] Scott D. Sagan, "Why Do States Build Nuclear Weapons? Three Models in Search of a Bomb." *International Security* 21 (1996–1997): 54–86.
[69] Hymans points to the strength of legal-rational organizations to explain why the Great Powers successfully developed nuclear weapons while other countries have not. Jacques E. C. Hymans, *Achieving Nuclear Ambitions: Scientists, Politicians, and Proliferation.* New York: Cambridge University Press, 2012.

The following section briefly discusses three of the principal disincentives, which have been (1) the high economic cost of nuclear development, (2) the increased security risks coupled with a lack of foreseeable military utility, and (3) domestic and international normative sanctions against the acquisition of nuclear weapons. Yet the Great Power states also faced those same disincentives. Indeed, the costs were actually higher for the Great Power states, especially on the economic and security dimensions. Regardless, the Great Power states eagerly embraced the costs and risks that accompany nuclear status.

Economic Costs

One of the major drawbacks to the development of a nuclear capability is the cost of research plus the expense of building, maintaining, and updating an arsenal of nuclear missiles.[70] All of the Great Power states incurred gigantic costs in the development of nuclear capability. For instance, nuclear weapons comprised one-quarter of the overall French defense budget in the 1960s, and the nuclear arms race captured a large percentage of the Soviet defense budget as well.[71] One study estimated that the United States spent $5.8 trillion on nuclear weapons from 1940 to 1996 – roughly the size of the entire U.S. Gross National Product in 1980.[72]

Small powers today face lower costs in the development of nuclear capability. Developments in nuclear physics and engineering have made broad knowledge about nuclear science widely available, although the particular details of engineering a nuclear device still requires considerable expert knowledge.[73] Moreover, a small power need not maintain an entire nuclear force of intercontinental ballistic missiles, submarines, and bombers to be perceived as a credible force. These lower economic costs have allowed states such as Israel and India to test nuclear weapons.

---

[70] Solingen, "The Political Economy of Nuclear Restraint"; Etel Solingen, *Nuclear Logics: Contrasting Paths in East Asia and the Middle East*. Princeton: Princeton University Press, 2007.

[71] Gordon, *A Certain Idea of France*, 35; Holloway, *Stalin and the Bomb*, 365.

[72] The United States spent $5.8 trillion on nuclear weapons from 1940 to 1996 and continues to spend $35 billion annually; Stephen I. Schwartz, *Atomic Audit: The Costs and Consequences of US Nuclear Weapons since 1940*. Washington, DC: Brookings Institution, 1998.

[73] Donald MacKenzie and Graham Spinardi, "Tacit Knowledge, Weapons Design, and the Uninvention of Nuclear Weapons." *American Journal of Sociology* 101.1 (1995): 44–99.

Nevertheless, the substantial economic costs of nuclear development have posed a significant deterrent against acquiring nuclear capability for many countries.

In addition, states that choose to forego nuclear weapons may be rewarded through an array of economic incentives. For instance, Pakistan has received large amounts of economic aid in return for its opacity on its nuclear status.[74] Huge financial incentives exist for other states to disavow nuclear acquisition as well. As Reiss notes, "For North Korea, Ukraine, Kazakhstan, and Belarus, for example, it literally became profitable to renounce nuclear weapons or constrain nuclear activities."[75]

In contrast, the economic costs of nuclear statehood have been astronomically high for the Great Powers, even with their sizable resources. Some scholars have argued that the high economic costs of maintaining a nuclear arsenal contributed to the downfall of the Soviet Union.[76] Others have claimed that the economic prosperity of states such as Japan and Germany has been due in part to their lack of maintenance of large standing armies and huge nuclear arsenals. The economic drawbacks of nuclear statehood have been substantial for the Great Powers. Yet they willingly paid those costs that deterred non–Great Power states.

Security Costs

An even more substantial drawback of a nuclear arsenal is that it actively reduces the security of a state.[77] During the Cold War, the nuclear arsenals of each Great Power were primarily targeted toward other Great Powers. The open avowal of nuclear capability was tantamount to declaring open season on oneself as a nuclear target to the other Great Powers. Although nobody was assured of security in a nuclear world, the nuclear powers placed themselves in the front line as the target for a first strike. These costs were sufficient to deter many states from acquiring nuclear capability. The risks were not lower for the Great Powers; instead, the

---

[74] T. V. Paul, *Power versus Prudence: Why Nations Forgo Nuclear Weapons*. Montreal: McGill-Queen's University Press, 2000, 134.

[75] Mitchell Reiss, *Bridled Ambition: Why Countries Constrain Their Nuclear Capabilities*. Baltimore: Johns Hopkins Press, 1995, 3.

[76] Rhodes, *Arsenals of Folly*.

[77] Kenneth N. Waltz, "Nuclear Myths and Political Realities." *The American Political Science Review* 84 (1990): 731–745 argues that proliferation would increase world security, but does not explain why this has not led to widespread proliferation.

mark of a Great Power was a state that was willing to accept the greater security risks that accompany nuclear acquisition.

In contrast, nonnuclear states expected some degree of protection from a Great Power patron. Moreover, their lower probability of being targeted by the nuclear missiles of another Great Power gave them (somewhat) greater security. Several states that sought to develop nuclear capability were faced with the loss of this nuclear protection and decided to forego nuclear weapons because of the significant decrease in security that would occur. For instance, in South Korea, "the development of nuclear weapons would have placed at risk the existing American military commitment."[78] In the case of Sweden, "[e]mployment of nuclear arms by Stockholm ... would likely have resulted in national suicide by provoking overwhelming retaliation" and not only would "nuclear weapons not deter aggression, they would in fact attract an attack, 'like flypaper.'" Japanese decision-makers also realized their increased vulnerability, where "the mere possession of nuclear weapons by Japan would almost have certainly guaranteed that the country would have been a target in a nuclear war."[79] In addition, even if a state were to develop nuclear capability, it would be of limited utility against the massive arsenals of one of the superpowers.[80]

These economic and security costs to nascent nuclear states are not hypothetical, but have resulted in active economic and military sanctions.[81] At times, attempts to acquire nuclear capability have resulted in military threat. For instance, the United States bombed Libya in 1982 due to international fears that Qaddafi was developing the capability to prepare uranium for use in a fission bomb. The U.S. invasion of Iraq in 2002 was also legitimated on the (erroneous) grounds that weapons of mass destruction were being developed.[82]

Yet keep in mind that the security risks of nuclear capability were even higher for the Great Powers than for nascent nuclear states. The nuclear arsenals of the Great Powers were certainly top targets for a Great Power enemy. Uncertainties about second-strike ability have made it far from

---

[78] Reiss, *Without the Bomb*, 103.   [79] Reiss, *Without the Bomb*, 62, 135.

[80] Reiss, *Without the Bomb*, 62, 135.

[81] Ariel E. Levite, "Never Say Never Again: Nuclear Reversal Revisited." In *Going Nuclear: Nuclear Proliferation and International Security in the 21st Century*, edited by Michael E. Brown, Owen R. Cote Jr., Sean M. Lynn-Jones, and Steven E. Miller, 297–326. Cambridge, MA: MIT Press, 2010.

[82] Robert Jervis, *Why Intelligence Fails: Lessons from the Iranian Revolution and the Iraq War*. Ithaca: Cornell University Press, 2010.

clear that even a monstrous nuclear arsenal could protect a Great Power in the event of nuclear attack. As discussed earlier in the case of Britain, France, and China, each recognized the dangers of leaving the nuclear umbrella of their superpower ally. The security risks were higher, not lower, for a Great Power. Again, the difference lay in the willingness of the Great Power state to take on those risks as a marker of Great Power status.

International Norms

A third disincentive to nuclear proliferation has been international and domestic norms.[83] The Great Powers have helped foster a cultural perception in the international community against nuclear proliferation.[84] In this climate, newly nuclear states face international censure for the violation of international treaties.[85] As Hagarty notes, "In the covert culture embraced by subsequent proliferants, nuclear capabilities have been acquired secretly and often in violation of international norms and national laws against the spread of nuclear weapons."[86]

The Nuclear Proliferation Treaty (NPT) is the strongest international instrument developed to prevent new states from gaining nuclear weapons. Ratified by nearly every country in the world, the NPT forbids the acquisition of nuclear weapons by signatory states. Yet the NPT allows the Great Powers to keep the nuclear weapons that they have, even though they are signatories of the treaty. Thus, one of the major consequences of the treaty has been to demarcate which states are legitimate nuclear "haves" and which are the "have-nots."

---

[83] Nina Tannenwald, *The Nuclear Taboo: The United States and the Non-Use of Nuclear Weapons Since 1945.* Cambridge: Cambridge University Press, 2007; Nina Tannenwald, "The Nuclear Taboo: The United States and the Normative Basis of Nuclear Non-Use." *International Organization* 53 (1999): 433–468.

[84] Härald Muller, "The Internationalization of Principles, Norms, and Rules by Governments: The Case of Security Regimes." In *Regime Theory and International Relations*, edited by Volker Rittberger, 361–390. Oxford: Clarendon Press, 1995; Sagan, "Why Do States Build Nuclear Weapons?"; Roger K. Smith, "Explaining the Non-Proliferation Regime: Anomalies for Contemporary International Relations Theory." *International Organization* 41 (1987): 253–281.

[85] Peter Liberman, "The Rise and Fall of the South African Bomb." In *Going Nuclear: Nuclear Proliferation and International Security in the 21st Century*, edited by Michael E. Brown, Owen R. Cote Jr., Sean M. Lynn-Jones, and Steven E. Miller, 255–296. Cambridge, MA: MIT Press, 2010.

[86] Devin T. Hagerty, *The Consequences of Nuclear Proliferation: Lessons from South Asia.* Cambridge, MA: MIT Press, 1998, 40.

Domestic norms, heightened by social movements in Germany, Japan, Canada, Australia, New Zealand, and other places, have also actively worked against national acquisition in several cases.[87] Wittner claims that "aroused world opinion" led to the development of international treaties restricting nuclear testing such as the atmospheric test ban treaty of 1963, the nuclear nonproliferation treaty of 1968, the first strategic nuclear arms controls, and other nuclear arms control measures.[88] Yet social movements against nuclear weapons in Great Power states such as the United States, Britain, and France did not prevail. This difference might not reflect disparities in the effectiveness of these social movements, but instead indicate the greater willingness of Great Power governments to accept the normative costs of nuclear capability, as well as the economic and security costs.

In short, the difference between the nuclear and nonnuclear states is not caused by different price tags in the economic, security, and normative costs of nuclear capability. Instead, the difference lies in the willingness of a state to accept those costs. Policy-makers in the Great Power states simply regard the high expenses and greater vulnerability, as well as the normative disapprobation that goes with nuclear capability, as the price of power. All the Great Powers were willing to take the expensive gamble that at some point a use would be found for nuclear weapons, even if that could not be foreseen at the time of the decision. States that eschewed Great Power status faced similar economic, political, and normative costs of nuclear capability. Without the desire for Great Power status, those costs were perceived as unnecessary.

THE SUPERPOWER ARMS RACE

Throughout the arms race, many military experts insisted that the mere number of nuclear weapons was an inadequate indicator of their military utility.[89] The unprecedented destructive capabilities of the fusion bomb meant that a single one could destroy a city. Regardless, each superpower strove for numerical superiority throughout the Cold War. Drawing on

---

[87] David S. Meyer, *A Winter of Discontent: The Nuclear Freeze and American Politics.* New York: Praeger, 1990; Wittner, *Resisting the Bomb*; Moore, *South Africa and Nuclear Proliferation*; Küntzel, *Bonn and the Bomb*.

[88] Wittner, *Resisting the Bomb*, 466.

[89] Newhouse, *War and Peace in the Nuclear Age*; Freedman, *The Evolution of Nuclear Strategy*; Thomas C. Schelling and Morton H. Halperin, *Strategy and Arms Control.* New York: Twentieth Century Fund, 1961.

the argument in Chapter 2, the scorecard of the arms race in the eyes of the international community was measured by the quantity of nuclear weapons regardless of the strategic utility of those weapons. This simple logic of numeric superiority can be traced back to lessons "learned" from the Napoleonic wars, in which the size of military forces – the army with more men, the navy with more ships – determined the outcome of the battles.[90] Although the advent of the atomic bomb meant that the meaning of the numbers had changed, the rubric for thinking about military power had not. As Luttwak grumbled, "Outside the narrow circle of the technical experts ... [g]ross numbers and crude qualitative factors provide the only indices of strategic power which are widely recognized."[91]

The naive view would be to assume that the thousands of nuclear missiles in each superpower's arsenal were warranted by their intrinsic utility. One might imagine, with teleological logic, that this buildup indicated the vast utility of nuclear missiles. Yet nuclear strategists throughout the Cold War were plagued by what Jervis has termed the paradox of unusability – that the fantastic destructive potential of nuclear weapons rendered them inappropriate for real-world scenarios.[92] Not only would the combatant states likely be obliterated; a nuclear barrage would incur incalculable damages worldwide. Nuclear strategists came to the uneasy recognition that numerical superiority in missiles was a poor indicator of capability. In the paradoxical world of nuclear weapons, more was not necessarily better.

Realist scholars argued, however, that the buildup in nuclear weapons was necessary for deterrence – to prevent their use. According to this logic, the Soviet Union was deterred from launching a nuclear strike by the equal ability of the United States to launch a first or second strike against the Soviet Union. There has been much debate over what size of a nuclear force would provide sufficient deterrence. The deterrence argument is difficult to prove or disprove based on available evidence – namely, the absence of direct nuclear exchange during the Cold War. The Soviet Union may have been deterred by the policies and nuclear arsenal of the United States. Then again, U.S. deterrence may have had the

[90] Jervis, *The Illogic of American Nuclear Strategy*, 60.
[91] Edward Luttwak, cited in Steven Kull, *Minds at War: Nuclear Reality and the Inner Conflicts of Defense Policymakers*. New York: Basic Books, 1988, 121.
[92] Jervis, *The Meaning of the Nuclear Revolution*. See also Scott D. Sagan, *Moving Targets: Nuclear Strategy and National Security*. Princeton: Princeton University Press, 1989.

same impact as an anti–pink elephant campaign – presumed effective because no pink elephants have been sighted.

The magnitude of controversy over nuclear strategy points to the fundamental ambiguity that underlies nuclear planning. As Morris notes, "The fact that some of the most intelligent people in the world have argued all sides of these questions for forty years, and argued them with a religious fervor and ferocity, is a clue that there are no answers."[93] Rhodes similarly observes:

So much confusion, so much paranoia, so many good intentions, so much hard work, technical genius, cynicism, manipulation, buckpassing, buckpocketing, argument, grandstanding, risk-taking, calculation, theorizing, goodwill and bad, rhetoric and hypocrisy, so much desperation, all point to something intractable behind the problem of how to deploy sufficient and appropriate nuclear arms to protect one's nation from a nuclear-armed opponent ... there is no military solution to safety in the nuclear age.[94]

Despite the debate, and despite strategic calculations of the optimal numbers of weapons needed for deterrence, the growth of the U.S. and Soviet nuclear arsenals grew alarmingly in the latter decades of the Cold War. Rather than leading the way, strategists flailed about, seeking to rationalize the nuclear escalation that had already occurred. Early on, the Great Powers had acquired nuclear weapons first, hoping to figure out what to do with them later. This pattern continued throughout the Cold War. "The former director of the Lawrence Livermore Laboratory, John S. Foster, Jr. adds, 'We were making it up as we went along.'"[95] Robert McNamara, perhaps the key decision-maker on nuclear strategy during the Kennedy and Johnson administrations, was once asked: "Why the United States built so many more [nuclear weapons] than it realistically needed during the Cold War?" McNamara responded, "Each individual decision along the way seemed rational at the time ... But the result was insane."[96] As McNamara mused, "[E]ach of the decisions, taken by itself, appeared rational or inescapable. But the fact is that they were made without reference to any master plan or long-term objective. They have led to nuclear arsenals and nuclear war plans that few of the participants anticipated or would, in retrospect, wish to support."[97]

[93] Charles R. Morris, *Iron Destinies, Lost Opportunities: The Arms Race between the USA and the USSR, 1945–1987.* New York: Harper and Row, 1988, 439.
[94] Rhodes, *Arsenals of Folly*, 101.   [95] Rhodes, *Arsenals of Folly*, 83.
[96] Quoted in Rhodes, *Arsenals of Folly*, 99.   [97] Quoted in Rhodes, *Arsenals of Folly*, 99.

This seemingly irrational expansion of the superpower nuclear arsenals can be explained by turning the dynamics of the arms race on its head. Drawing on the arguments in Chapter 4, competition among the Great Powers was the primary motivator of their interest in acquiring nuclear weapons. The superpowers expanded their nuclear arsenals primarily in order to outstrip the other. Regardless of their military utility, nuclear weapons became the means by which each superpower could prove its superiority over the other. This section briefly outlines three episodes in which the dynamics of one-upmanship, rather than sober calculation, drove the nuclear arms race.

The Race Is On

Until 1949, the United States possessed a nuclear monopoly, as the only state with atomic weapons. Subsequent scholarship, however, has recognized that the United States extracted little political advantage from this situation.[98] As Henry Kissinger pointed out, although "the United States was virtually immune to Soviet retaliation ... possession of [the atomic bomb] did not enable us to prevent a hostile power [the Soviet Union] from expanding its orbit and developing a capability to inflict a mortal blow on the United States."[99] Holloway similarly concludes: "There is little evidence to suggest that the United States was able to use the bomb to compel the Soviet Union to do things it did not want to do."[100]

By the late 1950s the United States was still comfortably in the nuclear lead. Confusion over the size of the Soviet arsenal was to catapult the United States even further ahead.[101] President Eisenhower had sought to put the brakes on military expenditures during his tenure, and was confident that the U.S. nuclear arsenal was substantially larger than that of the Soviets. However, U.S. missile estimates were kept top secret and were known only to the highest security circles, which did not include most military planners or Congressmen. Lacking data, U.S. pundits punted about various estimates of Soviet missile strength. Depending on initial assumptions, a sizable gap could be extrapolated between the projected U.S. and Soviet arsenals, beginning in the mid-1960s. John F. Kennedy,

---

[98] Newhouse, *War and Peace in the Nuclear Age.*
[99] Kissinger, *Nuclear Weapons and Foreign Policy,* 11–12.
[100] Holloway, *Stalin and the Bomb,* 271–272.
[101] Thomas W. Wolfe, *Soviet Power and Europe 1945–1970.* Baltimore: Johns Hopkins University Press, 1970, 85; Newhouse, *War and Peace in the Nuclear Age,* 118; Morris, *Iron Destinies,* 189–90.

the Democratic presidential candidate, made much of these figures, suggesting that the Republican administration had been lax in the maintenance of American nuclear security. These concerns were amplified by the rhetoric of the Soviet premier, Nikita Khrushchev, who "sought to persuade the world ... that the strategic balance had shifted to the advantage of the Soviet Union" through a "detailed pattern of missile claims and related strategic threats."[102] Following the recent proof of Soviet technological superiority in the launching of Sputnik in 1959, the United States and the rest of the world were willing to believe the United States was falling behind in the missile race.[103]

This strategy of threat amplification was to backfire on both Kennedy and Khrushchev. Once Kennedy arrived at the White House, he learned that the United States actually had a sizable numerical superiority in missiles, rather than the inferiority that had been claimed. The U-2 data was indisputable, although some Air Force generals hopefully "suggested that a medieval tower and a Crimean war memorial might be missile sites in disguise."[104] But "Kennedy would have courted political embarrassment if, after having hammered away at the shortcomings of the nation's nuclear forces during this campaign, he admitted upon taking office that his charges had been unfounded."[105] Consequently, the Kennedy administration increased missile production leading to a missile gap in the 1960s, but in the other direction – an unanticipated larger disparity in favor of U.S. superiority in nuclear missiles.

By 1962, the United States could launch 3,000 nuclear missiles by strategic bomber, in addition to 183 ICBMs and 144 missiles on submarines. The United States was also beginning deployment of the Minuteman missile, an effective solid-propellant ICBM. In contrast, the Soviet Union had a total of no more than 300 nuclear weapons that could be launched at the United States and only 30 ICBMs.[106] As Morris claims, "The accelerated Kennedy/McNamara missile buildup was a momentous decision, arguably one of a handful of turning points in the arms competition

---

[102] Wolfe, *Soviet Power and Europe 1945–1970*, 85.
[103] Newhouse, *War and Peace in the Nuclear Age*, 118.
[104] Morris, *Iron Destinies*, 189–190.
[105] Michael Mandelbaum, *The Nuclear Question: The United States and Nuclear Weapons, 1946–1976*. Cambridge: Cambridge University Press, 1979, 86.
[106] Pavel Podvig (ed.), *Russian Strategic Nuclear Forces*. Cambridge, MA: MIT Press, 2001, 5; Peter R. Beckman, Larry Campbell, Paul W. Crumlish, Michael N. Dobkowski, and Steven P. Lee. *The Nuclear Predicament: Nuclear Weapons in the Cold War and Beyond*, second edition. Englewood Cliffs: Prentice Hall, 1992, 91.

between the United States and the Soviet Union ... It greatly aggravated a nuclear force imbalance that was already lopsidedly in favor of the United States, and did so with little regard to any perceived strategic necessity. To the degree that any strategic criterion at all was proposed ... that was actually developed well after the essential decisions were already taken."[107]

For Khrushchev, convincing the United States that the Soviet Union "had gained the upper hand in global military power ... [had] the unwelcome effect of stimulating the United States to throw its immense resources more fully than before into the missile race."[108] The U.S. superiority was to make itself felt in the Cuban missile crisis of 1962. At the time, the nuclear missile balance was 17:1 in favor of the United States. U.S. decision-makers apparently did not consider using nuclear weapons to settle the crisis; according to Rhodes, "there was never any question on the U.S. side of initiating a nuclear attack."[109] Nevertheless, the overwhelming conventional military superiority of the United States in the context of Cuba – an island only a few hundred miles from the U.S. mainland – was overpowering compared to the Soviet force. Consequently, Kennedy won this round of the Cold War. "Although Kennedy carefully refrained from public boasting, it was evident to all which side had backed down."[110]

Scholars have agreed that the Soviet leaders did not yield due to fear of a nuclear reprisal.[111] Nonetheless, the Soviets believed that they had been forced to retreat in the face of the American numerical superiority in nuclear weapons. As the Soviet Deputy Foreign Minister V. V. Kuznetsov warned American diplomat John McCloy in 1962, "Never will we be caught like this again."[112] Wolfe notes, "Militarily, the Cuban missile gambit not only failed [from the Soviet perspective] as a shortcut method of altering the strategic balance, but it also served to reconfirm American superiority."[113] Beckman and colleagues elaborate, "[T]he 'never again' syndrome implied that the Soviet Union would not tolerate such a political loss of face again. Strategic parity seemed to be the cure-all; the United States would not make such humiliating demands and the Soviet

---

[107] Morris, *Iron Destinies*, 192.   [108] Wolfe, *Soviet Power and Europe*, 87.

[109] Rhodes, *Arsenals of Folly*, 99.

[110] Chalmers M. Roberts, *The Nuclear Years: The Arms Race and Arms Control, 1945–70*. New York: Praeger, 1970, 60.

[111] Rhodes, *Arsenals of Folly*.

[112] Quoted in Newhouse, *War and Peace in the Nuclear Age*, 68.

[113] Wolfe, *Soviet Power and Europe*, 99.

Union could do as it desired under a condition of parity."[114] Although the nuclear arsenals were not a military factor during the Cuban Missile crisis, the political game of nuclear one-upmanship and its aftermath centered on numerical superiority in missiles as a primary arena of super-power competition.

The Soviets Catch Up

In the late 1960s, the Soviet Union put a huge effort into building more and better nuclear missiles. While the number of U.S. ICBMs remained relatively constant at 1,054, the Soviet ICBM arsenal increased from 30 in 1962 to 850 in 1968 to more than 1,500 by 1972.[115] The Soviets also expanded their submarine ballistic missile force and improved their strategic air forces. This massive expansion, beginning in 1965, "would enable the Soviet Union to achieve rough nuclear parity with the United States by the end of the decade."[116]

Scholars have attributed the Soviet buildup in part to the loss of face from the Cuban missile crisis. "Humiliation in Cuba," writes Gates, "galvanized the Soviets into action. The USSR proceeded to undertake the largest military buildup in history over a twenty-five-year period, with profound consequences for the international balance of power, for the United States, and ultimately, and fatefully, for the Soviet economy and state."[117] Rhodes claims, the Soviet Union was "frightened and deeply humiliated ... [t]hat the United States could force the leaders of the Soviet Union to remove their missiles from Cuba."[118] "The missile crisis reinforced the earlier decisions by the Politburo to expand the Soviet missile force in order to remove the asymmetry in the nuclear balance."[119] "[T]he arms build-up carried out by the Brezhnev-Kosygin regime probably derived its initial momentum ... from the regime's resolve to alter the image of a Soviet Union strategically inferior to its principal Western adversary."[120] The breakaway of China in the mid-1960s created a new potential nuclear enemy; the world was becoming more dangerous for the Soviet Union.

---

[114] Beckman, *The Nuclear Predicament*, 135.
[115] Robert M. Gates, *From the Shadows*. New York: Simon and Schuster, 1996, 29.
[116] Ronald E. Powaski, *March to Armageddon: The United States and the Nuclear Arms Race, 1939 to the Present*. New York: Oxford University Press, 1987, 106.
[117] Gates, *From the Shadows*, 29.   [118] Rhodes, *Arsenals of Folly*, 94.
[119] Beckman, *The Nuclear Predicament*, 135.
[120] Wolfe, *Soviet Power and Europe*, 264.

For the Soviets as well as the Americans and the international community in general, superiority was measured in numbers rather than strategic requirements. "The new Soviet leadership [under Brezhnev] decided to directly challenge the U.S. superiority in strategic nuclear weapons by reaching parity in the major types of intercontinental nuclear weapons," leading to "the most intense nuclear arms race of the Cold War."[121] The Soviet nuclear buildup was not based on internal calculations of Soviet defense requirements. Post–Cold War analysis has revealed that "Soviet strategic doctrine in the mid-1960s ... was not refined enough to help determine force levels."[122] Instead, the Soviet Union was intent on showing the world their ability to match the United States. "The precise size of the force was based largely on the size of the U.S. forces, more for its symbolic numerical equivalence than any formal doctrinal requirement."[123]

The Americans, on the other hand, were for the first time attending to the question of sufficiency where nuclear weapons were concerned.[124] Robert McNamara, Secretary of Defense under both Kennedy and Johnson, "attempted to deal explicitly with the question of how much power America needed during a time when it was technically at peace with the Soviet Union."[125] Armed with calculations from nuclear strategists, McNamara developed the plan for the American nuclear triad – ICBMs on the land, strategic bombers in the air, and nuclear-armed submarines for the sea. McNamara gave numbers for the optimal size of these forces, stabilizing the ICBM force around 1,000 missiles.

The need for stability in the American arsenal was an idea that had been simmering in think tanks since the 1950s. By the mid-1960s, U.S. analysts could see that the Soviet Union would soon achieve parity in nuclear missiles. The United States would no longer be able to rely on overwhelming superiority as its nuclear doctrine.[126] Instead, McNamara drew on theories of second-strike capability that the defense intellectuals had been brewing. Under this logic, the Soviet Union would be deterred from launching a nuclear attack if the United States had a sufficiently large nuclear force so that a devastating counterstrike could be launched in return.

[121] Steven J. Zaloga, *The Kremlin's Nuclear Sword: The Rise and Fall of Russia's Strategic Nuclear Forces, 1945–2000*. Washington, DC: Smithsonian Institution Press, 2002, 101.

[122] Zaloga, *The Kremlin's Nuclear Sword*, 101.

[123] Zaloga, *The Kremlin's Nuclear Sword*, 101.

[124] Alain C. Enthoven and K. Wayne Smith. *How Much Is Enough? Shaping the Defense Program, 1961–1969*. New York: Harper and Row, 1971.

[125] Morris, *Iron Destinies*, 179.   [126] Powaski, *March to Armageddon*, 114.

McNamara was willing to allow the Soviet Union to reach strategic parity with the United States rather than escalate the arms race further. In his view, expanding the U.S. arsenal beyond the minimum needed for a second strike would merely "accelerate the arms race, achieving no useful military purpose and contributing to arms race instability."[127] Moreover, an excessive increase in missiles "was bound to be economically counter-productive," since increasing the number of missiles would not create a military advantage.[128] In the ironic world of nuclear logic, an excess of missiles would be inefficient, since the effectiveness of the first and second waves of missiles meant no Soviet cities would be left for a third or fourth strike to destroy.

In short, "McNamara's goal had become *stability*."[129] By the early 1970s, there was general agreement among U.S. decision-makers that the Soviet Union had reached strategic nuclear parity with the United States.[130] The SALT treaty, signed in 1972, had for the first time set ceilings for U.S. and Soviet arsenals. "Never before," Kissinger said, 'have the two world's most powerful nations ... placed their central armaments under formally agreed limitation and restraint.'"[131] As Holloway notes, "The Agreements themselves were a public and visible sign of the success of the ... [Soviet] drive to catch up with the United States."[132] According to the deterrence theories of the 1960s, this parity would allow mutual security.

The United States Ups the Ante

Unfortunately, the Soviet Union did not seem to have reached the same conclusion. The United States had resigned itself to a state of nuclear parity with its closest enemy and reluctantly regarded the Soviet Union as a nuclear equal. However, the Soviet Union continued to pour resources into expanding its nuclear forces rather than slackening its pace. From the U.S. perspective, the Soviet Union seemed to be aiming for superiority, not parity. During the mid-1970s, a strong conservative voice arose within the United States, arguing that Soviet intentions to launch a nuclear war

---

[127] Beckman, *The Nuclear Predicament*, 98–99, italics removed.
[128] Powaski, *March to Armageddon*, 115.
[129] Beckman, *The Nuclear Predicament*, 98–99.
[130] Beckman, *The Nuclear Predicament*, 137.
[131] Quoted in Powaski, *March to Armageddon*, 144.
[132] David Holloway, *The Soviet Union and the Arms Race*. New Haven: Yale University Press, 1983, 48.

had prompted the quest for Soviet nuclear superiority. This position became policy in the Reagan administration, leading the United States to place itself on a bellicose footing to arm itself physically and morally in order to deter the Soviet Union.

In the mid-1970s, conservative voices within the United States argued that U.S. quiescence during the Soviet buildup of the late 1960s had signaled complacency to the Soviet Union. The McNamara doctrine of stability was reviled as sheep-like stupidity in the face of a predator. "[U]nlike its previous responses to strategic gap alarms," the United States "had stood by during the rapid Soviet strategic build-up of the late sixties without lifting the fixed ceiling it had set for its own strategic forces in the early sixties," allowing the Soviet Union to seize "an opportunity to forge ahead of the United States."[133] Conservative critics lambasted:

By their inaction, successive administrations had lost strategic superiority over the Soviets, "welcomed" the loss of for its presumed "benign effects" on Soviet policy, frozen the new inferiority into place through SALT, and constructed theories of "stability" to justify their folly. They had refused to comprehend the Soviet Union as a "unique adversary," and had failed to recognize Soviet military superiority until it was almost too late to reverse.[134]

One major piece of evidence in support of this argument was the observation that the Soviet arsenal was expanding – and why would the Soviets increase their nuclear weapons if they were not planning to use them? Richard Pipes, one of the leading voices of conservative dissent, argued that "détente is not compatible with an unabated Soviet military effort for which no reasonable defense justification exists. As long as the USSR keeps on multiplying its arsenal and increasing the variety of military options open to it, its professions of peaceful intent must be viewed with skepticism."[135] An influential report by defense intellectuals concluded:

The pace of the Soviet armament effort in all fields is staggering; *it certainly exceeds any requirement for mutual deterrence* ... So does the high proportion of the national budget devoted to direct military expenditures ... *the Soviets may well expect to achieve a degree of military superiority which would permit a dramatically more aggressive pursuit of their hegemonial objectives.*[136]

---

[133] Wolfe, *Soviet Power and Europe*, 503–504.   [134] Morris, *Iron Destinies*, 352.
[135] Richard Pipes, editor, *Soviet Strategy in Europe*. New York: Crane, Russak and Co., 1976, 44.
[136] Quoted in Rhodes, *Arsenals of Folly*, 125; italics in the original.

A second piece of evidence was the aggressive Soviet discourse that Western analysts had been aware of but previously discounted. Major Soviet military journals throughout the 1960s and 1970s stated the Soviet objective of military superiority, and all three editions of the influential Soviet *Military Strategy* declared: "[T]he creation and constant maintenance of quantitative and qualitative superiority over the enemy in this means of armed combat and in the methods of its use represents one of the most important tasks of construction of the armed forces in the contemporary epoch."[137] Such statements gave credence to Reagan's belief that "the Soviets had never accepted MAD [deterrence theory] as the basis of their nuclear strategy. Instead, they believed that a nuclear war could be won."[138]

Subsequent scholarship has suggested that the United States may have erred in these estimates of Soviet nuclear expansion, much as it erred in the "missile gap" of the early 1960s and had also failed to note a missile lag in the other direction the late 1960s. Instead, "these confident estimates of a steady acceleration in Soviet military spending were wrong ... 'New information indicates,' says the CIA, 'that the Soviets did not field weapons as rapidly after 1976 as before. Practically all major categories of Soviet weapons were affected – missiles, aircraft, and ships.'"[139]

Nor could U.S. strategic experts explain how the Soviet expansion of its nuclear arsenal contributed to military advantage. "With each aspect of the [Soviet] build-up [in the 1970s] it was difficult to explain how the Soviet strategic or political position had really benefited."[140] U.S. thinkers had questioned whether the United States had gained advantage during its own period of superiority – the Soviet Union would likely be as little advantaged. Perhaps the Soviets even had their own military-industrial complex that was "as wasteful and extravagant as comparable US programmes."[141]

Nonetheless, these speculations "could not dispel the nagging doubt that the USSR was arming itself because it felt this to be advantageous ... It might be mistaken, but if it acted upon such beliefs, however wrong,

[137] William T. Lee and Richard F. Staar, *Soviet Military Policy: Since World War II*. Stanford: Hoover Institution Press, 1986, 29.
[138] Powaski, *March to Armageddon*, 187.
[139] Honoré M. Catudal, *Soviet Nuclear Strategy from Stalin to Gorbachev*. Berlin: Verlag, 1989, 110.
[140] Freedman, *The Evolution of Nuclear Strategy*, 330.
[141] Freedman, *The Evolution of Nuclear Strategy*, 330.

the consequences for everyone could be extremely dangerous."[142] Finally, the Soviet invasion of Afghanistan in 1979 as well as Soviet military forays into Angola and other Third World countries seemed to confirm that the Soviet Union was testing its military prowess through aggressive wars.[143]

Consequently, the United States began a huge increase in military expenditures, beginning during the Carter administration and reaching even greater heights under Reagan.[144] "To combat this perceived military imbalance, Reagan initiated the largest peacetime expansion of U.S. military forces since World War II."[145] Defense spending nearly doubled during the first years of the Reagan administration, revived major weapons proposals such as the B-1 bomber and the neutron bomb, and spurred the development of new systems such as the MX missile, the Trident submarine, and ballistic missile defense.[146]

Within the United States, liberal critics argued that the expansion of the nuclear arsenal had led to little increase in real security.[147] As Richard Stubbings, a federal defense analyst, noted, "[T]here is increasing controversy over the extent to which our real defense capabilities have improved. Many experts, on all sides of the political spectrum, have criticized the inefficiency of the recent defense buildup."[148] Media stories took advantage of exorbitantly priced toilet seats and hammers. As Morris concludes, "[T]he fact remains that the huge upsurge in spending has purchased a very modest increment in fighting capabilities, far less than might reasonably be expected from a 50 percent real increase in outlays."[149]

Nevertheless, the United States did surge ahead in one-upmanship over the Soviet Union. The Soviets reacted much as the Americans had a decade previously. Wolf observed that "the reaction in Moscow was one of barely controlled panic" to the record defense budget of $157 billion under Carter.[150] When Ronald Reagan became president, the already enlarged U.S. defense budget was greatly expanded. From the Soviet perspective, "the massive Reagan administration arms buildup threatened what the Soviet leadership perceived to be rough nuclear

[142] Freedman, *The Evolution of Nuclear Strategy*, 330.
[143] Rhodes, *Arsenals of Folly*, 138.   [144] Rhodes, *Arsenals of Folly*, 150.
[145] Catudal, *Soviet Nuclear Strategy from Stalin to Gorbachev*, 94.
[146] Powaski, *March to Armageddon*, 184.
[147] James Fallows, *National Defense*. New York: Random House, 1981.
[148] Quoted in Morris, *Iron Destinies*, 375.   [149] Morris, *Iron Destinies*, 376.
[150] Rhodes, *Arsenals of Folly*, 145; Wolfe, *Soviet Power and Europe*.

parity between the two nations."[151] The Soviet Union believed the United States was arming itself for a major nuclear attack. As Soviet premier Brezhnev believed, "They are working on new systems of weapons of mass destruction – we know this very well – in closed American engineering and construction offices."[152] The U.S. focus on strengthening the communications and command structure as well as the initiation of the Strategic Defense Initiative communicated an even more sinister commitment to actually launch a nuclear attack. "As seen from current Soviet perspective, an extensive U.S. program to prepare the command structure to support a nuclear campaign will be understood as a sign of increased willingness to initiate war."[153] Due to these U.S. initiatives, "'Never, perhaps, in the postwar decades,' Gorbachev would summarize later, 'has the situation in the world been as explosive ... as in the first half of the eighties.'"[154]

By the end of the Cold War, the United States and the Soviet Union each had staggeringly large nuclear arsenals with tens of thousands of nuclear warheads each.[155] Early in the Cold War, Eisenhower "had originally thought that about 20 to 40 ICBMs would be more than enough to round out a bomber-based deterrent," but by the end of his administration, a plan for 1,100 nuclear missiles was under way.[156] In the 1960s, White House analysts determined that diminishing returns occurred after 450 missiles for the simple reason that there were an insufficient number of Soviet targets.[157] Despite decades of effort, military strategists on both sides had largely failed to develop strategic doctrines in which these enormous arsenals would provide military or political advantage.

Rather than actual military utility, the primary motivation for the nuclear arms race was simply Great Power one-upmanship. As Snyder pointed out early in the arms race, "a quantitatively inferior force carries a serious psychological liability ... national self-respect and prestige are bound to suffer from a policy which deliberately accepts a permanent inferiority in nuclear striking power."[158] The superpowers paid dearly to maintain national self-respect and prestige. In the end, the desire for one-upmanship outweighed the real economic and security costs involved in the nuclear arms race.

[151] Rhodes, *Arsenals of Folly*, 150.   [152] Rhodes, *Arsenals of Folly*, 144.
[153] Rhodes, *Arsenals of Folly*, 150.   [154] Rhodes, *Arsenals of Folly*, 167.
[155] Morris, *Iron Destinies*.   [156] Morris, *Iron Destinies*, 183.
[157] Morris, *Iron Destinies*, 190–191.   [158] Snyder, *Deterrence and Defense*, 117–18.

CONCLUSION

How do states identify those assets or capabilities that will increase their power? This chapter has argued that the military power conferred by nuclear weapons was "learned" from the events of the Second World War. Yet the ambiguity of history implies that the effect of the atomic bomb on the Japanese in 1945 might not be generalizable to other countries or to modern nuclear missiles with their exceedingly greater destructive capacity. Instead, the Great Powers poured their wealth into the acquisition of nuclear weapons that had little impact on their effective military power. As Morris sums up, "[I]f such outlays are measured against the achievement of any other conceivable political or military objective, it is remarkable how little has been accomplished."[159]

Instead, the enormous economic and political investment in nuclear weapons did not increase the security of the Great Power states. Most conspicuous is the case of the Soviet Union, where the possession of a massive nuclear arsenal did not prevent the failure and collapse of the state. As Reiss notes, the "most startling ... is the recognition that an awesome collection of thirty thousand nuclear weapons – the world's largest arsenal – could not preserve the Soviet empire or, indeed, even prevent the collapse of the Soviet Union itself."[160]

From the perspective of the United States, Richard J. Barnet observes that although the United States might have been reckoned the most powerful country in the world after the Second World War, "it has not won a decisive military victory since 1945 despite the trillions spent on the military and the frequent engagement of its military forces."[161] Instead, Barnet adds, "It is one of history's greatest ironies that at the very moment when the United States had a monopoly of nuclear weapons, possessed most of the world's gold, produced half the world's goods on its own territory, and laid down the rules for allies and adversaries alike, it was afraid."[162] As Smoke noted in 1989, "The simplest observation to be made about the last few decades [of the Cold War] is that the American people now find themselves less secure than they ever have been."[163]

Paradoxically, states hoping to acquire power may find themselves at greater risk as a result of their ambitions. Iraq is one recent example of a state to suffer the costs of campaigning for recognition as a regional

---

[159] Morris, *Iron Destinies*, 418.   [160] Reiss, *Bridled Ambition*, 322–323.
[161] Quoted in Rhodes, *Arsenals of Folly*, 298.   [162] Rhodes, *Arsenals of Folly*, 298.
[163] Smoke, *National Security and the Nuclear Dilemma*, 290.

power. Previous bids for power, such as that of Japan, Italy, and Germany, also met with disaster in the Second World War. Those states that managed to hold on to their Great Power status suffered as well – France, Britain, and the Soviet Union experienced economic declines following the Second World War, despite the maintenance of their Great Power status. Thus the high economic costs and security risks that accompany the pursuit of power have historically been quite exorbitant for states.

States may desire power, but cannot penetrate the ambiguity of which resources will contribute to power. The story of the disappointing quest for military power is commonplace, as a broad review of the history of the European Great Powers shows. Being a Great Power does not always enhance state security – instead, the wars the Great Powers engage in are usually the greatest threats these states face. Nor does victory in one war ensure safety from future wars. Instead, Great Power states pour resources into acquiring indicators of military capability that are hoped to ensure victory and security. History frequently takes a left turn, however, leading to the abandonment of those costly technologies while the Great Powers rush to acquire the next token of power that promises security.

8

The Construction of U.S. Cold War Interests

"Had the Korean war not actually taken place, we would never have believed that it could have."[1]

The modern Great Power system emerged in Europe, and for centuries the primary economic, political, and strategic competitions had centered on that continent. After the Second World War, however, the superpowers began to compete over non-Western countries that traditional political calculations had long discounted. How did peripheral areas such as Korea and Vietnam come to be seen as sufficiently valuable to figure in the grand competitions between the Great Powers? As historian Bruce Cumings muses, "Why ... would a hegemonic power successively repeat this remarkable diversion of its attention on the peripheral, indulge this instinct for the toenail?"[2] In previous eras, the Great Powers had focused their energies on gaining allies that were believed to contribute militarily to an alliance. This sudden interest in militarily weak allies was historically unprecedented.

Scholars generally agree that there was little of objective military value at stake in Korea, Vietnam, and many of the other targets of U.S. intervention during the Cold War. Consequently, it is difficult to construct a simple instrumental account of Great Power involvement. Instead, scholars developed the concept of the proxy war – in which states fight each other through intermediary states – to explain the Cold War

[1] Henry A. Kissinger, *Nuclear Weapons and Foreign Policy*. New York: Harper and Brothers, 1957, 43.
[2] Bruce Cumings, *The Origins of the Korean War: Volume II The Roaring of the Cataract, 1947–1950*. Princeton: Princeton University Press, 1990, 17.

competition for states outside of Europe. Realists argued that the bipolar division of power between the United States and the Soviet Union inevitably led to confrontation.[3] The superpowers were deterred from a direct confrontation over the more valuable landscape of Europe because of the fear of nuclear holocaust. Proxy wars developed as a sort of a displaced aggression, in which the superpowers expended economic and military resources in squabbles of little objective value.

This chapter argues that the hostility between the United States and the Soviet Union can be understood as a constructed rivalry that was based on contingent interpretations made under ambiguity, rather than an inevitable outcome of the balance of power. U.S. policymakers chose an interpretation in which the Soviet Union sought world domination, even though historical evidence suggested other plausible interpretations. This chapter develops an account of the construction of Cold War interests leading up to the U.S. involvement in Korea in 1950.

First, U.S. policymakers began to construct the Soviet Union as its major rival. In 1945, it was far from clear that the United States and the Soviet Union would end up as enemies. Indeed, scholars have puzzled over how these allies in the Second World War could have turned so quickly to mutual hostility. U.S. policymakers made a series of interpretations to make sense of ambiguous actions of the Soviet Union. In particular, U.S. decision-makers placed the Soviet Union in the role of Nazi Germany in order to make sense of events and plan for future conflicts. Retrospectively, however, historians have questioned the reasonableness of this interpretation.

Second, the value of allies in the non-Western world was built on a particular theory for the prevention of future global conflicts. This theory, like many discussed in this book, was based on "lessons" of the prior war. In this case, the cause of the Second World War was attributed to European appeasement of Hitler, specifically in the ceding of peripheral territory to Germany at a conference in Munich. This theory was generalized to apply to the territorial ambitions of the Soviet Union on a global scale. The principal value of U.S. credibility toward allies in non-Western countries was the theoretical prevention of another Munich.

Third, the newly constructed rivalry between the superpowers resulted in familiar patterns of competition and one-upmanship, described in

---

[3] Kenneth N. Waltz, *Theory of International Politics*. Reading: Addison-Wesley, 1979; John J. Mearsheimer, *The Tragedy of Great Power Politics*. New York: W. W. Norton and Company, 2001.

Chapter 2. The United States entered into competitions with the primary goal of increasing its reputation by one-upmanship over its chief rival, the Soviet Union. In the case of the Korean War, U.S. decision-makers had initially seen little instrumental value in the Korean peninsula. Yet when events suggested the possibility of triumphing over the Soviet Union, the United States immediately moved to declare war in 1950.

THE CONSTRUCTION OF A RIVAL

Scholars of the Cold War have been puzzled by the rapidity with which the Soviet Union, a key ally during the Second World War, turned into the implacable Cold War enemy of the United States. Much of the historical literature on the origins of the Cold War has been focused on describing the process by which U.S. political leaders ascertained that the Soviet Union had become an inimical threat only a year or two after being an ally in the Second World War. Numerous theories have been developed, ranging from the portrayal of the Soviet Union as inevitably set on world domination to those portraying the Soviet Union as the hapless goat of American capitalist interests. As Paterson has observed, "The dizzying array of explanations demonstrates that there have been no pat answers and certainly little agreement among scholars ... Doubt must dog any careful student of Soviet behavior."[4] This proliferation of scholarly theories demonstrates the ambiguity of Soviet antagonism, since multiple plausible interpretations have been put forth to explain the same set of events.

Realist scholars have argued that the enmity between the United States and the Soviet Union was the inevitable outcome of the balance of power. Waltz writes, "In the great-power politics of a bipolar world, who is a danger to whom is never in doubt."[5] Realists claimed that military power was more evenly distributed among the Great Powers in previous historical eras, allowing multiple combinations and alliances. The second half of the twentieth century was historically unprecedented in having two Great Powers of equivalent military capability. These two Great Powers would necessarily divide the international system into two camps, and each would seek to expand its influence at the expense of the other.

[4] Thomas G. Paterson, *On Every Front: The Making and Unmaking of the Cold War*. New York: W. W. Norton and Company, 1992, 165.

[5] Kenneth N. Waltz, "The Origins of War in Neorealist Theory." In *The Origin and Prevention of Major Wars*, edited by Robert I. Rotberg and Theodore K. Raab, 39–52. Cambridge: Cambridge University Press, 1988, 46.

From the realist perspective, the enmity between the United States and the Soviet Union was inevitable, based on the underlying distribution of power.

Yet much of the historical scholarship on the origins of the Cold War suggests that the antagonism between the United States and the Soviet Union was contingent rather than inevitable.[6] As Gaddis argues, the empirical facts did not simply speak for themselves. Instead he observes, "How well-founded that alarm was – how accurately it reflected the realities that shaped Soviet policy – are issues upon which there are legitimate grounds for disagreement."[7] This ambiguity is highlighted by three generations of U.S. scholarship, each of which gave radically different interpretations for the same ambiguous set of facts. In addition, the early actions of the Soviet Union also led to considerable confusion among Western diplomats about the postwar intentions of the Soviet Union. In the end, the United States chose an interpretation that allowed the Soviet Union to reprise the role of Nazi Germany in the American construction of the theorized causes of the Second World War.

Three Generations of U.S. Scholarship

This section briefly recounts three divergent interpretations of the hostility of the Soviet Union toward the West developed by three generations of U.S. scholars.[8] U.S. scholarship can be broadly divided into three perspectives on the degree of competition between the Soviet Union and the United States: (1) the dominant interpretation of the 1950s in which the Soviet Union, driven by Marxist-Leninist ideology, was aggressively poised to take over the world[9]; (2) the revisionist interpretation of the

---

[6] For example, see Deborah Welch Larson, *Origins of Containment: A Psychological Explanation*. Princeton: Princeton University Press, 1985; Deborah Welch Larson, *Anatomy of Mistrust*. Ithaca: Cornell University Press, 1997. Der Derian provides a discourse-based analysis in James Der Derian, *On Diplomacy: A Genealogy of Western Estrangement*. New York: Basil Blackwell, 1987.

[7] John Lewis Gaddis, *The Long Peace: Inquiries into the History of the Cold War*. Oxford: Oxford University Press, 1987, 47.

[8] Simon J. Ball, *The Cold War: An International History, 1947–1991*. New York: St. Martin's Press, 1998; David S. Painter, *The Cold War: An International History*. London: Routledge, 1999.

[9] Herbert Feis, *From Trust to Terror: The Onset of the Cold War, 1945–1950*. New York: W.W. Norton and Company, 1970; Louis J. Halle, *The Cold War as History*. New York: Harper and Row, 1967; George F. Kennan, "Mr. 'X' Reassesses His Brainchild." In *The Evolution of the Cold War*, edited by Richard H. Miller, 70–75. Huntington: Robert E. Krieger, 1979 [1967].

1960s, which claimed that the USSR was a scapegoat created by the United States to justify its own aggressive capitalist policies[10]; and (3) the "post-revisionist" interpretation, developed in the 1980s, in which the Cold War was the result of mutual insecurity created by the efforts of the Soviet Union and the United States to each ensure its own well-being.[11]

These three different interpretations provide different accounts of the postwar Soviet occupation of Eastern Europe, which was one of the major incidents that contributed to the perception of Soviet hostility by the U.S. government and public. During the Second World War, the Allies had divided Europe among themselves in the pursuit of German defeat. The Western states had mostly recalled their armies at the end of the war. The Soviet Union, on the other hand, continued to occupy much of the territory gained as a result of the war, including Eastern Europe and Soviet-occupied Germany.

The first generation of scholarship, which was dominant in the 1950s, interpreted the actions of the Soviet Union as indicators of its pursuit of world domination. From this perspective, the Soviet occupation of Eastern Europe was the first step in a hostile takeover of the world. The occupation of Eastern Europe was widely perceived by the American public and government officials as indicating Soviet territorial ambitions, which were generally assumed to include the eventual occupation of Western Europe. As Halle wrote with alarm, "The Soviet Union had suddenly, as if by sleight of hand, effected the military conquest of the eastern half of Europe."[12] Feis wrote in 1947: "Who, observing such malign actions ... could continue to believe that the Soviet Government would permit freedom or democracy in the Western sense, or show regard for any agreements which obligated them to tolerate opposition?"[13]

---

[10] Joyce Kolko and Gabriel Kolko, *The Limits of Power: The World and United States Foreign Policy, 1945–1954*. New York: Harper and Row, 1972; Arthur Jr. P. Schlesinger, chapter 2 in *The Origins of the Cold War*, by Lloyd C. Gardner, Arthur Schlesinger Jr., and Hans J. Morgenthau, 41–78. Waltham: Ginn-Blaisdell, 1970 [1967]; William Appleman Williams, *The Tragedy of American Diplomacy*. New York: Delta, 1962 [1959].

[11] John Lewis Gaddis, *Strategies of Containment: A Critical Appraisal of Postwar American National Security Policy*. Oxford: Oxford University Press, 1982; John Lewis Gaddis, *The United States and the Origins of the Cold War, 1941–1947*. New York: Columbia University Press, 1972; Melvyn P. Leffler, *A Preponderance of Power: National Security, the Truman Administration, and the Cold War*. Stanford: Stanford University Press, 1992; Ralph B. Levering, *The Cold War, 1945–1987*, second edition. Arlington Heights: Harlan Davidson, 1988.

[12] Halle, *The Cold War as History*, 1.   [13] Quoted in Feis, *From Trust to Terror*, 174.

This generation of scholars argued that the Soviet Union was driven by Marxist-Leninist ideology to develop a communist sphere that would exclude the capitalist countries.[14] Gradually, this sphere would grow until it had "contained" the United States, isolating it economically and politically. As a 1946 issue of *Life* declared, "Already Poland, the Baltic States, Rumania, Bulgaria, Yugoslavia and Albania are behind the Iron Curtain. Huge armies hold Hungary and half of Germany and Austria .... One ... must also wonder whether they will ultimately be satisfied with less than dominion over Europe and Asia."[15] From this perspective, the Soviet Union was an implacable enemy, analogous to Nazi Germany, which had to be resisted by the West at all costs.

A second interpretation, developed by revisionist historians in the 1960s, saw the Soviet occupation of Eastern Europe as provoked primarily by U.S. actions.[16] Scholars such as Williams, Kolko, Gardner, Schlesinger, and Morgenthau argued that the aggressive capitalist policies followed by the United States after the Second World War provoked the Soviet Union to protect its own economic sphere in Eastern Europe. For instance, Williams interpreted the U.S. Marshall Plan as "an American strategy for setting and maintaining conditions on economic development in eastern Europe and the Soviet Union."[17] These American economic pressures in turn forced the Soviet Union to increase repression and gain political control in Romania, Bulgaria, Czechoslovakia, and Soviet-held Germany. The Soviets believed that their economic and political controls in Eastern Europe were "defensive measures to protect Soviet security and its rightful fruits of victory over the Axis."[18] From this perspective, the Soviet Union had been provoked by the United States into some regrettable acts of oppression, but was not necessarily fundamentally opposed to the United States.

The third interpretation, labeled "post-revisionist," was developed in the 1980s. Scholars in this camp posited that the Cold War was based on

---

[14] Feis, *From Trust to Terror*; Halle, *The Cold War as History*; Kennan, "Mr. 'X' Reassesses His Brainchild"; Walter LaFeber, *America, Russia, and the Cold War.* New York: John Wiley, 1967.

[15] Norman A. Graebner, "Myth and Reality: America's Rhetorical Cold War." In *Critical Reflections on the Cold War: Linking Rhetoric and History*, edited by Martin J. Medhurst and H. W. Brands, 20–37. College Station: Texas A&M University Press, 2000, 20–21.

[16] Kolko, *The Limits of Power*; Lloyd C. Gardner, Arthur Schlesinger, Jr., and Hans J. Morgenthau, *The Origins of the Cold War.* Waltham: Ginn-Blaisdell, 1970; Schlesinger, "chapter 2"; Williams, *The Tragedy of American Diplomacy.*

[17] Williams, *The Tragedy of American Diplomacy*, 274.

[18] Paterson, *On Every Front*, 102.

mutual insecurity arising from efforts of the Soviet Union and the United States to ensure their own well-being.[19] Both superpowers were seeking security, although at times their quest for their own security inadvertently appeared threatening to the other. From this perspective, the Soviets were simply "consolidat[ing] their security in Eastern Europe." Yet the Americans regarded these actions "as the first step toward [an invasion of] Western Europe."[20]

The post-revisionist historians suggest that the Soviet occupation of Eastern Europe was based on a misunderstanding. British and American officials had tacitly agreed during the Second World War to the postwar Soviet occupation of Eastern Europe, but President Roosevelt did not inform the U.S. public, or even Vice President Truman, of this secret wartime agreement.[21] Consequently, with Roosevelt's death, the U.S. government and public were left with the perception that the Soviet Union had violated its wartime agreements. From the Soviet perspective, however, it was abiding by terms that had been agreed on by the United States. From the post-revisionist perspective, both superpowers were innocent of unwarranted territorial ambitions, but each superpower's attempts to ensure its own security increased suspicion and hostility of the other.

This summary of scholarship is intended to emphasize the ambiguity of the empirical facts available to U.S. policymakers, rather than to claim, post hoc, that one interpretation was empirically correct. Each of these three radically divergent interpretations of Soviet behavior was based on roughly the same set of empirical facts available to U.S. scholars in the postwar period. Analogous to the cavalry debates of the late nineteenth century, the facts available to policymakers allowed multiple interpretations. Nevertheless, the U.S. interpretation of Soviet aggression proved highly consequential for the U.S.-Soviet relationship and for the world in the latter half of the twentieth century.

Initial Assessments

Ambiguity over the motivations of the Soviet Union can be seen not only in the scholarly literature of the Cold War but in the interpretations of

---

[19] Gaddis, *The United States and the Origins of the Cold War*, *Strategies of Containment*, *The Long Peace*; Leffler, *A Preponderance of Power*; Levering, *The Cold War*; Simon J. Ball, *The Cold War: An International History, 1947–1991*. New York: St. Martin's Press, 1998, 3.

[20] Schlesinger, "chapter 2," 68.

[21] Schlesinger, "chapter 2"; Gaddis, *The United States and the Origins of the Cold War*.

U.S. policymakers in the early postwar years. In the famous words of Winston Churchill, the Soviet Union was "a riddle wrapped in a mystery inside an enigma."[22] Ball, another Cold War historian, complained that "trying to identify the ambitions of the Stalinist regime is akin to gazing into a crystal ball."[23] In the early postwar years, U.S. policymakers were urgently trying to figure out the role that the United States would play as a Great Power. The ambiguous behavior of the Soviet Union only contributed to their confusion.

In the second half of the twentieth century, the United States had emerged as one of the leading Great Powers. As argued in Chapter 2, this status was the result of the wartime performance and victory of the Allies in the Second World War. However, Britain and the Soviet Union also shared in the victorious outcome of the Allies. Indeed, when the term "superpower" was coined in 1944, it included Britain as well as the United States and the Soviet Union.[24]

Ambiguity was evident in the relationships among these Powers in the first few years following the Second World War. Initially, the United States envisioned a bipolar world in which Britain and the Soviet Union would be the superpowers while the United States played a secondary role. In 1945, U.S. policymakers "saw the United States more as a mediator between Britain and Russia than as a permanent ally of either one of them."[25] A U.S. Joint Chief of Staffs report in 1944 had assessed: "The greatest likelihood of eventual conflict" would be between Britain and Russia, each attempting to maintain its sphere of influence.[26] As Gaddis notes, "As late as April, 1946, Truman could still speculate publicly about the possibility of a contest for world influence between London and Moscow, with Washington acting as an impartial umpire."[27]

Alternately, the United States considered Britain as a potential enemy. The other Great Powers had also foreseen conflict between the United States and Britain. For instance, Hitler had based his war plans in part on the likelihood of Anglo-American conflict over their control of Atlantic trade.[28] The Soviet Union was also "ready to assume inevitable Anglo-American discord," since the tenets of Leninism theorized Britain and the

[22] Winston Churchill, BBC radio address "The Russian Enigma," October 1, 1939.
[23] Paterson, *On Every Front*, 165.   [24] Ball, *The Cold War*, 6–7.
[25] Gaddis, *The Long Peace*, 27.   [26] Schlesinger, "chapter 2," 59.
[27] Gaddis, *The Long Peace*, 55.
[28] Manfred Messerschmidt, "German Military Effectiveness between 1919 and 1939." In *Military Effectiveness: Volume II: The Interwar Period*, edited by Allan R. Millett and Williamson Murray, 218–255 Boston: Allen and Unwin, 1988.

United States as economic and political rivals of each other.[29] However, Britain chose to drop out of the three-way Great Power competition, ceding its place to the United States. The postwar relationship between the United States and Britain grew warmer rather than colder.

U.S. policymakers were unsure how to interpret the motivations of the Soviet Union in the early postwar years. Initially, U.S. President Truman had been favorably impressed by Stalin and thought they could get along together. Truman wrote in his diary at Potsdam that "I can deal with Stalin ... He is honest – but smart as hell."[30] Truman regarded early difficulties "simply as failures of communication" and was inclined "to give the Kremlin the benefit of the doubt: to assume ... that difficulties with Moscow had arisen out of misunderstandings rather than fundamental conflicts of interest."[31] Truman claimed in 1945 that the problems with the Soviet Union "could be solved 'amicably if we gave ourselves time.'"[32]

Yet the Soviet Union gave puzzling mixed messages from the Western point of view. At one conference, five postwar peace treaties were harmoniously signed by the Soviet Union, "including some that had been adopted in the face of stiff Russian objection."[33] British Foreign Secretary Bevin exclaimed, "I believe we have entered the first stage of establishing concord and harmony between the Great Powers."[34] Yet the Soviets refused to sign a treaty on German demilitarization at another conference, which was interpreted by the Americans as a sign that "the Soviets were more interested in expansionism than security."[35] Another possible interpretation was the lack of experience between Western and Soviet diplomats, due to the recent birth of the Soviet Union in 1917. At least one U.S. ambassador to the Soviet Union in the early Cold War years "subscribed to the dictum ... that 'there are no experts on the Soviet Union; there are only varying degrees of ignorance.'"[36]

U.S. policymakers felt the imperative to identify enemies as quickly as possible. New to its role as one of the leading Great Powers, the United States had been forced out of its previous apathy toward international

[29] David Reynolds, "The European Dimension of the Cold War." In *Origins of the Cold War: An International History*, edited by Melvyn P. Leffler and David S. Painter, 125–138. London: Routledge, 1994, 131.

[30] Quoted in Gaddis, *The Long Peace*, 31.   [31] Gaddis, *The Long Peace*, 32, 34.

[32] Quoted in Daniel Yergin, *Shattered Peace: The Origins of the Cold War and the National Security State*. Boston: Houghton Mifflin, 1977, 141.

[33] Feis, *From Trust to Terror*, 168.   [34] Feis, *From Trust to Terror*, 170.

[35] Paterson, *On Every Front*, 66.   [36] Quoted in Paterson, *On Every Front*, 165.

affairs. Following the errors of the Second World War, the United States felt great urgency to identify and prepare for its military opponent in the upcoming Third World War. In the early postwar years, the lack of an identified enemy created a great deal of anxiety and "an obvious gap in Washington's thinking about the postwar world."[37] Interestingly, neither of the aggressors in the previous war, Germany or Japan, was considered a threat by U.S. planners, despite the concern of many European statesmen over a potential rise of German military power.

In this context of ambiguous behavior by the Soviet Union coupled with the demand to proactively identify future enemies, U.S. policymakers desperately searched for a satisfying interpretation of the Soviet Union. The Long Telegram written by George Kennan – who was serving as deputy chief at the U.S. embassy in the Soviet Union – was seized upon as bringing clarity to a vexingly ambiguous situation and allowed U.S. decision-makers to move forward.

The Resolution of Ambiguity

The historical scholarship suggests the initial ambiguity of the relationship between the United States and the Soviet Union. A range of plausible interpretations of Soviet behavior was supported by the empirical facts. Yet such ambiguity was intolerable for U.S. policymakers who needed to make immediate decisions about the postwar world. Therefore, in short order, an interpretation of the Soviet Union was developed that corresponded with the nascent "lessons" drawn from the Second World War. While these lessons will be described in the next section, one implication was that the Soviet Union came to be seen as the replacement for Nazi Germany, and Stalin as the understudy of Hitler. As Levering summarizes, "[H]istorians have noted ... how many tended to view Stalin as another Hitler bent on world domination."[38] The interpretation of the Soviet Union as the enemy corresponded neatly with the U.S. attempts to avoid a replay of the Second World War.

Once in place, this interpretation became locked into the thinking of the U.S. foreign policy establishment. "Once Truman and the men around him perceived developments of the 1940's as parallel to those of the 1930's, they applied this moral and hence resolved to behave toward the Soviet Union as they believed their predecessors should have behaved

---

[37] Gaddis, *The Long Peace*, 40.   [38] Levering, *The Cold War*, 24.

toward the expansionist states of their time."[39] As the United States became more suspicious of the Soviet Union, the apparent hostility of the Soviets served as a self-fulfilling prophecy. As the United States increasingly adopted the perspective of the Soviet Union as its primary rival, U.S. decision-makers were increasingly able to interpret ambiguous incidents with the Soviet Union as reinforcing that interpretation.[40]

Events immediately following the Second World War were quite ambiguous, yet provided fodder for those who viewed the Soviet Union as hostile. As Paterson notes retrospectively, "considerable evidence suggests that in the 1945–1946 period, the Soviet Union was uncertain, halting, and defensive in its relations with the eastern European nations and did not have a master plan for the region."[41] As Cold War historian Leffler concludes, "In their overall assessment of Soviet long-term intentions, however, [U.S.] military planners dismissed all evidence of Soviet moderation, circumspection, and restraint ... Information not confirming prevailing assumptions either was ignored in overall assessments of Soviet intentions or was used to illustrate that the Soviets were shifting tactics but not altering objectives."[42]

Even in the case of Eastern Europe, American attention focused on the particular cases of Soviet behavior in Poland, Hungary, Romania, and Bulgaria, but "did not seriously grapple with contradictory evidence," as Leffler points out, "disregard[ing] numerous signs of Soviet weakness, moderation, and circumspection." For instance, Soviet troops withdrew on schedule from Norway, Manchuria, and Bornholm, and the Soviet Union extensively demobilized its armies in Eastern Europe as well.[43] Although the Soviet Union installed governments in Poland and Romania, it allowed a non-communist regime in Finland and did not interfere with elections in Hungary and Czechoslovakia in the early postwar years. "Yet Truman and his advisers ... took Soviet actions in Poland, Rumania, and Bulgaria to be indicative of what the Soviet government intended to do everywhere else" and "apparently paid little attention to occurrences in Finland, Hungary, or Czechoslovakia."[44]

[39] Ernest R. May, *"Lessons" of the Past: The Use and Misuse of History in American Foreign Policy*. London: Oxford University Press, 1979 [1973], 32.
[40] Feis, *From Trust to Terror*, 174.   [41] Paterson, *On Every Front*, 116.
[42] Melvyn P. Leffler, "National Security and US Foreign Policy." In *Origins of the Cold War: An International History*, edited by Melvyn P. Leffler and David S. Painter, 15–52. New York: Routledge, 1994, 31.
[43] Leffler, "National Security and US Foreign Policy," 30.
[44] May, *"Lessons" of the Past*, 44–45.

Much of the U.S. historical scholarship on the origins of the Cold War has suggested the contingency of antagonism between the superpowers. As Gaddis muses on U.S. concerns in the early years of the Cold War, "How well-founded that alarm was – how accurately it reflected the realities that shaped Soviet policy – are issues upon which there are legitimate grounds for disagreement."[45] May sums up: "[T]here is no quick and simple answer to the question of why and how American leaders so rapidly adopted the view that Russia, the war-time ally, should be regarded, and responded to, as a dangerous enemy."[46]

Nevertheless, the United States and the Soviet Union certainly became enemies during the Cold War, despite initial interpretations of ambiguous incidents that might – and subsequently have been – interpreted otherwise. As Gaddis writes, the definition of the Soviet Union as the primary enemy reduced "[a] generalized sense of vulnerability" for U.S. policy-makers.[47] Not coincidentally, the identification of the Soviet Union as the enemy in the next major war corresponded with the developing theory of the unfolding of the Third World War.

LEARNING FROM HISTORY

After a period of fumbling and uncertain interpretation, U.S. policy-makers had identified the Soviet Union as the enemy of the future. The construction of the Soviet Union as the enemy corresponded with the nascent theory of the origins of war that had been "learned" from the events of the Second World War. The development of these two theories supported each other. Fitting Stalin into the role of Hitler lent support to the appearance of malign Soviet intent, while the perceived territorial ambitions of the Soviet Union reinforced the perceived lessons of the negotiations at Munich.

Interpreting the Past

In *Lessons of History*, Ernest R. May argued that critical decisions by U.S. policymakers during the Cold War were driven by their overgeneralization of a single historical event. U.S. decision-makers gave undue attention to the events of Munich in 1938 as the key to explaining the onset of the Second World War. This event was abstracted into a general theory in

---

[45] Gaddis, *The Long Peace*, 47.   [46] May, *"Lessons" of the Past*, 19.
[47] Gaddis, *The Long Peace*, 40.

which the territorial ambitions of dictators were understood as a major cause of war. Early U.S. successes in the Cold War were taken as confirmation of the theory, which solidified into the broad paradigm for U.S. actions. May concluded that instead of straightforwardly learning from history, the overgeneralization of the events at Munich led to systematic and highly consequential errors in U.S. foreign policy.

American planning had been dismally inaccurate for the Second World War, particularly in the catastrophic failure to predict the Japanese invasion of Pearl Harbor. In the aftermath of the Second World War, U.S. policymakers were determined to improve their planning. As Gaddis notes, "Nothing shaped American plans to prevent future wars more than a determination to avoid mistakes of the past."[48] In order to prevent war, U.S. decision-makers needed a theory of the origins of war.

Following in the traditional footsteps of military planners, U.S. policymakers drew on their interpretations of the last major war to provide guidelines for the wars of the future, as argued in Chapter 3. U.S. policymakers theorized that the appeasement of Hitler at Munich in 1938 was the key event that initiated the Second World War. During the Munich Conference in 1938, Hitler had demanded that the Western states allow Germany to annex the Sudetenland – a German-speaking region of western Czechoslovakia. Western diplomats, led by British Prime Minister Chamberlain and French Minister Daladier, acceded to Germany's request. At the time, European diplomats believed they had successfully averted major war through this concession. Despite the economic and strategic value of the Czechoslovakian region, British and French diplomats assessed the value of the region as lower than the costs of war. However, the subsequent German invasion of Poland in 1939 was interpreted by Western diplomats as indicating that Hitler had greater territorial ambitions than the unification of German-speaking peoples, impelling Britain and France to declare war.

According to the theory, Germany had been emboldened by the successful negotiations at Munich and began to nip away at strategically peripheral areas in Austria, Czechoslovakia, and Poland. This resulted in a buildup of nearly irresistible momentum, which launched the Second World War and allowed Germany to dominate nearly the whole of Europe by 1942. May summarizes the lesson: "World War II had been made inevitable . . . because the Western democracies had not recognized

---

[48] Gaddis, *The United States and the Origins of the Cold War*, 1.

early enough the menace to them of the expansionist drive of Fascism and had not resisted its initial manifestations."[49]

The importance of Munich in the Second World War was generalized by U.S. thinkers into a broad theory of the causes of interstate war. Known colloquially as the domino theory, it was to become infamous as the motivation behind the Vietnam War. The domino theory abstracted the events at Munich into a general principle in which ambitious dictators would begin territorial expansion by capturing a weak and peripheral state of little worth to the other Great Power states. If not contested – if the dictator was appeased – this domino would provide a toehold to the annexation of the next few dominos, which would also be of relatively low value. Continued appeasement would eventually produce an avalanche that would be nearly impossible to stop and would end with the dictator acquiring territory of considerable value. Conversely, world war could be prevented in the early stages if the first few dominoes were prevented from falling. As Graebner summarizes, "The domino theory ... served as a dramatic warning that a peripheral contest could, if not resolved, become one of pivotal importance."[50]

The universal applicability of the domino theory can be debated on several fronts. In the first place, there is controversy over the causes of the Second World War. Scholars have put forth several other candidate explanations besides the events at Munich. John Maynard Keynes argued that the high reparations and severe treaty conditions required of Germany after the First World War encouraged the rise of Hitler and German ambitions.[51] Taylor argued that the war was simply the outcome of normal balance-of-power European politics.[52] Others have blamed the peculiar charisma of Hitler and the innate aggressiveness of Nazi Germany under the Third Reich. Regardless of the range of possible explanations, the Munich analogy became the dominant explanation of the causes of the Second World War for U.S. decision-makers.

Secondly, even if the appeasement of Hitler was the fundamental cause of the Second World War, the appeasement of dictators does not

---

May, *"Lessons" of the Past*, 32.

Norman A. Graebner, "Myth and Reality: America's Rhetorical Cold War." In *Critical Reflections on the Cold War: Linking Rhetoric and History*, edited by Martin J. Medhurst and H. W. Brands, 20–37. College Station: Texas A&M University Press, 2000, 32.

John Maynard Keynes, *The Economic Consequences of the Peace*. London: Macmillan, 1919.

A. J. P. Taylor, *The Origins of the Second World War*. New York: Atheneum, 1962.

necessarily generalize into a common cause of interstate conflict. Indeed, appeasement has not historically been perceived as a common cause of war. For instance, appeasement did not figure to any appreciable degree in the origins of the First World War or the Franco-Prussian War. Nor is there any empirical reason to assume that, had the Third World War occurred, its origins would have replicated those of the Second World War. In short, U.S. leaders followed the typical error of preparing for the last war rather than considering the full range of precursors to major interstate wars.

Not only appeasement but the dynamic of falling dominoes also appears to have been peculiar to the events of the Second World War. Empirically, there have been few historical cases in which major interstate wars began by an aggressor state nibbling away at peripheral regions. Scholars have also contested the domino theory of momentum in which previous victories increase the ease of toppling a domino.[53] As Graebner reflects, "[T]he concept of falling dominoes had no precedent in history. Territorial expansion had always rested on naked military force."[54] Instead, the pacification of unimportant territorial stepping-stones arguably sapped energy and resources away from the main objective of the aggressor.

Scholars have since contested the assumptions of the domino theory. For instance, Snyder notes the difficulty of calculating the probabilities of linked events – even if one domino were to fall to communism, its connection to other dominoes is complex and their fall is probabilistic rather than certain.[55] Jervis has questioned the assumption that states will leap to side with the Great Power who has the dominoes, arguing that realism suggests instead that states will tend to oppose a runaway Great Power.[56] At the time, however, only a handful of critics contested the logic of the domino theory, which was to motivate U.S. interventions in Korea and Vietnam, among others.

---

[53] Jervis, "Domino Beliefs and Strategic Behavior." In *Dominoes and Bandwagon: Strategic Beliefs and Great Power Competition in the Eurasian Rimland*, edited by Robert Jervis and Jack Snyder, 20–50. Oxford: Oxford University Press, 1991; Jack Snyder, "Introduction." In *Dominoes and Bandwagon: Strategic Beliefs and Great Power Competition in the Eurasian Rimland*, edited by Robert Jervis and Jack Snyder, 3–19. Oxford: Oxford University Press, 1991.

[54] Graebner, "Myth and Reality," 25.   [55] Snyder, "Introduction," 10.

[56] Robert Jervis, "Systems and Interaction Effects." In *Coping with Complexity in the International System*, edited by Jack Snyder and Robert Jervis, 25–46. Boulder: Westview Press, 1993; Jervis, "Domino Beliefs and Strategic Behavior."

Retrospectively, scholars have roundly criticized the application of the Munich analogy to the Soviet Union and pointed to the fallacies of the domino theory. As Graebner points out, "To base policy vis-à-vis the Soviet Union on the Munich syndrome was a misreading of the past and an application of metaphors, images, and historical analogies without any examination of their applicability." Yet regardless of the appropriateness of the lessons learned from history, these lessons were to be enormously consequential for the United States, the Soviet Union, and the host of states that were to be affected by the superpower competition of the Cold War.

Extrapolating to the Future

U.S. policymakers ran into a snag in fitting the Soviet Union into the role of Nazi Germany. Unlike prewar Nazi Germany, the Soviet Union had been decimated by its wartime experiences. As Graebner points out, "Nowhere did the Munich rhetoric of 1947 correspond to the realities of 1938. What the West faced at Munich was open German aggression on a massive scale ... But in 1947, no Soviet forces awaited orders to advance against a neighboring state."[57] U.S. planners might have interpreted this lack of military capability as implying a lack of threat. Instead, a corollary to the domino theory was developed whereby populations could be overwhelmed by the psychological attraction of communism without the need for military attack. In the U.S. Cold War model, the Soviet Union would suborn allies using the ideological appeal of communism on psychologically and economically weakened peoples. This particular formulation created a historically unprecedented value for credibility as a military resource.

In the early postwar period, U.S. military planners were confident that the Soviet Union did not pose a direct military threat to the United States. The forces of the Soviet Union had dropped from more than 11 million in 1945 to less than 3 million in 1948.[58] In addition, the Soviet army lacked modern technological weaponry, particularly the absence of a modern navy, a strategic air force, and nuclear weapons. As one account summarizes, "Much of the Soviet army's equipment was broken or obsolete; as late as 1950 half of its transportation was horse-drawn."[59] U.S. military planners agreed that the lack of naval and air power in the early postwar

[57] Graebner, "Myth and Reality," 25–26.   [58] Paterson, *On Every Front*, 179.
[59] Paterson, *On Every Front*, 178.

years meant that the Soviet Union could not offer a direct military threat to the United States or to Western Europe.

Moreover, U.S. policymakers agreed that the Soviet Union lacked the motivation to start a war in Europe in the short term. George Kennan, the original inventor of the doctrine of containment, claimed in 1946 that "[n]either the Russian economy nor the Russian people were in any condition to stand another conflict so soon after the last," and that "there was no way that Russia could appear as a military threat."[60] As Gaddis summarizes, "At no point ... did these officials [in Washington in 1947] seriously anticipate a Soviet military attack in Europe. Estimates of Moscow's intentions, whether from the Pentagon, the State Department, or the intelligence community, consistently discounted the possibility that the Russians might risk a direct military confrontation within the foreseeable future."[61] Kennan concluded, "It was perfectly clear to anyone with even a rudimentary knowledge of the Russia of that day, that the Soviet leaders had no intention of attempting to advance their cause by launching military attacks with their own armed forces across frontiers."[62]

Yet the apparent lack of both capability and motivation did not deter U.S. policymakers from slotting the Soviet Union into the role of Nazi Germany, despite the obvious discrepancies between the two states. Instead, it was posited that since the Soviet Union did not pose a military threat to Western Europe, it must be able to subdue countries without military force. U.S. policymakers devised a new mechanism of war: the ideological appeal of communism coupled with the dispirited morale of war-weary peoples would allow communist victory without military invasion. Cold War thinkers hypothesized that "the real Soviet danger ... lay in the limitless promise of Soviet ideological expansion," which "rendered military aggression irrelevant."[63]

This fear of psychological subordination may have been historically rooted in the wartime concerns over German "fifth columns" during the Second World War, in which German-friendly British citizens were feared to be working within Britain to enable a German invasion of the English Channel. As Gaddis notes, the "ideological dimension" of the domino theory appeared reasonable to U.S. policymakers "when considered

---

[60] Quoted in Gaddis, *Strategies of Containment*, 34–35; George F. Kennan, "Containment Then and Now." *Foreign Affairs* 65 (1987): 885–890.
[61] Gaddis, *The Long Peace*, 41.
[62] David Horowitz, "Introduction." In *Containment and Revolution*, edited by David Horowitz, 9–12. London: Anthony Blond, 1967, 11.
[63] Graebner, "Myth and Reality," 21.

against the record of how Nazi Germany had used 'fifth columns' before the war."[64] While the "fifth columnists" ended up having little apparent impact on military outcomes, the mechanism of psychological subterfuge was planted in the minds of postwar thinkers.

This emphasis on the importance of psychological factors was supported by Soviet claims that capitalism would fall as a result of the economic forces of history rather than through military force. According to both the U.S. and Soviet theories, the economic and spiritual depletion that resulted from the Second World War created vulnerability to the promises of communism. Extrapolating from the factors theorized to have led to the rise of Hitler in Depression-era Germany, U.S. planners feared that "the combined dislocations of war and reconstruction" might create a "psychological malaise" that would demoralize the peoples of Western Europe and Japan and "make themselves vulnerable, through sheer lack of self-confidence, to communist-led coups, or even to communist victories in free elections."[65] This tenet implied the Soviet Union "possessed the power and will to incite or support Communist-led revolutions everywhere" and that "[i]deological expansionism, assuring future Soviet triumphs without war ... enable[d] the Soviet Union to extend its presence over vast distances without military force."[66]

In comparison with the land-based forces used in the Second World War, the posited psychological mechanisms of communist aggression were almost invisible. Given that psychological rather than military forces were theorized as the mechanism for revolution, the hand of the Kremlin could be suspected in every nascent communist, or even nationalist, rebellion. As the British Embassy noted disapprovingly of the United States in 1946, "The tendency is increasingly marked ... to detect the Soviet mind or hand behind every move which seems to threaten or embarrass the United States or its friends."[67] In the later decades of the Cold War, any group against U.S. interests would be accused of communism.

What is perhaps even more amazing, this model proved robust despite the substantial changes in the military capability of the Soviet Union. In 1949, the Soviet Union tested an atomic weapon; in the 1950s, it developed intercontinental ballistic capabilities and created a deep-sea navy with nuclear-armed submarines. Despite these changes that made a Soviet invasion of the European heartland more plausible, the importance

---

[64] Gaddis, *The Long Peace*, 38.   [65] Gaddis, *Strategies of Containment*, 35.
[66] Graebner, "Myth and Reality," 22.   [67] Gaddis, *The Long Peace*, 38.

of psychological subordination was not reconsidered. Instead, U.S. policymakers continued to operate throughout the Cold War as if psychological warfare was one of the major mechanisms for Soviet invasion.

During the Cold War, only a "miniscule minority" criticized the domino theory before the mid-1960s.[68] Indeed, it is startling to realize how little these assumptions were questioned even into the 1960s and beyond.[69] Although decisions about Vietnam were highly controversial, debates were centered on the appropriateness of the application of these principles. The principles themselves remained largely unquestioned. As the Pentagon Papers noted in relation to the decisions over Vietnam, "The domino theory and the assumptions behind it were never questioned."[70] Another Vietnam historian notes: "The decision-makers of 1965 felt that ... [the U.S. policies of the late 1940s] still had validity despite the enormous changes that had taken place in the world."[71] Furthermore, the correctness of the U.S. domino theory seemed to be confirmed by the failure of the Soviet Union to invade Europe and initiate the Third World War.[72] As Lebow and Stein agree, "The efficacy of deterrence ... was confirmed tautologically."[73]

Even today the theorized danger of appeasement remains prominent in the minds of U.S. decision-makers and the American public. Its validity has been strengthened by the apparent "victory" of the United States over the Soviet Union in the Cold War. Much of the rhetoric of the United States in both the first and the second Gulf Wars relied on the imagery of the domino theory. For instance, Karnow notes that William Bush Sr. "equated Saddam Hussein with Adolf Hitler, asserting that inaction would 'reward aggression,' as appeasement of the Nazis had during the 1930s."[74] More importantly, the domino theory played an essential role in the competitions of the Cold War, encouraging the superpowers to compete over credibility as measured by the scorecard of allies. The theorized value of credibility proved highly consequential

[68] Richard H. Miller, "Introduction." In *The Evolution of the Cold War*, edited by Richard H. Miller, 3–12. Huntington: Robert E. Krieger, 1979, 8.

[69] Walter Lippmann, *The Cold War: A Study in U.S. Foreign Policy*. New York: Harper and Row, 1947, offered one of the few public critiques of containment theory.

[70] New York Times, *The Pentagon Papers*. New York: Quadrangle Books, 1971, 8.

[71] George C. Herring, *America's Longest War: The United States and Vietnam, 1950–1975*, second edition. New York: Alfred A. Knopf, 1986, 141.

[72] Graebner, "Myth and Reality," 25.

[73] Richard Ned Lebow and Janice Gross Stein, *We All Lost the Cold War*. Princeton: Princeton University Press, 1994, 15.

[74] Stanley Karnow, *Vietnam: A History*. New York: Viking, 1991, 30.

in the postwar world, resulting in U.S. interventions in Korea, Vietnam, and a score of other places.

THE COLD WAR COMPETITION FOR KOREA

Why did the United States decide that interventions in Korea, Vietnam, and other countries in the non-Western world were in the national interest? I argue that the Cold War value of peripheral allies lay not in their instrumental utility, but rather was a token of one-upmanship in the global competition between the United States and the Soviet Union. This is particularly evident in the case of Korea, which suddenly jumped in its perceived value after it was invaded by the armies of North Korea (which U.S. policymakers incorrectly assumed were backed by the Soviet Union).

The instrumental perspective posits that decision-makers develop cost-benefit calculations to decide which territories or resources are worth the costs of contention.[75] If an opponent places a high value on a territory that one considers to be worthless, a rational decision-maker should cede the territory as simply not worth the cost of a fight.[76] This simple instrumental logic fails abysmally to explain the alteration of U.S. calculations of value once its Great Power rivals – the Soviet Union and China – appeared to enter the contest for Korea.[77]

Instead, the case of Korea provides evidence that it is Great Power competition that creates a national interest, in contrast to the conventional formulation that assumes calculated interests lead to competition. In this topsy-turvy formulation, the calculation of value of an object depends substantially on signs of interest from a rival Great Power state rather than the intrinsic value of a resource. If a Great Power rival places a high value on a territory that has been assessed as having low value, decision-makers are likely to recalculate, upping the value on the territory. This dynamic has been shown in previous chapters, particularly in the Great Power interest in the acquisition of nuclear weapons.

---

[75] Robert Axelrod, *Conflict of Interest: A Theory of Divergent Goals with Applications to Politics.* Chicago: Markham Publishing Company, 1970; James D. Morrow, *Game Theory for Political Scientists.* Princeton: Princeton University Press, 1994.

[76] Ron E. Hassner, "To Halve and to Hold: Conflicts over Sacred Space and the Problem of Indivisibility." *Security Studies* 12 (2003): 1–33; Morrow, *Game Theory for Political Scientists.*

[77] Morton H. Halperin, "The Korean War." In *The Use of Force: International Politics and Foreign Policy*, edited by Robert J. Art and Kenneth N. Waltz, 216–234. Boston: Little, Brown and Company.

The Korean War similarly highlights the recalculation of the value of Korea from the U.S. perspective once it becomes a potential site for one-upmanship over its Great Power rivals. The value of South Korea to U.S. policymakers was undeniably enhanced by the presumption of Great Power competition on the part of the United States, despite the fact that subsequent scholarship has established that the Soviet Union was not actually involved in the initiation of the conflict.

Instrumental Calculations. Early in the Cold War, U.S. policymakers had sought to draw a line demarcating those areas that were critical to the United States. Such a line was necessary for U.S. containment policy, allowing U.S. policymakers to firmly restrict the Soviet Union behind the line. If the line were drawn too generously, however, U.S. resources would be depleted. Initially, George Kennan, the architect of U.S. containment policy, had proposed the protection of regions of key economic and military resources – essentially, Western Europe and Japan. Kennan argued that "that there were only five regions of the world – the United States, the United Kingdom, the Rhine valley with adjacent industrial areas, the Soviet Union, and Japan – where the sinews of modern military strength could be produced in quantity."[78] The four regions that were not already under Soviet control needed to be protected by the United States and its Western European allies, but the rest of the world did not merit such attention. It was obvious to U.S. policymakers that seeking to protect too many regions would overstretch U.S. resources. Thus in the late 1940s, "Kennan found little resistance ... to his insistence on the need to distinguish vital from peripheral interests."[79]

Yet the formation of the doctrine of containment quickly moved from the fairly objective waters of instrumental military resources to the murky depths of international perceptions. Initially, the emphasis on psychological mechanisms of invasion was applied to the potential for Soviet influence in geographically nearby Western European states such as France and Italy. These states were thought to be in danger of communist takeover as a result of the existence of institutionalized communist political parties, whose participation in elections might lead to the installation of a Communist Party–dominated government in a Western European state.

As the Cold War proceeded, however, its geographic scope expanded, and U.S. policymakers began to view communism anywhere as a victory for the Soviet Union. Thus the civil war in Greece and Soviet demands in

[78] Kennan, "Mr. 'X' Reassesses his Brainchild," 72.
[79] Gaddis, *Strategies of Containment*, 59.

Turkey were perceived as part of the superpower struggle for credibility, despite being peripheral to the "sinews of modern military strength." Regardless, U.S. policymakers moved to intervene, since according to the domino theory, "Greece and Turkey had become symbols of the status quo; their fall, like that of Austria, the Sudetenland, and Czechoslovakia after 1938, would ... 'undermine the foundations of international peace and hence the security of the United States.'"[80]

Even from this expanded point of view of economic and strategic value, however, U.S. policymakers had evaluated Korea as being of quite low value for U.S. interests. Indeed, the United States had actually withdrawn its troops from Korea in 1949, as "the defense of South Korea was not a vital strategic interest of the United States."[81] The Truman administration had explicitly calculated that Korea was an area "whose loss to Soviet control, however regrettable, would not immediately endanger American security." Not only did the region lack economic resources (in the late 1940s), but "the task of defending [Korea] against [the Soviet Union], given the distances and logistical problems involved, would be immense." Moreover, should the Soviets seek to occupy Korea, they would face the obstacle of "the rising tide of nationalism among the people of those regions."[82]

As a result, U.S. policymakers explicitly drew the U.S. defensive line to exclude Korea. In what is now perceived as an infamous blunder, Secretary of State Dean Acheson publicly declared that the U.S. Pacific line of containment stretched essentially from Alaska to Japan to the Philippines, explicitly excluding Korea.[83] From the point of economic and strategic resources, this exclusion of Korea seemed reasonable – even rational – to U.S. policymakers. Yet this assessment of the value of Korea failed to take into account the nature of Great Power status competition.

Recalculation and Great Power rivalry. A few weeks after the Acheson speech, a communist-led North Korean army invaded South Korea. Although this conflict was beyond Acheson's line – and thus should not have led to intervention according to the clearly defined U.S. policy at the time – U.S. policy was immediately and dramatically revised in light of these events. The American government immediately leaped to the conclusion that the Soviet Union was behind the North Korean invasion. As soon as this apparent Soviet interest in the Korean peninsula became manifest, "the Truman administration, with a rapidity that surprised itself

---

[80] Graebner, "Myth and Reality," 25.   [81] Gaddis, *The Long Peace*, 94.
[82] Gaddis, *Strategies of Containment*, 60.   [83] Gaddis, *The Long Peace*, 75.

as well as its adversaries, committed air, naval, and ground forces to repel the invasion."[84] In addition, the value of much of the rest of Asia was hurriedly recalculated, leading to increased U.S. commitments in Vietnam and Taiwan as well.[85]

U.S. policymakers at the time had assumed that "the powerful Communist movements in China and Indochina were totally under Moscow's command."[86] Subsequent scholarly work has produced little evidence for the belief that the Kremlin controlled a monolithic communism that was expanding worldwide. Historians have also debated at length the amount of influence Stalin played in the North Korean invasion that touched off the Korean War. Recent historical scholarship suggests that the attack was predominantly planned and instigated by Kim Il Sung, the leader of North Korea, although both Stalin and the Chinese leadership assented to the invasion.[87]

Although the Soviet Union was peripheral to the invasion of Korea, the Munich analogy was evident in the minds of U.S. policymakers in their discussions of involvement in Korea. President Truman wrote in his memoirs, "My thoughts ... kept coming back to the 1930s – to Manchuria-Ethiopia-the Rhineland-Austria-and finally to Munich. If the Republic of Korea was allowed to go under, some other country would be next, and then another, just like in the 1930s."[88] Presidential candidate Eisenhower in 1952 also recalled analogies to Munich: "World War II should have taught us all one lesson: To vacillate, to hesitate, to appease – even by merely betraying unsteady purpose – is to feed a dictator's appetite for conquest and to invite war itself."[89] In the minds of U.S. decision-makers, the analogy of South Korea to Munich and the applicability of the domino theory were straightforward.[90] As Gaddis summarizes, "The blatant nature of the North Korean attack made resistance necessary, in the eyes of administration officials, not because South Korea was important in and of itself, but because any demonstration of aggression left unopposed would only encourage further aggressions elsewhere."[91]

Costs of Intervention. Nevertheless, the U.S. decision to intervene in Korea was costly. The war drained resources and forfeited opportunity costs that might otherwise have been spent on preparing for the expected war in Europe. Estimates suggest that the United States spent $20 billion

---

[84] Gaddis, *The Long Peace*, 94.   [85] Gaddis, *The Long Peace*, 72–73.
[86] Graebner, "Myth and Reality," 29.   [87] Levering, *The Cold War*, 44.
[88] Quoted in Graebner, "Myth and Reality," 31.   [89] Gaddis, *The Long Peace*, 97.
[90] Quoted in Graebner, "Myth and Reality," 31.   [91] Gaddis, *The Long Peace*, 97.

on the Korean War plus another $5 billion in aid after the war and suffered an estimated 54,000 casualties.[92] The Western allies also made major commitments to the Korean War. Moreover, the war expended resources that might have been used to protect the United States or its European allies on other fronts. Scholars such as Jervis have argued that the Korean War was critical in setting parameters of U.S. policy such as high defense budgets, the perception of a unified Sino-Soviet bloc, a fear that small wars would escalate into major ones, and anticommunist commitments all over the world.[93] The perceived need to prevent communism from gaining a toehold in Asia and to counter the actions of a rival Great Power made these real and potential costs acceptable to the United States.

The value of Korea had not been foreseen in U.S. Cold War policy, despite explicit pre-invasion calculations of its value. As Secretary of State Henry Kissinger wrote, "Korea caught us completely unprepared ... Our strategic thinking had defined but two causes of war: a surprise attack on the continental United States and military aggression against Western Europe."[94] The United States was unprepared for the Korean War because the value of South Korea derived from the need for one-upmanship against the Soviet Union rather than from its calculable instrumental value. South Korea became valuable to the United States only once it appeared to be of value to the Soviet Union. In turn, this reassessment was based on the assumptions of the domino theory that had been developed from an overgeneralization of the origins of the Second World War. Consequently, the chief value at stake in the Korean War, as well as numerous other conflicts of the Cold War, was to serve as a marker of victory in the Great Power competition between the United States and the Soviet Union.

CONCLUSION

The Cold War has already been relegated to the dusty attics of history, along with other inexplicable things our ancestors got worked up over, such as the sinking of the *Maine* in Havana harbor or the loss of the

---

[92] Richard Whelan, *Drawing the Line: The Korean War, 1950–1953*. Boston: Little, Brown and Company, 1990, 373.

[93] Robert Jervis, "The Impact of the Korean War on the Cold War." *The Journal of Conflict Resolution* 24 (1980): 563–592.

[94] Kissinger, *Nuclear Weapons and Foreign Policy*, 43.

Lusitania. Today's college students have difficulty understanding what the Cold War was all about. In part, this lack of comprehension is due to the effects of teleology, in which it seems that the way history turned out was the only way it could have happened. Since World War III did not take place between the superpowers, the very real fears of people during the Cold War seem misplaced to later generations. Indeed, the perspective of the current generation is closer to wondering what "could anyone ever have had to fear ... from a state that turned out to be as weak, as bumbling, and as temporary as the Soviet Union?"[95]

Realists assume that military planners can correctly assess the threats in the international system and identify which Great Power states will be hostile in the future. Great Power politicians are able to assess strategic and economic resources in order to take advantage or deny access to rivals. Since the United States "won" the Cold War, U.S. decision-makers must have correctly assessed these threats.

In contrast, historical scholarship suggests that the assumptions of Cold War politicians were based on ambiguous empirical facts. U.S. decision-makers floundered to make sense of the complexities of the postwar world. As states repositioned themselves in the international hierarchy in the early postwar years, evidence of Soviet hostility toward the United States was ambiguous. Evaluations of military capability suggested that the Soviet Union lacked the means to threaten Europe or the United States militarily. Nevertheless, U.S. decision-makers developed interpretations to make sense of their situation, drawing on historical interpretations of the Second World War. When the army of North Korea invaded the South, these assumptions made it seem essential that the United States move to counter Soviet aggression.

Even during the Cold War, questions were raised about the instrumental value of some of these interests. Many scholars questioned the utility of the vast U.S. nuclear arsenal, which cost trillions of dollars. Political scientists in the 1960s widely argued that the U.S. involvement in Vietnam contradicted U.S. interests. Others argued that the support of authoritarian dictators in non-Western states went against U.S. humanitarian and democratic interests. These criticisms were grounded in a conventional instrumental perspective that assumed careful analysis could discern which interests would contribute to U.S. goals and which actions were not justified by the costs.

[95] John Lewis Gaddis, *The Cold War: A New History*. New York: Penguin Press, 2005, x.

Instead, it may be that the interests of a state cannot be reliably identified a priori. The dynamics of Great Power competition themselves create the interests of the day. In this case, the United States' identification of the Soviet Union as the implacable enemy of Western capitalism and democracy and the domino theory were fundamental to the construction of the realities of the Cold War. Drawing on these theories, the impetus of Great Power competition motivated the superpowers to fight costly wars in Asia, Africa, and Latin America. Once constructed, these political realities were consequential and could not be "pretended" out of existence. Nevertheless, the foundations of the construction were grounded in ambiguity rather than incontrovertible fact.

9

Conclusion

"The prime threat to the security of modern great powers is ... themselves. Their greatest menace lies in their own tendency to exaggerate the dangers they face, and to respond with counterproductive belligerence. The causes of this syndrome pose a large question for students of international relations."[1]

This book has attempted to develop a new answer to the centuries-old question: Why do states go to war? The conventional view is that states fight out of necessity in order to ensure security in a dangerous world. At least in recent centuries, however, the Great Power conflicts have been more akin to duels within a highly structured pecking order. Rather than obdurate empirical realities, the identities and issues that are the basis for the competition turn out to be social constructions embedded in world society.

This conclusion will consider broader implications for our understandings of war, and also pursue some more specific points regarding power, military planning, and security. As Van Evera's chapter-opening quote suggests, states that participate in the Great Power competitions expose themselves to tremendous risk, raising questions about the relation between power and objective security. Later, the chapter turns to questions that might have arisen in the reader's mind: (1) Do the book's insights about Great Power war apply to other kinds of wars, such as interstate wars between non–Great Power states, civil wars, or conflicts involving non-state actors? (2) What historical factors led to the

---

[1] Stephen Van Evera, *Causes of War: Power and the Roots of Conflict*. Ithaca: Cornell University Press, 1999, 192.

prominence of military power as the primary determinant of status in the international system? That is, how did this distinctive system of Great Power competition come into being? (3) Do these arguments generalize to other types of issues or organizations? Finally, I return to a question raised in the introduction: (4) Is enduring peace possible?

RETHINKING GREAT POWER WAR

This book builds on insights and puzzles that many have noted, such as the old adage that states are always "fighting the last war" and Fearon's recognition that war involves systematic misperception. The foundation stones for the book's argument may be easy to accept, especially when articulated in conditional form. Sometimes the complexity of war defies the best efforts of military planners. Sometimes countries have difficulty evaluating their own power, or that of their competitors. Sometimes states presume that "winners" are superior in many ways, even though victory may have been the product of historically specific circumstances or chance. Sometimes states resolve ambiguity by drawing oversimplified lessons from the victors of prior wars. Sometimes these lessons – about the sources of power or the utility of particular strategies or technologies – become widely accepted tropes that propel new competitions. Sometimes threats are ambiguous, and vagaries of interaction and interpretation can construct rivalries. Sometimes Great Power competition devolves into one-upmanship or wild goose chases over things that prove to have little value. Sometimes military competition yields disaster.

These conditional claims can, with varying degrees of effort, be reconciled with traditional perspectives in the international relations literature. However, the implications of the book become much more radical when the foundation stones are assembled and stated less conditionally, when "sometimes" becomes "often" or "always." For instance, the preceding chapters argue that states generally do a poor job of evaluating their own power and that of their rivals. Occasional difficulties in evaluating power, discerning optimal strategies, or identifying strategic interests and threats are to be expected in a world of imperfect information and fallible leaders. Endemic difficulties, however, pose a fundamental challenge to the materialisms that underlie conventional analysis in international relations. If power and strategy and interests are unknowable, or worse, the product of social interpretation rather than hard material realities, then the image of interstate war as a fight for survival amid anarchy becomes difficult to sustain. The Great Powers are jumping at shadows rather than systematically enhancing their security.

This book ultimately seeks to invert conventional understandings. The most important realities of the system are not the hard material objects that states command or fight over – for instance, the properties of technology that render weapons threatening, or the features of territory that render it strategically valuable. Rather, the preeminent features of the system are the social "realities" that construct and channel competition: the identities and roles established in the international community, the social hierarchy of the system, and the widely accepted military understandings and theories that place attention and value on some resources rather than others. It is the latter that are the key to understanding the character of Great Power war.

Again, dueling offers a useful analogy. In some contexts, elites engage in risky combat over issues of honor and symbolic value. One can try to identify the "real" material stakes that underlie conflict, but the scripted nature of dueling calls for a more anthropological approach. Dueling is a property of the society: social roles, identities, and obligations propel certain kinds of individuals to engage in duels in certain situations. To understand such behavior, one must identify the features of the context that give rise to it. Of course, it is easy to recognize dueling as an arbitrary social construction, because one can point to many societies and historical periods without such traditions. It is harder to see Great Power warfare as a social construction, because of its dominance in recent centuries, and consequently the alternatives are less apparent.

Ultimately, Great Power war is a property of an international system, or "world society," that is filled with meaning, rules, and identities. As previous chapters argue, being a Great Power means donning an identity and accepting a distinctive role within a social system. When a country inhabits the role of a Great Power, it is perceived very differently. Suddenly, even the most trivial territorial disagreement may be seen in a new light – as a hint of broader ambitions, a challenge to the credibility of others, or the first of many dominos. The possibility of being swept up into rivalry and combat becomes ever present, just as personal insults – in some societies – gave rise to duels.

This suggests new directions for future research. Most obviously, work could further explore the ways that Great Power war is ordered by shared identities and meanings that are established in the international community. We tend to imagine that war involves raw and unadulterated competition, as when the Mongol hordes swept across the countryside. That may have been the case in some historical periods, when the international community was not well established. But the distinctive feature of European war is the amount of order and agreement. Everyone in Europe knew that Bismarck's Ems telegram would incite the French to war because of deeply shared understandings about the rules and meanings of diplomatic communication. Likewise, everyone knew that the French acquisition of nuclear weapons represented a boost in status, even if the operational utility of those weapons remained uncertain.

Scholars need to unpack the shared grammar of Great Power competition and explore how it evolves over time. This book describes some dynamics, such as the importance of disruptions at the peak of the status hierarchy, which prompt a cascade of new interpretations and meanings. Also, previous chapters highlight the central role of European military theorists, who operate as an epistemic community, generating shared understandings of power and interests that guide competition. Moreover, Chapter 8 points to the importance of sense-making and interaction amid uncertainty, through which potential rivalries may emerge. And every chapter addresses the endemic ambiguity involved in military affairs, which is insufficiently appreciated. It is also important to explore the origins of this distinctive system. In the following sections I offer some preliminary reflections on the issue.

Within this overarching framework, the book offers more specific insights about key concepts, including power, strategy, and interests. Here, I reprise some key points and offer additional reflections.

Tokens of Power

More than anything, this book provides the basis for rethinking power. Assessments of military power are fundamental to interstate war and politics. However, the difficulty of evaluating power is evident throughout history. For instance, states frequently bite off more than they can chew. Aggressor states are defeated about 40 percent of the time across the nineteenth and twentieth centuries, an astonishing figure.[2]

The reason for these errors is that states confront vast ambiguity in identifying those factors that will reliably increase state power and

---

[2] Meredith Reid Sarkees and Frank Wayman, *Resort to War: 1816–2007*. Washington, DC: CQ Press, 2010.

security. Under ambiguity, decision-makers tend to be influenced by widely accepted social facts at hand, particularly the Great Power hierarchy, the actions of a Great Power rival, and the widely accepted "lessons" of prior wars. True interests are ambiguous, and so competition often devolves into the sweetness of outdoing a rival, with concomitant intangible boosts in status. Great Power states expend resources and human lives chasing after symbolic tokens of power.

The recognized Great Power hierarchy becomes the basis for evaluating military power, and there is usually a great deal of consensus about it in the international community. However, the presence of consensus does not mean that evaluations of power are reliable or accurate. Instead, the Great Power hierarchy is built on overgeneralizations of history, most importantly the belief that military victory reflects generalized military capability rather than chance and circumstance. Consequently, evaluations of power often prove flawed in retrospect. Putatively powerful states such as France, Germany, and recently the Soviet Union have been ignominiously defeated or dismembered. Conversely, seemingly weaker states have at times been surprisingly victorious. States often pursue material attributes that offer the illusion of power but ultimately prove irrelevant in the next major war.

Military Planning and Error

This book calls for greater attention to error in military affairs. The omnipresence of error actually makes sense when one considers the tremendous ambiguity and complexity of military planning. Taking into account the inevitability that errors will occur, decision-makers might prudently take a more cautious approach to war.

The twin assumptions that military competition compels states to be rational and that winners generally reflect best practices – which give rise to the "efficient war hypothesis" – are deeply problematic. Military planners, who are under tremendous pressure to draw up plans, necessarily make such simplifying assumptions to move forward. Academics, however, have no justification for accepting such strong assumptions without equally compelling empirical evidence.

Nevertheless, the notion that war is rational, functional, and inevitable still pervades the military history literature, and consequently the profusion of errors evident in any military campaign is given only marginal significance. To the extent that it is addressed, error is often treated as idiosyncratic and exceptional – the result of foolish individual decision-makers[3] or the inertia of bureaucratic institutions.[4] Groups of decision-makers may have acted as "yes-men" rather than honestly pointing out the deficiencies in war plans.[5] Underlying these criticisms is the assumption that error could be minimized or eliminated if individuals or organizations had done a better job.

To be sure, militaries certainly do take steps to reduce error. Military organizations routinely analyze past practices to identify and rectify mistakes. Whole rooms in the Pentagon are devoted to volumes of analyses documenting the lessons learned from previous missions and battles. As discussed in Chapter 3, militaries are very effective at improving when they are facing straightforward problems and consistent conditions. However, the overall ability to distill and transfer broad lessons to future wars is quite limited. Military planners are gravely handicapped by the futility of forecasting complex events with few comparable wars to draw on. Since the specifics of a battle are often the result of idiosyncratic conditions, nearly all that one can know is that the next war is likely to be substantially different than the last. Militaries can improve their effectiveness in specific ways, but the range of possible errors is very large. Thus it should not be surprising that war plans typically go awry. The omnipresence of these errors is not due primarily to foolish individuals or flawed institutions. Instead, it is a consequence of the vast ambiguities of war. Making optimal decisions in the face of vast unknowns is simply not a reasonable task.

Errors are inevitable in military decision-making. From this perspective, it might be prudent for decision-makers to be more cautious in their military plans.[6] Militaries and publics nearly always go to war with the belief that they will win. If the ambiguities of war were fully recognized, decision-makers might come to view war as a risky and often foolish option, especially when the stakes are critical. By analogy, an investor would be ill advised to put his life savings into risky stocks with a 40 percent chance of losing their principal. If decision-makers had greater

[3] Norman F. Dixon, *On the Psychology of Military Incompetence*. London: Cape, 1976; Geoffrey Regan, *Someone Had Blundered*. London: Batsford, 1987; Dominic D. P. Johnson, *Overconfidence and War*. Cambridge, MA: Harvard University Press, 2004.

[4] Eliot A. Cohen and John Gooch, *Military Misfortunes*. New York: Free Press, 1990; Barbara W. Tuchman, *The March of Folly*. London: Abacus, 1984; Ian Roxborough, Organizational Innovation." *Sociological Forum* 15 (2000): 367–372.

[5] Graham T. Allison, *Essence of Decision: Explaining the Cuban Missile Crisis*. Boston: Little, Brown, 1971.

[6] Johnson, *Overconfidence and War*.

appreciation for the risks of war, there might be more enthusiasm for less costly diplomatic mechanisms. Vacillation and hesitation have at times proven to be the wrong strategies – yet aggression and boldness may carry even greater risks. Given the exceptional costliness of war, it might be better to err on the side of less aggression.

Nevertheless, each generation believes that it has finally gotten it right; that it alone has avoided the mistakes of previous cohorts. The current generation is no exception. I have been told that the United States has plans for virtually every contingency and that methods have been refined to fight any possible enemy the United States might face. This optimism may be borne out in some cases. In a coin toss, the penny comes up heads some of the time. Yet history suggests that military planning looks impressive only as long as there has been a string of successes. When flipping a coin, betting on heads will inevitably lose in the long run. As Jervis muses, "[N]o formula will eliminate misperception ... Faced with ambiguous and confusing evidence, decision-makers must draw inferences that will often prove to be incorrect."[7]

War and Security

Great Power competition is the centerpiece of the interstate system. The interests or "tokens of power" over which Great Powers compete defines the international political agenda in each historical era, affecting the welfare of all. Arms races and wars drain treasuries and political energies, and usually result in tremendous loss of life. It is often assumed that Great Power conflicts are generally worth the cost because they afford greater power and security in the long run. However, there is little evidence that Great Power competitions reliably bring about lasting benefits. The glory of being at the top of the Great Power hierarchy is often fleeting.

The benefits of military victory – often achieved at great cost – are frequently elusive. Organski and Kugler have shown that the winner of interstate war generally gains little.[8] Liberman similarly hesitates to claim that the profits of occupying territory are worth the costs and risk of defeat. He concludes: "When external costs are taken into account,

[7] Robert Jervis, *Perception and Misperception in International Politics*. Princeton: Princeton University Press, 1976, 409.

[8] A. F. K. Organski and Jacek Kugler, "The Costs of Major Wars: The Phoenix Factor." *The American Political Science Review* 71 (1977): 1347–1366.

conquest pays only when unopposed."[9] Even the exchange of intrinsically valuable territory, such as the provinces of Alsace-Lorraine and Strasbourg (part of the settlement of the Franco-Prussian War and again in the First World War), is often a symbolic afterthought. Fertile as these lands are, it would be difficult to claim that their acquisition offset the costs of these two wars – particularly for Germany, which ended up losing the provinces in the end. As Kennan remarked in 1951, while musing on American involvement in the First World War, "Looking backward today on these endless disputes between our government and the belligerents over neutral rights, it seems hard to understand how we could have attached so much importance to them."[10]

The preceding chapters argue that Great Power competitions essentially devolve into struggles for status. The rules of the international system encourage the Great Powers to compete against rivals, and those competitions frequently escalate far beyond the value of the objects of contention. Entrenched in rhetorics of strategic rationality, decision-makers rarely note the irrelevance of goals pursued so fervently in prior generations. The history of Great Power war can be read as a series of wild goose chases, with resources and effort spent to acquire symbolic tokens that provide little utility in the next era. As Van Evera notes, "[T]he aftermath of the world's great security wars ... often reveal[s] that the belligerents' security fears were illusory," moreover, "even the winners would avoid many wars if they foresaw the price of victory."[11] George Kennan agrees: "When you tally up the total score of the two [World] wars, in terms of their ostensible objective, you find that if there has been any gain at all, it is pretty hard to discern."[12]

Instead, Great Power competitions ultimately endanger security. It is difficult to imagine a threat to the security of Great Power states greater than war with another Great Power. And yet, in order to be recognized as a Great Power, a state must enter into competitions and engage in one-upmanship against these states. Consequently, Great Powers repeatedly compete against precisely those states with the capacity to injure them. As a consequence of the First World War, for instance, Austria lost Hungary, the Ottoman Empire was partitioned and lost much influence, and Germany lost Alsace-Lorraine and its colonies. After the Second World War,

---

[9] Peter Liberman, *Does Conquest Pay?* Princeton: Princeton University Press, 1996, 151.

[10] George F. Kennan, *American Diplomacy, 1900–1950.* Chicago: University of Chicago Press, 1951, 64.

[11] Van Evera, *Causes of War*, 191, 15.   [12] Kennan, *American Diplomacy*, 56.

Germany was divided in two and Japan was occupied and shorn of her overseas colonies. Similarly, a huge arsenal of nuclear weapons was unable to prevent the loss of a quarter of the territory of the Soviet Union in the competition of the Cold War. Even successful Great Powers have the tendency to continue fighting and overextend. It is ultimately an empirical question to be explored in future research, but these arguments suggest that engagement in Great Power competitions might generally undermine security rather than strengthen it.

BEYOND GREAT POWER WARS

This book focuses on Great Power wars for two reasons. First, the Great Power wars are central to the international system, shaping the political contours and patterns of military competition of each era. As argued in Chapter 3, it is Great Power victories that produce the lessons and shared understandings that propel future conflict. Second, the dynamics of rivalry and one-upmanship are most clear-cut among the states that are competing for position in the Great Power hierarchy. Great Power states gain status by defeating another Great Power, but gains to status are minimal for asymmetric wars. For instance, the U.S. victories in Grenada or Panama did little to enhance American status in the international community. Moreover, this book focuses on the Great Power wars because they are the hardest cases to test the arguments regarding ambiguity of power, strategy, and interests. If even the most advanced militaries are confounded by ambiguity and miscalculation, this suggests that these processes are fundamental.

That said, many of the patterns described in this book apply, with some caveats, to asymmetric wars between a Great Power and a smaller power and to wars between regional powers fighting over status within a local hierarchy. Such dynamics are less evident in civil wars, although some parallels can be drawn.

Great Power Asymmetric Wars

Although there is constant competitive tension among the Great Powers, even the Great Powers are not continually at war with each other. The majority of wars are fought between a Great Power and a substantially weaker state. As argued in Chapters 2 and 4, states enact their role as a Great Power state by expanding their interests beyond their borders. Each Great Power historically had a territorial sphere of interest in which it exerted its influence over smaller states. Influence might be exercised through a number of mechanisms, including diplomatic, economic, and political levers. But part of the role of being a Great Power requires the willingness to use armed aggression in support of its interests, to enter into military scuffles both large and small. The chapters of this book have relatively little to say about *which* potential asymmetric conflicts will escalate into warfare. Some seem to be driven by wider "lessons" of recent Great Power wars, but many are not. Often, the stakes in such conflicts are small and the interests unclear. It seems difficult to predict a priori which will escalate; often decision makers themselves are surprised by the turn of events.

What can be predicted is that Great Power identity and concerns about status loom large in asymmetric conflict. The U.S. involvement in Vietnam exemplifies this. Herring raises the puzzle: "Why did the United States make such a vast commitment to an area of so little apparent importance?"[13] Instrumental military or economic interests for the United States have been difficult to identify in the case of Vietnam. "Few scholars ... contend that Americans were guided by a belief that Vietnam's natural resources and markets were critical to U.S. prosperity."[14] Instead, the national interest that compelled American involvement in Vietnam was primarily status and international prestige.

As many scholars have recounted, the United States stumbled into the conflict in Vietnam and then found itself unable to withdraw due to concerns about loss of status in the eyes of domestic, regional, and international audiences.[15] The United States was playing for Great Power stakes against its rivals: China and, indirectly, the Soviet Union. The United States feared that withdrawing from Vietnam would lead to a decrease in credibility in the eyes of the world – its current allies, its potential allies, and its enemies.[16] While a victory in Vietnam would have provided only modest benefits to its Great Power status, American policymakers feared that defeat would have a resounding negative impact.

---

[13] George C. Herring, *America's Longest War: The United States and Vietnam, 1950–1975*, second edition. New York: Alfred A. Knopf, 1986, x.

[14] Mark Lawrence, *Assuming the Burden: Europe and the American Commitment to War in Vietnam*. Berkeley: University of California Press, 2005, 4.

[15] Stanley Karnow, *Vietnam: A History*. New York: Viking, 1991; George Kahin, *Intervention*. New York: Anchor, 1987.

[16] New York Times, *The Pentagon Papers*. New York: Quadrangle Books, 1971.

Ultimately, the United States did lose in Vietnam.[17] This defeat did not cause the United States to be demoted in the Great Power hierarchy; asymmetric wars tend not to prompt a reconsideration of the overall status order (in sharp contrast to wars involving aspiring Great Powers). However, the United States did lose prestige in multiple arenas. Lyndon B. Johnson did not run for reelection following the disaster of the Tet offensive in 1968. The United States ceded influence over southeast Asia to China, which proceeded to fight a series of wars in Laos, Cambodia, and Vietnam to establish its own regional dominance in the next decade. And on the international front, the United States refrained from becoming directly involved in another interstate war until the end of the Cold War.[18] While it is always dangerous to draw causal inferences from historical events, the defeat in Vietnam does appear to have had some costs in status and prestige for the United States.

The case of Vietnam exemplifies other themes of this book as well, especially the fundamental ambiguity of power. Perhaps the key puzzle has been how the military forces of Vietnam were able to defeat a superpower. As Herring puts it, "Why, despite the expenditure of more than $150 billion, the loss of more than 58,000 lives, the application of its great technical expertise, and the employment of a huge military arsenal, did the world's most powerful nation fail to achieve its objectives and suffer its first defeat in war, a humiliating and deeply frustrating experience for a people accustomed to success?"[19] Summers wrote: "Neither our civilian nor our military leaders dreamed that a tenth-rate undeveloped country like North Vietnam could possibly defeat the United States, the world's dominant military and industrial power."[20] As discussed in Chapter 2, the rubric for understanding power was derived from previous Great Power wars. These factors turned out to be inappropriate for wars that took place under the quite different conditions of Southeast Asia.

Vietnam also highlights the difficulty of applying lessons from disparate military contexts. The Americans faithfully applied the lessons from

---

[17] Although the United States was not defeated on the battlefield, its withdrawal from Vietnam in 1973 was viewed nationally and internationally as a sign of defeat.

[18] The United States did intervene, openly or covertly, in several civil wars and created its own occasion for intervention in Grenada. However, according to the definitions of the Correlates of War dataset, the United States was not involved in any interstate wars between 1975 and 1989 (Sarkees and Wayman, *Resort to War*).

[19] Herring, *America's Longest War*, x.

[20] Colonel Harry G. Summer, Jr., *On Strategy: A Critical Analysis of the Vietnam War*. Novato: Presido Press, 1982, 120.

previous wars, primarily wars fought in the European context. As Summers writes, "One of the most frustrating aspects of the Vietnam war from the Army's point of view is that ... we succeeded in everything we set out to do ... On the battlefield itself, the Army was unbeatable ... Yet, in the end, it was North Vietnam, not the United States, that emerged victorious."[21] Kolko notes in retrospect, "Victory in war is not simply the result of battles, and nowhere in the twentieth century has this been truer than in Vietnam."[22] Historically, however, victory *has* often simply been the result of battles. The fact that battle success did not translate to victory in Vietnam highlights the complexity and multiple contingencies of war. Recipes that worked in the past – and seem certain to work in the future – may nevertheless fail to bring victory.

Regional Competitions

Many of the arguments about Great Power warfare, outlined in previous chapters, can be generalized to conflicts between states competing within regional hierarchies. In particular, one can observe similar patterns of status competition and one-upmanship. In the last half-century, contests for regional dominance have led to wars between India and Pakistan, India and China, and Iran and Iraq. These regional hierarchies follow similar rules of status as do the Great Power competitions, but on a local scale.

In the postwar world, South America, the Middle East, the Indian subcontinent, and Africa have developed regional competitions for status, with dynamics of rivalry and competition similar to those of the Great Power competitions. Akin to that of the Great Powers, regional competition has led to enduring rivalries in the Middle East and the Indian subcontinent. On other continents, the regional powers have sought to establish their position in the local hierarchy primarily by pursuing the military resources defined by the Great Power hierarchy.

For example, the "opaque" status of nuclear-capable states has served to demarcate an intermediate position between the openly nuclear Great Powers and the nonnuclear small powers. Argentina, Brazil, India, Pakistan, South Africa, and Israel either developed "opaque" nuclear capability or initiated and abandoned a program for the development of nuclear

---

[21] Summer, *On Strategy*, 1.

[22] Gabriel Kolko, *Anatomy of a War: Vietnam, the United States, and the Modern Historical Experience*. New York: New Press, 1994, 545.

weapons.[23] These nuclear competitions can be seen as contests for regional status, much as the Great Powers competed over nuclear weapons as symbolic tokens of power.

Given the smaller scope of the regional audience, regional powers will be more affected by the local political context, particular personalities of leaders, and domestic opinion. Regional powers may be more easily swayed from their quest to achieve regional status. A new governmental regime, bringing different personalities into play, might lead a state to seek regional status or to drop out of the competition. The South African transition from an apartheid regime to a democratic regime, for instance, led to a reduction in its efforts to become a regional military power.[24] Since the Great Powers are playing to a world audience, domestic changes in regime tend to have less effect on their efforts to maintain Great Power status.[25] The broader scope of the international audience creates greater stability in Great Power competitive efforts, for good or ill.

Fundamentally, the symbolic stakes of a war depend on an international community that provides the audience and the arena for the competition. In the cases of regional competitions, the rules of the game are those laid out for the Great Powers. The regional powers are playing in the minor leagues, so to speak. While the rules are the same, the stakes and rewards are not as high.

Civil Wars

As I argued in my previous book, *Neverending Wars*, the international community profoundly influences the character and course of civil wars.[26] Great Power competition provides resources and identities that fuel local conflicts. Moreover, the postwar norms and rules in the international community tend to "lock in" national boundaries in ways

[23] Scott D. Sagan, "Why Do States Build Nuclear Weapons? Three Models in Search of a Bomb." *International Security* 21 (1996–1997): 54–86.

[24] Peter Liberman, "The Rise and Fall of the South African Bomb." In *Going Nuclear: Nuclear Proliferation and International Security in the 21st Century*, edited by Michael E. Brown, Owen R. Cote Jr., Sean M. Lynn-Jones, and Steven E. Miller, 255–296. Cambridge, MA: MIT Press, 2010.

[25] Great Powers may still be highly influenced by domestic politics, however. See Jacques Hymans, *The Psychology of Nuclear Proliferation: Identity, Emotions, and Foreign Policy*. Cambridge: Cambridge University Press, 2006.

[26] Ann Hironaka, *Neverending Wars: The International Community, Weak States, and the Perpetuation of Civil War*. Cambridge, MA: Harvard University Press, 2005.

that propel conflict. Beyond that, one of the arguments developed in this book certainly applies to civil wars: ambiguity dogs the efforts of military planners in a civil war as much as in a Great Power war. As in the case of Great Power war, planners and insurgents may look to the international system to resolve ambiguity. The lessons of Great Power wars – or exemplary successful insurgencies – often diffuse to civil war participants.

However, certain key arguments of previous chapters, such as the dynamics of status competition and one-upmanship, do not typically extend to subnational conflicts. Whereas regional conflicts tend to look like microcosms of Great Power status competition, civil wars frequently do not. The key difference in a civil war is the lack of a stable context and set of players needed to have ordered competition for status and power. Unlike the Great Power hierarchy, which is maintained despite the wars among the Great Powers themselves, civil wars frequently undermine the social basis of the hierarchies for which parties contend. Consequently, while some parallels can be drawn, civil wars are typically quite different from Great Power wars and only rarely involve status competition.[27]

Domestic arenas are notable for their instability. As argued in my previous book, civil wars in the contemporary period tend to be extremely disorganized affairs.[28] In many cases, there is no agreed-on governmental structure over which contenders are competing. Instead, various subgroups in the opposition coalition vary widely in their aims. These "patchwork coalitions," as I termed them, reflect broad variation in the underlying constituencies. Given the disorganized social landscape in which many contemporary civil wars occur, there is no coherent audience or agreed-on rules regarding status and prestige. The level of disorganization also implies that civil war contenders will have less capacity to draw stylized "lessons" from their prior experience.

For instance, in the case of Vietnam (which involved a civil war, in addition to an asymmetric conflict with the United States), the competitive dynamics of one-upmanship posited for Great Power rivalries did not apply to the chaotic governmental structure within South Vietnam.

---

[27] Fearon argues that when the domestic audience is stable, it can have influence on the escalation of international crises. James D. Fearon, "Domestic Political Audiences and the Escalation of International Disputes." *The American Political Science Review* 88.3 (1994): 577–592.

[28] Hironaka, *Neverending Wars*.

While local politicians did develop rivalries with other politicians, the lack of an orderly state structure and domestic constituency could not provide a stable venue for competition. Within the government of South Vietnam, indicators of "power" changed with alarming rapidity; officials popular in one season might be executed in the next. As Lawrence notes, "The enormously complex Vietnamese political situation defied easy categorization, as nationalists, communists, royalists, and many other elements jockeyed for power in the turbulent years following the Second World War."[29] In this civil war context, local dynamics of one-upmanship and status competition did not emerge.

Domestic political actors in contemporary civil wars are rarely fighting primarily for status in the way that Great Powers contend in the international community. This is largely due to the lack of a stable environment beyond the scope of the conflict. In contrast, the Great Power competition for status is possible because of the existence of a broader international status system that transcends the specific competitors. Consequently, the Great Power dynamics described in this book are mainly observed in interstate wars.

WAR IN EUROPEAN HISTORY

A central question remains: How did this distinctive system of Great Power identities and competition emerge? For centuries, war has served as the fundamental ordering principle of the Great Power status hierarchy in the international community. Realist scholars theorized war as an inevitable consequence of states seeking to survive in an anarchic world. However, from a social construction perspective, this emphasis on military power is itself a historically contingent result of Europe's distinctive political history, geography, and culture. As Alexander Wendt argued in his seminal article, "Anarchy Is What States Make of It," counterfactual international communities might be based on quite different hierarchical principles.[30] At least in theory, other values, such as economic prowess, might have formed the basis of an international status hierarchy.

The type of wars posited in this book – wars fought over status and prestige – occur when there is a strong international community

---

[29] Lawrence, *Assuming the Burden*, 9.
[30] Alexander Wendt, "Anarchy Is What States Make of It: The Social Construction of Power Politics." *International Organization* 46 (1992): 391–425.

organized around a military hierarchy.[31] The former condition certainly did not always apply to Europe, and scholars such as Wendt suggest that the latter is by no means inevitable. I discuss some other possible configurations that could have been created by different communities and different hierarchies.

World society scholars have emphasized that the contemporary international order is one in which common discourses and global institutions such as the United Nations have created a cohesive international community, despite the lack of a formal world government.[32] In contrast, Europe of the Dark Ages might be considered a weak and poorly integrated international community. For example, some scholars argue that "Europe" cannot be said to have existed before 1400 or so.[33] As discussed earlier in the book, the Great Power dynamics of competition require a stable international community as observers. If a broader community does not exist, there can be no agreed-on indicators of power and mechanisms of competition. Consequently, Great Power competitive dynamics will not ensue.

For example, in premodern Europe, individual princes fought among themselves for territory or resources. The international community was too weak to support a stable hierarchy of Great Powers in which states could develop rivalries and symbolic competitions. Two kings might develop a rivalry, but the death of one typically ended the rivalry. Even if one ruler were to climb to the top of the international pecking order, the lack of stable structure meant his achievements were unlikely to last, as Charlemagne was to discover. Thus Europe before 1000 CE did not evince the enduring Great Power rivalries that were to follow. Contests such as the Hundred Years War between England and France or the dynastic wars of the Habsburgs would not occur for several more centuries.

---

[31] See Andreas Wimmer, *Waves of War: Nationalism, State Formation and Ethnic Exclusion in the Modern World*. New York: Cambridge University Press, 2013; Andreas Wimmer and Brian Min, "From Empire to Nation-State: Explaining Wars in the Modern World, 1816–2001." *American Sociological Review* 71.6 (2006): 867–897; and Andreas Wimmer and Yuval Feinstein, "The Rise of the Nation-State across the World, 1816 to 2001." *American Sociological Review* 75.5 (2010): 764–790 for one aspect of the formation of international society.

[32] Ann Hironaka, *Greening the Globe: World Society and Environmental Change*. Cambridge: Cambridge University Press, 2014; John W. Meyer, John Boli, George M. Thomas, and Francisco O. Ramirez. "World Society and the Nation-State." *American Journal of Sociology* 103 (1997): 144–181.

[33] Norman Davies, *Europe: A History*. New York: Harper Perennial, 1998.

The type of competitions described in this book also hinge on the fact that military power has served as the basis for the Great Power hierarchy in recent centuries. However, alternative bases for a Great Power hierarchy are hypothetically possible. Scholars such as Wallerstein and Braudel have theorized international orders centered on economic competition.[34] Or, in principle, one could envision an international community focused on religious values such as the Holy Roman Empire or perhaps even social worlds structured around human rights or environmental protection.

Thus, in principle, an international order might be focused primarily on economic competition, rather than on military power, as the foundational measure of status.[35] Current economic leaders such as Japan and Germany have acquired economic power without concomitant investment in military resources, as did the United States in the nineteenth century. An historical example might include premodern European trade with Asia.[36] Economically powerful states might invest in military resources to protect their merchant ships, but this military power would not serve as a primary source of prestige in itself. Instead, prestige would be based on economic properties such as control of the spice trade or production of manufactured goods. In this world, military power would be ancillary and provide merely instrumental value in support of economic power.

One contemporary example might be the European Community, in which economic power provides the major form of political currency.[37] In this system, strong international institutions allow societal resources to be more fully devoted to economic development, and status in the system rests on indicators of economic strength. This is not necessarily a utopian

---

[34] Immanuel Wallerstein, *The Modern World System I: Capitalist Agriculture and the Origins of the European World-Economy in the Sixteenth Century*. Berkeley: University of California Press, 2011; Fernand Braudel, *The Mediterranean and the Mediterranean World in the Age of Philip II*. Berkeley: University of California Press, 1996; Daniel Chirot, *Social Change in the Modern Era*. New York: Harcourt Brace Jovanovich, 1986; Daniel Chirot and Thomas D. Hall, "World-System Theory." *Annual Review of Sociology* 8 (1982): 81–106.

[35] For a fascinating account of the contemporary world from this perspective, see Daniel W. Drezner, *All Politics Is Global: Explaining International Regulatory Regimes*. Princeton: Princeton University Press, 2008.

[36] Janet L. Abu-Lughod, *Before European Hegemony: The World System A.D. 1250–1350*. Oxford: Oxford University Press, 1991.

[37] Internally, the European Union may be based primarily on economic power, but it also exists in a world in which the military Great Power system is dominant. Thus states such as the United Kingdom and France attempt to acquire status in both systems.

system, since scholars have pointed out many issues of inequality that arise within social systems organized in terms of economic power.[38] However, such a system is likely to be typified by lower levels of military conflict.

How did the distinctive European system arise? The issue surely deserves detailed scrutiny, but I speculate that path-dependent processes led to the preeminence of military power as the foundation for international status, which endured even after a strong international community emerged. After the fall of the Roman Empire in the west, the European system was anarchic and military capability was central to the ability of kings to maintain their political power.[39] In this context, the elite status culture and the expectations regarding interstate relations centered on military competition and prowess. These components later became the elements of a nascent world society. By the seventeenth and eighteenth centuries, the strength of domestic and regional institutions meant that European politics was no longer a pure anarchy; a European-wide society had emerged and became increasingly institutionalized. As Wendt suggests, there came into being the possibility for different global orders, including ones that did not center on military prestige. However, the historical legacy of the Dark Ages persisted. Great Power military competition had become institutionalized as the dominant basis of interstate relations. Akin to duels – which were also prevalent in this period – the wars of the Great Power states both reflected and further reinforced an international Great Power hierarchy founded on military power. Military prowess remains the ordering logic of the international hierarchy, an institutionalized anachronism, even though the initial conditions of the Dark Ages are long gone.

BEYOND WAR

Some of the arguments developed to explain Great Power wars may apply to other domains of activity. In particular, states may draw lessons to resolve ambiguity whenever they pursue complex goals within a clearly defined social hierarchy. One example might be economic planning.

---

[38] David Graeber, *Debt: The First 5,000 Years*. London: Melville House, 2011. Also, see the world systems literature.

[39] Scholars tend to treat this as inevitable, but there are few parallel cases to evaluate the generalizability of such claims.

Governments are under tremendous pressure to pursue pro-growth policies, but the optimal policies are not usually obvious. As in the case of military planning, states seek to learn from exemplar countries, for instance, drawing oversimplified lessons about the virtues of free markets and privatization in the 1980s.[40] Again, the role of scholars and epistemic communities may play an important role in diffusion.[41]

More generally, one might expect similar patterns of competition and episodic "learning" whenever organizations pursue complex tasks under ambiguity in small, hierarchical groups. David Strang's work, which inspired key arguments in this book, shows that corporate firms routinely draw lessons from leading organizations within their industry. Small communities of stratified firms, such as the highly connected world of Wall Street may be especially prone to such dynamics. Seemingly successful innovations spread rapidly through the financial sector, for instance the mortgage-backed securities that ultimately contributed to the financial disaster of 2008.[42] As in the case of states, there is a tendency to see organizational learning as reflecting optimal behavior among firms. Yet the "winners" might not reflect best practices and that the "lessons" from the past may prove useless – or worse – in the future.

The real world is filled with ambiguity and complexity. Organizations that are forced to navigate complexity must necessarily use simplifications to plan and act. Whenever such organizations are embedded in a community, there is the potential for planners and leaders to draw on socially constructed realities or "lessons" to fill in the gaps and resolve uncertainties. And when social communities feature a sharp status hierarchy, there may be a tendency for organizations to be drawn in the direction of climbing the status hierarchy, which provides a clear goal in a sea of ambiguity.

IS ENDURING PEACE POSSIBLE?

This book offers a reinterpretation of Great Power competition. Classical theories suggest that competition is inevitable without a strong world

[40] Dani Rodrik, *Economics Rules: The Rights and Wrongs of the Dismal Science.* New York: W. W. Norton, 2015.

[41] Marion Fourcade-Gourinchas and Sarah L. Babb, "The Rebirth of the Liberal Creed: Paths to Neoliberalism in Four Countries." *American Journal of Sociology* 108.3 (2002): 533–579.

[42] Kim Pernell-Gallagher, "Learning from Performance: Banks, Collateralized Debt Obligations, and the Credit Crisis." *Social Forces* 94.1 (2015): 31–59.

state to impose order. By contrast, this book argues that patterns of Great Power warfare are the result of a distinctive set of identities, rules, and expectations that have become historically entrenched in the international community. On one hand, this suggests that war is by no means inevitable: historically constructed arrangements may shift over time. However, to label Great Power competition as socially constructed does not mean that it is a mere figment of the imagination that can simply be wished away. As scholars such as Foucault have observed, deeply embedded societal formations are durable, and the process of change may take a long time.

One could imagine several ways that the system of Great Power competition could change. For one, the international community could fragment or dissolve, due to a global catastrophe such as nuclear war or environmental collapse. In the absence of a stable hierarchy of players and shared identities and frames, competition would become less orderly and status competition would be less commonplace.

Of greater interest here, the identities and shared understandings across the international community could evolve in ways that no longer privilege Great Power military competition. Indeed, some have suggested such changes are already under way.[43] State identities could shift in ways that de-emphasize hierarchy and competition altogether. Or more likely, competition and status hierarchies might be defined along dimensions other than military power. Optimistically, one might hope that economic success might come to replace military power as the primary axis of Great Power status and competition. One hint of this possibility is the high status enjoyed by Germany and Japan, despite their clear disavowal of military power. Another indicator might be the lack of interstate war in the world generally, particularly the low rate of involvement of the European states in interstate wars since the end of the Second World War.

At this historical moment, the United States stands at the apex of both military power and economic power. Its prolific military agenda suggests and reinforces the centrality of the military power in defining the international hierarchy. However, the rules of the international system are not solely up to a single Great Power. The shift toward economic issues as the

---

[43] John Mueller, *The Remnants of War*. Ithaca: Cornell University Press, 2004; John Mueller, *Retreat from Doomsday: The Obsolescence of Major War*. New York: Basic Books, 1989; Joshua S. Goldstein, *Winning the War on War: The Decline of Armed Conflict Worldwide*. New York: Dutton, 2011; Steven Pinker, *The Better Angels of our Nature: Why Violence Has Declined*. New York: Viking, 2011.

basis for social organization in Europe suggests that change in the centuries-old basis of military power might be possible.

In itself, however, the simple absence of Great Power war is not sufficient to claim that war is obsolete.[44] Ninety-nine years passed between the end of the Napoleonic Wars and the beginning of the First World War. At the dawn of the twentieth century, optimists were celebrating the end of war.[45] The nineteenth-century lull in Great Power war was notable, but did not erase the identities and logics underlying Great Power competition – as the events of 1914 would sadly demonstrate.

In order for the Great Power hierarchy to shift away from a military basis and toward an economic basis, the international community must undergo a fundamental shift in its valuation of military power. Rather than viewing war as a necessary means by which to further national interest, an alternate set of frames would need to become entrenched. One mechanism might be the "learning" processes described in Chapter 3. Were the military Great Powers to repeatedly destroy themselves in war (for instance, following Germany's pattern) or collapse (e.g., the Soviet Union), new lessons might diffuse across world society, painting military competition as a foolish risk rather than a source of advantage. In this case, war might someday be viewed as an expensive and unnecessary – even obsolete – mechanism of international diplomacy.

Alternatives, such as economic prowess, might instead come to be seen as the principle basis for national success and status. If that occurred, states might dismantle their militaries in favor of economic (or other) ends. However, the potential negative lessons of Germany and the Soviet Union have not fully taken hold – perhaps because they were mainly seen as triumphs of a competing Great Power, the United States. Germany's legacy may have affected parts of Europe, but it has only caused minor ripples in the overall ocean of international relations. A hypothetical future collapse of the United States would go much further in undermining perceptions regarding the importance of war and military competition.

This book began with the claim that we must understand the causes of Great Power war before we can predict whether Great Power peace is

---

[44] Bradley A. Thayer, "Humans, Not Angels: Reasons to Doubt the Decline of War Thesis." *International Studies Review* 15 (2013): 405–411; Jack S. Levy and William R. Thompson, "The Decline of War? Multiple Trajectories and Diverging Trends." *International Studies Review* (2013): 16–24.

[45] Charles DeBenedetti, *The Peace Reform in American History*. Bloomington: Indiana University Press, 1980.

likely to endure. It is not yet clear whether the current quiescence among the Great Powers in the twenty-first century is a lull between conflicts or the start of a fundamental shift in the identities, understandings, and expectations of the system as a whole that may signal the end of Great Power war. History suggests that it is usually a mistake to underestimate the potential for hubris and folly of Great Powers. In a complex and ambiguous world – with much flexibility of interpretation – states may come to perceive new threats and construct new rivalries. The numerous military activities of the United States, despite the absence of significant rivals, are one indication that logics of Great Power competition have not faded. One hopes that wiser heads will prevail, but it is conceivable that the United States may construct new rivalries, perhaps with China or some as-yet-unforeseen competitor.

While the short-term prognosis is uncertain, the arguments outlined over the course of this book are fundamentally optimistic. Classic perspectives see Great Power rivalry and war as inevitable, driven by survival imperatives. By contrast, this book suggests that such competitions are instead the enduring legacy of an arbitrary but deeply entrenched set of roles and identities in world society. On one hand, this implies that the horrific destruction of war is even more foolish than people imagine, an anachronistic form of dueling that somehow persists to this day. On the other hand, it affords hope that war is not inevitable: cultural changes in world society have the potential to end centuries of Great Power competition. Indeed, one theme of the book is that the epistemic community of scholars shapes the understandings and lessons of war. Prior scholarship has almost without exception reinforced the idea that war is rational and necessary for survival. By rethinking war and documenting the ambiguities and perils of warfare that have been systematically overlooked, scholars may help states learn new lessons from history and chart a new path forward.

Bibliography

Abu-Lughod, Janet L. *Before European Hegemony: The World System A.D. 1250–1350*. Oxford: Oxford University Press, 1991.

Addington, Larry H. *The Patterns of War since the Eighteenth Century*. Bloomington: Indiana University Press, 1994 [1984].

Alasuutari, Pertti. *The Synchronization of National Policies: Ethnography of the Global Tribe of Moderns*. New York: Routledge, 2016.

Albertini, Luigi. *The Origins of the War of 1914*. Oxford: Oxford University Press, 1952.

Allison, Graham T. *Essence of Decision: Explaining the Cuban Missile Crisis*. Boston: Little, Brown, 1971.

Allison, Graham T. and Morton H. Halperin. "Bureaucratic Politics: A Paradigm and Some Policy Implications." *World Politics* 24 (1972): 40–79.

Aron, Raymond. *The Century of Total War*. Garden City: Doubleday, 1954.

Arrow, Kenneth J. *The Limits of Organization*. New York: W.W. Norton and Company, 1974.

Avant, Deborah. *Political Institutions and Military Change: Lessons from Peripheral Wars*. Ithaca: Cornell University Press, 1994.

"From Mercenary to Citizen Armies: Explaining Change in the Practice of War." *International Organization* 54 (2000): 41–72.

"Political Institutions and Military Effectiveness: Contemporary United States and United Kingdom." In *Creating Military Power: The Sources of Military Effectiveness*, edited by Risa A. Brooks and Elizabeth A. Stanley, 80–105. Stanford: Stanford University Press, 2007.

Axelrod, Robert. *Conflict of Interest: A Theory of Divergent Goals with Applications to Politics*. Chicago: Markham Publishing Company, 1970.

Ball, Simon J. *The Cold War: An International History, 1947–1991*. New York: St. Martin's Press, 1998.

Baran, Paul A. and Paul M. Sweezy. *Monopoly Capital: An Essay on the American Economic and Social Order*. New York: Monthly Review Press, 1968.

Barnett, Michael and Martha Finnemore. *Rules for the World: International Organizations in Global Politics.* Ithaca: Cornell University Press, 2004.

Beaufre, Général d'Armée André. "Liddell Hart and the French Army, 1919–1939." In *The Theory and Practice of War*, edited by Michael Howard, 129–142. Bloomington: Indiana University Press, 1965.

Beck, Colin J. "The World-Cultural Origins of Revolutionary Waves: Five Centuries of European Contention." *Social Science History* 35.2 (2011): 167–207.

Beckman, Peter R., Larry Campbell, Paul W. Crumlish, Michael N. Dobkowski, and Steven P. Lee. *The Nuclear Predicament: Nuclear Weapons in the Cold War and Beyond*, second edition. Englewood Cliffs: Prentice Hall, 1992.

Bernstein, Jeremy. *Hitler's Uranium Club.* Woodbury: American Institute of Physics, 1996.

Betts, Richard K. "Is Strategy an Illusion?" *International Security* 25(2003): 5–50.

Biddle, Stephen. *Military Power: Explaining Victory and Defeat in Modern Battle.* Princeton: Princeton University Press, 2006.

Bidwell, Shelford and Dominick Graham. *Fire-Power: British Army Weapons and Theories of War 1904–1945.* London: George Allen and Unwin, 1982.

Blechman, Barry and Douglas Hart. "The Political Utility of Nuclear Weapons: The 1973 Middle East Crisis." In *Strategy and Nuclear Deterrence*, edited by Steven E. Miller, 273–297. Princeton: Princeton University Press, 1987.

Bloomfield, Lincoln P. *Forward to Without the Bomb: The Politics of Nuclear Nonproliferation*, edited by Mitchell Reiss, vii–x. New York: Columbia University Press, 1988.

Bluth, Christoph. *Britain, Germany, and Western Nuclear Strategy.* Oxford: Clarendon Press, 1995.

Boli, John and George M. Thomas. "World Culture in the World Polity: A Century of International Non-Governmental Organization." *American Sociological Review* 62 (1997): 171–190.

Constructing World Culture: International Nongovernmental Organizations since 1875. Stanford: Stanford University Press, 1999.

Bond, Brian. "Doctrine and Training in the British Cavalry, 1870–1914." In *The Theory and Practice of War*, edited by Michael Howard, 95–128. Bloomington: Indiana University Press, 1965.

British Military Policy between the Two World Wars. Oxford: Clarendon Press, 1980.

The Pursuit of Victory: From Napoleon to Saddam Hussein. New York: Oxford University Press, 1996.

Bond, Brian and Williamson Murray. "The British Armed Forces, 1918–39." In *Military Effectiveness: Volume II: The Interwar Period*, edited by Allan R. Millett and Williamson Murray, 98–130. Boston: Allen and Unwin, 1988.

Boot, Max. *War Made New: Technology, Warfare, and the Course of History, 1500 to Today.* New York: Gotham, 2006.

Borer, Douglas A. *Superpowers Defeated: Vietnam and Afghanistan Compared.* London: Frank Cass, 1999.

Bottome, Edgar M. *The Missile Gap.* Cranbury: Associated University Presses, 1971.

Boyle, Elizabeth Heger. *Female Genital Cutting: Cultural Conflict in the Global Community*. Baltimore: Johns Hopkins University Press, 2002.

Boyle, Elizabeth H., Minzee Kim, and Wesley Longhofer. "Abortion Liberalization in World Society, 1960–2009." *American Journal of Sociology*, 121 (2015): 882–913.

Boyle, Elizabeth Heger, and Sharon E. Preves. "National Politics as International Process: The Case of Anti-Female-Genital-Cutting Laws." *Law & Society Review* 34 (2000): 703–737.

Braudel, Fernand. *The Mediterranean and the Mediterranean World in the Age of Philip II*. Berkeley: University of California Press, 1996.

Brodie, Bernard. *Strategy in the Missile Age*. Princeton: Princeton University Press, 1959.

Brodie, Bernard and Fawn M. *From Crossbow to H-Bomb*. Bloomington: Indiana University Press, 1973.

Brooks, Risa A. "Introduction: The Impact of Culture, Society, Institutions, and International Forces on Military Effectiveness." In *Creating Military Power: The Sources of Military Effectiveness*, edited by Risa A. Brooks and Elizabeth A. Stanley, 1–26. Stanford: Stanford University Press, 2007.

Shaping Strategy: The Civil-Military Politics of Strategic Assessment. Princeton: Princeton University Press, 2008.

Brooks, Risa A. and Elizabeth A. Stanley, (Eds.) *Creating Military Power: The Sources of Military Effectiveness*. Stanford: Stanford University Press, 2007.

Brose, Eric Dorn. *The Kaiser's Army: The Politics of Military Technology in Germany during the Machine Age, 1870–1918*. Oxford: Oxford University Press, 2001.

Brown, Michael E., Owen R. Coté Jr., Sean M. Lynn-Jones, and Steven E. Miller, (Eds.) *Offense, Defense, and War*. Cambridge, MA: MIT Press, 2004.

Bueno de Mesquita, Bruce, Alastair Smith, Randolph M. Siverson, and James D. Morrow. *The Logic of Political Survival*. Cambridge, MA: MIT Press, 2003.

Carr, E.H. *Great Britain as a Mediterranean Power*, Cust Foundation Lecture, University College, Nottingham, 1937.

Carr, Edward Hallett. *The Twenty Years' Crisis, 1919–1939: An Introduction to the Study of International Relations*. New York: Palgrave, 2001[1939].

Carruthers, Bruce G. and Wendy Nelson Espeland. "Accounting for Rationality: Double-Entry Bookkeeping and the Rhetoric of Economic Rationality." *American Journal of Sociology* 97 (1991): 31–69.

Catudal, Honoré M. *Soviet Nuclear Strategy from Stalin to Gorbachev*. Berlin: Verlag, 1989.

Challener, Richard D. *The French Theory of the Nation in Arms, 1866–1939*. New York: Columbia University Press, 1952.

Childs, John. *Armies and Warfare in Europe, 1648–1789*. Manchester: Manchester University Press, 1982.

Chirot, Daniel. *Social Change in the Modern Era*. New York: Harcourt Brace Jovanovich, 1986.

Chirot, Daniel and Thomas D. Hall. "World-System Theory." *Annual Review of Sociology* 8 (1982): 81–106.

Church, William Conant. *Ulysses S. Grant and the Period of National Preservation and Reconstruction.* Garden City: Garden City Publishing Company, 1926.

Churchill, Winston. BBC radio address "The Russian Enigma," October 1, 1939.

Citino, Robert M. *Armored Forces: History and Sourcebook.* Westport: Greenwood Press, 1994.

Quest for Decisive Victory: From Stalemate to Blitzkrieg in Europe, 1899–1940. Lawrence: University Press of Kansas, 2002.

Clark, Ian and Nicholas J. Wheeler. *The British Origins of Nuclear Strategy, 1945–1955.* Oxford: Clarendon Press, 1989.

Claude, Inis L., Jr. *Power and International Relations.* New York: Random House, 1962.

Clausewitz, Carl von. *On War*, edited and translated by Michael Howard and Peter Paret. Princeton: Princeton University Press, 1989.

Clodfelter, Micheal. *Warfare and Armed Conflicts: A Statistical Reference*, vols. 1–2. Jefferson: McFarland and Co, 1992.

Cohen, Eliot A and John Gooch. *Military Misfortunes: The Anatomy of Failure in War.* New York: Free Press, 1990.

Colaresi, Michael P. *Scare Tactics: The Politics of International Rivalry.* Syracuse: Syracuse University Press, 2005.

Colaresi, Michael P., Karen Rasler, and William R. Thompson. *Strategic Rivalries in World Politics: Position, Space and Conflict Escalation.* Cambridge: Cambridge University Press, 2007.

Cole, Wade M. "Sovereignty Relinquished? Explaining Commitment to the International Human Rights Covenants, 1966–1999." *American Sociological Review* 70 (2005): 472–495.

"Human Rights as Myth and Ceremony? Reevaluating the Effectiveness of Human Rights Treaties, 1981–2007." *American Journal of Sociology* 117 (2012): 1131–1171.

Cole, Wade M. and Francisco O. Ramirez. "Conditional Decoupling: Assessing the Impact of National Human Rights Institutions, 1981 to 2004." *American Sociological Review* 78 (2013): 702–725.

Copeland, Dale C. *The Origins of Major War.* Ithaca: Cornell University Press, 2000.

Corum, James S. *The Roots of Blitzkrieg: Hans von Seeckt and German Military Reform.* Lawrence: University Press of Kansas, 1992.

"A Comprehensive Approach to Change: Reform in the German Army in the Interwar Period." In *The Challenge of Change: Military Institutions and New Realities, 1918–1941*, edited by Harold R. Winton and David R. Mets, 35–73. Lincoln: University of Nebraska Press, 2000.

Craig, Gordon A. *Europe since 1815.* New York: Holt, Rinehart and Winston, 1966.

Cumings, Bruce. *The Origins of the Korean War: Volume II The Roaring of the Cataract, 1947–1950.* Princeton: Princeton University Press, 1990.

Cyert, Richard M. and James G. March. *A Behavioral Theory of the Firm.* Cambridge: Blackwell Publishers, 1963.

Dafoe, Allen, Jonathan Renshon, and Paul Huth. "Reputation and Status as Motives for War." *Annual Review of Political Science* 17 (2014): 371–393.

Dahl, Robert A. "The Concept of Power." *Behavioural Science* 2 (1957): 201–215.

Davies, Norman. *Europe: A History.* New York: Harper Perennial, 1998.

Debs, Alexandre and Nuno P. Monteiro. "Known Unknowns: Power Shifts, Uncertainty, and War." *International Organization* 68 (2014): 1–31.

Der Derian, James. *On Diplomacy: A Genealogy of Western Estrangement.* New York: Basil Blackwell, 1987.

DiCicco, Jonathan M. and Jack S. Levy. "Power Shifts and Problem Shifts: The Evolution of the Power Transition Research Program." *The Journal of Conflict Resolution* 43 (1999): 675–704.

Diehl, Paul F. and Gary Goertz. *War and Peace in International Rivalry.* Ann Arbor: University of Michigan Press, 2000.

DiMaggio, Paul J. and Walter W. Powell. "The Iron Cage Revisited: Institutional Isomorphism and Collective Rationality in Organizational Fields." *American Sociological Review* 48 (1983): 147–160.

Dixon, Norman F. *On the Psychology of Military Incompetence.* London: Cape, 1976.

Dobbin, Frank. *Forging Industrial Policy: The United States, Britain, and France in the Railway Age.* New York: Cambridge University Press, 1994.

Inventing Equal Opportunity. Princeton: Princeton University Press, 2011.

Dobson, John M. *America's Ascent: The United States Becomes a Great Power, 1880–1914.* DeKalb: Northern Illinois University Press, 1978.

Dorn, Walter Louis. *Competition for Empire, 1740–1763.* New York: Harper Brothers, 1940.

Doughty, Robert A. *The Seeds of Disaster: The Development of French Army Doctrine, 1919–1939.* Hamden: Archon, 1985.

"The French Armed Forces, 1918–40." In *Military Effectiveness: Volume II: The Interwar Period,* edited by Allan R. Millett and Williamson Murray, 39–69. Boston: Allen and Unwin, 1988.

Drezner, Daniel W. *All Politics Is Global: Explaining International Regulatory Regimes.* Princeton: Princeton University Press, 2008.

"Military Primacy Doesn't Pay (Nearly As Much As You Think)." *International Security* 38 (2013): 52–79.

Drori, Gili S., John W. Meyer, and Hokyu Hwang. *Globalization and Organization: World Society and Organizational Change.* New York: Oxford University Press, 2006.

Drori, Gili S., John W. Meyer, Francisco Ramirez, and Evan Schofer. *Science in the Modern World Polity: Institutionalization and Globalization.* Stanford: Stanford University Press, 2003.

Duffield, John S. *World Power Forsaken: Political Culture, International Institutions, and German Security Policy after Unification.* Stanford: Stanford University Press, 1998.

Duffield, John S., Theo Farrell, Richard Price, and Michael C. Desch. "Isms and Schisms: Culturalism versus Realism in Security Studies." *International Security* 24 (1999): 156–180.

Duffy, Christopher. *The Army of Frederick the Great.* Vancouver: Douglas David and Charles Limited, 1974.

Dupuy, Trevor N. *A Genius for War: The German Army and General Staff, 1807–1945*. Englewood Cliffs: Prentice-Hall, 1977.

Echevarria, Antulio J. II. *After Clausewitz: German Military Thinkers before the Great War*. Lawrence: University of Kansas Press, 2000.

Eden, Lynn. *Whole World on Fire: Organizations, Knowledge, and Nuclear Weapons Devastation*. Ithaca: Cornell University Press, 2004.

Enthoven, Alain C. and K. Wayne Smith. *How Much Is Enough? Shaping the Defense Program, 1961–1969*. New York: Harper and Row, 1971.

Espeland, Wendy Nelson and Mitchell L. Stevens. "Commensuration as a Social Process." *Annual Review of Sociology* 24 (1998): 313–343.

Evangelista, Matthew. *Innovation and the Arms Race: How the United States and the Soviet Union Develop New Military Technologies*. Ithaca: Cornell University Press, 1988.

Fallows, James. *National Defense*. New York: Random House, 1981.

Farrell, Theo. *Weapons without a Cause: The Politics of Weapons Acquisition in the United States*. New York: Palgrave Macmillan, 1996.

"Culture and Military Power," *Review of International Studies* 24 (1998): 407–416.

"Constructivist Security Studies: Portrait of a Research Program." *International Studies Review* 4 (2002): 49–72.

The Norms of War: Cultural Beliefs and Modern Conflict. Boulder: Lynne Rienner, 2005a.

"World Culture and Military Power." *Security Studies* 14(3): (2005b), 448–488.

"Global Norms and Military Effectiveness: The Army in Early Twentieth-Century Ireland." In *Creating Military Power: The Sources of Military Effectiveness*, edited by Risa A. Brooks and Elizabeth A. Stanley, 136–157. Stanford: Stanford University Press, 2007.

"Improving in War: Military Adaptation and the British in Helmand Province, Afghanistan, 2006–2009." *Journal of Strategic Studies* 33.4 (2010): 567–594.

Farrell, Theo and Terry Terriff. *The Sources of Military Change: Culture, Politics, Technology*. Boulder: Lynne Rienner, 2002.

Fazal, Tanisha. *State Death: The Politics and Geography of Conquest, Annexation and Occupation*. Princeton: Princeton University Press, 2007.

Fearon, James D. "Domestic Political Audiences and the Escalation of International Disputes." *The American Political Science Review* 88.3 (1994): 577–592.

"Rationalist Explanations for War." *International Organization* 49 (1995): 379–414.

Feis, Herbert. *From Trust to Terror: The Onset of the Cold War, 1945–1950*. New York: W. W. Norton and Company, 1970.

Ferguson, Niall. *The Pity of War*. New York: Basic Books, 2000.

Fey, Mark and Kristopher W. Ramsay. "Mutual Optimism and War." *American Journal of Political Science* 51 (2007): 738–754.

Filson, Darren and Suzanne Werner. "A Bargaining Model of War and Peace." *American Journal of Political Science* 46 (2002): 819–838.

Finnemore, Martha. *National Interests in International Society*. Ithaca: Cornell University Press, 1996a.

"Norms, Culture, and World Politics: Insights from Sociology's Institutionalism." *International Organization* 50.2 (1996b): 325–347.

Fischer, Fritz. *Germany's Aims in the First World War*. New York: W. W. Norton, 1967.

War of Illusions: German Policies from 1911 to 1914. London: Chatto and Windus, 1975.

Fourcade, Marion. *Economists and Societies: Discipline and Profession in the United States, Britain, and France, 1890s to 1990s*. Princeton: Princeton University Press, 2010.

Fourcade-Gourinchas, Marion, and Sarah L. Babb. "The Rebirth of the Liberal Creed: Paths to Neoliberalism in Four Countries." *American Journal of Sociology* 108.3 (2002): 533–579.

Frank, David John and Jay Gabler. *Reconstructing the University: Worldwide Shifts in Academia in the 20th Century*. Stanford: Stanford University Press, 2006.

Freedman, Lawrence. *The Evolution of Nuclear Strategy*, third edition. Basingstoke: Palgrave Macmillan, 2003.

Strategy: A History. Oxford: Oxford University Press, 2013.

Friedland, Roger and Robert R. Alford. "Bringing Society Back In: Symbols, Practices, and Institutional Contradiction." In *The New Institutionalism in Organizational Analysis*, edited by Walter W. Powell and Paul J. DiMaggio, 232–263. Chicago: University of Chicago Press, 1991.

Fuller, J. F. C. *Armament and History*. New York: Charles Scribner's Sons, 1945.

A Military History of the Western World, Volume III. New York: Funk and Wagnalls, 1956.

The Conduct of War, 1789–1961. New Brunswick: Rutgers University Press, 1961.

Gaddis, John Lewis. *The United States and the Origins of the Cold War, 1941–1947*. New York: Columbia University Press, 1972.

Strategies of Containment: A Critical Appraisal of Postwar American National Security Policy. Oxford: Oxford University Press, 1982.

The Long Peace: Inquiries into the History of the Cold War. Oxford: Oxford University Press, 1987.

The Cold War: A New History. New York: Penguin Press, 2005.

Gallo-Cruz, Selina. "Organizing Global Nonviolence: The Growth and Spread of Nonviolent INGOs, 1948–2003." *Research in Social Movements, Conflict, and Change* 34 (2012): 213–256.

Gardner, Lloyd C., Arthur Schlesinger, Jr., and Hans J. Morgenthau. *The Origins of the Cold War*. Waltham: Ginn-Blaisdell, 1970.

Gartner, Scott Sigmund. *Strategic Assessment in War*. New Haven: Yale University Press, 1997.

Gat, Azar. *The Origins of Military Thought from the Enlightenment to Clausewitz*. Oxford: Clarendon Press, 1989.

War in Human Civilization. Oxford: Oxford University Press, 2006.

Gates, Robert M. *From the Shadows.* New York: Simon and Schuster, 1996.

George, Alexander L. and Richard Smoke. *Deterrence in American Foreign Policy: Theory and Practice.* New York: Columbia University Press, 1974.

Gilpin, Robert. *War and Change in World Politics.* Cambridge: Cambridge University Press, 1981.

"The Theory of Hegemonic War." *The Journal of Interdisciplinary History* 18 (1988): 591–613.

Glaser, Charles L. *Rational Theory of International Politics: The Logic of Competition and Cooperation.* Princeton: Princeton University Press. 2010.

Gleditsch, Nils Petter, Steven Pinker, Bradley A. Thayer, Jack S. Levy, and William R. Thompson. "The Decline of War." *International Studies Review* 15 (2013): 396–419.

Goddard, Stacie E. *Indivisible Territory and the Politics of Legitimacy: Jerusalem and Northern Ireland.* New York: Cambridge University Press, 2010.

Goemans, Hein E. *War and Punishment: The Causes of War Termination and the First World War.* Princeton: Princeton University Press, 2000.

Goertz, Gary and Jack S. Levy (eds.). *Explaining War and Peace: Case Studies and Necessary Condition Counterfactuals.* New York: Routledge, 2007.

Goldman, Emily O. "The Spread of Western Military Models to Ottoman Turkey and Meiji Japan." In Theo Farrell and Terry Terriff (eds.), *The Sources of Military Change: Culture, Politics, Technology,* 41–68. Boulder: Lynne Rienner, 2002.

"International Competition and Military Effectiveness: Naval Air Power, 1919–1945." In Brooks, Risa A. and Elizabeth A. Stanley (eds.), *Creating Military Power: The Sources of Military Effectiveness,* 158–185. Stanford: Stanford University Press, 2007.

Power in Uncertain Times: Strategy in the Fog of Peace. Stanford: Stanford University Press, 2011.

Goldman, Emily O. and Leslie C. Eliason (eds.). *The Diffusion of Military Technology and Ideas.* Stanford: Stanford University Press, 2003.

Goldschmidt, Bertrand. *Atomic Rivals,* translated by Georges M. Temmer. New Brunswick: Rutgers University Press, 1990.

Goldstein, Joshua S. *Winning the War on War: The Decline of Armed Conflict Worldwide.* New York: Dutton, 2011.

Gordon, Philip H. *A Certain Idea of France: French Security Policy and the Gaullist Legacy.* Princeton: Princeton University Press, 1993.

Graeber, David. *Debt: The First 5,000 Years.* Brooklyn, NY: Melville House, 2011.

Graebner, Norman A. "Myth and Reality: America's Rhetorical Cold War." In *Critical Reflections on the Cold War: Linking Rhetoric and History,* edited by Martin J. Medhurst and H.W. Brands, 20–37. College Station: Texas A&M University Press, 2000.

Gray, Colin S. *Modern Strategy.* Oxford: Oxford University Press, 1999.

Grenville, J.A.S. *Europe Reshaped, 1848–1878.* Hassocks: Harvester Press, 1976.

"Diplomacy and War Plans in the United States, 1890–1917." In *The War Plans of the Great Powers, 1880–1914,* edited by Paul M. Kennedy, 23–28. London: George Allen and Unwin, 1979 [1961].

Grieco, Joseph M. "Realist International Theory and the Study of World Politics." In *Thinking in International Relations Theory*, edited by Michael W. Doyle and G. John Ikenberry, 163–201. Boulder: Westview, 1997.

Griffin, Larry J., Joel A. Devine, and Michael Wallace. "Monopoly Capital, Organized Labor, and Military Expenditures in the United States, 1949–1976." *American Journal of Sociology* 88 (1982): S113–S153.

Griffith, Paddy. *Military Thought in the French Army, 1815–51*. Manchester: Manchester University Press, 1989.

Habeck, Mary R. *Storm of Steel: The Development of Armor Doctrine in Germany and the Soviet Union, 1919–1939*. Ithaca: Cornell University Press, 2003.

Hafner-Burton, Emilie M. and Kiyoteru Tsutsui. "Human Rights in a Globalizing World: The Paradox of Empty Promises." *American Journal of Sociology* 110 (2005): 1373–1411.

Halle, Louis J. *The Cold War as History*. New York: Harper and Row, 1967.

Hallett, Tim and Marc J. Ventresca. "Inhabited Institutions: Social Interactions and Organizational Forms in Gouldner's *Patterns of Industrial Bureaucracy*." *Theory and Society* 35 (2006): 213–236.

Halperin, Morton H. "The Korean War." In *The Use of Force: International Politics and Foreign Policy*, edited by Robert J. Art and Kenneth N. Waltz, 216–234. Boston: Little, Brown and Company, 1971.

Bureaucratic Politics and Foreign Policy. Washington, DC: The Brookings Institution, 1974.

Hannigan, Robert E. 2002. *The New World Power: American Foreign Policy, 1898–1917*. Philadelphia: University of Pennsylvania Press, 2002.

Harris, J.P. *Men, Ideas and Tank: British Military Thought and Armoured Forces, 1903–1939*. Manchester: Manchester University Press, 1995.

Hassner, Ron E. "To Halve and to Hold: Conflicts over Sacred Space and the Problem of Indivisibility." *Security Studies* 12.4 (2003): 1–33.

"The Path to Intractability Time and the Entrenchment of Territorial Disputes." *International Security* 31 (2006): 107–138.

War on Sacred Grounds. Ithaca: Cornell University Press, 2009.

Hastings, Max. *Catastrophe 1914: Europe Goes to War*. New York: Knopf, 2013.

Haveman, Heather A. "Between a Rock and a Hard Place: Organizational Change and Performance Under Conditions of Fundamental Environmental Transformation." *Administrative Science Quarterly* 37 (1992): 48–75.

"Follow the Leader: Mimetic Isomorphism and Entry into New Markets." *Administrative Science Quarterly* 38 (1993): 593–627.

Healy, Kieran. *Last Best Gifts: Altruism and the Market for Human Blood and Organs*. Chicago: University of Chicago Press, 2006.

Heinemann, W. "The Development of German Armoured Forces 1918–40." In *Armoured Warfare*, edited by J.P. Harris and F.H. Toase, 51–69. New York: St. Martin's Press, 1990.

Herrera, Geoffrey L. and Thomas G. Mahnken. "Military Diffusion in Nineteenth-Century Europe: The Napoleonic and Prussian Military Systems." In *The Diffusion of Military Technology and Ideas*, edited by

Emily O. Goldman and Leslie C. Eliason, 205–242. Stanford: Stanford University Press, 2003.

Herring, George C. *America's Longest War: The United States and Vietnam, 1950–1975*, second edition. New York: Alfred A. Knopf, 1986.

Herrmann, David G. *The Arming of Europe and the Making of the First World War*. Princeton: Princeton University Press, 1996.

Herwig, Holger H. *The First World War: Germany and Austria-Hungary 1914–1918*. New York: Bloomsbury Academic, 1996.

"Command Decision Making: Imperial Germany, 1871–1914." In *The Fog of Peace and War Planning*, edited by Talbot C. Imlay and Monica Duffy Toft, 100–125. New York: Routledge, 2006.

Herwig, Holger H. and D.F. Trask. "Naval Operations Plans between Germany and the USA, 1898–1913." In *The War Plans of the Great Powers, 1880–1914*, edited by Paul M. Kennedy, 39–74. London: George Allen and Unwin, 1979 [1970].

Hicks, Alexander. *Social Democracy and Welfare Capitalism: A Century of Income Security Politics*. Ithaca: Cornell University Press, 1999.

Hironaka, Ann. *Neverending Wars: The International Community, Weak States, and the Perpetuation of Civil War*. Cambridge, MA: Harvard University Press, 2005.

Greening the Globe: World Society and Environmental Change. Cambridge: Cambridge University Press, 2014.

Hobsbawm, Eric J. *The Age of Extremes: A History of the World, 1914–1991*. New York: Pantheon Books, 1994.

Holloway, David. *The Soviet Union and the Arms Race*. New Haven: Yale University Press, 1983.

Stalin and the Bomb: The Soviet Union and Atomic Energy 1939–1956. New Haven: Yale University Press, 1994.

Holmes, Richard. *The Road to Sedan: The French Army 1866–70*. London: Royal Historical Society, 1984.

Holsti, Kalevi J. *Peace and War: Armed Conflicts and International Order, 1648–1989*. Cambridge: Cambridge University Press, 1991.

Homer-Dixon, Thomas F. and Marc A. Levy. "Environment and Security." *International Security* 20 (1995–1996): 189–198.

Horowitz, David. "Introduction." In *Containment and Revolution*, edited by David Horowitz, 9–12. London: Anthony Blond, 1967.

Horowitz, Michael. "The Spread of Nuclear Weapons and International Conflict: Does Experience Matter? *Journal of Conflict Resolution* 53 (2009): 234–257.

Horowitz, Michael C. *The Diffusion of Military Power: Causes and Consequences for International Relations*. Princeton: Princeton University Press, 2010.

Howard, Michael. *The Franco-Prussian War: The German Invasion of France, 1870–1871*. New York: Macmillan, 1962.

Studies in War and Peace. New York: Viking Press, 1970.

War in European History. Oxford: Oxford University Press, 1976.

"Men against Fire: Expectations of War in 1914." In *Military Strategy and the Origins of the First World War*, edited by Steven E. Miller, Sean

M. Lynn-Jones and Stephen Van Evera, 3–19. Princeton: Princeton University Press, 1991 [1984].

The Lessons of History. New Haven: Yale University Press, 1991.

The First World War. Oxford: Oxford University Press, 2002.

Huntington, Samuel P. "Why International Primacy Matters." *International Security* 17 (1993): 68–83.

Huth, Paul K. 1996. *Standing Your Ground: Territorial Disputes and International Conflict*. Ann Arbor: University of Michigan Press.

Hymans, Jacques. *The Psychology of Nuclear Proliferation: Identity, Emotions, and Foreign Policy*. Cambridge: Cambridge University Press, 2006.

Achieving Nuclear Ambitions: Scientists, Politicians, and Proliferation. New York: Cambridge University Press, 2012.

Ikenberry, G. John. *After Victory: Institutions, Strategic Restraint, and the Rebuilding of Order after Major Wars*. Princeton: Princeton University Press, 2001.

"Liberal Order Building." In *To Lead the World: American Strategy after the Bush Doctrine*, edited by Melvyn P. Leffler and Jeffrey W. Legro, 85–108. New York: Oxford University Press, 2008.

Ikle, Fred. *Every War Must End*. New York: Columbia University Press, 1991.

Imlay, Talbot C. and Monica Duffy Toft (eds.), *The Fog of Peace and War Planning*. New York: Routledge, 2006.

Jackson, Julian. *The Fall of France*. Oxford: Oxford University Press, 2003.

Jepperson, Ronald L., Alexander Wendt, and Peter J. Katzenstein. "Norms, Identity, and Culture in National Security." In *The Culture of National Security: Norms and Identity in World Politics*, edited by Peter J. Katzenstein, 33–75. New York: Columbia University Press, 1996.

Jervis, Robert. *Perception and Misperception in International Politics*. Princeton: Princeton University Press, 1976.

"Cooperation Under the Security Dilemma." *World Politics* 30 (1978): 167–214.

"The Impact of the Korean War on the Cold War." *The Journal of Conflict Resolution* 24 (1980): 563–592.

The Illogic of American Nuclear Strategy. Ithaca: Cornell University Press, 1984.

The Meaning of the Nuclear Revolution: Statecraft and the Prospect of Armageddon. Ithaca: Cornell University Press, 1989.

"Domino Beliefs and Strategic Behavior." In *Dominoes and Bandwagon: Strategic Beliefs and Great Power Competition in the Eurasian Rimland*, edited by Robert Jervis and Jack Snyder, 20–50. Oxford: Oxford University Press, 1991.

"Systems and Interaction Effects." In *Coping with Complexity in the International System*, edited by Jack Snyder and Robert Jervis, 25–46. Boulder: Westview Press, 1993a.

"International Primacy: Is the Game Worth the Candle?." *International Security* 17 (1993b): 52–67.

System Effects: Complexity in Political and Social Life. Princeton: Princeton University Press, 1997.

Why Intelligence Fails: Lessons from the Iranian Revolution and the Iraq War. Ithaca: Cornell University Press, 2010.

Jervis, Robert, Richard Ned Lebow, and Janice Gross Stein. *Psychology and Deterrence.* Baltimore: Johns Hopkins Press, 1985.

Johnson, David. E. *Fast Tanks and Heavy Bombers.* Ithaca: Cornell University Press, 1998.

Johnson, Dominic D.P. *Overconfidence and War: The Havoc and Glory of Positive Illusions.* Cambridge, MA: Harvard University Press, 2004.

Johnson, Dominic D.P. and Dominic Tierney. *Failing to Win: Perceptions of Victory and Defeat in International Politics.* Cambridge, MA: Harvard University Press, 2006.

Johnson, Dominic D.P. and Monica Duffy Toft. "Grounds for War: The Evolution of Territorial Conflict." *International Security* 38 (2013–2014): 7–38.

Joll, James. *The Origins of the First World War.* New York: Longman, 1992.

Jones, Howard. *Crucible of Power: A History of American Foreign Relations from 1897,* second edition. Lanham: Rowman and Littlefield, 2008.

Kagan, Donald. 1995. *On the Origins of War and the Preservation of Peace.* New York: Doubleday.

Kahin, George. *Intervention.* New York: Anchor, 1987.

Kahn, Herman. *On Thermonuclear War.* Princeton: Princeton University Press, 1961.

Kahneman, Daniel, Paul Slovic, and Amos Tversky. *Judgment under Uncertainty: Heuristics and Biases.* Cambridge: Cambridge University Press, 1982.

Kaiser, David. *Politics and War.* Cambridge, MA: Harvard University Press, 1990.

Kaldor, Mary. *New and Old Wars.* Stanford: Stanford University Press, 1999.

Karnow, Stanley. *Vietnam: A History.* New York: Viking, 1991.

Katzenbach, Jr., Edward L. "The Horse Cavalry in the Twentieth Century." In *The Use of Force: International Politics and Foreign Policy,* edited by Robert J. Art and Kenneth N. Waltz, 277–297. Boston: Little, Brown and Company, 1971 [1958].

Katzenstein, Peter J. (ed.). *The Culture of National Security: Norms and Identity in World Politics.* New York: Columbia University Press, 1996.

Kaufman, Stuart J., Richard Little, and William C. Wohlforth (eds.). *The Balance of Power in World History.* New York: Palgrave Macmillan, 2007.

Kennan, George F. *American Diplomacy, 1900–1950.* Chicago: University of Chicago Press, 1951.

"Mr. 'X' Reassesses His Brainchild." In *The Evolution of the Cold War,* edited by Richard H. Miller, 70–75. Huntington: Robert E. Krieger. Excerpted from Memoirs, 1979 [1967].

"Containment Then and Now." *Foreign Affairs* 65 (1987): 885–890.

Kennedy, Paul M. "The First World War and the International Power System." *International Security* 9 (1984): 7–40.

The Rise and Fall of the Great Powers: Economic Change and Military Conflict from 1500 to 2000. New York: Random House, 1986.

Keohane, Robert O. "Institutional Theory and the Realist Challenge after the Cold War." In *Neo-Realism and Neo-Liberalism*, edited by David A. Baldwin, 269–300. New York: Columbia University Press, 1993.

Keynes, John Maynard. *The Economic Consequences of the Peace*. London: Macmillan, 1919.

Khong, Yuen Foong. *Analogies at War: Korea, Munich, Dien Bien Phu, and the Vietnam Decisions of 1965*. Princeton: Princeton University Press, 1992.

Kier, Elizabeth. "Culture and Military Doctrine: France between the Wars." *International Security* 19 (1995): 65–93.

Imagining War: French and British Military Doctrine between the Wars. Princeton: Princeton University Press, 1997.

Kiesling, Eugenia C. *Arming against Hitler: France and the Limits of Military Planning*. Lawrence: University Press of Kansas, 1996.

"Resting Uncomfortably on its Laurels: The Army of Interwar France." In *The Challenge of Change: Military Institutions and New Realities, 1918–1941*, edited by Harold R. Winton and David R. Mets, 1–34. Lincoln: University of Nebraska Press, 2000.

King, Gary, Robert O. Keohane, and Sidney Verba. *Designing Social Inquiry: Scientific Inference in Qualitative Research*. Princeton: Princeton University Press, 1994.

Kirby, M. and R. Capey. "The Air Defence of Great Britain, 1920–1940: An Operational Research Perspective." *The Journal of the Operational Research Society* 48 (1997): 555–568.

Kissenger, Henry A. *Nuclear Weapons and Foreign Policy*. New York: Harper and Brothers, 1957.

"American Strategic Doctrine and Diplomacy." In *The Theory and Practice of War*, edited by Michael Howard, 271–292. Bloomington: Indiana University Press, 1975.

Kolko, Gabriel. *Anatomy of a War: Vietnam, the United States, and the Modern Historical Experience*. New York: New Press, 1994.

Kolko, Joyce and Gabriel Kolko. *The Limits of Power: The World and United States Foreign Policy, 1945–1954*. New York: Harper and Row, 1972.

Krasner, Stephen D. "Logics of Consequences and Appropriateness in the International System." In *Organizing Political Institutions*, edited by Morten Egeberg and Per Laegrid, 181–214. Oslo: Scandinavian University Press, 1999.

Krasner, Stephen D. (ed.). *Problematic Sovereignty*. New York: Columbia University Press, 2009.

Krepinevich, Andrew F. "Cavalry to Computer: The Pattern of Military Revolution." *The National Interest* 37 (1994): 30–42.

Kroenig, Matthew. "Nuclear Superiority and the Balance of Resolve: Explaining Nuclear Crisis Outcomes." *International Organization* 67 (2013): 141–171.

Krücken, Georg. "Learning the 'New, New Thing': On the Role of Path Dependency in University Structures." *Higher Education* 46 (2003): 315–339.

Krücken, Georg and Gili S. Drori (eds.). *World Society: The Writings of John Meyer*. New York: Oxford University Press, 2010.

Kugler, Jacek, and Douglas Lemke (eds.). *Parity and War: Evaluations and Extensions of "The War Ledger."* Ann Arbor: University of Michigan Press, 1996.

Kull, Steven. *Minds at War: Nuclear Reality and the Inner Conflicts of Defense Policymakers.* New York: Basic Books, 1988.

Kydd, Andrew. "Which Side Are You On? Bias, Credibility and Mediation." *American Journal of Political Science* 47 (2003): 597–611.

LaFeber, Walter. *America, Russia, and the Cold War.* New York: John Wiley, 1967.

Lake, David A. "Escape from the State of Nature: Authority and Hierarchy in World Politics." *International Security* 32 (2007): 47–79.

Hierarchy in International Relations. Ithaca: Cornell University Press, 2009.

Larson, Deborah Welch. *Origins of Containment: A Psychological Explanation.* Princeton: Princeton University Press, 1985.

Anatomy of Mistrust: U.S.-Soviet Relations during the Cold War. Ithaca: Cornell University Press, 1997.

Larson, Deborah Welch, T.V. Paul, and William C. Wohlforth. "Status and World Order." In *Status in World Politics*, edited by T.V. Paul, Deborah Welch Larson, and William C. Wohlforth, 3–32. Cambridge: Cambridge University Press, 2014.

Lawrence, Mark. *Assuming the Burden: Europe and the American Commitment to War in Vietnam.* Berkeley: University of California Press, 2005.

Lebow, Richard Ned. *A Cultural Theory of International Relations.* Cambridge: Cambridge University Press, 2008.

Forbidden Fruit: Counterfactuals and International Relations. Princeton: Princeton University Press, 2010a.

Why Nations Fight: Past and Future Motives for War. Cambridge: Cambridge University Press, 2010b.

Lebow, Richard Ned and Janice Gross Stein. *We All Lost the Cold War.* Princeton: Princeton University Press, 1994.

Lee, Chang Kil and David Strang. "The International Diffusion of Public-Sector Downsizing: Network Emulation and Theory-Driven Learning." *International Organization* 60 (2006): 883–909.

Leffler, Melvyn P. *A Preponderance of Power: National Security, the Truman Administration, and the Cold War.* Stanford: Stanford University Press, 1992.

"National Security and US Foreign Policy." In *Origins of the Cold War: An International History*, edited by Melvyn P. Leffler and David S. Painter, 15–52. New York: Routledge, 1994.

Levering, Ralph B. *The Cold War, 1945–1987*, second edition. Arlington Heights: Harlan Davidson, 1988.

Levinthal, Daniel A. and James G. March. "The Myopia of Learning." *Strategic Management Journal* 14 (1993): 95–112.

Levite, Ariel E. "Never Say Never Again: Nuclear Reversal Revisited." In *Going Nuclear: Nuclear Proliferation and International Security in the 21st Century*, edited by Michael E. Brown, Owen R. Cote Jr., Sean M. Lynn-Jones and Steven E. Miller, 297–326. Cambridge, MA: MIT Press, 2010.

Levitt, Barbara and James G. March. "Organizational Learning." *Annual Review of Sociology* 14 (1988): 319–338.

Levy, Jack S. "Misperception and the Causes of War: Theoretical Linkages and Analytical Problems." *World Politics* 36 (1983a): 76–99.

War in the Modern Great Power System, 1495–1975. Lexington: University Press of Kentucky, 1983b.

"Declining Power and the Preventive Motivation for War." *World Politics* 40 (1987): 82–107.

"Preferences, Constraints, and Choices in July 1914." *International Security* 15.3 (1990–1991): 151–186.

"Learning and Foreign Policy: Sweeping a Conceptual Minefield." *International Organization* 48 (1994): 279–312.

"Preventive War and Democratic Politics." *International Studies Quarterly* 52 (2008): 1–24.

Levy, Jack S. and John A. Vasquez (eds.). *The Outbreak of the First World War: Structure, Politics and Decision-Making.* Cambridge: Cambridge University Press, 2014.

Levy, Jack S. and William R. Thompson. "Balancing on Land and at Sea: Do States Ally against the Leading Global Power?" *International Security* 35 (2010a): 7–43.

Causes of War. Malden: Wiley-Blackwell, 2010b.

"The Decline of War? Multiple Trajectories and Diverging Trends." *International Studies Review* 15 (2013): 16–24.

Lewis, John Wilson and Xue Litai. *China Builds the Bomb.* Stanford: Stanford University Press, 1988.

Liberman, Peter. *Does Conquest Pay?* Princeton: Princeton University Press, 1996.

"The Rise and Fall of the South African Bomb." In *Going Nuclear: Nuclear Proliferation and International Security in the 21st Century*, edited by Michael E. Brown, Owen R. Cote Jr., Sean M. Lynn-Jones, and Steven E. Miller, 255–296. Cambridge, MA: MIT Press, 2010.

Liddell Hart, Basil H. *The Real War, 1914–1918.* Boston: Little, Brown and Company, 1930.

Tanks, Volume One 1914–1939. London: Cassell, 1959.

History of the Second World War. New York: G.P. Putnam's Sons, 1970.

Lieber, Keir A. *War and the Engineers: The Primacy of Politics over Technology.* Ithaca: Cornell University Press, 2005.

"The New History of World War I and What It Means for International Relations Theory." *International Security* 32.2 (2007): 155–191.

Lieber, Kier A. and Daryl Press. "The End of MAD? The Nuclear Dimension of U.S. Primacy." *International Security* 30 (2006): 7–44.

Lim, Alwyn and Kiyoteru Tsutsui. "Globalization and Commitment in Corporate Social Responsibility: Cross-National Analyses of Institutional and Political-Economy Effects." *American Sociological Review* 77 (2012): 69–98.

Lippmann, Walter. *The Cold War: A Study in U.S. Foreign Policy.* New York: Harper and Row, 1947.

Logsdon, John M. *The Decision to Go to the Moon: Project Apollo and the National Interest*. Cambridge, MA: MIT Press, 1970.

Lord, Robert Howard. *The Origins of the War of 1870*. New York: Russell and Russell, 1966.

Lounsbury, Michael and Marc Ventresca. "The New Structuralism in Organizational Theory." *Organization* 10 (2003): 457–480.

Lovell, Sir Bernard. *The Origins and International Economics of Space Exploration*. Edinburgh: Edinburgh University Press, 1973.

Luard, Evan. *The Blunted Sword: The Erosion of Military Power in Modern World Politics*. New York: New Amsterdam Books, 1988.

Lukacs, John. *The Last European War*. Garden City: Anchor Press, 1976

Luttwak, Edward N. *Strategy and Politics*. New Brunswick: Transaction Books, 1980.

Luvaas, Jay. *The Military Legacy of the Civil War: The European Inheritance*. Chicago: University of Chicago Press, 1959.

"European Military Thought and Doctrine, 1870–1914." In *The Theory and Practice of War*, edited by Michael Howard, 69–94. Bloomington: Indiana University Press, 1965.

Lyall, Jason and Isaiah Wilson, III. "Rage against the Machines: Explaining Outcomes in Counterinsurgency Wars." *International Organization*. 63 (2009): 67–106.

Lynn, John A. 1999. *The Wars of Louis XIV, 1667–1714*. New York: Longman.

Mackenzie, Donald. *Inventing Accuracy: A Historical Sociology of Nuclear Missile Guidance*. Cambridge, MA: MIT Press, 1993.

Mahnken, Thomas G. *Uncovering Ways of War: U.S. Intelligence and Foreign Military Innovation, 1918–1941*. Ithaca: Cornell University Press, 2002.

"Beyond Blitzkrieg: Allied Responses to Combined-Arms Armored Warfare during World War II. In *The Diffusion of Military Technology and Ideas*, edited by Emily O. Goldman and Leslie C. Eliason, 243–366. Stanford: Stanford University Press, 2003.

Mandel, Robert. *The Meaning of Military Victory*. London: Lynne Rienner, 2006.

Mandelbaum, Michael. *The Nuclear Question: The United States and Nuclear Weapons, 1946–1976*. Cambridge: Cambridge University Press, 1979.

Maoz, Zeev and Ben D. Mor. *Bound by Struggle: The Strategic Evolution of Enduring International Rivalries*. Ann Arbor: University of Michigan Press, 2002.

March, James G. "The Power of Power." In *Varieties of Political Theory*, edited by David Easton, 39–70. Englewood Cliffs: Prentice Hall, 1966.

"Bounded Rationality, Ambiguity, and the Engineering of Choice." *The Bell Journal of Economics* 9 (1978): 587–608.

"Decisions in Organizations and Theories of Choice." In *Perspectives on Organization Design and Behavior*, edited by Andrew H. Van de Ven and William F. Joyce, 205–244. New York: John Wiley and Sons, 1981a.

"Footnotes to Organizational Change." *Administrative Science Quarterly* 26 (1981b): 563–577.

"Exploration and Exploitation in Organizational Learning." *Organization Science* 2 (1991): 71–87.

March, James G. and Johan P. Olsen. "The New Institutionalism: Organizational Factors in Political Life." *The American Political Science Review* 78 (1984):734–749.

"The Institutional Dynamics of International Political Orders." *International Organization* 52 (1998): 943–969.

March, James G., Lee S. Sproull, and Michal Tamuz. "Learning from Samples of One or Fewer." *Organization Science* 2 (1991): 1–13.

Martel, William C. *Victory in War: Foundations of Modern Strategy*, revised second edition. Cambridge: Cambridge University Press, 2011.

Massie, Robert K. *Castles of Steel: Britain, Germany, and the Winning of the Great War at Sea*. New York: Random House, 2003.

Matloff, Maurice. 1975. "The American Approach to War, 1919–1945." In *The Theory and Practice of War*, edited by Michael Howard, 213–243. Bloomington: Indiana University Press.

May, Ernest R. *Imperial Democracy: The Emergence of America as a Great Power*. New York: Harcourt, Brace and World, 1961.

"The U-Boat Campaign." In *The Use of Force: International Politics and Foreign Policy*, edited by Robert J. Art and Kenneth N. Waltz, 298–315. Boston: Little, Brown and Company, 1971 [1959].

"Lessons" of the Past: The Use and Misuse of History in American Foreign Policy. London: Oxford University Press, 1979 [1973].

Strange Victory: Hitler's Conquest of France. New York: Hill and Wang, 2000.

McDermott, J. "The Revolution in British Military Thinking from the Boer War to the Moroccan Crisis." In *The War Plans of the Great Powers, 1880–1914*, edited by Paul M. Kennedy, 99–117. London: George Allen and Unwin, 1979 [1974].

McElwee, William. *The Art of War: Waterloo to Mons*. Bloomington: Indiana University Press, 1974.

McKay, Derek and H.M. Scott. *The Rise of the Great Powers, 1648–1815*. New York: Longman, 1983.

McKercher, B.J.C. and Roch Legault. 2001. "Introduction." In *Military Planning and the Origins of the Second World War in Europe*, edited by B.J.C. McKercher and Roch Legault, 1–10. Westport: Praeger.

McMeekin, Sean. *The Russian Origins of the First World War*. Cambridge, MA: Belknap Press, 2011.

McNeill, William H. *The Rise of the West*. Chicago: University of Chicago Press, 1964.

The Pursuit of Power: Technology, Armed Force, and Society since A.D. 1000. Chicago: University of Chicago Press, 1982.

Mearsheimer, John J. *Liddell Hart and the Weight of History*. Ithaca: Cornell University Press, 1988.

The Tragedy of Great Power Politics. New York: W.W. Norton and Company, 2001.

"Hitler and the Blitzkrieg Strategy." In *The Use of Force: Military Power in International Politics*, edited by Robert J. Art and Kenneth N. Waltz, 152–166. Lanham: Rowman and Littlefield, 2009.

Mercer, Jonathan. *Reputation and International Politics*. Ithaca: Cornell University Press, 1996.

Merton, Robert K. "The Self-Fulfilling Prophecy." *The Antioch Review* 8.2 (1948): 193–210.

Messerschmidt, Manfred. "German Military Effectiveness between 1919 and 1939." In *Military Effectiveness: Volume II: The Interwar Period,* edited by Allan R. Millett and Williamson Murray, 218–255. Boston: Allen and Unwin, 1988.

Meyer, John W. "World Society, Institutional Theories, and the Actor." *Annual Review of Sociology* 36 (2010): 1–20.

Meyer, John W., John Boli, and George M. Thomas. "Ontology and Rationalization in the Western Cultural Account." In *Institutional Structure: Constituting State, Society, and the Individual,* edited by George M. Thomas, John W. Meyer, Francisco O. Ramirez, and John Boli, 12–37. Newbury Park: Sage, 1987.

Meyer, John W., John Boli, George M. Thomas, and Francisco O. Ramirez. "World Society and the Nation-State." *American Journal of Sociology* 103 (1997): 144–181.

Meyer, John W. and Ronald L. Jepperson. "The 'Actors' of Modern Society: The Cultural Construction of Social Agency." *Sociological Theory* 18 (2000): 100–120.

Miller, Benjamin. *States, Nations, and the Great Powers: The Sources of Regional War and Peace.* Cambridge: Cambridge University Press, 2007.

Miller, Gregory D. *The Shadow of the Past: Reputation and Military Alliances Before the First World War.* Ithaca: Cornell University Press, 2012.

Miller, Richard H. (ed.). *Introduction to the Evolution of the Cold War.* Huntington: Robert E. Krieger, 1979.

Miller, Steven E. and Sean M. Lynn-Jones. *Preface to* Military Strategy and the Origins of the First World War, edited by Steven E. Miller, Sean M. Lynn-Jones, and Stephen Van Evera, xi–xix. Princeton: Princeton University Press, 1991.

Millett, Allan and Williamson Murray (eds.). *Military Effectiveness.* Boston: Allen & Unwin, 1988.

Mitchell, Allan. *Victors and Vanquished: The German Influence on Army and Church in France after 1870.* Chapel Hill: University of North Carolina Press, 1984.

Mombauer, Annika. *The Origins of the First World War: Controversies and Consensus.* New York: Longman 2002.

Morgenthau, Hans J. *Politics among Nations.* New York: Alfred A. Knopf, 1973 [1948].

Morris, Charles R. *Iron Destinies, Lost Opportunities: The Arms Race between the USA and the USSR, 1945–1987.* New York: Harper and Row, 1988.

Morrow, James D. *Game Theory for Political Scientists.* Princeton: Princeton University Press, 1994.

Morton, Jeffrey S. and Harvey Starr. "Uncertainty, Change, and War: Power Fluctuations in the Modern Elite Power System." *Journal of Peace Research* 38 (2001): 49–66.

Moskos, Jr., Charles C. "The Concept of the Military-Industrial Complex: Radical Critique or Liberal Bogey?" *Social Problems* 21 (1974): 498–512.

Moul, William. "Power Parity, Preponderance, and War between Great Powers, 1816–1989." *The Journal of Conflict Resolution* 47 (2003): 468–489.

Mueller, John. *Retreat from Doomsday: The Obsolescence of Major War.* New York: Basic Books, 1989.

The Remnants of War. Ithaca: Cornell University Press, 2004.

Murray, Williamson. "Armored Warfare: The British, French, and German Experiences." In *Military Innovation in the Interwar Period,* edited by Williamson Murray and Allan R. Millett, 6–49. Cambridge: Cambridge University Press, 1996.

Nenniger, Timothy K. "American Military Effectiveness in the First World War." In *Military Effectiveness: Volume I, The First World War,* edited by Allan R. Millett and Williamson Murray, 116–156. Boston: Allen and Unwin, 1988.

Newhouse, John. *War and Peace in the Nuclear Age.* New York: Alfred A. Knopf, 1988.

New York Times. *The Pentagon Papers.* New York: Quadrangle Books, 1971.

O'Connell, Robert L. *Of Arms and Men: A History of War, Weapons, and Aggression.* Oxford: Oxford University Press, 1989.

Ogorkiewicz, Richard M. *Armor: A History of Mechanized Forces.* New York: Frederick A. Praeger, 1960.

O'Neill, Barry. *Honor, Symbols, and War.* Ann Arbor: University of Michigan Press, 1999.

2006. "Nuclear Weapons and National Prestige." Cowles Foundation Discussion Paper No. 1560.

Organski, A.F.K. *World Politics.* New York: Alfred A. Knopf, 1958.

Organski, A.F.K. and Jacek Kugler. "The Costs of Major Wars: The Phoenix Factor." *The American Political Science Review* 71 (1977): 1347–1366.

The War Ledger. Chicago: University of Chicago Press, 1980.

Orton, J. Douglas and Karl E. Weick. "Loosely Coupled Systems: A Reconceptualization." *The Academy of Management Review* 15 (1990): 203–223.

Painter, David S. *The Cold War: An International History.* London: Routledge, 1999.

Paterson, Thomas G. *Soviet-American Confrontation: Postwar Reconstruction and the Origins of the Cold War.* Baltimore: Johns Hopkins University Press, 1973.

On Every Front: The Making and Unmaking of the Cold War. New York: W.W. Norton and Company, 1992.

Paul, T.V., Deborah Welch Larson, and William C. Wohlforth (eds.). *Status in World Politics.* New York: Cambridge University Press, 2014.

Pernell-Gallagher, Kim. "Learning from Performance: Banks, Collateralized Debt Obligations, and the Credit Crisis." *Social Forces* 94.1 (2015): 31–59.

Perrow, Charles. *Complex Organizations: A Critical Essay,* third edition. New York: Random House, 1986.

The Next Catastrophe: Reducing our Vulnerabilities to Natural, Industrial, and Terrorist Disasters. Princeton: Princeton University Press, 2011.

Pinker, Steven. *The Better Angels of Our Nature: Why Violence Has Declined.* New York: Viking, 2011.

Poast, Paul. 2013. "Can Issue Linkage Improve Treaty Credibility?" *Journal of Conflict Resolution* 57 (2013): 739–764.

Podvig, Pavel (ed.). *Russian Strategic Nuclear Forces.* Cambridge, MA: MIT Press, 2001.

Porch, Douglas. *The March to the Marne: The French Army 1871–1914.* Cambridge: Cambridge University Press, 1981.

Posen, Barry R. *The Sources of Military Doctrine: France, Britain, and Germany between the World Wars.* Ithaca: Cornell University Press, 1984.

Powaski, Ronald E. *March to Armageddon: The United States and the Nuclear Arms Race, 1939 to the Present.* New York: Oxford University Press, 1987.

Lightning War: Blitzkrieg in the West, 1940. Hoboken: John Wiley and Sons, 2003.

Powell, Robert. "Uncertainty, Shifting Power, and Appeasement." *The American Political Science Review* 90 (1996): 749–764.

In the Shadow of Power: States and Strategies in International Politics. Princeton: Princeton University Press, 1999.

"The Inefficient Use of Power: Costly Conflict with Complete Information." *American Political Science Review* 98 (2004): 231–241.

"War as a Commitment Problem." *International Organization* 60 (2006): 169–203.

"Persistent Fighting and Shifting Power." *American Journal of Political Science* 56 (2012): 620–637.

Powell, Walter W. and Paul J. DiMaggio. *The New Institutionalism in Organizational Analysis.* Chicago: University of Chicago Press, 2012.

Press, Daryl G. *Calculating Credibility: How Leaders Assess Military Threats.* Ithaca: Cornell University Press, 2005.

Price, Richard M. *The Chemical Weapons Taboo.* Ithaca: Cornell University Press, 1997.

Quester, George H. *Nuclear Diplomacy: The First Twenty-Five Years.* New York: Dunellen, 1970.

The Politics of Nuclear Proliferation. Baltimore: Johns Hopkins Press, 1973.

Ramirez, Francisco O. and John Boli. "The Political Construction of Mass Schooling: European Origins and Worldwide Institutionalization." *Sociology of Education* 60 (1987): 2–17.

Ramirez, Francisco O. and John W. Meyer. "Comparative Education: The Social Construction of the Modern World System." *Annual Review of Sociology* 6 (1980): 369–399.

Rasler, Karen A. and William R. Thompson. *War and State Making: The Shaping of the Global Powers.* Boston: Unwin Hyman, 1989.

The Great Powers and Global Struggle, 1490–1990. Lexington: University of Kentucky, 1994.

"Explaining Rivalry Escalation to War: Space, Position, and Contiguity in the Major Power Subsystem." *International Studies Quarterly* 44 (2000): 503–530.

"Strategic Rivalries and Complex Causality in 1914." In *The Outbreak of the First World War: Structure, Politics and Decision-Making*, edited by Jack S. Levy and John A. Vasquez, 65–86. New York: Cambridge University Press, 2014.

Rasler, Karen, William R. Thompson, and Sumit Ganguly. *How Rivalries End*. Philadelphia: University of Pennsylvania Press, 2013.

Rathbun, Brian C. "Uncertainty about Uncertainty: Understanding the Multiple Meanings of a Crucial Concept in International Relations Theory." *International Studies Quarterly* 51 (2007): 533–557.

Regan, Geoffrey. *Someone Had Blundered: A Historical Survey of Military Incompetence*. London: B.T. Batsford, 1987.

Reich, Simon and Richard Ned Lebow. *Good-Bye Hegemony! Power and Influence in the Global System*. Princeton: Princeton University Press, 2014.

Reiss, Mitchell. *Without the Bomb: The Politics of Nuclear Nonproliferation*. New York: Columbia University Press, 1988.

Bridled Ambition: Why Countries Constrain Their Nuclear Capabilities. Baltimore: Johns Hopkins Press, 1995.

Reiter, Dan. *Crucible of Beliefs: Learning, Alliances, and World Wars*. Ithaca: Cornell University Press, 1996.

How Wars End. Princeton: Princeton University Press, 2009.

Reiter, Dan and Curtis Meek. "Determinants of Military Strategy 1903–1994: A Quantitative Empirical Test." *International Studies Quarterly* 43 (1999): 363–387.

Reiter, Dan and Allen C. Stam. *Democracies at War*. Princeton: Princeton University Press, 2002.

Resende-Santos, João. *Neorealism, States, and the Modern Mass Army*. Cambridge: Cambridge University Press, 2007.

Reynolds, David. "The European Dimension of the Cold War." In *Origins of the Cold War: An International History*, edited by Melvyn P. Leffler and David S. Painter, 125–138. London: Routledge, 1994.

Rhodes, Richard. *The Making of the Atomic Bomb*. New York: Simon and Schuster, 1986.

Arsenals of Folly: The Making of the Nuclear Arms Race. New York: Alfred A. Knopf, 2007.

Rider, Toby J., Michael G. Findley, and Paul Diehl. "Just Part of the Game? Arms Races, Rivalry, and War." *Journal of Peace Research* 48 (2011): 85–100.

Ritter, Gerhard. *The Schlieffen Plan: Critique of a Myth*. New York: Frederick A. Praeger, 1958.

Roberts, Chalmers M. *The Nuclear Years: The Arms Race and Arms Control, 1945–70*. New York: Praeger, 1970.

Rodrik, Dani. *Economics Rules: The Rights and Wrongs of the Dismal Science*. New York: W.W. Norton, 2015.

Ropp, Theodore. *War in the Modern World*. Durham: Duke University Press, 1959.

Rosen, Stephen Peter. *Winning the Next War: Innovation and the Modern Military*. Ithaca: Cornell University Press, 1991.

Rosenau, James N. *The Scientific Study of Foreign Policy*. New York: Free Press, 1971.

Ross, Steven. 2001. "American War Plans." In *Military Planning and the Origins of the Second World War in Europe*, edited by B.J.C. McKercher and Roch Legault, 145–166. Westport: Praeger.

Rothenberg, Gunther E. 1978. *The Art of Warfare in the Age of Napoleon*. Bloomington: Indiana University Press.

Roxborough, Ian. "Organizational Innovation: Lessons from Military Organizations." *Sociological Forum* 15 (2000): 367–372.

Sagan, Scott D. "1914 Revisited: Allies, Offense, and Instability." *International Security* 11 (1986): 151–175.

The Limits of Safety: Organizations, Accidents, and Nuclear Weapons. Princeton: Princeton University Press, 1993.

"Why Do States Build Nuclear Weapons? Three Models in Search of a Bomb." *International Security* 21 (1996–1997): 54–86.

Sagan, Scott D. and Kenneth N. Waltz. *The Spread of Nuclear Weapons: A Debate Renewed*. New York: Norton, 2002.

Sarkees, Meredith Reid and Frank Wayman. *Resort to War: 1816–2007*. Washington, DC: CQ Press, 2010.

Schelling, Thomas C. and Morton H. Halperin. *Strategy and Arms Control*. New York: Twentieth Century Fund, 1961.

Scheinman, Lawrence. *Atomic Energy Policy in France under the Fourth Republic*. Princeton: Princeton University Press, 1965.

Schlesinger, Jr., Arthur P. Chapter 2 in *The Origins of the Cold War*, by Lloyd C. Gardner, Arthur Schlesinger, Jr. and Hans J. Morgenthau, 41–78. Waltham: Ginn-Blaisdell, 1970 [1967].

Schlesinger, Stephen and Stephen Kinzer. *Bitter Fruit: The Untold Story of the American Coup in Guatemala*. Garden City: Anchor, 1982.

Schneiberg, Marc and Sarah A. Soule. "Institutionalization as a Contested, Multi-Level Process: Rate Regulation in American Fire Insurance." In *Social Movements and Organization Theory*, edited by Jerry Davis, Doug McAdam, Dick Scott, and Mayer Zald, 122–160. Cambridge: Cambridge University Press, 2005.

Schofer, Evan, Ann Hironaka, David John Frank, and Wesley Longhofer. "Sociological Institutionalism and World Society." In *The Wiley-Blackwell Companion to Political Sociology*, edited by Edwin Amenta, Kate Nash, and Alan Scott, 57–68. New York: Wiley-Blackwell, 2012.

Schulzinger, Robert D. *U.S. Diplomacy since 1900*. Oxford: Oxford University Press, 2002.

Schweller, Randall L. *Unanswered Threats: Political Constraints on the Balance of Power*. Princeton: Princeton University Press, 2006.

Sechser, Todd S. "Goliath's Curse: Coercive Threats and Asymmetric Power." *International Organization* 64 (2010): 627–660.

Sechser, Todd S. and Fuhrmann, Matthew. "Crisis Bargaining and Nuclear Blackmail." *International Organization*. 67 (2013): 173–195.

Senese, Paul D. and John A. Vasquez. *The Steps to War: An Empirical Study*. Princeton: Princeton University Press, 2008.

Sharman, Jason. "War, Selection, and Micro-States: Economic and Sociological Perspectives on the International System." *European Journal of International Relations* 21 (2015): 194–214.

Shimshoni, Jonathan. "Technology, Military Advantage and World War I: A Case of Military Entrepreneurship." *International Security* 15 (1990–1991): 187–215.

Simpson, John. *The Independent Nuclear State: The United States, Britain and the Military Atom.* New York: St. Martin's Press, 1983.

Singer, J. David and Melvin Small. *The Wages of War, 1816–1965.* Ann Arbor: Inter-University Consortium for Political Research, 1974.

Siverson, Randolph M. and Michael D. Ward. "The Long Peace: A Reconsideration." *International Organization* 56 (2002): 679–691.

Slantchev, Branislav. "The Principle of Convergence in Wartime Negotiations." *American Political Science Review* 47 (2003): 621–632.

Smith, Alastair and Allan C. Stam. "Bargaining and the Nature of War." *The Journal of Conflict Resolution* 48 (2004): 783–813.

Smith, Rupert. *The Utility of Force: The Art of War in the Modern World.* New York: Knopf, 2007.

Smoke, Richard. *National Security and the Nuclear Dilemma: An Introduction to the American Experience,* second edition. New York: Random House, 1987.

Snyder, Glenn H. *Deterrence and Defense: Toward a Theory of National Security.* Princeton: Princeton University Press, 1961.

Snyder, Jack. "Civil-Military Relations and the Cult of the Offensive, 1914 and 1984." *International Security* 9 (1984a): 108–146.

The Ideology of the Offensive: Military Decision Making and the Disasters of 1914. Ithaca: Cornell University Press, 1984b.

Introduction in *Dominoes and Bandwagon: Strategic Beliefs and Great Power Competition in the Eurasian Rimland,* edited by Robert Jervis and Jack Snyder, 3–19. Oxford: Oxford University Press, 1991a.

Myths of Empire: Domestic Politics and International Ambition. Ithaca: Cornell University Press, 1991b.

"Better Now Than Later: The Paradox of 1914 as Everyone's Favored Year for War." *International Security* 39 (2014): 71–94.

Snyder, Jack and Robert Jervis (eds.). *Coping with Complexity in the International System.* Boulder: Westview Press, 1993.

Solingen, Etel. *Nuclear Logics: Contrasting Paths in East Asia and the Middle East.* Princeton: Princeton University Press, 2007.

"The Political Economy of Nuclear Restraint." In *Going Nuclear: Nuclear Proliferation and International Security in the 21st Century,* edited by Michael E. Brown, Owen R. Cote Jr., Sean M. Lynn-Jones, and Steven E. Miller, 36–77. Cambridge, MA: MIT Press, 2010.

Soysal, Yasemin Nuhoğlu. *Limits of Citizenship: Migrants and Postnational Membership in Europe.* Chicago: University of Chicago, 1994.

Spector, Ronald. "The Military Effectiveness of the US Armed Forces, 1919–39." In *Military Effectiveness: Volume II: The Interwar Period,* edited by Allan R. Millett and Williamson Murray, 70–97. Boston: Allen and Unwin, 1988.

Steefel, Lawrence D. *Bismarck, the Hohenzollern Candidacy, and the Origins of the Franco-German War of 1870.* Cambridge, MA: Harvard University Press, 1961.

Stevens, Mitchell L. *Creating a Class: College Admissions and the Education of Elites*. Cambridge, MA: Harvard University Press, 2009.

Stevenson, David. *Armaments and the Coming of War*. Oxford: Clarendon Press, 1996.

"Militarization and Diplomacy in Europe before 1914." *International Security* 22 (1997): 125–161.

Stoecker, Sally W. *Forging Stalin's Army: Marshal Tukhachevsky and the Politics of Military Innovation*. Boulder: Westview Press, 1998.

Strachan, Hew. *European Armies and the Conduct of War*. London: George Allen and Unwin, 1983.

Strang, David. *Learning by Example: Imitation and Innovation at a Global Bank*. Princeton: Princeton University Press, 2010.

Strang, David and John W. Meyer. "Institutional Conditions for Diffusion." *Theory and Society* 22 (1993): 487–511.

Strang, David and Michael W. Macy. "In Search of Excellence: Fads, Success Stories, and Adaptive Emulation." *The American Journal of Sociology* 107 (2001): 147–182.

Strang, David and Sarah A. Soule. "Diffusion in Organizations and Social Movements: From Hybrid Corn to Poison Pills." *Annual Review of Sociology* 24 (1998): 265–290.

Suchman, Mark C. and Dana P. Eyre. "Military Procurement as Rational Myth: Notes on the Social Construction of Weapons Proliferation." *Sociological Forum* 7 (1992): 137–161.

Sullivan, Patricia L. "War Aims and War Outcomes: Why Powerful States Lose Limited Wars." *The Journal of Conflict Resolution* 51 (2007): 496–524.

Who Wins: Predicting Strategic Success and Failure in Armed Conflict. Oxford: Oxford University Press, 2012.

Summer, Jr., Harry G. Colonel. *On Strategy: A Critical Analysis of the Vietnam War*. Novato: Presido Press, 1982.

Swidler, Ann. "Culture in Action: Symbols and Strategies." *American Sociological Review* (1986): 273–286.

"What Anchors Cultural Practices." In *The Practice Turn in Contemporary Theory*, edited by Theodore R. Schatzki, Karin Knorr Cetina, and Eike von Savigny, 74–92. London: Routledge, 2001.

Tannenwald, Nina. "The Nuclear Taboo: The United States and the Normative Basis of Nuclear Non-Use." *International Organization* 53 (1999): 433–468.

The Nuclear Taboo: The United States and the Non-Use of Nuclear Weapons Since 1945. Cambridge: Cambridge University Press, 2007.

Tarrow, Sidney. *War, States and Contention: A Comparative Historical Study*. Ithaca: Cornell University Press, 2015.

Taylor, A.J.P. *The Struggle for Mastery in Europe, 1848–1918*. Oxford: Clarendon Press, 1954.

The Origins of the Second World War. New York: Atheneum, 1962.

War by Time-Table: How the First World War Began. London: MacDonald and Company, 1969.

Tetlock, Philip E. "Theory-Driven Reasoning about Plausible Pasts and Probable Futures in World Politics: Are We Prisoners of Our Preconceptions?" *American Journal of Political Science* 43 (1999): 335–366.

Tetlock, Philip E. and Aaron Belkin (eds.). *Counterfactual Thought Experiments in World Politics: Logical, Methodological, and Psychological Perspectives.* Princeton: Princeton University Press, 1996.

Thayer, Bradley A. "Humans, Not Angels: Reasons to Doubt the Decline of War Thesis." *International Studies Review* 15 (2013): 405–411.

Thompson, William R. (ed.). *Great Power Rivalries.* Columbia: University of South Carolina Press, 1999.

"Identifying Rivals and Rivalries in World Politics." *International Studies Quarterly* 45 (2001): 557–586.

"Status Conflict, Hierarchies, and Interpretation Dilemmas." In *Status in World Politics*, edited by T.V. Paul, Deborah Welch Larson, and William C. Wohlforth, 219–245. Cambridge: Cambridge University Press, 2014.

Tilly, Charles (ed.). *The Formation of National States in Western Europe.* Princeton: Princeton University Press, 1975.

Coercion, Capital, and European States, AD 990–1992. Cambridge, MA: Blackwell, 1992.

Toft, Monica Duffy. "Indivisible Territory, Geographic Concentration, and Ethnic War." *Security Studies* 12 (2002): 82–119.

Toft, Monica Duffy and Talbot Imlay. "Strategic and Military Planning under the Fog of Peace." In *The Fog of Peace and War Planning: Military and Strategic Planning under Uncertainty*, edited by Talbot C. Imlay and Monica Duffy Toft, 1–10. London: Routledge, 2006.

Tomz, Michael. *Reputation and International Cooperation: Sovereign Debt across Three Centuries.* Princeton: Princeton University Press, 2007.

Trachtenberg, Marc. "The Meaning of Mobilization in 1914." *International Security* 15 (1990–1991): 120–150.

Travers, Tim. *How the War Was Won: Command and Technology in the British Army on the Western Front, 1917–1918.* London: Routledge, 1992.

Tuchman, Barbara W. *The Guns of August.* New York: Macmillan, 1962.

The March of Folly: From Troy to Vietnam. London: Abacus, 1984.

Turner, Leonard C.F. *Origins of the First World War.* New York: W.W. Norton and Company, 1970.

Van Creveld, Martin L. *Technology and War: From 2000 B.C. to the Present.* New York: Free Press, 1989.

The Transformation of War. New York: Free Press, 1991.

Nuclear Proliferation and the Future of Conflict. New York: Free Press, 1993.

"The Cult of the Offensive and the Origins of the First World War." *International Security* 9 (1984): 58–107.

Causes of War: Power and the Roots of Conflict. Ithaca: Cornell University Press, 1999.

Vasquez, John A. *The War Puzzle.* New York: Cambridge University Press, 1993.

The War Puzzle Revisited. New York: Cambridge University Press, 2009.

Vaughan, Diane. *The Challenger Launch Decision: Risky Technology, Culture, and Deviance at War.* Chicago: University of Chicago Press, 1996.

Wagner, R. Harrison. "Bargaining and War." *American Journal of Political Science* 44 (2000): 469–484.

Wallerstein, Immanuel. *The Modern World System I: Capitalist Agriculture and the Origins of the European World-Economy in the Sixteenth Century.* Berkeley: University of California Press, 2011.

Walt, Stephen M. *The Origins of Alliances.* Ithaca: Cornell University Press, 1987.

Waltz, Kenneth N. *Theory of International Politics.* Reading, MA: Addison-Wesley, 1979.

"The Origins of War in Neorealist Theory." In *The Origin and Prevention of Major Wars*, edited by Robert I. Rotberg and Theodore K. Raab, 39–52. Cambridge: Cambridge University Press, 1988.

"Nuclear Myths and Political Realities." *The American Political Science Review* 84 (1990): 731–745.

Wawro, Geoffrey. *Warfare and Society in Europe, 1792–1914.* London: Routledge, 2000.

The Franco-Prussian War: The German Conquest of France in 1870–1871. Cambridge: Cambridge University Press, 2003.

Weber, Max with Guenther Roth and Claus Wittich (eds.). *Economy and Society: An Outline of Interpretive Sociology.* Berkeley: University of California Press, 1978 [1956].

Weick, Karl E. "Educational Organizations as Loosely Coupled Systems." *Administrative Science Quarterly* 21 (1976): 1–19.

Sensemaking in Organizations. Thousand Oaks: Sage, 1995.

The American Way of War: A History of United States Military Strategy and Policy. New York: Macmillan, 1973.

The Age of Battles: The Quest for Decisive Warfare from Breitenfeld to Waterloo. Bloomington: Indiana University Press, 1991.

Weisiger, Alex. *Logics of War: Explanations for Limited and Unlimited Conflicts.* Ithaca: Cornell University Press, 2013.

Weldes, Jutta, Mark Lafffey, Hugh Gusterson, and Raymond Duvall (eds.). *Cultures of Insecurity: States, Communities and the Production of Danger.* Minneapolis: University of Minnesota Press, 1999.

Wendt, Alexander. "Anarchy Is What States Make of It: The Social Construction of Power Politics." *International Organization.* 46 (1992): 391–425.

Social Theory of International Politics. Cambridge: Cambridge University Press, 1999.

Werner, Suzanne. "Deterring Intervention: The Stakes of War and Third Party Involvement." *American Journal of Political Science* 44 (2000): 720–732.

Wetzel, David. *A Duel of Giants: Bismarck, Napoleon III, and the Origins of the Franco-Prussian War.* Madison: University of Wisconsin Press, 2001.

Whelan, Richard. *Drawing the Line: The Korean War, 1950–1953.* Boston: Little, Brown and Company, 1990.

Wight, Martin. *Power Politics*, edited by Hedley Bull and Carsten Holbraad. London: Leicester University Press, 1978.

Williams, William Appleman. *The Tragedy of American Diplomacy.* New York: Delta, 1962 [1959].

Williamson, Jr., Samuel R. *Austria-Hungary and the Origins of the First World War.* New York: Palgrave Macmillan, 1991.

Wilson, Ward. "The Winning Weapon? Rethinking Nuclear Weapons in Light of Hiroshima." *International Security* 31 (2007): 162–179.

Wimmer, Andreas. *Waves of War: Nationalism, State Formation, and Ethnic Exclusion in the Modern World.* New York: Cambridge University Press, 2013.

Wimmer, Andreas and Brian Min. "From Empire to Nation-State: Explaining Wars in the Modern World, 1816–2001." *American Sociological Review* 71 (2006): 867–897.

Wimmer, Andreas and Yuval Feinstein. "The Rise of the Nation-State across the World, 1816 to 2001." *American Sociological Review* 75 (2010): 764–790.

Winton, Harold R. "Tanks, Votes, and Budgets: The Politics of Mechanization and Armored Warfare in Britain, 1919–1939." In *The Challenge of Change: Military Institutions and New Realities, 1918–1941,* edited by Harold R. Winton and David R. Mets, 74–107. Lincoln: University of Nebraska Press, 2000.

Wohlforth, William C. *The Elusive Balance: Power and Perceptions during the Cold War.* Ithaca: Cornell University Press, 1993.

"Unipolarity, Status Competition, and Great Power War." *World Politics* 61 (2009): 28–57.

"Status Dilemmas and Interstate Conflict." In *Status in World Politics,* edited by T.V. Paul, Deborah Welch Larson, and William C. Wohlforth, 115–140. Cambridge: Cambridge University Press, 2014.

Wolfe, Thomas W. *Soviet Power and Europe 1945–1970.* Baltimore: Johns Hopkins Press, 1970.

Wolfers, Arnold. *Discord and Collaboration: Essays on International Politics.* Baltimore: Johns Hopkins Press, 1962.

Wolford, Scott, Dan Reiter, and Clifford J. Carrubba. "Information, Commitment, and War." *The Journal of Conflict Resolution* 55 (2011): 556–579.

Yergin, Daniel. *Shattered Peace: The Origins of the Cold War and the National Security State.* Boston: Houghton Mifflin, 1977.

Zacher, Mark W. "The Territorial Integrity Norm: International Boundaries and the Use of Force." *International Organization* 55 (2001): 215–250.

Zaloga, Steven J. *The Kremlin's Nuclear Sword: The Rise and Fall of Russia's Strategic Nuclear Forces, 1945–2000.* Washington, DC: Smithsonian Institution Press, 2002.

Zeitlin, Maurice. 1974. "Military Spending and Economic Stagnation." *The American Journal of Sociology* 79 (1974): 1452–1456.

Zisk, Kimberly Marten. *Engaging the Enemy: Organization Theory and Soviet Military Innovation, 1955–1991.* Princeton: Princeton University Press, 1993.

Zook, Jr., David H. and Robin Higham. *A Short History of Warfare.* New York: Twayne, 1996.

Zubin, Terence. *Inventing the Schlieffen Plan: German War Planning, 1871–1914.* Oxford: Oxford University Press, 2002.

Index

VII) 192 Hiroshima / Nagasaki: —
   A bomb's use   I DISAGREE
194 A.A. here goes too far — but has a
   Point. See "overkill"
197 wrong on Stalin's fears.
212 But she's right on the
⇒ |over production of bombs
   223 in the end USSR ruined itself.

_____

VIII Who started the Cold War?
   235 Th S understands much of E.E.
⇒ 238 Domino theory: Munich to V. Nam
   242 Fear of psychological
Leffler   subversion — on both sides
is better 247 Korea? arguments —
   + 1930s dominoes —
⇒! (249) very good on how the
      present forgets history + old
      fears (250) and constructing
                  fear.

_____

IX) CONCLUSION
   255 - 259 3 main points
      to keeping power
      planning
      security
   260 Vietnam error
   262 regional versions + civil wars
   /263

265-272 veers off into
weak history +
doubtful utopianism.

③ The int'l. system + the thesis,
④

7. The results of single wars can be misleading -

17. Great powers fight wars to remain great
   powers.

18 Pyrrhic victories are common.

Ⅰ) 24-25 From realism to constructivism
   to world society theory

35) Great power, tautological perception
based on outcome of last war (AN
EXAGERATION, BUT NOT TOTALLY)

Ⅱ) 45) Great powers often lose wars
   (US, FR, etc.)

52. to be a great power you have to
want it... + compete.

66-7 Being a great power is
   costly- + often futile (US, USSR)

Ⅲ) THE WRONG LESSONS of 1870 Fr-Pr war
   + the cavalry illusion

→ 103 Great powers fight wars over
Ⅳ) status + prestige. and 117 "honor"
                                        face
   [m.n-vietnam] (119) MOON
   + 1870 NⅢ + Bismarck

Ⅴ) The idiocy of WWI, based on
   "lesson of history of 1870-1

Ⅵ) WW Ⅱ - mostly France's
   defeat + chance - Blitzkrieg